D1448545

Labour Country

Political Radicalism
and Social Democracy
in South Wales

1831-1985

Labour Country

Political Radicalism
and Social Democracy
in South Wales

1831-1985

DARYL LEEWORTHY

PARTHIAN

Parthian, Cardigan SA43 1ED
www.parthianbooks.com
First published in 2018
© Daryl Leeworthy 2018
ISBN 9781912681006
Edited by Dai Smith
The Modern Wales series receives support from the Rhys Davies Trust
Front cover painting Kevin Sinnott, *Struggle or Starve*, 2016, oil on linen,
850 x 1100 mm with kind permission of the artist.
Typeset by Elaine Sharples
Printed by Opolgraf, Poland
Published with the financial support of the Welsh Books Council
British Library Cataloguing in Publication Data
A cataloguing record for this book is available from the British Library.
Every attempt has been made to secure the permission of copyright
holders to reproduce archival and printed material.

*For Jayne Louise Leeworthy (née Salway),
1968-2000, and Agnes Leeworthy
(née Carruthers), 1928–.*

CONTENTS

ABBREVIATIONS

AL	*Aberdare Leader*
ALS	Aberdare Local Studies, Aberdare Library
ASLEF	Associated Society of Locomotive Engineers and Firemen
ASRS	Amalgamated Society of Railway Servants
BDN	*Barry Dock News*
BH	*Barry Herald*
BL	British Library
BodL	Bodleian Library, Oxford
BSP	British Socialist Party
CA	Carmarthenshire Archives, Carmarthen
CarmJ	*Carmarthen Journal*
CBC	County Borough Council
CC	County Council
CJ	*Caerphilly Journal*
CLP	Constituency Labour Party
CLS	Cardiff Local Studies Department, Cathays Heritage Centre
CMG	*Cardiff and Merthyr Guardian*
CPGB	Communist Party of Great Britain
CT	*Cardiff Times*
DH	*Daily Herald*
DLP	Divisional Labour Party
DW	*Daily Worker*
EC	Executive Committee
EEx	*Evening Express*
GA	Glamorgan Archives, Cardiff
GFP	*Glamorgan Free Press*
GG	*Glamorgan Gazette*

GwA	Gwent Archives, Ebbw Vale
IISH	International Institute of Social History, Amsterdam
ILP	Independent Labour Party
IRSH	*International Review of Social History*
LHASC	Labour History Archive and Study Centre, Manchester
LL	*Labour Leader*
LRC	Labour Representation Committee
LSE	London School of Economics
MEx	*Merthyr Express*
MFGB	Miners' Federation of Great Britain
MG	*Merthyr Guardian*
MM	*Monmouthshire Merlin*
MT	*Merthyr Telegraph*
MWF	Miners' Welfare Fund
NLW	National Library of Wales, Aberystwyth
NS	*Northern Star*
NUM	National Union of Mineworkers
NUR	National Union of Railwaymen
NUT	National Union of Teachers
PC	*Pontypridd Chronicle*
PFP	*Pontypool Free Press*
PLS	Pontypridd Local Studies, Pontypridd Library
PO	*Pontypridd Observer*
PSOE	Spanish Socialist Workers' Party / Partido Socialista Obrero Español.
RBA	Richard Burton Archives, Swansea University
RDC	Rural District Council
RGASPI	Russian State Archive of Socio-Political History, Moscow
RL	*Rhondda Leader*
RPA	Robin Page Arnot Papers, Hull History Centre, Hull
SCOLAR	Special Collections and Archives, Cardiff University

ABBREVIATIONS

SDF	Social Democratic Federation
SDP	Social Democratic Party
SLP	Socialist Labour Party
SPGB	Socialist Party of Great Britain
SSS	Socialist Sunday School
SWA	*South Wales Argus*
SWCC	South Wales Coalfield Collection, Swansea University
SWDN	*South Wales Daily News*
SWDP	*South Wales Daily Post*
SWE	*South Wales Echo*
SWLP	*South Wales Labour Pioneer*
SWMF	South Wales Miners' Federation
SWML	South Wales Miners' Library, Swansea University
TCLP	Trades Council and Labour Party
TG	*Tarian y Gweithiwr*
TLC	Trades and Labour Council
TLS	Treorchy Local Studies, Treorchy Library
TNA	The National Archives, Kew, London.
UDC	Urban District Council
VWC	John E. Morgan, *A Village Worker's Council: A Short History of the Lady Windsor Lodge, South Wales Miners' Federation* (Pontypridd, 1950)
WCML	Working Class Movement Library, Salford
WGA	West Glamorgan Archives, Swansea
WHR	*Welsh History Review*
WM	*Western Mail*

PREAMBLE

For the greater part of the twentieth century, one party held the momentum of political and social change in South Wales: the Labour Party. Its role in society, its ability to effect alterations in the landscape, to project hope and expectation and aspiration, was defined by its dominant position across politics, social organisation, and culture. In the twenty-first century, it is easy to think of the Labour Party – and the labour movement more generally – as a defence mechanism, as conservative and too attached to the legacies of the past, for that is how they have governed in devolved Wales, but for generations the labour movement – and its political wing – aspired towards radical change and inspired it. For many socialists in the late-nineteenth and early twentieth centuries the idea that the revolution was at hand, that it was possible to smell, hear, and see the utopia of the New Jerusalem, was a powerful guiding force.[1] Its effects are still with us, just. There was once little in Ebbw Vale or Pontardawe besides the steel industry; little in Treherbert, Maerdy[2], or Ynysybwl besides the mining of coal[3]; but the labour movement – particularly its most dynamic leader – in Gwyn Thomas's words 'took the image of this place out of the valleys ... and presented it, its imperfections, its struggles, its humour, as a challenge to those parts of Britain that have never been scarred by poverty or the monstrous toil that heavy industry exacts from beauty'.[4] This was Labour Country.

But what exactly do I mean by those terms: 'South Wales' and 'Labour Country'? For nineteenth-century compilers of trades directories, the southern part of Wales extended from the Bristol Channel to the northern fringes of Cardiganshire and Breconshire. Today, as encountered on blue motorway signposts,

1

perhaps, South Wales is more geographically contained: at its greatest extent, it includes the old counties of Glamorgan and Monmouthshire with the former industrial fringes of Carmarthenshire and Breconshire. In essence: the coalfield with its allied ports and the rural hinterland that lies in between. The South Wales encountered in the pages that follow, which I refer to as Labour Country, was more than geography. It is a version of the American Wales identified by Sir Alfred Zimmern shortly after the First World War, and since explored in social and cultural terms by generations of labour historians. 'Of American Wales, the Wales of the coalfield and the industrial working class', Zimmern wrote, 'let me only say ... what a joy it has been to pass a too fleeting and infrequent weekend among men and women who really care for ideas and love the search for truth'.[5] American, then, because of the enormous industrial and demographic capacity of the coalfield; because of the vibrancy of the society and culture made by an immigrant population; and because, like America, it was young and curious about the world. To rediscover it I employ not the teleology of a telescopic viewfinder but rather the shake of a kaleidoscope for its shards of the unexpected, the glints and colours of a changing, now vanished, experience.

At the heart of what made South Wales different was its frontier experience. This was a nineteenth-century industrial frontier that, by the First World War, had reshaped itself into an urban society. When the population of Wales was calculated in 1801, it stood at around half a million. A century later, it had risen to more than two million and four-fifths of the Welsh lived in Glamorgan and Monmouthshire. Glamorgan's population in 1801 had been around seventy five thousand people, but by the outbreak of the First World War it was in excess of one million. Here was the rise of South Wales measured in its rawest material terms, that of people and of potential labour. Few places experienced this rise more acutely, more tellingly, than the Rhondda. The five hundred or so people that comprised Rhondda's population in 1801 or the four hundred living in the neighbouring parish of Llanwynno could have little imagined existing in a place, as was the case in 1911, of more than one hundred and fifty thousand on the one hand or more than forty thousand on the other. Nowhere grows that dramatically without calling on, and absorbing, resources – notably people – from elsewhere. The alternative was a steady, if unimpressive, growth and eventual decline, as occurred in Pembrokeshire and Cardiganshire. Therein, in those western counties, lies the story of what would have happened to Wales in the absence of the industrial dynamo: the permanent periphery.

The people who moved to South Wales from all over the world had to make a society and a culture from scratch. Houses, streets, sewage systems, cemeteries, churches and chapels, schools and hospitals, courts of law, council offices, theatres and cinemas, public meeting places, libraries, these things and more had to be constructed in communities that simply did not exist – or were little more than hamlets or villages or a collection of hillside farms – before the industrial revolution. In the chaotic novelty of those first decades of settlement, when muddy roads and privies offered little tangible difference from the rural existence scratched out by scores of previous generations – they may even have provided some comfort in the rawness of change – facets of modern civilisation such as the public park, library, and hospital, were but a dream. But as one generation gave way to the next and new ideas came to the fore, this industrial frontier came alive with simmering tensions and far-reaching aspirations. The liberalism which encompassed social radicalism, religious independence, national self-consciousness, and industrial and commercial interests, eventually struggled to adapt to demands for industrial democracy from below, giving rise first to an annexe – the Lib-Labs – and then to a rival, the Labour Party.

Central to this story was coal. Coal powered the iron industry in Merthyr Tydfil, the copperworks in Swansea, and propelled South Wales into a new, industrial existence. Industry encouraged scientific interest and the establishment of new production techniques, it linked South Wales to global networks of trade, and it made investors extremely wealthy.[6] The imperial grandeur of Cardiff's civic centre and its docklands coal exchange were a testament to that nineteenth-century largesse, as was the commercial opportunity, indicated by the surviving shop buildings, to be found in industrial towns such as Barry and Pontypridd. Until the 1870s, the primary destination for South Wales coal was the domestic iron industry. Of the nine million tons of coal produced in the mid-1850s more than one third was consumed by iron production. The export market at that time accounted for just one million tons.

By 1900, however, coal output had leapt to nearly forty million tons per annum, half of which was exported, and a further five million tons used to power steam ships. The amount used for iron production remained the same – around three and a half million tons.[7] South Wales overtook the coalfields in the North East of England as the principal source of coal for the Royal Mail and the Royal Navy (the Admiralty was the South Wales Coalfield's best customer), and steam coal was found on many of the commercial passenger liners, merchant vessels, and the navies of rival empires.[8] By the early twentieth century, South Wales was home to great coal combines, such as Powell Duffryn, and to smaller independent coal companies, which harnessed the substantial profitability of the coalfield for the business elite. Profit was not redistributed into the hands of the miners themselves, whose wage packets included stoppages for everything from candles to pick sharpening to a contribution to the colliery doctor's retainer.

If the difference between company profit and an individual's wage packet provided one reason for the emergence of the labour movement, so too did the character of work in the coalfield – particularly work underground which was done almost universally by hand. The introduction of technology – cutting machines – which had a substantial impact on Scottish collieries where around a fifth of coal was machine cut by 1913, had a negligible presence in South Wales. There the amount was around one per cent, although geological conditions made the use of technology unviable in most cases.[9] Consequently, South Wales miners worked, on average, the longest hours of any mineworker in Britain.[10] Small wonder that miners' leaders, such as A. J. Cook, frequently appealed to the ethical considerations of the majority of people who were not miners when responding to industrial action. Mining was extremely hard and physically arduous work with the act of hewing coal and other associated tasks accompanied by dangers of gas, roof collapse, and flooding. As Cook put it in the 1920s,

I wonder if those who abuse the miners were made to work even for one year in the pits, hauling nine hours a day down hot narrow galleries, lying half naked at the coalface, sweating at a narrow seam, working in water or excessive heat, living in a miner's row and taking home, week by week, a miner's average pay. With a risk of terrible mutilation and death ever present. I wonder if these people would be quite so sure that it was those paid agitators who made the miner's struggle for better treatment?[11]

The historical contours of South Wales, well mapped by historians, are now overwhelmingly familiar, as are the causes of complaint evident in Cook's speech. From the Merthyr Rising in 1831 and the Chartist Rising in Newport in 1839, which marked the beginnings of the working-class movement that was to come to prominence in the twentieth century, we move swiftly on to the start of democracy in the 1860s, the arrival of the Liberal Party as its political manifestation, and the election of the pacifist radical Henry Richard at Merthyr in 1868. William Abraham, Mabon, followed suit as MP for Rhondda in 1885. From the 1890s, the complexion altered significantly. The formation of the South Wales Miners' Federation in 1898 galvanised miners and provided a vital means of fusing together political and industrial radicalism. Keir Hardie's election at Merthyr two years later, Wales's first independent Labour MP, further signalled that change was on the horizon if not yet a political revolution. By the time the people of Mid Rhondda took to the streets in 1910, battling against the injustices of Edwardian capitalism and the compromises made by that earlier generation of labour leaders, the miners had switched allegiance from the Liberal Party to Labour and it was not long before the first local councils changed hands either.

After the First World War, after the Russian Revolutions of 1917, the political and intellectual environment altered completely – from 1922, the Labour Party was the largest parliamentary party in South Wales and ran most of the local councils. The transition of power from Liberal to Labour took place, however, in the context of a rapidly deteriorating economy. This prompted the miners' last stand in 1926, it led to the mass protests against unemployment, poverty, and deprivation in the 1930s, it fuelled widespread outmigration and depopulation in industrial areas, and convinced much of the labour movement that the survival of the social democratic ideas and values which were being put into practice municipally rested on winning control of central government and manifesting social democracy at all levels of society. The programme of nationalisation which accompanied the Labour governments of 1945-1951, of coal mining in 1947 and healthcare and the railways in 1948, was a fulfilment of that collective desire never to return to the experiences of the interwar Depression. In the decades that followed, amidst pit closure programmes from both Conservative and Labour governments in the 1950s and 1960s, there were attempts to diversify the economies of mining communities, but neither party was able to revitalise the dynamics of South Walian social democracy. In the 1970s, radicalism was temporarily revived, with those miners who remained calling once more for a living wage, a more secure job, and better prospects. The twin strikes of 1972 and 1974 offered hope, the election of the Conservatives in 1979 dismay, and the 1984-5 miners' strike the final curtain. Social democracy as it once was ceased to exist.

But what do we find when we step away from the mapping and remapping of these contours, from the telling and retelling of 'mainstream' events and the actions of leading politicians and trade union leaders, and concentrate on all that swirled around them and emanated from them? To dance, in effect, around the Labour Party, the political core of Labour Country, but also with it. After all, South Wales – Labour Country – is relatively easy to grasp from its demographic and political changes, they can be expressed by a graph or by colours on a map, but the social and cultural meaning of this place is far more complex, as are the twin legacies of political radicalism and a strong social democratic tradition. These complex legacies and intertwined meanings are what lie at the heart of this book and its connected studies in political radicalism and social democracy. *Labour Country* is, at once, a study of institutions, ideas, and people; it is about the interactions between those elements; and it is about the social, cultural, and political consequences of those interactions. It may indeed have been the case that the middle classes set the tone for nineteenth-century urban reform, as in Merthyr and Cardiff, but the grassroots impulse was not packed away after the bloody insurrection of 1831 and reopened in Tonypandy in 1910.[12] It persisted, together with the high infant mortality rates and low life expectancy which the liberal middle classes ignored except where they were politically useful.

The counterpoint both to liberal governance conducted by the middle classes, on the one hand, and to the conservative, paternalistic alliance between the industrial-aristocratic elite and the great mass of the working population, on the other, were the co-operative societies, trade unions, and friendly societies, in which the origins of a popular social democracy lie. These institutions were the manifestation of a grassroots, mutualist alternative to a society whose terms were established by industrial and commercial interests. Once the middle class had won control of local affairs, a clash between working-class mutualism and middle-class liberal reformism was inevitable. The choice made in this book, then, is to explore the making of that grassroots alternative rather than, as is so often the case in the existing historical literature, to place the narrative arc of the nineteenth century into the hands of liberal reformers once the radicalism of the 1830s has been rehearsed. It is a choice made in order to respond both to whiggish models of history which stress consistent, inevitable progress and to the nationalist models of history that deny the validity of the South Walian industrial dynamo as a specific, indeed overwhelming, maker of modern Wales. It is, invariably, also a rejoinder to more traditional labour histories, which place institutions and collectivities, unions and politics, the doers rather than the dreamers, in the foreground. What follows examines the paths travelled by the agitators and activists whose aspirations responded to, but also helped to shape, the mosaic world of

South Wales. In this sense, *Labour Country* is, to borrow Dai Smith's phrase, a 'cubist' history.[13]

This begs the question, however, of how to approach writing about those alternatives and what sources inform such a history. There is, put simply, no single archive that informs this study: everyday politics, perhaps as opposed to their expression through ideas and in institutions, are multifaceted and not easily pared down to singularities. The challenge lies not so much in finding source material but in spotting the trends and patterns – the hints at alternative choices – which are present in the archival record. Inevitably sources are held in numerous different locations and survive in numerous languages, not just English and Welsh, itself a reflection of the global character of South Wales. Newspaper readers in Reykjavik, Tallinn, Helsinki, or Stockholm, knew about colliery disasters in places that even people in Birmingham or London would have had trouble placing on a map; readers in Paris, Moscow, Berlin, or Madrid, could read interviews with the leading figures of the South Wales Miners' Federation; police officers in Bristol, Bath, and Swindon, knew to look out for particular individuals with Rhondda addresses; and Spanish and Italian anarchists the world over knew of Abertillery, Dowlais, Ammanford, and Abercraf. The borders of Labour Country have always been porous and have always been global. And, yes, imperial.[14]

The early twentieth century, as mapped in those sources, was an age of globalisation long before the term was popularised by economists in the 1980s as a way of describing, as the sociologist Anthony Giddens put it, the 'intensification of worldwide social relations'.[15] But the politics described here were local, as much as they were informed by globalised networks of information and political philosophies. They were, in effect, 'glocalised' – a term employed by the sociologist Roland Robertson to emphasise the agency of peoples at the local level when responding to globalising influences in ways that reinforce local cultural traditions and possibilities.[16] Cardiff, the principal city of the world of South Wales, linked together Joseph Conrad, Eugene O'Neill, Paul Robeson and Bertolt Brecht.[17] The list of consuls for the port of Cardiff, published regularly in city directories from the 1890s onwards, served as evidence enough of a region connected to the outside world in myriad ways.[18] Thus we cannot truly hope to understand South Wales and its importance by refashioning the past as the pursuit of nationhood in which south Wales appears but South Wales does not.

Mass digitisation of newspapers has similarly opened up the past, serving at once to expand our knowledge of both great historical themes and everyday minutiae. I believe that the unprecedented range of archival material I have been thus able to access puts a great deal, even of what is familiar, into a different light, and certainly allows an accretion of detail which is, like a novel perhaps, redolent of past lives. We can know, for instance, the lengths that coffee house owners went to sell their various blends of coffee to a willing public. We can know just how many foreign musicians managed to keep their heads above water by giving language instruction to company clerks in the docks of Barry, Cardiff, and Swansea. We can know that shorthand writers set up their own society and published their own journal – in shorthand of course – with a separate society for those who mastered Rev. R. H. Morgan's adaptation for the Welsh language. And we can know just when and where vegetarianism first became an organised movement in Wales: in Cardiff in July 1898.[19] Hardly a coincidence that it took place at the time of the coal lockout. Not to be outdone by Cardiff, vegetarian societies were soon established in Barry, Newport, and Swansea, and an intrepid Mrs Churchill ran her own vegetarian stores on Salisbury Road in Cathays.[20] Perhaps the first in a long line of radical stores to be established in that part of Cardiff. Promoters of vegetarianism at that time felt that the challenges faced by miners and their families during the lockout might encourage the take up of vegetarianism on economic grounds. The butcher's bill, observed one activist, was a considerable item for family budgets. Vegetarians responded to the lockout by travelling to the coalfield and handing out recipes to miners' wives to help them make the most of the fruits and vegetables they could afford.[21]

Of course, the central story of nineteenth- and twentieth-century South Wales is not so much the story of militant vegetarians, Welsh-speaking shorthand writers, or French-speaking office clerks, although they undoubtedly form part of a total history; rather, the core story is that of the growth of the state and how organisations with a particular set of ideas sought either to harness its power or to curtail it. Before the changes to local government in 1894, which dragged South Wales out of its rural past, sub-parliamentary administration was often a matter of accident, and for coalfield towns administered by sanitary authorities and local boards of health, the notion of 'government' at all was a distant one. Chance saw Aberdare prosper with many of the institutions of civilisation that Merthyr, with its absentee barons of industry and frustrated would-be middle-class reformers, lacked until the twentieth century. After 1894, the local authority became a much more efficient branch of the state. It became a living organisation which mirrored, through its workforce and strict hierarchy of power, the divisions of contemporary society. There were posts of influence, posts of prestige, and positions of labour. The scramble for jobs in local government throughout the twentieth and twenty-first centuries highlights the long-standing importance of the public sector as employer, and the ways in which local government existed as a life buoy amid economic storms. In November 1932, for instance, just two council jobs in the Rhondda attracted nearly seven hundred applications, a figure that included two councillors, a tax inspector, a school teacher, and a cinema manager.[22]

The state, particularly after the First World War, provided jobs and it was also increasingly central to the implementation of Labour's ideas for change. As Keir Hardie explained to voters in Aberdare in 1901, the purpose and great potential of independent Labour representation in local government lay in 'helping to improve the locality in which you live, helping to improve the conditions under which you live, and helping to uplift your class from the position it occupies into that of a self-respecting unit in the life of the nation'.[23] In the view of other early Labour activists, such as Tom Morris, Labour's regional organiser in Wales after the First World War, local government was the 'most democratic institution at our very doors which can be made a powerful lever for social reform through its administrative powers'.[24] In this sense, the process of municipalisation described in the pages that follow was simply the construction or incorporation of local services under the control and auspices of municipal officials such as local councillors and their committees, the clerk of the council, or the council surveyor and medical officer. The expansion of this process to central government after the Second World War, from this perspective, was a logical one.

Yet it was not an entirely inevitable progression. There was a clear debate about shifting from 'the ideology of "workers' control" (roughly 1910-23) into an implicit acceptance of state-ownership as the best solution (c.1926-1950)', just as alternatives to state socialism faded in the interwar years.[25] For a period, notably in the 1920s, Labour sought to balance the pursuit of power in the name of the working class with continuing to support efforts that fostered empowerment and self-help through socialised means. This was especially apparent in healthcare, which was typically funded through voluntary organisations such as the Tredegar Medical Aid Society and its equivalent in other communities, but was also in evidence in the provision of recreation grounds, libraries, cinemas, ambulances, and so on. But such a model was vulnerable to economic turbulence, and most in the Labour Party came to recognise that the collapse, during the long depression of the 1930s, of the financial supports that had underpinned voluntary action was reason enough to embrace the greater resources and stability of the state. It was, after all, local authorities which stepped in across the coalfield to protect valuable resources, such as miners' welfare grounds, when the resources of the voluntary committees dissipated. No surprise, therefore, that local authority spending across Britain rose from one hundred and forty million pounds in 1913 to five hundred and thirty three million in 1939: Labour were willing partners, and beneficiaries, of this expansion.[26]

Those who lived in Labour Country were, justifiably, proud of their achievements in the face of considerable adversity and material hardship. When King Edward VIII toured South Wales in mid-November 1936 and declared 'something must be done' (he abdicated a few weeks later, and not much was done), he was taken to the co-operative farm at Boverton run by the Welsh Land Settlement Society, he was shown around the intermediate training centre at Pentrebach, and he was shown the sorry carcass of the former steel works at Dowlais. He was also shown Dinas Park, built by the unemployed members of the Ton Pentre Miners' Welfare Association on the site of a disused coal tip. He might just as easily have been shown the headquarters of the Ynysybwl Co-operative Society in Pontypridd, a multi-storey emporium in the town's market square which the society had acquired shortly after the First

World War, or the miners' hospital in Caerphilly, or one of a network of over one hundred miners' institutes and welfare halls. The scale of ambition and the extent to which that ambition was brought into being is one of the greatest success stories of modern Britain, and ought to be hailed as a triumph of working-class ingenuity and determination – in short, as a triumph of socialism in a democracy.

Opinion has long differed as to the nature of that triumph. In the late-1940s and early 1950s, when long-standing political activists and co-operators such as William Hazell, Ted Stonelake, and John E. Morgan, sat down to write the histories of their movements up to the present day, they surveyed a landscape of social, political, and economic activity that was changing. Where once there had been vivid voluntary effort and local, democratically accountable initiative, there was now the state; a transfer that sat uncomfortably with them all. As Alun Burge has recorded of Hazell, it 'pained him'. Burge continues:

> Hazell's reservations about other aspects of the welfare state come through clearly. He believed that there needed to be more individual discipline in the welfare state, which he referred to as 'over-paternal'. ... He thought there was a loss in everything being 'planned and geometrical, orderly and tidy'. ... He pointed out that as the state became omnipotent, so distrust grew of its efficiency and referred to calls for management of the nationalised coal and railway industries to be decentralised.[27]

Likewise, for John E. Morgan, for all his delight in raising the National Coal Board flag over the Lady Windsor Colliery on 1 January 1947, and the confirmation that this gave to a lifetime's commitment to socialism, it was clear that the achievements of his 'village workers' council' ought not to be overridden by nationalisation. He wrote:

It should be remembered that the pioneers had to create and establish the institutions that we now enjoy, and to lay the foundations of others upon which we have since built. Let us recapitulate some of them –

An institute, owned and controlled by the workmen.

A successful cinema, the profits of which accrue to the workmen.

A hospital and convalescent homes fund.

A highly efficient ambulance service.

...Abolition of house-rents being retained at the office.

Improved colliery approaches.

A people's park and welfare ground.

Majority Labour representation on the District Council (later it became 100%).

...More pleasing still it is to record the Committee's attempt to take private profit out of the housing of the people at Ynysybwl by forming a Garden Village.[28]

A few years later, Morgan could have added a small paddling pool to the list. Indeed, the influence of labour activists delivered nursery education, maternity clinics, infant welfare centres, community libraries, and leisure facilities. They changed the political, social, cultural, and built landscape. At a time when the South Wales Coalfield resembles the flotsam and jetsam of deindustrialisation – the new kind of bleak, as the writer Owen Hatherley has put it – it behoves us to reflect on the achievements of earlier generations, to relate them to the South Wales that has come about in the aftermath of their destruction, and to reflect on the relationship between the state and the people.

When Wales voted very narrowly for devolution in 1997, with a majority of less than seven thousand votes, commentators, particularly those on the left, enthused that the

Assembly might lead to a new Wales.[29] To take up the words of Ron Davies, the then Secretary of State for Wales, there was a feeling that perhaps, at last, it was a 'very good morning in Wales'. In his *Wales: A Question for History* published that year, Dai Smith wondered whether 1997 might turn out to be 'the single most important year in the Welsh twentieth century. Or not, since no single constitutional reform ... can effect that scale of cultural change by mere political direction or administrative action'. Compared to the despair that followed the 1979 referendum when historians such as Gwyn A. Williams wrote of Wales voting itself out of existence, such cautious optimism was understandable. But how far has the 'New Wales' come in responding to the radical legacy of the South Wales Coalfield and using it as the basis of a social democratic settlement for the twenty-first century? That leaves fewer grounds for optimism today than twenty years ago. Speaking at an Index on Censorship event at the Chapter Arts Centre in November 2014, Dai Smith returned to the essential themes of his work of the early 1980s:

Imagine if you will a country of around three million people, in which seven hundred and fifty thousand people – a quarter of the entire population of the country – live in one extended conurbation which is more populous than that country's two largest cities put together. A conurbation in which from eighty to ninety five percent are native born (that is more than first or second generation), a true heartland in other words, one which formed the politics, the society, and the culture of that country's last century like nothing else and like nowhere else in the country. So much so that in the eyes of outsiders that part became the whole to the continued distress of those who would shun the reality of that country. Shun it, shunning that populous huge sector, shunning it by demonising the population, by caricaturing them, by despising them, by arguing, quite seriously, for decanting them in swathes from the communities that they have made, so that they can live forcibly together near the only work apparently feasible for them in the city, not in the so-called region. Imagine how strange that country would be. Open your eyes and think of Wales.[30]

It is hardly the image of a self-confident nation that has learned to embrace the sum of its parts. The element – the elephant in the room – that is missing from twenty-first century Wales is the culture, society, and politics of the valleys themselves. The collapse of the Labour citadel into a static, bureaucratic, devolved machine has starved the valleys of their potential to be, once more, the engine of Welsh (and British) life. There can be no starker reminder of the failure of South Walian social democracy to renew itself than the seemingly uniform decision of the former coalfield to leave the European Union in June 2016.

Looking back at the rise and fall of that social democracy to locate possible remedies for renewal, we will not find a joined-up answer within the framework of a nationalist perspective. The real legacy of the coalfield's radicalism and democratic tradition lies in grassroots, communitarian lines of solidarity that had relatively little to do with the concept of a nation but recognised fully the need to rely on the stable resources of the state for the benefit of ordinary people. The step-by-step decline evident since the 1970s reflects, in part, Labour's managerialism in office and its tendency, in Wales, to be caught in the headlights of nationalism, left and right. Devolution's current slide towards a failure to engage its electorate is tantamount to an unwillingness to look properly at the possibilities and problems of state-supported grassroots activity. The miners' welfare fund, which bequeathed a network of recreation grounds, swimming pools, and welfare halls, was a tax on industrial profits redistributed to the communities which did the work, but which crucially reverted to the state when the money ran out to sustain them voluntarily. The medical aid societies rested on a foundation of a levy of wages that was pooled to provide healthcare for all and became the model for the National Health Service. And the co-operative societies, too, were apparent as beacons of collective action that spoke to another potential way of doing things in a socialist manner. In this way solidarity – as well as the struggle for it – did not mean with the trade union alone, but with society as a whole. The South Wales that was formed by the rise and fall of coal mining, and by the concomitant rise and fall of social democracy, was driven by this kind of solidarity. It did not mean, nor could it mean, uniformity, either of personnel or of policies.

It is now almost two centuries since the red flag was first raised on the Waun overlooking Merthyr Tydfil in 1831, the starting point of a journey that has, by now, come to an end. The defeat of the miners in 1985 shattered any meaningful possibility of mirroring the political activism of the past; as miners' institutes stood empty and vandalised, and were then burned down or demolished, the visible symbols of what was once possible in South Wales disappeared. For two generations, South Wales was lit up by a popular politics that fulfilled the ambitions of the two generations that preceded them and gifted to the two generations that followed a remarkable legacy. Nurseries, infant welfare clinics, recreation grounds, hospitals, swimming pools, libraries, public halls, cinemas, dedicated men and women who ran their own newspapers and shops, educated themselves in ways that today's university students can only dream of, looked after refugees, sent vital aid into warzones, and even fought and died to protect the principles of democracy. That was the essence of the South Wales of Aneurin Bevan and

Gwyn Thomas. South Wales today lives in their shadow, and what follows is their history, and of the individuals, hitherto somewhat discarded if not ignored, whom I champion and namecheck in the pages which follow. How the story continues is another matter, an outcome dependent on knowing and acknowledging their history.

Notes

[1] See, for example, the letter sent by the then secretary of the Aberdare Divisional Labour Party, Edmund Stonelake, to Goronwy Jones of Ynysybwl, 12 February 1941. In it Stonelake reflected that when he was a young man, like many of his socialist comrades, he had considered the revolution to be at hand. RBA, MNA/PP/61/5 (Goronwy Jones Papers). The letter was sent amidst the People's Vigilance Committee controversy in the early part of the Second World War. Established by the Communist Party, it was an attempt to maintain the spirit of the popular front of the late 1930s. The central feature of the committee was the People's Convention held on 12 January 1941. Goronwy Jones was lodge chairman at the Lady Windsor Colliery at the time. He was expelled from Labour together with the lodge secretary, John E. Morgan, for his support for the Convention. See John E. Morgan, *VWC*, 47 and the letters contained in NLW, Pontypridd Miners' Agents' Papers: Goronwy R. Jones of Ynysybwl, File 1 (Correspondence, 1941-1969). See also James Jupp, *The Radical Left in Britain, 1931-1941* (London, 1982), ch. 11.

[2] Although contemporary spelling of Maerdy varied, sometimes with an 'e' and at other times – as Thomas Isaac Jones's nickname discussed below demonstrates – without, I have followed present practice except insofar as sources use 'Mardy'. These instances have been left as they were found. Likewise I have favoured Llanelli over Llanelly. Elsewhere, I have employed the most commonly used spellings in use today. Thus, Aberdare is preferred to Aberdâr; Rhymney to Rhymni; Ynysybwl to Ynys-y-bŵl, and so forth.

[3] This is a point underlined in many of the oral history interviews undertaken by the Coalfield History Project in the 1970s. For an indicative recording see those with Abel Morgan, Ynysybwl. SWML, AUD/310, 'Interview with Abel Morgan, 9 October 1972'; AUD/311, 'Interview with Abel Morgan, May 1972'.

[4] Gwyn Thomas, *Shades of Gwyn Thomas: Programme Two, Ebbw Vale* (HTV Wales, 1996). This was a repeat of the original broadcast made in 1960.

[5] Alfred Zimmern, *My Impressions of Wales* (London, 1921).

[6] J. H. Morris and L. J. Williams, *The South Wales Coal Industry, 1841-1975* (Cardiff, 1958), 77.

[7] B. R. Mitchell, *Economic Development of the British Coal Industry, 1800-1914* (Cambridge, 1984), 7, 17; Michael Asteris, 'The Rise and Fall of South Wales Coal Exports, 1870-1930', *WHR* 13, no. 1 (1986).

[8] Steven Gray, *Steam Power and Sea Power: Coal, the Royal Navy, and the British Empire, c.1870-1914* (London, 2017).

[9] Mitchell, *Economic Development*, 83.

[10] As above, *Economic Development*, 138.

[11] A. J. Cook, *Appeal to the Workers of Britain* (Lansbury's Labour Weekly Record, c. 1926). Available online: http://www.bishopsgate.org.uk/content/1430/Recordings-of-Talks [Accessed: 2 November 2017]

[12] Joe England, *Merthyr: The Crucible of Modern Wales* (Cardigan, 2017); Neil Evans, 'The Welsh Victorian City: The Middle Class and National Consciousness in Cardiff, 1850-1914', *WHR* 12, no. 3 (1985), 350-387.

[13] Dai Smith, 'Excesses of the Past or Stopping the Narrative', *Llafur* 8, no. 4 (2003), 109. See also his *Out of the People: A Century in Labour* (Aberystwyth, 2000).

[14] Gwyn A. Williams, 'Imperial South Wales', in his *The Welsh in their History* (London, 1982).

[15] Anthony Giddens, *The Consequences of Modernity* (Cambridge, 1991), 64.

[16] Roland Robertson, 'Glocalization: Time-Space and Homogeneity-Heterogeneity', in Mike Featherstone, Scott Lash and Roland Roberts (eds.), *Global Modernities* (New York, 1995), 25-44.

[17] The Brecht story, which also refers to Barry Dock, is an appendix to a collected volume of his short stories. Bertolt Brecht, 'The Life of the Boxer Samson-Körner', in idem (ed. John Willett and Ralph Manheim), *The Short Stories of Bertolt Brecht* (London, 2015 edn). On Conrad in Wales see Dai Smith, *Aneurin Bevan and the World of South Wales* (Cardiff, 1993), 115, 343. Eugene O'Neill, 'Bound East for Cardiff' in *The Provincetown Plays* (New York, 1916), 6-25.

[18] Dai Smith, *In the Frame: Memory in Society, Wales 1910 to 2010* (Cardigan, 2012), xii-xiii.

[19] *SWE*, 16 July 1898.

[20] *BH*, 9 December 1898; *EEx*, 18 February 1899; *CT*, 9 December 1899; *Weekly Mail*, 16 December 1899.

[21] *SWE*, 19 September 1898; *SWDN*, 12 October 1898.

[22] *GFP*, 5 November 1932.

[23] Keir Hardie, *Labour Representation on Different Bodies: An Address* (Aberdare, 1901), 7. Copy consulted at Aberdare Library.

[24] *GFP*, 10 January 1908. Chris Williams, 'An Able Administrator of Capitalism? The Labour Party in the Rhondda, 1917-21', *Llafur* 4, no. 4 (1987), 20-33.

[25] Dai Smith, 'The Future of Coalfield History', *Morgannwg* 19 (1975), 57-70, p. 64. See also, idem, 'What Does History Know of Nail Biting?', *Llafur* 1, no. 2 (1973) and Chris Williams, 'The South Wales Miners' Federation', *Llafur* 5, no. 3 (1990), 45-56.

[26] This is discussed in Daryl Leeworthy, *Fields of Play: The Sporting Heritage of Wales* (Aberystwyth, 2012). See also my 'Workers' Fields: Sport, Landscape, and the Labour Movement in South Wales, 1858-1958' (Unpublished PhD thesis, 2011).

[27] Alun Burge, *William Hazell and the Gleaming Vision: A Co-operative Life in South Wales, 1890-1964* (Talybont, 2014), 195.

[28] John E. Morgan, *VWC*, 70.

[29] Leighton Andrews, *Wales Says Yes* (Bridgend, 1999); Denis Balsom and J. Barry Jones (eds.), *The Road to the National Assembly for Wales* (Cardiff, 2000).

[30] The speech is available online: https://www.youtube.com/watch?v=4H9XtrQ5OR0 [Accessed: 10 March 2018].

PART I

Building South Wales

CHAPTER ONE

Making a Working Class

This is to give you a notice Argoed Colliers you cannot leave your old ways. Levi Harris – Chas. Williams, the two Devils and John Morgan take a work under price 14s a week and Wilks long legged devil pray on G-d for mercy. O Lord look on thy situation – they shall be in hell before Monday morning – and you all Brothers if you will work with such a people I will break your bones – And after you can't work in any work.[1]

Notice left at Argoed Colliery, 16 May 1834

This notice signed with the hieroglyph of a bull – the mark of the *Tarw Scotch* (Scotch Cattle) – was found at the Argoed Colliery near Tredegar in May 1834.[2] One of scores of similar notices left at collieries and ironworks across Monmouthshire and the eastern parts of Glamorgan in the 1820s, 1830s, and 1840s, it forewarned of a visit by a group of men, with blackened faces and wearing disguises, who would proceed to terrorise those workers who had accepted wage reductions or worsened conditions, thus broken ranks with the rest of the workforce and undermined solidarity.[3] At times, particularly in moments of deepest crisis, the Scotch Cattle took aim at the masters themselves. In her journal, Lady Charlotte Guest commented on 18 June 1834 that some of the local ironmasters had received letters threatening their lives; the next morning one such letter arrived at Dowlais threatening to bring the Scotch Cattle in early July 'unless all the Irish were discharged from the works'. She reflected, 'I was far from well during the morning'.[4] Two days later, the threats made to workers at Argoed Colliery were carried out. Three houses were attacked by a roving gang and shots fired. One of those alleged to have taken part, a 20-year-old Somerset man called Aaron Smallcombe, was arrested having been identified by a little girl woken up when the Scotch Cattle entered the house she was living in.[5]

When the case came before the Assizes that summer, Smallcombe was acquitted because the girl, Rebecca Rogers, was too young to be able to legitimately testify against him in court.[6] Nevertheless, the evidence given by adult witnesses in the case gives a good sense of the terror that could be inflicted by the Scotch Cattle as they moved from house to house, from village to village. The sounds that they made – 'a sort of bellowing noise, resembling the noise made by oxen' – was undoubtedly a key part of this terroristic impression, and was well remembered by Mary Rogers, Rebecca's mother.[7] Others recalled being awoken by the blowing of a horn and the rattling of chains that announced the arrival of the cattle in the middle of the night.[8] What they saw when their eyes opened were men with blackened faces, wearing deliberately unusual clothes – whether women's clothes, turned in jackets, or their Sunday best. The leaders amongst them were disguised with cattle skins and masks, and occasionally wore horns on their heads. And they all carried tools of destruction: stones, the handles of mandrels, and axes. The work tools, indeed, that were essential to their livelihood, along with such projectiles that could be gathered, stored, and carried easily to the site of harassment.[9]

There can be little doubt that the motivations of the Scotch Cattle reflected economic and industrial circumstances: the fragility of working class life in communities governed by wage labour (but not a living wage) and the exploitative truck system which meant workers were paid in shop goods at the company store instead of money that they then possessed.[10] In a letter sent to the Home Office in April 1832, John Moggridge of

Blackwood, a Monmouthshire magistrate, explained that those carrying out violence in Fleur-de-Lys were motivated by the fact that they had been 'recently paid in shop goods instead of in money'. This had left the workers at the mercy of the company stores. Moggridge noted that the 'obnoxious shop [was] nearly demolished'. The deliberate focus of the cattle was clear to him, since 'these disturbers of the peace came from a distance, and were directed only as to the particular objects of their vengeance'.[11] The Marquess of Bute, in a letter sent to Lord Melbourne a few weeks later, expressed similar sentiments.

> I believe the great majority of the workmen at Merthyr to be well disported to remain quiet; there are some parts in that neighbourhood, but of comparatively trifling important as to numbers, where they are in a more inflammable state, the fact is that there is a very great difference in the wages and conditions of the workmen at the various ironworks and mines connected with them, arising from the different system of management. [...] This inequality of wages falls very severely upon many respectable men and families but it affects too many who are not very able or willing to understand why their wages are lower without injustice to themselves.[12]

In his reports to the Home Office, the garrison commander at Brecon, Colonel Love, offered more sympathy with the rioters, noting that 'in the course of our enquiry [it appeared] that the truck system is by no means entirely abandoned, and that [...] the workmen may have just cause of complaint'.[13] These views were given a wider airing at a meeting of the ironmasters and the magistrates of Glamorgan, Monmouthshire and Breconshire at the Angel Inn in Abergavenny on 4 May 1832. During the meeting, they resolved to end the truck system, thereby bringing an end to the probable cause of the disturbances in the valleys. They also came to collective agreement to 'suppress the [Scotch Cattle] and to defeat and bring to justice all persons guilty of these flagrant outrages' and as part of that determination to take steps to establish a new permanent police force. This would replace the ad hoc swearing in of special constables, a system which had been found wanting.[14]

But what of the working-class men who joined the Scotch Cattle gangs? Their antagonism towards the truck system and the bondage that resulted from it was quite clear, as was their desire to collectively shield their wages from price fluctuations in the market. On several occasions prior to the passage of the 1831 Truck Act, parliament had passed legislation outlawing aspects of the practice, most notably in 1817, but these acts failed to prevent the presence of truck shops in South Wales.[15] The system operating in Glamorgan and Monmouthshire was not outright bondage resulting from compulsion to deal with the employer's shop or be paid in goods as a condition of employment, rather it was a 'compulsion to deal with the truck shop only if one drew an irregular anticipation of wages accrued but not yet due to be paid' – a system of 'credit' which tied workers to their employers. Those workers who did not draw an advance on their wages, or drew it on the designated 'draw day' (typically mid-way through the payment cycle) were not obliged to spend their money in the shop. Those who took part of their wages at any other time had to spend the clear majority – typically around eighty per cent – in the truck shop.[16]

The operation of this kind of truck was most prevalent in the valleys of Monmouthshire. As Thomas Evans, principal agent for the Guest Iron Works at Dowlais, explained in his evidence to the parliamentary select committee on payment of wages in 1842, the truck system prevailed 'considerably in Monmouthshire, but not in the neighbourhood of Merthyr Tidvil; within two miles of us, at the Romney [sic] and other iron-works in Monmouthshire, it prevails; the nearest to us is two miles'.[17] The key complaint from workers focused on the prices that were charged at the truck shops. One collier from Newbridge, who gave evidence to the committee, related how it was possible to buy the same amount of everyday items in Newport for thirteen shillings, and four pence, as were charged for one pound (or twenty shillings) in the truck shop of Abercarn. 'It squeezes us very badly', he remarked.[18] The Chairman of the Merthyr Board of Guardians, himself a trader, explained similarly that there was at least six pence difference in the cost of flour in Merthyr and Dowlais compared to the prices being charged in Rhymney, a situation that was much worse when buying butter, bacon and cheese. The workers 'were extremely anxious to get their money from the receiving officer at Merthyr on the Saturday, instead of being paid in the district, so as to be able to lay it out in the shops at Merthyr'.[19]

Aside from deliberate manipulation of where they received parish relief payments (which was not always feasible), workers and their families had few legal means of redress. With the near universal operation of truck in the valleys of Monmouthshire, workers had no means of escaping it. Truck thrived on workers caught in the trap of having to live hand to mouth and having no visible escape route. It was exacerbated by housing conditions which reflected the role of speculators in meeting housing demand. In the words of one government inspector, writing about Merthyr:

The best of the workmen's houses are, for the most part, those erected by the different iron companies for such as labour in connexion with their establishments. Some of these appear to have been unsold, especially at Dowlais. Speculators of various kind seem to have built courts, alleys and rows of houses, wherever opportunities presented themselves, in order to meet the demand for the rapid increase of the town, without regard to any order or system, and without any control as to lines, the form of the streets, or arrangements for drainage.[20]

The differences were largely superficial, however, since 'the absence of piped water and any sanitary facilities was universal'.[21] Merthyr had its shanty towns and some residents even sought shelter under bridges when no other option was available to them.[22] Dowlais was no different, with most of the eight thousand residents in the town by the middle of the nineteenth century crammed, as many as ten per house, into buildings that had two or three rooms at most.[23] Half a century later, nothing had changed. As a delegation from the Merthyr branch of the Independent Labour Party explained to the town's primarily Liberal councillors in 1901, there were houses no more than three hundred yards from the town hall where families were living nine in a room. When one of them died, the others had to live, sleep, eat, and do the washing, with the body laid out on the table, until the funeral was held. As to why nothing was done by the authorities, the ILP delegation explained to party members at a subsequent branch meeting that 'we did not think [they] were in sympathy'.[24] Such was the impact of liberalism on the material lives of the poor.

Housing, wages, and free access to a market of goods and services, in which working people were not exploited, provide the contextual themes of this chapter, which explores the range of efforts by working people to try and ameliorate, through politics and different models of consumption, the circumstances in which they lived. Friendly societies, co-operatives, trade unions, and the first generation of labour politicians, were the immediate ancestors of the formalised labour movement of the twentieth century. Steadily there emerged a new political language too, labourism, and those who preached its gospel.

The most prominent of these was William Abraham, Mabon, the charismatic but singular leader of the Rhondda miners. His rise to prominence in the 1870s and his election as the first MP for the Rhondda in 1885, marked a new period in the history of Labour Country.

Towards a Friendly Society

By the 1830s, efforts to forge mutualised responses to speculative industrialisation were already several years old. Gwyn Alf Williams, writing of the late-eighteenth century, the time of the American and French Revolutions, called this a 'time of beginnings'.[25] It was when the Welsh population began to grow, when the ideas that emerged from (and in opposition to) the revolutions abroad kick-started political thought, and when dissent of both a political and religious kind was fast becoming the order of the day.[26] Out of this fermentation came the friendly societies, voluntary associations which gathered subscriptions from members and provided assistance in times of need: whether those needs derived from a loss of income during illness or injury, or came in old age when work became difficult and the idea of a state pension was more than a century away, or came on the death of a family member with the money being used to enable a family to survive after losing a breadwinner. But friendly societies were about more than social insurance, they were co-operatives, trade unions, and an early phase in the women's movement providing women with a clear political voice.[27] No surprise then that, as Ieuan Gwynedd Jones noted, 'there were more members of Friendly Societies than of chapels'.[28]

The earliest friendly societies in Wales developed in the mid-eighteenth century, just as the agricultural and industrial revolutions began to alter the fabric of life, and they tended to be based on a community, rather than a trade or those who drank in a particular public house, as would be the case in the nineteenth century.[29] The Union Club of Swansea, founded in the early 1760s, was probably the first in Glamorgan.[30] When official registration of friendly societies was introduced in 1794, it revealed over thirty societies in existence across Glamorgan; within a decade this had grown to over one hundred and twenty.[31] In all, the registered societies boasted a combined membership of some twelve thousand people at a time when Glamorgan had a population of around seventy thousand. By the time of the Merthyr Rising in 1831, there were nearly two hundred registered societies in Glamorgan – over thirty of them in Merthyr alone.[32] Although not every friendly society submitted to the registration regime, these figures nevertheless give some indication of their organisational strength.

But what of their purpose and meaning beyond the provision of insurance and mutual aid? Some friendly societies, although not all, provided an environment in which working-class visions of society could be thought about and acted upon. For E.P. Thompson, they were a 'unifying cultural influence' and bridged the gap between eighteenth century forms of popular organisation and later nineteenth century forms such as Chartist lodges, co-operatives, and the labour movement.[33] If working-class visions of society, as Raymond Williams argued, may be understood as collectivist and mutual, brought together by the effects of capitalist production and distribution, then friendly societies represented a working-class means of ameliorating those effects.[34] One consequence of efforts to bind communities together for collective purpose was the institution of rules and regulations designed to preserve integrity. The United Blaina Society of Nantyglo, for instance, enjoyed no support from the ironmasters and met at a public house, its business was conducted in Welsh and members swore an oath of absolute secrecy to maintain the security of the society.[35] Those who joined the politically-radical Vulcan Friendly Society, based at the Swan Inn in Dowlais, were compelled to go one stage further and not join another society.[36]

If workers recognised the possibilities of the friendly society, so too did employers – and in various ways. Some, such as the owners of the Melingriffith Tin Works near Cardiff or the Nantyglo Iron Works in Monmouthshire, provided a degree of sponsorship to works-based friendly societies. The Melingriffith Friendly Society, established for men in 1786 and for women in 1803, met in the club facilities set aside by the tinmasters for the clerks and managerial staff at the works.[37] This provided the societies with considerable stability, and they thrived: celebrating their anniversary in 1860, the men's society drew deliberate attention to their financial status – some two thousand, three hundred pounds in the bank – and the continued enrolment of young members.[38] Combining with gentry and clergy others formed friendly societies of their own to propagate a value system based on individual improvement. Of prominence was the Society for the Improvement of the Working Population in the County of Glamorgan established at a meeting in the Bear Inn, Cowbridge, on 21 January 1831. Chaired by Benjamin Heath Malkin, a Cambridge graduate, close friend of William Blake, and recently retired professor of history at the University of London, the society aimed at diffusing 'a knowledge, generally, of the circumstances on which the well-being of the labourers and their families depends'.[39]

For several months, the gentry in South Wales, southern England, and parts of northern England, had been animated by the work of 'Captain Swing', an anonymous incendiary figure at the head of a rural revolt against the mechanisation of agriculture.[40] Swing's presence in Wales was relatively slight, the *Cambrian* newspaper could even boast that 'no part of the Principality has the destructive spirit of outrage, lately so prevalent in many districts of the kingdom'.[41] Nevertheless, several letters 'signed' by Swing were sent to the gentry in Glamorgan and Monmouthshire, and shortly before Christmas 1830 a number of hayricks and wheat stacks were burnt at farms near St Nicholas and Llantwit Major.[42] There were also complaints about agricultural unemployment near Llantrisant.[43] It was enough to encourage the authorities in both counties to swear in a number of special constables as a precautionary measure: a gathering of magistrates in Chepstow, for instance, saw nearly eight hundred afforded these powers. It was symptomatic of the tension between gentry and labourer, between the authorities and the wider working population: as was reported in the press, 'suspicious characters will be closely watched and not permitted to perambulate the county without interruption'.[44] The meeting in Cowbridge in January 1831 was just one possible response.

Within a month of its foundation, the Society for the Improvement of the Working Population in the County of Glamorgan had attracted a healthy membership of sixty and received the patronage of the Marquess of Bute.[45] Alongside Malkin, the society's officers were Francis Taynton (treasurer) and Charles Redwood (secretary). Taynton was linked to Malkin through marriage (Malkin's sister-in-law was Taynton's wife) and worked as a solicitor. He also served as clerk to the Cowbridge corporation. Redwood, later the author of *The Vale of Glamorgan: Scenes and Tales among the Welsh* (1839) and friend and correspondent of Thomas and Jane Carlyle, was also a solicitor. Resident at Llandough, he was considered 'at all times ready and willing, by professional advice or otherwise, to assist in extricating out of their difficulties the poor and unfortunate'.[46] The Redwood family were notable for their Quaker beliefs and, particularly in the case of Charles's uncle Isaac, whom Elijah Waring later described as a 'constant and energetic friend', for their support of Iolo Morganwg.[47] Both Waring and Isaac

Redwood were members of the society. As was Edward Bradley, a prominent local land agent, whose name appeared in a Swing letter sent to Edward Picton, the Rector of Llandow:

Newport Decr 10th 1830
Reverend Father no machinery no tythe to the Clergy no Bradley Agency &c I have just been paying a Visit at Duffrin. The Honbl. W. B. Grey I shall vissit [sic] you Shortly as bold as the General entered Badajoss it is my intention to see your house burnt down to the ground take this hint
Swing
PS more wages to workmen.[48]

The society's membership was generally reflective of the gentry and clergy of Cowbridge and its neighbours. Central to the political motivations of the society was the allegiance of several members, including Malkin, to the Whig Party. These included Edward Romilly, the Whig MP for Ludlow (1832-1835), Charles Vachell, who served as mayor of Cardiff (1849-50), Walter Coffin, colliery owner, mayor of Cardiff (1848-49) and its MP (1852-57), and local magistrate (and former High Sheriff of Glamorgan) Llewellyn Traherne. Like many Whigs, this group were active in the anti-slavery movement organising petitions for 'the earliest practicable abolition of slavery in the British Colonies'.[49] And they took seriously the value of education, believing it necessary to establish a network of free libraries in the boroughs of Glamorgan, to set up infant schools, and to promote opportunities for lifelong learning.[50] These values were taken from two sources: the Society for the Diffusion of Useful Knowledge (SDUK) and the Society for the Promotion of Christian Knowledge (SPCK). The latter had had a long presence in Cowbridge founding a diocesan library there in 1711 and many of the local clergy were involved in the Cowbridge Clerical

Book Club, founded in 1817 as the successor to the Cowbridge Book Society of 1736, that provided lending items for the library by means of membership subscription.

The SDUK, on whose general committee two of Malkin's sons sat, was more significant. Malkin sought – and gained – the support of Henry Brougham MP, the SDUK's founder, for the Cowbridge society, and the SDUK provided a large set of pamphlets and books that enabled the establishment of the society's itinerating libraries.[51] Towards the end of 1831, the Cowbridge society was even reformed as the Glamorganshire local committee of the SDUK with Malkin, the Reverend R. B. Paul of Llantwit Major, and William Williams of Aberpergwm, serving as the officers.[52] This followed the example of the Monmouth committee established by John H. Moggridge in 1830, and the Swansea Mechanics' Institute founded a few years earlier in 1826.[53] The main priority of the Cowbridge society (and its equivalents) was indeed 'to diffuse a knowledge, generally, of the circumstances on which the well-being of the labourers and their families depends', language very much in keeping with the aims of the SDUK. But this was also about transforming the habits of working people and a desire from above to instil in them 'prudential and industrious' behaviour.[54] To propagate these ideas, the society published a number of 'Cowbridge tracts' (twelve in total), one of which was entitled 'On the Advantages of Friendly Societies'. It offered the belief that through membership of a society a poor man could claim:

> Poor as I am, I am obliged to no man for a farthing, and therefore consider myself as independent as any gentleman or farmer in the parish.[55]

The society made good on this claim by establishing the 'Cowbridge and Lanblethian Friendly Society', formally registering it in January 1832. Although there is no clear evidence that it actually functioned, the society nevertheless remained on the official register for several years.[56]

What occurred in Cowbridge in 1831 was an example of middle-class organisation and an attempt at using the resources of the middle class to create institutions that would instil order and a certain form of morality and respectability in the working population. But it was a misreading of the way in which friendly societies and collective organisation were used by working people as a form of radical expression. Whereas the middle classes established museums and libraries complete with Roman artefacts, stuffed animals, rocks, and old coins, as was the case in Neath in 1835, there were clear political undercurrents within working-class institutions.[57] This division was clearest in Merthyr and Dowlais, where the Guests set up their mechanics' institute and formed a local committee of the Society for the Diffusion of Useful Knowledge, and the workers set about establishing branches of the first national miners' union: the Friendly Associated Coal Miners Union Society (FACMUS).[58] These fault lines, made starkly apparent during Chartist agitation, were so significant that when the leading middle-class participants died towards the end of the nineteenth century, mention was made in their obituaries. Matthew Moggridge, mayor of Swansea, president of the Royal Institution of South Wales, and magistrate for both Glamorgan and Monmouthshire, was seen on his death in 1882 as an 'advanced' Liberal but nevertheless firmly opposed to Chartism and its antecedents.[59]

The FACMUS arrived in Merthyr in the aftermath of the 1831 rising. In a letter to the Home Office sent on 3 July, the Marquess of Bute reported that a large placard called 'The Workman's Manual' giving details of how to hold legal union meetings was in the hands of magistrates in the town and he hoped to be able to report more details soon.[60] And in August, wealthier citizens of Merthyr petitioned the Home Secretary not to withdraw the troops stationed in the town because of the presence of 'strangers calling themselves delegates from some parts of England'.[61] By September, the press were reporting that 'the firemen and miners and colliers of that district [Merthyr], and in the collieries in Monmouthshire and Glamorganshire, have formed themselves into clubs or lodges, upon the principle of those which have excited so much bad feeling in the North of England'. The *Monmouthshire Merlin* continued:

> The professed object of these societies, as set forth in their *printed* rules, is for mutual assistance when out of employment, and to *prevent the reduction of their wages*.[62]

The ironmasters at the Dowlais Iron Works and the Plymouth Iron Works refused to have anything to do with those men who had joined the union, thus prompting a lockout.[63] In a letter to Bute, Robert Beaumont, the mineral agent for the Bute Estate in Glamorgan, described the scene:

> There has been almost a suspension of labour at the Dowlais and Plymouth Iron Works. Owing to the workmen throughout the different works having entered into the union society, Dowlais Company and Messrs Hills resolved to put a stop to the continuance of such proceeding and so determined were the workmen to follow their new system that they preferred quitting their work to renouncing the society.

To test the workers' resolve, the Dowlais works began importing fresh labour and some of the older miners renounced the union and returned to work. Beaumont recorded that the only aid flowing into the district had come from South Wales: 'no aid has been afforded to them from England'.[64]

His suggestion that the workers would soon be forced back proved premature. On 1 November, John B. Bruce, the stipendiary magistrate, wrote to the Home Office warning that 'a very large portion of the workmen [are] still holding out and refusing to abandon the miners, the funds of which are very nearly exhausted, a crisis may very reasonably be shortly expected'.[65] The crisis was already visible on the streets. Crowds filled the streets of Merthyr and Dowlais, half starved, beggars were a common sight, and the tension remained at fever pitch. 'How long [will] they [...] be peaceable with stomachs only half filled', Bruce wrote despairingly.[66]

In the event, it took until the end of November before the miners finally renounced the union and were taken back on. The *Cambrian* crowed, 'It is with feelings of great satisfaction that we announce to our readers, that the men engaged in the extensive iron works of Dowlais and Plymouth, at Merthyr Tydfil, have returned to their usual employments, having utterly renounced all connexion with the "Union Societies" lately formed there'.[67] The preachers, elders, and other members of the Welsh Calvinistic Methodists at Tredegar met on 19 October to denounce the union declaring that 'none will in future be received as members of our connexion, who belong to the above "union clubs"'. And the Select Vestry at Merthyr – the predominant civil authority in the town – refused relief because the miners had removed themselves from work 'voluntarily'.[68] The screw turning of the ironmasters and civic institutions had apparently worked. Even an unfortunate chapel minister from Dowlais was reprimanded by Josiah John Guest for having been present at a union meeting; he apologised to the ironmaster in the strongest of terms.[69] The men too, were in the mood to be contrite. On 23 November, William Thompson, former lord mayor of London, and a proprietor of the Penydarren Iron Works, held a general meeting of his workforce at the works.

He encouraged his men to 'abjure the clubs'. To bring peace, he even offered an amnesty to the leading organisers of the trade union clubs. The *Monmouthshire Merlin* wrote triumphantly, 'the Union is now [...] *as dead as a herring!*'[70]

1831 was not an end, but a beginning. In 1834, fresh disturbances amongst miners and ironworkers of Glamorgan and Monmouthshire prompted the *Monmouthshire Merlin* to warn that 'various illegal associations have of late been established by designing persons, in and about the iron districts of South Wales, under the designation of Trades' Union Clubs, and other plausible titles'. There was some dissent from the general pattern – at the Blaenavon Iron Works, for instance, workers refused to join the union clubs – but in the western part of the county, membership was strong, as it was in Newport.[71] At Pontypool and at the Cyfarthfa Works in Merthyr, men rushed to join the trade union.[72] The ironmasters again threw down their gauntlets threatening to lockout their workforce unless they quit the union clubs immediately. The Independent Order of Odd Fellows at Merthyr and Tredegar threatened members with expulsion if they joined a trade union: at Merthyr one man was thrown out of the order, he protested that he feared losing his job if he left the trade union, and at Tredegar the rules were altered to bar any odd fellow from ever joining a union. So much for the *pax et amor* – peace and love – which was the order's motto.[73]

But a different kind of motto was in vogue in Merthyr that year: 'labour is the source of wealth'. Drawn from the writing of Adam Smith, it served as the guiding impulse of Wales's first working-class newspaper, *Y Gweithiwr* (The Workman).[74] Bilingual and radical in politics, the paper was edited by John Thomas, a former Unitarian minister and schoolmaster, and Morgan Williams, then twenty-four years old, a master-weaver and fast emerging as a leading figure of Merthyr's working-class movement.[75] It was printed by W. Williams of High Street, Brecon, a former Merthyr resident. The surviving copy, published in March 1834, gives a clear sense of the fiery politics of the editors. There are fierce denunciations of the 'stupid and imbecile aristocracy', a warning that 'the crisis is coming', angry declaration against the hated Court of Requests (the debtors' court), and reflections on the hypocrisy of secret oaths being acceptable for middle- and upper-class members of society, but being illegal for workers. Morgan Williams even went so far as to declare that:

> Labour cannot be destroyed, for it will produce, it will fashion into every shape the rude ores of Nature, and whether untaxed bread or a social revolution be Britain's destiny, after all labour will be the source of wealth.

Much of this sort of language is underscored by the pen of John Bruce who sent the copy to the Marquess of Bute encouraging him to ask the government to suppress it as seditious. 'I think a public notice', mused Bruce, 'would effectively frighten the printer, unless, indeed, it were thought worthwhile to punish the authors'.[76] It is not known when *Y Gweithiwr* ceased publication, but it likely fell victim to the successful efforts of the ironmasters to eradicate trades unionism in the district that summer.

What the ironmasters failed to do, however, was quash printed outlets for working-class opinion, and thereby the steady growth of political activism. In 1836, the government reduced the newspaper stamp duty to a penny, encouraging the newspaper trade. Whereas *Y Gweithiwr*, as an unstamped newspaper, rode the boundary of illegality, Merthyr's 'proto-Chartist' press in the form of the *Merthyr and Cardiff Chronicle* was a legal, stamped newspaper.[77] The *Chronicle* developed out of the *South Wales Reporter* published by Josiah Thomas Jones, a Congregationalist minister and printer from Caernarfon who moved to Merthyr in April 1836. The first edition appeared on 4 March 1837 and was deliberately aimed at those with 'the humblest resources'. Its main target was the truck shop. Financial difficulties and low circulation caused the newspaper to fold at the end of May, but with the promise of a new title.[78] That title was the *Merthyr and Cardiff Chronicle* and its first issue appeared on 8 July. One of the most regular contributors was Morgan Williams, who pressed the case for the formation of branches of the Working Men's Association and for participation in the formation of a new Literary and Scientific Institution for the town.[79]

The Merthyr branch of the Working Men's Association was founded in October 1838 and Morgan Williams was elected secretary. This followed the formation of a branch of the Association at Carmarthen in 1837, the first in Wales. On Christmas Day, 1838, a major rally was held at Merthyr with thousands marching behind the Chartist colours of green, white and blue. The purpose of the event – the largest Chartist meeting held in Wales up to this point – was to elect someone to represent the town at the National Chartist Convention. The Charter was read in Welsh and English. Williams and his comrades may have felt confident that they were 'bringing the Merthyr working classes into a national crusade' but the ironmasters and their families looked on with concern. Lady Charlotte Guest wrote in her diary of the event that, 'the meeting was considered a failure.[80] No violent language was used. It is supposed that the strength of the Merthyr Chartists is about seven hundred'.[81] She was wrong. There were soon Chartist branches across the coalfield: at Dowlais, Tredegar, Nantyglo, Blackwood, and Swansea.[82] Early in the New Year, Chartism had become 'a mass movement' and could boast as many as fifty branches and nearly twenty five thousand members.[83]

The press held the key to this simmering working-class activity, as did the lodge structure learned from the friendly societies.

Lewis Weston Dillwyn, MP for Glamorganshire, wrote to the Marquess of Bute on 9 May 1839 expressing concern at the 'slow effect of the poison which they [the Chartist press] are always spreading among the Labouring Classes [...] last week a vast number of the papers which I sent one to your Lordship were publicly and gratuitously distributed'.[84] A similar situation prevailed at Pontypridd, Merthyr, Aberdare, and Gelligaer.[85] By July, meetings were being held at Cardiff with a view to forming a Chartist branch. The journeymen tailors, shoemakers, and masons who formed the core of the branch met regularly at the Red Lion Hotel. Members were admitted upon payment of a one penny subscription in the manner of a friendly society.[86] In Merthyr, the Chartists had their own uniform consisting of a flannel waistcoat in a design created at Morgan Williams's weaving shop in Penyrheolgerrig. It too was a symptom of the society structure learned previously. A local magistrate described the effects of the 'uniform' at a church rally in Merthyr:

> The Church became unusually filled with workmen and women very decently draped and a good many of them (the greater number) distinguished by the Chartist Badge, viz blue ribbon attached to the button hole, and flannel waistcoat of a peculiar pattern. Their leader here in point of literary talent is Morgan Williams, a weaver, who no doubt has suggested the flannel waistcoat badge for his own benefit. The church was filled to suffocation – it is computed that about 2,000 were inside the church and that 1,000 remained outside – not the slightest disturbance took place.[87]

In the manner of the more ceremonial friendly societies, the Merthyr Chartists organised an annual Christmas Day festival, events to celebrate Tom Paine's birthday, and a myriad of discussion classes.[88] And by 1840 they had their own newspaper once more, *Udgorn Cymru* (the Trumpet of Wales): it appeared fortnightly between March 1840 and October 1842.[89] Its motto, drawn from Thessalonians in the New Testament, *profwch pob beth, deliwch yr hyn sy' dda* (prove all things, hold onto that which is good), was indicative of its questioning nature and the proto-co-operative of shareholders that owned the newspaper published under the name 'The Working Men's Press and Publications'.[90]

Udgorn Cymru caused alarm amongst the magistrates of Merthyr and they established a monitoring committee which met weekly at the Castle Inn. They endeavoured to secure copies of unstamped periodicals, particularly the *Udgorn*, and bring their existence to the attention of the government. They also read the *Northern Star*, the noted Chartist newspaper published in Leeds, for information of activities in South Wales and shared this information with magistrates across the region.[91] One effect of this surveillance was a warning issued by the government and sent to the publishers of *Udgorn* stating that they could not publish news unless the paper was stamped.[92] To compensate, the paper published articles on subjects such as the inaccessibility of the law to ordinary people and the need to disestablish the church.[93] Lack of news, however, dampened the paper's effectiveness and by October 1841 the publishers had resolved to published a stamped edition in order to aid the Chartist cause. The government kept the publishers waiting six months before sending the stamps, a delay that was attributed to a desire to prevent the publication of genuine working-class news.[94] Bute certainly understood the importance of the newspaper. As he wrote to Lord Normanby, 'but for the publication [... of] the *Udgorn* and the *Advocate* [...] very little would be heard of Chartism in the district'.[95]

The hostility of the non-Chartist press to the Chartist movement ensured that any coverage was highly partial but

Bute's assessment perhaps underestimates the significance of alternative means of communication and organisation. The old adage of 'actions speak louder than words' offers some indication of those alternatives. In June 1841, the superintendent of police at Merthyr, Thomas Lewis, submitted a report to Bute on recent attempts by local Chartists to force down the price of meat.[96] However much this was ignored by the newspapers, it could hardly fail to be noticed by the people of Merthyr. In fact, Chartists across the country were busy setting up co-operative stores with the purpose of 'building a way out of the competitive world but this time closely connected to the question of state power'.[97] Shops and campaigns on food prices were a signal that democratic control had consequences and meaning for consumption as well as production. The co-operative model employed by the Chartists for their newspapers and shops was about proving, through action, that an alternative way of doing things was possible. This was the greatest success of early nineteenth century labour agitation and the 'great arch' linking that period to what came later.

Labour's Great Arch

The earliest Chartist co-operative store in Wales was formed in Pontypridd.[98] On 24 October 1840, the *Northern Star* – Britain's leading Chartist newspaper – carried a letter from Thomas Morgan, a carpenter in the town, stating that 'the Chartists of Newbridge [as Pontypridd was then known], and the adjoining villages, seeing that the whole of the shopkeepers are against the principles of Universal Suffrage, have come to the determination of opening a co-operative store for themselves'.[99] Within a week, the would-be co-operators had been inundated with rules and advice from those running Chartist co-operatives around the country, and they set to work forming the Pont-y-Ty-Prydd Provision Company.[100] It faced considerable challenges, not least the hostility of wholesalers who refused to engage with a 'political' enterprise. In a letter to the *Northern Star* in August 1841, Dr William Price reflected on these travails:

> Sir – as the Pont-y-Ty-Prydd Provision Company experiences much difficulty in obtaining what they want from the wholesale dealers, *for ready money*, will you be so good as to make the fact known in the columns of the *Star*, in order that some of your Chartist correspondents may refer us to some houses who do not consider it their interest to make a political distinction between the money of Chartist companies, and that of the factions. To remove all doubt on this point, I beg to transcribe a copy of *one* of these invidious distinctions.

The letter Price refers to was from Joseph Travers and Sons, a London wholesale grocer's:

> Sir – we are in receipt of your favour, and are much obliged for the preference of your order, but had rather decline the account altogether, as we are only in the habit of doing business with regular grocers, and not companies of the description you represent.[101]

Ironically, the Travers family were considered advanced Liberals in metropolitan circles and their offices in St Swithins Lane were at the heart of the Anti-Corn Law League agitations. Their refusal to do business with the store, however, was indicative of the wider challenges that the Chartists had in pursuing an alternative, democratic method of business. Despite such refusals to supply goods, the store survived and in 1842 it could provide considerable support – through credit – to workers from the town's Brown Lenox Chainworks on strike against reduced wages and rising unemployment. One hostile newspaper took aim:

> The reduction being proposed being very moderate, certainly not at all commensurate with the depressed state of the times, ought to have been accepted by the workmen: but unfortunately they are entirely at the command of a certain doctor in the neighbourhood who, although receiving his bread from the works, makes it his study to create and keep dissension between master and man to the utmost of his power, and in this instance has taken steps to provide the workers with provisions to a large amount.[102]

The doctor was William Price who had been employed at the chain works as medical officer since 1823. By 1842 the store was registered with the county clerk of the peace under the Friendly Societies Acts as the 'Commercial Company of Co-operatives', thereby indicating the full embrace of the co-operative principle by members.[103] There were also meetings held at an 'association room' above the store at which members discussed the campaign for political rights, amongst other matters.[104] But the level of credit extended to the workers at the chain works proved too much and the company folded at the end of the year. A second Chartist store was opened in Cardiff, but not until 1852.[105]

Co-operative societies and Chartist stores were a robust response to the prevalence of truck and other forms of consumer credit which exploited workers. Unsurprisingly, co-operatives grew substantially during periods of industrial unrest, when wage reductions or the absence of wages altogether impacted upon living standards. In Merthyr in 1854, a shoemakers' strike resulted in a manifesto issued to employers stating that unless wages were improved, workers would set up a co-operative instead. They met to discuss forming such a society.[106] But it was not until 1857 that the Merthyr Co-operative Society came into existence. With an inaugural membership of one hundred, the society was an immediate success.[107] Over the next few months the society endeavoured to secure premises, initially on a small scale, and by the summer of 1858 in a much larger store on Dynevor Street in Georgetown; this enabled them to expand into the boot and shoe trade by the autumn.[108] When the Merthyr Society expanded in 1859, it looked to Troedyrhiw, where forty members were already resident. The following year the branch shop was opened throughout the day – previously it had been open in the evenings only. 'This is a strong indication', recorded the *Merthyr Telegraph* approvingly, 'of the plant taking deep root and flourishing'.[109] By 1860, there were moves to establish an independent society at Dowlais and attempts to encourage a society in Rhymney and Brynmawr, both taking inspiration from Merthyr.[110]

The Dowlais Co-operative and Industrial Society eventually came into being in 1866. Whilst the society began small – with just fourteen members enrolled at the outset – it grew rapidly with between three and four hundred members registered by the time the stores opened at 14 and 15 Upper Union Street early in 1867.[111] Elsewhere in South Wales, the early 1860s proved similarly crucial to the development of consumer cooperation. The Cwmbach Co-operative Society, the first co-operative society to survive in the long-term, was established in 1859, as was the Pontypool Industrial Co-operative Society.[112] The Pioneer Industrial Society in Pontypridd, founded in 1860, picked up Dr William Price's mantle of nearly twenty years earlier, growing considerably in its first few years of operation. The same year saw the formation of the Bute Docks Industrial and Provident Society which ran a store on Alice Street. It was started, recorded the *Cardiff Times*, 'by a small band of intelligent, earnest working men'.[113] It also saw the foundation of the Tredegar Co-operative

Society.[114] Newport's Working Men's Industrial Co-operative Society was formed in April 1861 – the shop itself opening a few months later. Within a year the society had a membership of a hundred and by the middle of the decade could report 'satisfactory progress'.[115] At the end of the 1870s, after nearly two decades of growth, Glamorgan had over twenty co-operative societies accounting for nearly two hundred thousand pounds of sales per annum and almost five thousand members.[116]

Co-operators proved the potential for democratic control of the means of consumption, and for much of the mid-nineteenth century co-operative societies were far more advanced than either trade unions or labour as a political force. They were an indication of the possibilities of a democratic model of public ownership, but as memories of the truck system faded, and parliamentary reform returned to the agenda, it was the question of political representation rather than consumption which demanded an answer. A generation of younger MPs, who took their intellectual cues from John Stuart Mill, called for parliamentary reform to forge a more effective link between the disenfranchised working class and the government, in order to avoid social disharmony. In Mill's view, parliamentary reform would lead to a better democracy since the state would no longer be governed in the interests of the upper and middle classes, and so would be more popular. As he explained:

Political discussions fly over the heads of those who have no votes, and are not endeavouring to acquire them. Their position, in comparison with the electors, is that of the audience in a court of justice, compared with the twelve men in the jury-box. [...] Whoever, in an otherwise popular government, has no vote, and no prospect of obtaining it will either be a permanent malcontent, or will feel as one whom the general affairs of society do not concern.

The campaign for parliamentary reform, which was essentially a mechanism for fashioning popular liberalism, reinvigorated a dormant political labour movement. It drew initially on the voices of old Chartists such as Morgan Williams. Speaking at a reform rally in Merthyr, Williams lamented that the 'bias of the people was not so political as it was twenty years ago'. His comments were echoed by another of those present who suggested that 'the apathy of some of the people [can] be traced to the fact that they had been deceived so often about Reform [...] they had lost faith'.[117] Their response was to make reform about the fulfilment of Chartism, not the Liberal cause – as the *Aberdare Times* complained 'firm liberals stopped away in consequence of the immoderate demands of the promoters'.[118] At another rally in mid-November 1866, one old Chartist noted that he had taken the chair at a similar campaign twenty years earlier and that 'he still held to the same opinion' that workers should have the vote. The facts of disenfranchisement in Merthyr before the 1867 Reform Act were stark: fewer than fifteen hundred electors, of which only one hundred and twenty-six were working class men.

The reawakening of Chartist sentiments, apparent in Cardiff as well as Merthyr, provided for a degree of fracture within organised liberalism.[119] For the most part this was a cleavage between those pushing for moderate franchise reform and those willing to subscribe to calls for universal male suffrage and the secret ballot, but it had implications for relations between the nascent labour movement and liberalism. Radicals drew on a wide variety of influences, including secularism and republicanism, as they sought to weaken the grip of liberalism on South Walian politics, even as it was still consolidating. They recognised that the only way to press labour's demands effectively was to establish a co-ordinating body to encourage co-operation – the trades council. In this way, they learned the lesson of the co-operative societies which was not to tackle the inequalities of consumer credit and living standards singularly but in a collective manner.

The combination of political reform and labour organisation was strongest in Cardiff, where it was taken up by the trades council. In an advertisement placed in the *Cardiff Times* in October 1866, the trades council informed readers that 'they are now prepared to enrol all persons desirous of becoming members of the London Reform League at 16, Wharton Street, Cardiff', their headquarters.[120] The following month, a meeting took place to organise a reform rally akin to those already held in Merthyr. In the chair was Richard Cory senior who expressed disquiet at the connection between the reform movement and the burgeoning trade union movement in the town. 'They had better form a new committee of reformers', he said, 'and have nothing to do with the trades unions or anything else'. The problem was once again universal male suffrage. Cory declared that 'he was for going no further than household suffrage' and in consequence refused to join the committee.[121] In the event, separate meetings were held, chaired by members of the trades council, to appeal directly to workmen on issues such as universal male suffrage and the secret ballot.[122] It was the trades council that subsequently organised working-class political activity ensuring that the lines of fracture between the Liberal Party and labour did not disappear.[123]

The split became even starker in Merthyr, where post-Chartist activism combined with a radical press and the national Labour Representation League to push for the election of Thomas Halliday, the President of the Amalgamated Association of Miners, as Wales's first independent Labour MP at the General Election of 1874.[124] As John Thomas Morgan, editor of the *Workman's Advocate* put it in a column in September 1873, 'The great majority of the electors are working men, pitmen, ironworkers, &c; then, surely, we are justly and fully entitled to one [seat]. One we seek, and one we are resolved to have. It is ours to advocate and urge the claims of labour'.[125] Another expressed the view in the *Bee-Hive* that he could not support Henry Richard because he had failed to support the recent strike.[126] This was the first genuine campaign in South Wales that pitted a would-be labour representative against the forces of liberalism.[127] In the event, Halliday secured a quarter of the vote but failed to displace the sitting Liberal MPs. Undeterred, Halliday's supporters set about forming the Merthyr and Dowlais Trades Council, which would represent the independent cause of labour and lay the groundwork for the election of a labour member at the next general election.[128] When the constituency Liberal Association tried to gain the upper hand, through the formation of a working men's Liberal Association in 1879, the approach was rejected. It continued to be refused throughout the 1880s.[129]

Halliday's campaign in 1874 was novel not only because it was the first attempt to get a labour candidate elected for a South Walian constituency, but also because of a rising (if small) tide of secularism and republicanism evident in Merthyr, as well as in Aberdare and Cardiff. Cardiff's branch of the National Secular Society (NSS) was established by 1868 as the Association of Controversialists and attracted members such as Dr William Price and speakers including Charles Bradlaugh, the leading secularist of the period.[130] The branch debated women's suffrage, the Irish Question, vegetarianism, and provided the basis for the Cardiff Republican Club which was established towards the end of 1872.[131] The Merthyr Republican Club, which was founded in January 1872, had a similar basis in secularism, but members were also content to criticise Henry Richard for his support for the monarchy and were active in encouraging Thomas Halliday and the Labour Representation League in their efforts to win the Merthyr seat.[132] By 1879, there were branches of the NSS in Cardiff, Newport, and

Merthyr, with branches established in Aberdare and Pontypool in the early 1880s.[133] The most successful branch in the 1880s and 1890s was at Swansea, which formed in 1886, with the focus of secularism shifting to the Rhondda, Cynon, and Taff valleys in the early twentieth century.[134]

None of these fractures or developments was strong enough to weaken the grip of the Liberal Party at this point, nor could the Labour Representation League and Thomas Halliday overthrow the political framework built around popular liberalism and the singular figure of Henry Richard. It was too secure to be so easily dislodged. In the event, it was not secularism or republicanism that was successful in weakening Liberal control of politics in South Wales but labourism – the assertion of the rights of labour – which became closely identified with Mabon. In the redistribution of parliamentary constituencies in 1885, Rhondda gained direct representation for the first time – the old Glamorganshire constituency being divided into five. At the subsequent general election, the Rhondda seat was won by Mabon standing as a 'Labour' candidate against the wishes of the Liberal Party. Mabon articulated a political language that stressed the independence of labour, the need for distinct organisation, and a 'loyalty to the Labour movement and to the wider working class'.[135] But why did Mabon succeed where others had failed? Why was it the Rhondda rather than Merthyr Tydfil that produced Wales's first 'Labour' MP? The answers to these questions lie in Mabon's rise through the ranks of the trade union movement in the 1870s and his enthusiasm for pragmatism where it might further the cause of those he represented.[136]

In The Shadow of the Valley

Mabon came to prominence through the Amalgamated Association of Miners, which was formed in Lancashire in

1869.[137] The first lodge formed in South Wales was at Aberdare in November that year, and by the end of 1870 there were nineteen lodges representing miners from over sixty collieries.[138] Most were concentrated in the Rhondda, the Cynon Valley, Merthyr, and the western valleys of Monmouthshire.[139] The following year, the union spread to western parts of Glamorgan and the anthracite coalfield. It was during this wave of expansion that Mabon became involved, becoming elected miners' agent for the district around the Waunarlwydd Colliery where he worked.[140] He rose rapidly, becoming secretary of the South Wales region in 1873 and the de facto leader of the South Wales miners – a position amplified by the fact that the region was the largest in the AAM.[141] There were certainly others on the coalfield who could have challenged him for the leadership of the South Wales miners: Isaac Connick, the agent for Merthyr, or Phillip Jones (Abertillery), Samuel Davies (Aberdare), and George Coles (Rhondda). Each wielded considerable influence in their districts but was never quite able to bring it to bear beyond their local base. Mabon was different. Time and again, the newspaper press remarked on his 'powerful' ability to communicate regardless of the district.

The press's enthusiasm for Mabon was clearly significant and they promoted him over his potential rivals presenting a miners' leader who was reasonable as well as effective. As the *Cardiff Times* put it: 'the most promising sign is that the men are now seeking the counsel and guidance of Mr William Abraham, who besides being a hearty sympathiser with the colliers, is also responsible and prudent'.[142] His were speeches pitched in the language of labour rights and the necessity of trades unions. As he observed at a meeting in Aberaman in August 1877: 'combine in order not only to attain [your] rights, but to have fair wages for [your] labour. The reductions which [you] have had to submit to of late years [...can be] attributed to the want of unionism'.[143] Mabon was certainly not the first working-class leader to adopt this kind of language – indeed, it may be argued that he learned it from Thomas Halliday, who used the theme with vigour during the 1874 general election campaign in Merthyr Tydfil. Nevertheless, he made it into a political creed which 'became a central ideological pillar of working-class political representation from that point on'.[144] As miners struggled to forge a union across South Wales in the late-1870s and early 1880s, they often adopted Mabon's language. At one meeting miners resolved that they needed 'a union to defend the rights of labour, and therefore advise the formation of lodges at the various collieries'.[145] At another, delegates passed resolutions in support of striking miners at Hirwaun who 'do not receive their rights of labour'.[146]

By then, Mabon had been appointed agent of the Rhondda Steam Coal Miners' Association, consolidating his position at the apex of trade union organisation in the coalfield. He articulated a sophisticated critique of prevailing political economy emphasising that the introduction of the sliding scale, which he oversaw in the mid-1870s, had set the value of labour not by supply and demand but by the products of that labour. It had 'created a new state of things', as he put it, and 'produced peace and concord between employers and the employed'.[147] In Mabon's reading of the industrial conflict over the previous generation, strike action was the direct result of fluctuations in wage payments that were linked to the supply and demand of labour. But there was another consequence of the sliding scale, namely the joint sliding scale committee which brought together coal owners and miners' leaders. This committee was the lynchpin in Mabon's approach to industrial relations: arbitration on the one hand, but respect for the rights of labour on the other. Miners were to take full part in the management of their industry and be recognised as doing so.

This extended to Mabon's political career as well. He diverged from official liberalism in the Rhondda only insofar as to press the case for the rights of labour. Others went further, extending his creed, but no sooner had Mabon been elected to parliament in 1885 than he sought to reunite liberalism and labour.

Such reconciliation with organised liberalism was important and quickly attended to because there was little purpose in maintaining a split. Mabon differed little from popular liberalism and by allying himself to that cause, he could make certain his position as MP. From the point of view of the Liberals, having Mabon as a spokesperson for the alliance between liberals and labour was attractive: they could maintain the leadership of the district that they had long held whilst demonstrating their 'progressive' tendencies through the person of Mabon.[148] Of course, the articulation of a distinctive labour voice even allied to the forces of liberalism (or set in competition with it) could not be undone. The Rhondda never again had a separate Liberal Association: instead the Rhondda Liberal Association (RLA) became the Rhondda Labour and Liberal Association. The name itself is telling. In other parts of South Wales where a merged association was either considered or brought into being, the 'labour' element was typically relegated to second position. In Abercarn, for instance, in Risca, Blaina, or Gower, these were Liberal and Labour Associations and not the other way around.[149]

Why the difference? In the Rhondda, it was the supporters of Mabon, the voices of labour, who captured the Liberal Association subsuming it into their own organisation, rather than a Liberal Association reaching out to labour that made for a different nomenclature. This took place between December 1885 and February 1886.[150] Two years later, an attempt was made to establish a Labour and Liberal Association in Merthyr Tydfil without success because potential working-class members abstained.[151] In 1889, similarly, one 'radical' from Aberdare encouraged the formation of an organisation on the same lines as the Rhondda Labour and Liberal Association, again without success.[152] A further move was made in 1892 with the support of D. A. Thomas, the then Liberal MP for Merthyr, and whilst this did result in the establishment of the Merthyr Tydfil Labour and Liberal Association, it was hardly a powerful organisation and quickly fell apart.[153] As the *Evening Express* noted pointedly in 1892, the initial meetings were 'somewhat of a frost' and with a lack of funds it was not 'overwhelmed with prosperity'.[154] Workers from Dowlais and elsewhere in the valley were notable absentees.[155] The failure to form a Labour and Liberal Association in Merthyr worried radicals in the town and one from Abercanaid wrote to the *Merthyr Times* in 1896 to warn that 'it is time for the Radicals of Merthyr to be up and doing, or they will wake up some day to see Merthyr represented by a Tory'.[156] But it was a misreading of the situation.

The political stirrings in Merthyr were coming not from the right but from the left. Just four years after that prophetic warning, with the support and encouragement of the fledgling South Wales Miners' Federation, at least in the Cynon Valley, if not in Dowlais, Keir Hardie was elected as the junior member for Merthyr Boroughs.[157] In Monmouthshire, too, labour candidates were capturing seats on urban district councils, school boards, and Boards of Guardians. Amongst them were Thomas Richards, Alfred Onions, and James Winstone. These men were the new leaders of the coalfield. They were a signal that the political world of South Wales had begun to change.

Notes

[1] *MG*, 17 May 1834.

[2] The best interpretation of the Scotch Cattle can be found in David J. V. Jones, 'The Scotch Cattle and their Black Domain', *WHR* 5, no. 3 (1971), 220-249. For other interpretations see: E. W. Evans, *The Miners of South Wales* (Cardiff, 1961); E. J. Jones, 'Scotch Cattle and Early Trades Unionism in Wales', in W. E. Minchinton (ed.), *Industrial South Wales, 1750-1914: Essays in Welsh Economic History* (London, 1969), 209-217. The essay was originally published in 1928. A more recent interpretation, guided by the linguistic turn, is that of Rhian E. Jones, 'Symbol, Ritual and Popular Protest in Early Nineteenth-Century Wales: The Scotch Cattle Rebranded', *WHR* 26, no. 1 (2012), 34-57; eadem, *Petticoat Heroes: Gender, Culture and Popular Protest in the Rebecca Riots* (Cardiff, 2015).

[3] 'Letter from John H. Moggridge, 1 January 1829', TNA, HO 40/23, ff. 1-2. Moggridge relates the involvement of the Scotch Cattle in the Monmouthshire strikes of 1827. See also his letter of 3 January, which relates a further revival of the cattle in 1829. 'Letter from John H. Moggridge, 3 January 1829', TNA, HO 40/23, ff. 5-6. These are now available for download from the National Archives as 'digital microfilm' by which means they – and all other references to material from HO 40, HO 41, and HO 52 – were consulted for the present book. Additional material from HO 52 was consulted on microfilm in Special Collections and Archives (SCOLAR) at Cardiff University.

[4] Earl of Bessborough (ed.), *Lady Charlotte Guest: Extracts from her Journal, 1833-1852* (London, 1950), 30.

[5] *MG*, 28 June 1834.

[6] *MG*, 9 August 1834. Rebecca Rogers was just seven years old. *Monmouthshire Merlin*, 9 August 1834.

[7] *MG*, 16 August 1834.

[8] *MG*, 17 May, 20 September 1834.

[9] This description draws on Jones, 'Scotch Cattle', 238.

[10] Ignotus, *The Last Thirty Years in a Mining District* (London, 1867), 3; 'Letter from Thomas Wood, Brecon, 6 October 1833', TNA, HO 52/23, ff. 52-4.

[11] 'Letter from John Moggridge, 11 April 1832', in TNA, HO 52/21, ff. 11-13. He had written similarly three years earlier stating that the 'prolific source of discontent which has been at the bottom of all the more serious disturbances with which that part of the country has been afflicted for the last fifteen years – the payment of wages in shop goods – again prevails'. TNA, HO 40/23, f. 36 'Letter from John H. Moggridge, 22 January 1829'.

[12] 'Letter from the Marquess of Bute to Viscount Melbourne, 28 April 1832', in TNA, HO 52/21, ff. 15-16.

[13] 'Report from Colonel Love, Cardiff, 20 April 1832', TNA, HO 40/30 f. 258.

[14] 'Minutes of a Meeting of Magistrates and Ironmasters, 4 May 1832', TNA, HO 40/30 ff. 266-7.

[15] The 1817 Act had been driven by John H. Moggridge, as a result of riots and the pillaging of truck shops in Monmouthshire the previous year. *The Cambrian*, 25 July 1817.

[16] George W. Hilton, 'The British Truck System in the Nineteenth Century', *Journal of Political Economy* 65, no. 3 (1957), 239, 244. See also the evidence given by Thomas Jones Phillips, clerk to the magistrates for Newport and Bedwellty, to the select committee investigating wages in 1842 which describes this process. *Report from the Select Committee on Payment of Wages* (1842), QQ. 1519-1532. On the 1831 Act see: G. W. Hilton, 'The Truck Act of 1831', *The Economic History Review* 10, no. 3 (1958), 470-9.

[17] *Report from the Select Committee on Payment of Wages*, Q. 1314. A point reiterated in evidence given by David William James, a trader from Merthyr, and chairman of the Board of Guardians. QQ. 1781-98.

[18] As above, QQ. 2282, 2289.

[19] As above, Q. 1813.

[20] H. T. de la Beche, 'Report on the sanitary condition of Merthyr Tydfil, Glamorganshire', *Second Report of the Commissioners Inquiring in the State of Large Towns and Populous Districts*, Parl. Papers, 1845, XVIII [610], Vol. 5, Appendix, Part 1, 146.

[21] Harold Carter and Sandra Wheatley, *Merthyr in 1851* (Cardiff, 1982), 10.

[22] Gwyn A. Williams, *The Merthyr Rising* (Cardiff, 1988 edn), 27.

[23] Kate Sullivan, '"The Biggest Room in Merthyr": Working Class Housing in Dowlais, 1850-1914', *WHR* 17, no. 2 (1994), 157. See also Martin Daunton, 'Miners' Houses: South Wales and the Great Northern Coalfield, 1880-1914', *International Review of Social History* 25 (1980).

[24] *EEx*, 7 November 1901.

[25] Gwyn A. Williams, *The Search for Beulah Land* (London, 1980), 1.

[26] This has been made clear by the findings of the Wales and the French Revolution research project. See: Mary-Ann Constantine and Dafydd Johnston (eds.), *'Footsteps of Liberty and Revolt': Essays on Wales and the French Revolution* (Cardiff, 2013).

[27] Patrick Joyce, *Work, Society and Politics: The Culture of the Factory in Later Victorian England* (London, 1991 edn), 289; Dot Jones, 'Do Friendly Societies Matter? A Study of Friendly Society Membership in Glamorgan, 1794-1910', *WHR* 12, no. 3 (1985), 336; W. H. Howse, 'The Early Friendly Societies of Radnorshire', *Radnorshire Society Transactions* 18 (1948), 27.

[28] Ieuan Gwynedd Jones, 'Language, Politics and the Emptying of the Churches in Wales', (unpublished paper, 1995) – a précis of his paper is given in *Journal of Welsh Religious History* 4 (1996), 101.

[29] Emma Lile, 'Friendly Societies in Aberystwyth and their contribution towards cultural and social life' *Ceredigion* 13, no. 1 (1997), 67.

[30] WGA, RISW/SFS/2: *Articles and Rules made and agreed to by a society of men calling themselves by the name of the Union Club* (Swansea, 1763).

[31] Gwyn A. Williams, 'Friendly Societies in Glamorgan, 1793-1832', *Bulletin of the Board of Celtic Studies* 18 (1959), 275-283; Dot Jones, 'Self-Help in Nineteenth-Century Wales: The Rise and Fall of the Female Friendly Society', *Llafur* 4, no. 1 (1984), 20.

[32] *MT*, 26 September 1857.

[33] E. P. Thompson, *The Making of the English Working Class* (London, 1963 edn), 462.

[34] Raymond Williams, *Culture and Society* (London, 1983 edn), 326.

[35] GwA, Misc MSS 1090, 'The Industry of South Wales with particular reference to Nantyglo'.

[36] *MG*, 17 December 1836; Williams, *Merthyr Rising*, 79.

[37] Jones, 'Self-Help', 15.

[38] *CMG*, 2 June 1860. A copy of the society's rules, dated 1858, rests in the Glamorgan Archives: DCH/51. The society later merged with the Shepherds Society. *Cardiff Times*, 3 October 1908.

[39] *The Cambrian*, 29 January 1831.

[40] Eric Hobsbawm and George Rudé, *Captain Swing* (London, 1970); Katrina Navickas, 'Captain Swing in the North: The Carlisle Riots of 1830', *History Workshop Journal* 71, no. 1 (2011), 5-28.

[41] *The Cambrian*, 11 December 1830.

[42] *Carmarthen Journal*, 24 December, 31 December 1830.

[43] CLS, Bute Collection, Box 9, letter 7 (21) 17: 'Letter from Lord Bute to E. P. Richards, 7 December 1830'.

[44] *The Cambrian*, 11 December 1830.

[45] *MM*, 26 March 1831.

[46] John Howells, 'Carlyle's Holidays in Wales', *Red Dragon* 5 (1884), 335.

[47] Elijah Waring, *Recollections and Anecdotes of Edward Williams* (London, 1850), 116.

[48] Cited in DJV Jones, *Before Rebecca: Popular Protests in Wales, 1793-1835* (London, 1973), 59.

[49] *The Cambrian*, 27 November 1830. Members of the society who spoke at this meeting included Elijah Waring, Dr. R. Rowland, James Reynolds, and B. H. Malkin. Waring and his fellow Quaker Charles Hayward were also active in the anti-slavery movement in Neath. *The Cambrian*, 20 November 1830.

[50] *The Cambrian*, 1 October 1831.

[51] *The Cambrian*, 4 June 1831; *MM*, 26 March 1831.

[52] *The Companion to the Almanac or Year-Book of General Information for the Year 1832* (London, 1832).

[53] *The Companion to the Almanac or Year-Book of General Information for the Year 1830* (London, 1830). The Swansea Mechanics' Institute was the first of its kind in Wales but dissolved in 1828. See: *Mechanics' Magazine* 760 (3 March 1838), 375; J. H. Moggridge, *Introductory Discourse Delivered at the Town-Hall, in Swansea, at the First Meeting of the Tradesman's and Mechanic's Institute for that*

Town and Neighbourhood, 1 December 1826 (Swansea, 1827); *The Cambrian*, 9 December 1826, 17 March, 24 March 1827.

[54] *The Cambrian*, 29 January 1831; *MM*, 5 February 1831.

[55] Cowbridge Tracts, No. 5, *On the Advantages of Friendly Societies* (Cardiff, 1831), 2, 163.

[56] *Return Relating to Friendly Societies* (London, 1837), 32.

[57] *The Cambrian*, 2 May, 9 May 1835.

[58] TNA, HO 41/8, 'Letter from Robert Peel to J. F. Foster, 25 October 1830'. Branches formed across Wales through 1830 and 1831, initially in North Wales. This was consulted via the National Archives' 'digital microfilm'.

[59] *The Cambrian*, 21 July 1882.

[60] TNA, HO 52/ 16, f. 128, 'Letter from Lord Bute, 3 July 1831'.

[61] TNA, HO 52/16, ff. 190-191 'Petition from the Householders of Merthyr, 1 August 1831'.

[62] *The Cambrian*, 10 September 1831.

[63] *MM*, 22 October, 19 November 1831.

[64] TNA, HO 52/16, f. 181, 'Letter from Robert Beaumont to Marquess of Bute, 19 October 1831'. A similar description was sent to Bute by J. B. Bruce on 5 October, see ff. 206-7. There were branches of the union in Blaenavon, Varteg, Abersychan, and Pontypool. *MM*, 1 October 1831.

[65] TNA, HO 52/16, f. 146, 'Letter from J. B. Bruce, 1 November 1831'.

[66] TNA, HO 52/16, 'Letter from J. B. Bruce, 23 October 1831'.

[67] *The Cambrian*, 26 November 1831.

[68] *The Cambrian*, 15 October 1831.

[69] 'L. Evans Evan to Josiah John Guest, 27 September 1831'. GA, DG/A/1/158: Dowlais Iron Company Collection, Letters. Reprinted in Madeleine Elsas (ed.), *Iron in the Making: Dowlais Iron Company Letters, 1782-1860* (Cardiff, 1960), 61.

[70] *MM*, 3 December 1831.

[71] *MM*, 2 August 1834; *The Cambrian*, 5 April 1834.

[72] *MM*, 15 March, 26 July 1834.

[73] *MG*, 5 July 1834. The same threat was levied at any member who joined the Scotch Cattle brigades.

[74] The only copy that has survived is contained in TNA, HO 52/25, ff. 36-8. The phrase was widely used by the early labour movement. In the Potteries, for example, workers employed it on advertising notices during agitation to form a national union in August 1831. Stoke-on-Trent Museums: Enoch Wood Scrapbook, 136/17046. Both are available digitally online.

[75] His father, William Williams, had been Merthyr's first printer and a close friend of Iolo Morganwg. Geraint H. Jenkins, 'The Urban Experiences of Iolo Morganwg', *WHR* 22, no. 3 (2005), 496.

[76] Note from J. B. Bruce, 5 May 1834' in TNA, HO 52/25, f. 36.

[77] Gwyn A. Williams, 'The Merthyr Election of 1835', *WHR* 10, no. 3 (1981), 372.

[78] *Merthyr and Cardiff Chronicle*, 4 March 1837, 27 May 1837.

[79] *Merthyr and Cardiff Chronicle*, 23 September, 30 September, 7 October, 14 October, 21 October, 28 October, 9 December 1837. The newspaper fizzled out shortly afterwards, the last edition being published on 16 December 1837.

[80] Joe England, 'Engaged in a Righteous Cause: Chartism in Merthyr Tydfil' *Llafur* 10, no. 3 (2010), 62-3.

[81] Guest, *Diaries*, 86.

[82] Charles Wilkins, *The History of Merthyr Tydfil* (Merthyr Tydfil, 1908), 423.

[83] Ryland Wallace, *Organise,* 9.

[84] CLS, Bute Papers XX, no. 8: 'Letter from L. W. Dillwyn to Lord Bute, 9 May 1839'.

[85] As above, Bute Papers XX, no. 4: 'Letter from Thomas W. Booker to Lord Bute, 2 May 1839'.

[86] As above, Bute Papers XX, no. 16: 'Letter from Charles C. Williams to Lord Bute, 18 July 1839'. There had been a friendly society founded at the Red Lion in 1816. GA, Q/D/F/56 'Friendly Benefit Society, Red Lion, Cardiff'.

[87] CLS, Bute Papers XX, no, 20: 'Letter from William Thomas to Lord Bute, 18 August 1839'.

[88] *NS*, 6 January 1844.

[89] Its publication was greeted by the prominent Chartist leader Henry Vincent, who was then serving a sentence in Monmouth Gaol

for making inflammatory remarks. LHASC, Labour Party Archives, LP/VIN/1/1/23, Letter from Henry Vincent to John Minikin, 28 February 1840.

[90] TNA, HO 40/57, 'Letter from Lord Bute to Lord Normanby, 20 October 1840'.

[91] CLS, Bute Papers XX, nos. 157-159. Minutes of meetings of Board of Magistrates, Castle Inn, Merthyr: 12 October, 16 October, 23 October, 6 November 1840.

[92] *Udgorn Cymru*, 1 April 1841.

[93] CLS, Bute Papers XX, no. 163. Translation of articles from *Udgorn Cymru*, 1 February 1841.

[94] *Udgorn Cymru* 1 April 1842.

[95] TNA, HO 40/57, 'Bute to Normanby, 5 October 1840'.

[96] CLS, Bute Papers XX, no. 164. Report of Thomas M. Lewis, 26 June 1841.

[97] Peter Gurney, 'Labor's Great Arch: Cooperation and Cultural Revolution in Britain, 1795-1926', in Ellen Furlough and Carl Strikwerda (eds.), *Consumers Against Capitalism? Consumer Cooperation in Europe, North America and Japan, 1840-1990* (Lanham, Maryland, 1999), 138.

[98] The shop was first noted by Brian Davies, 'Empire and Identity: The "Case" of Dr William Price', in David Smith (ed.), *A People and a Proletariat: Essays in the History of Wales, 1780-1980* (London, 1981), 72-93.

[99] *NS*, 24 October 1840.

[100] *NS*, 7 November 1840.

[101] *NS*, 21 August 1841.

[102] *CMG*, 14 May 1842.

[103] Friendly Societies: A Return Relating to Friendly Societies enrolled in the several counties of England & Wales, 1842. Parliamentary Papers, vol. 26, paper 73, 47.

[104] *NS*, 16 April 1842.

[105] *NS,* 13 March 1852.

[106] *CMG*, 25 February 1854.

[107] *MT*, 28 November 1857.

[108] *MT*, 26 June 1858, 27 November 1858.

[109] *MT*, 17 September 1859, 21 April 1860.

[110] *MT*, 1 September 1860. On Brynmawr see: *MT*, 2 January 1858.

[111] *MT*, 28 July 1866, 11 August 1866, 9 February 1867. Much smaller stores had initially opened in Mary Anne Street in the summer of 1866.

[112] *Illustrated Usk Observer and Raglan Herald*, 2 April 1859, 14 May 1859.

[113] *CT*, 28 July 1860.

[114] *MT*, 8 December 1860; *CMG*, 15 December 1860. See also Industrial and Provident reports for 1863 and 1864.

[115] *MM*, 3 May 1862, 30 April 1864. The printed records of the Newport society can be found at Newport Central Library including rule books from 1906 and 1924, and a series of annual reports from 1920-1949.

[116] *SWDN*, 28 June 1879. The largest society was Cwmbach with seven hundred and sixty three members. A further two hundred and eighty six were members of the Aberdare society and one hundred and seventy five were part of the Trecynon and Cwmdare society. Dowlais had over four hundred members as did the Taff Industrial and Provident in Troedyrhiw.

[117] *MEx*, 22 September 1866.

[118] *AT*, 24 November 1866. This was echoed, albeit with regret, in the *MT*, 24 November 1866.

[119] *CT*, 21 December 1866.

[120] *CT*, 12 October 1866.

[121] *CT*, 16 November 1866. The committee of the Cardiff branch of the London Reform Committee was: John Hogan, Thomas Cram, Alfred Preston, Thomas Wills, Luke Richards, Henry Jenks, William Harris, Robert Shaddick, George Barnes, John Hales, Edward Osborne, and Robert Fear. Thomas Jones (Chairman of Cardiff Trades Council) was elected president; Charles Matthews, treasurer; and Edmund Wilkins, secretary.

[122] *CT*, 23 November 1866.

[123] Martin Daunton, *Coal Metropolis: Cardiff, 1870-1914* (Leicester, 1977), 203; *CT*, 20 November 1869.

[124] For the wider British story see James Owen, *Labour and the Caucus: Working-Class Radicalism and Organised Liberalism in England, 1868-1888* (Liverpool, 2014). See also Eugenio Biagini, *Liberty, Retrenchment and Reform: Popular Liberalism in the Age of Gladstone, 1860-1880* (Cambridge, 1992).

[125] *Workman's Advocate* (Merthyr), 6 September 1873.

[126] *Bee-Hive*, 10 May 1873.

[127] *Bee-Hive*, 26 July 1873, 14 February 1874.

[128] *Workman's Advocate*, 23 May 1874, 15 June 1874. The leading members were William Evans, W. R. Jones (manager of the Abercanaid Co-operative Stores), and J. T. Morgan (editor of the *Workman's Advocate*).

[129] *MEx*, 29 March 1879. Although by this time the trades council itself had collapsed. *Aberdare Times*, 17 August 1878.

[130] *National Reformer*, 26 July 1868, 14 August 1870, 21 January 1872. On Aberdare see, *National Reformer*, 22 January 1871.

[131] *National Reformer*, 10 March, 31 March, 13 October 1872; *Cardiff Times*, 7 December 1872. Members included Edmund Wilkins (President) and A. J. Eddington (Secretary). *National Reformer*, 27 October 1872. Wilkins had been secretary of the Cardiff Reform League in 1866. *Cardiff Times*, 16 November 1866. Eddington had previously been the secretary of the Controversialists. He lived at 4 Richmond Place, Roath. The Republican Club met at the York Hotel. *National Reformer*, 20 April 1873.

[132] *MT*, 15 March 1872; *National Reformer*, 5 April 1868, 22 January 1871 28 January 1872. *CT*, 3 February 1872. For details on the other clubs see, Christopher Rumsey, *The Rise and Fall of British Republican Clubs, 1871-1874* (London, 2000), 105.

[133] *Secular Review*, 31 May 1879; *Freethinker*, 1 October 1882; *The National Secular Society Almanack for 1880*, 36.

[134] *Freethinker*, 5 March, 6 August 1905; *AL*, 14 September 1907; *RL*, 17 December 1910.

[135] Chris Williams, Democratic Rhondda: Politics and Society, 1885-1951 (Cardiff, 1996), 30.

[136] The classic portrait of Mabon is that by E. W. Evans. My thinking on the significance of Mabon as a pioneer of a new language of

labour, however, has been much influenced by Williams, *Democratic Rhondda*, ch. 2.

[137] Indeed, at the outset, the union was known as the Amalgamated Association of Miners of Lancashire, Cheshire and North Wales. *MM*, 27 November 1869. On the founding of the union see *Manchester Courier*, 24 August, 25 August 1869.

[138] *MT*, 4 December 1869

[139] *MM*, 29 November 1870. See also the delegates list printed in *MT*, 24 March 1871. *MT*, 6 October 1871.

[140] *Gwladgarwr*, 28 September 1872, 25 January 1873.

[141] *Welshman*, 14 February 1873. G. D. H. Cole, 'Some Notes on British Trade Unionism in the Third Quarter of the Nineteenth Century *IRSH* 2, no. 1 (1937), 12.

[142] *CT*, 14 October 1876.

[143] *CT*, 1 September 1877. See also the report of a meeting at Llanelli which passed a resolution affirming the need to 'protect the rights of labour'. *CT*, 17 November 1877.

[144] Williams, *Democratic Rhondda*, 43.

[145] *Carnarvon and Denbigh Herald*, 27 September 1879.

[146] *CT*, 27 May 1882.

[147] *Weekly Mail*, 15 September 1883. These comments were made at a mass meeting in Garnant. See also his comments from a mass meeting in the Rhondda in July 1884, when he moved for a single sliding scale rather than the three then in operation. *Weekly Mail*, 26 July 1884.

[148] Williams, *Democratic Rhondda,* 37-8.

[149] *The Cambrian*, 9 October 1891, 12 July 1895; *CT*, 4 June 1892; *EEx*, 20 June 1892; *Merthyr Times*, 7 November 1895. Nor was this a trend limited to these districts – it was an identifiable and common theme across the coalfield whenever the Liberal Association endeavoured to 'provide' a means of labour articulating its voice. See, for example, the discussions at Merthyr Vale and Aberaman in early 1896: *PC*, 31 January 1896; *Merthyr Times*, 6 February 1896.

[150] *PC*, 25 December 1885; 1 January, 19 February 1886.

[151] *SWE*, 7 November 1888; *CT*, 10 November 1888; 16 April, 21

May 1892. The 1888 attempt had been undertaken by the miners of Cyfarthfa but was rebuffed, when the Liberal Association tried in 1892, the workers' collective response was clear.

[152] *SWDN*, 25 January 1889.

[153] *SWDN*, 14 April 1892.

[154] *EEx*, 30 March; *WM*, 18 May 1892.

[155] *CT*, 16 April 1892.

[156] *Merthyr Times, 7 May 1896.*

[157] Even as late as June 1900, a matter of months before the election, the secretary of the Merthyr and Dowlais TLC complained of the 'liberalism of the miners and the difficulty gaining the choice of a true Labour man as candidate for the election'. LHASC, Labour Party Archive, LP/LRC/2/208, Letter from Dai Davies, 28 June 1900.

CHAPTER TWO

Bread of Heaven

The progressive age, that period from about 1890 through to the outbreak of the Great War in the summer of 1914, changed everything.[1] It was a period punctuated by landmarks in the formation of the labour movement: the creation of the Independent Labour Party in 1893, the long stoppage in the mining industry in 1898 that heralded the creation of the South Wales Miners' Federation, Keir Hardie's election as Wales's first independent Labour MP in Merthyr in 1900, the Taff Vale Judgement in 1901, the Osborne Judgement in 1909, the so-called Great Unrest after 1910, and the Trade Union Act of 1913 which enabled trade unions to create political and social funds (in effect to fund the Labour Party). Popular liberalism steadily ebbed away and workers embraced a different sort of politics: independent Labour. The nineteenth century had demonstrated the potential of the working-class movement, but it was in this period that that potential became manifest reality, especially in Merthyr and the Rhondda. The social democracy that came into existence in South Wales in the interwar years developed out of this generation of political organisers, who had come into consciousness in the last decade of the nineteenth century and the first of the twentieth. The ideas that they formulated, be they for political organisation, cultural and social activity, municipal governance, or self-education and self-improvement, were central to the labour movement. For *fin de siècle* South Wales was distinguished by remarkable social, cultural and economic confidence and outward political stability on the one hand, and by radical political ideas, activism and organisation on the other.

In September 1888, at the annual gathering of the Cardiff Cymmrodorion Society, Thomas Lemuel James, the 29th US Postmaster General, remarked on his experiences during a tour of his 'native' country. 'I am', he said by way of preface to his speech, 'a Welshman through and through'. He declared Cardiff to be the 'Chicago of Wales'.[2] A few weeks later, at the annual mayor's banquet, the American consul for Cardiff, Major Evan R. Jones, similarly remarked on the confidence and prosperity of the town.[3] Thereafter the epithet entered into the lexicon as a sign of progress and invoked as a sign of the times.[4] But it was also a way of cajoling the elite to act for the common good. Writing in the *Evening Express* in September 1893, one journalist put it bluntly: 'Cardiff is the Chicago of Wales, the most progressive, enterprising, go-a-head place in the kingdom – Cardiff is like time and tide: it waits for no one... But when it comes to public matters, what then? ... Cardiff waits'.[5] It was true of Liberal South Wales more generally. Young Turks began to ask questions of older Liberals, demanding greater public investment, improved civil liberties, and a society better able to articulate the aspirations of respectable working people. Others went further still, calling for socialist answers to questions to which liberalism seemed no longer able to respond.

There were deep-felt frustrations at the failure of popular liberalism to act in the best interests of society on a range of issues, notably housing and living standards, with echoes of the old moral economy and the rights of labour. But those frustrations with the failure of existing models of governance were by now manifesting themselves in the form of deliberately independent action. Underpinning this shift in working-class allegiance was both a radical system of ideas and organisations intent on implementing practical changes. This was a period in which a myriad of trade unions, co-operative societies, and political movements, were formed, ranging from the Marxist

Social Democratic Federation to the Independent Labour Party to the Fabian Society to small, impossibilist organisations such as the Socialist Party of Great Britain. Not all avenues explored in the 1890s and 1900s were equally fruitful, nor was politics necessarily more significant to the labour movement than trade union activity. In fact, the South Wales Miners' Federation was the most powerful labour institution in the region and the only one able to cohere entire communities. To be its president was, effectively, to be the most powerful working man in South Wales. Consequently, from its foundation in 1898 onwards, the SWMF was the key battleground between Lib-Lab, ILP, and even more radical approaches to political organisation.

This chapter follows the two major political organisations of the left – the Social Democratic Federation and the Independent Labour Party, from their formation in the 1880s and 1890s – exploring their impact on South Walian politics and the reasons for the ILP's eventual triumph over its rivals. It culminates in the creation of the SWMF. The boundaries between these organisations was often fluid, with ideas and personnel shared across them with little incongruity. Their purpose, after all, was not to create a fragmented left but to find the best mechanism by which to press the cause of labour industrially and politically, and that meant experimentation and a willingness to adapt to prevailing circumstances. Although the 1890s and 1900s can appear as but a prelude to the far more dramatic events after 1910, this was a formative period. Those who emerged during this period, such as James Winstone, Vernon Hartshorn, and Charles Stanton, went on to play a major role in shaping the politics of the South Wales Coalfield and it was vital in the development of several generations of Labour MPs, some of whom were in office until the 1960s, and the hierarchy of the Labour Party locally until at least the 1930s. It led to the remaking of South Wales.

The Arrival of Marxism

In 1881, the journalist and businessman, Henry Hyndman, founded the Democratic Federation, Britain's first socialist party, in London. It became the SDF in 1884. The party's formation followed Hyndman's abortive attempt to run as an independent during the 1880 general election.[6] After his withdrawal, he went on holiday and it was on that voyage to the United States that he began reading a new book: a French translation of Karl Marx's *Das Kapital*. 'I read hard at Marx', he wrote, 'and although I did not at the time fully grasp all the significance of his theories ... I came to the conclusion that the only way out of the existing social difficulties was the inevitable development from capitalism to socialism'.[7] Hyndman set about producing socialist literature with which to propagandise since 'there was then no literature to refer to, no books in English which could be obtained and read, either by the educated class or by the workers'.[8] One piece was an article in the literary journal *Nineteenth Century* which carried the title, 'The Dawn of a Revolutionary Epoch'. It was a signal of Hyndman's new creed.

One of those who joined the SDF in its early stages was John Spargo.[9] Born near Penryn in Cornwall on 31 January 1876, Spargo was the son of a stonecutter. His parents, Thomas (1850-1920) and Jane (1851-1900), divorced when John was two years old and he went to live with his poverty-stricken aunt. When John's father remarried in 1883, the young boy moved to live with him at his new home in Tuckingwell near Camborne. This new life was deeply unhappy: his father descended into alcoholism and his step-mother was strict and occasionally abusive. John found solace in the Methodism in which he had been immersed whilst living with his aunt, and he became an active member of the Band of Hope, a Sunday School teacher, and later a lay preacher. Methodism provided training and education that was otherwise denied, and proved as formative to the character of the adolescent John Spargo as the socialism he picked up in his later teens and early twenties. Years later, by then settled in the United States, he wrote a book on the relationship between religion and socialism, one which he felt was strong. 'Socialism', he wrote, 'appears as a great, vital and vitalizing religious principle'. He continued:

> The man who, because his life is torn by the economic struggle, sees in Socialism economic redemption, is right; the man who, because his soul rebels at the bondage of the mind, sees in Socialism mental and intellectual freedom, is right; and the man who, because his religious faith withers under the blight of capitalism, sees in Socialism the force which will make the religious life possible, is right. Each point of view is legitimate and all are necessary to a full comprehension of Socialism. And there are still other points of view – the point of view of Woman, for example, seeing in Socialism the breakdown of the last remnants of her servitude and the triumph of Sex Equality.[10]

And so, he concluded, 'the torch which all the prophets from Moses to Jesus bore aloft is to-day being borne onward by Socialist agitators'.

Religion provided some of the answers to the young man's questions, but could not help him deal with the economic and political injustices that he witnessed on a daily basis in Cornwall. As in South Wales, Cornish mines were dangerous places to work and the fruits of labour, in the form of bountiful profits, lined the pockets not of the workers themselves but of the landowners and those with 'rights' to the mineral wealth of the county. Such injustices drove a sense of rebellion and, as his political consciousness grew, Spargo had first moved towards the radical wing of the Liberal Party and its hero

William Gladstone. He became, he admitted later, fired 'by Gladstone and the Liberal political party ferment'.[11] Another influence was John Stuart Mill. He read and re-read Mill's *Principles of Political Economy*, first published in 1848, which Spargo later suggested had, in his self-teaching at least, 'prepared the way for Marx'.[12] In this he was hardly alone, but little in Spargo's life up to this point (he was only fifteen) suggested a move away from radical liberalism. In fact, Spargo's conversion from radical liberalism to socialism was, his reading apart, something of an accident.

A regular attendee at Mutual Improvement Society meetings at his local chapel, one evening Spargo was present at a talk delivered by the Christian Socialist James Adderley, then active in preaching the social gospel in the slums of the east end of London. A persistent and challenger interrogator, Spargo drew the ire of Adderley who lambasted the young man for his 'Marxism'. 'I was', he remembered, 'in receipt of a lecture on the failings of the teachings of Karl Marx. [But] I had never heard of Karl Marx'. His curiosity piqued, Spargo remained behind at the end of the lecture and spoke more calmly with Adderley who told him about a group of socialists in London gathered around Henry Hyndman. A quizzing letter was despatched from Cornwall to Hyndman a few days later, the reply being a copy of *England For All* and encouraging words about the SDF and how to join and subscribe to its newspaper, *Justice*. Spargo raced through the book, absorbing Marxian ideas as he did so, sent off his half a crown for *Justice*, and emerged the other end, aged just sixteen, a self-declared socialist. There was no branch of the SDF in Cornwall, nor much evidence of a socialist tradition. It left Spargo to immerse himself through self-education.

Then in 1895, aged nineteen, Spargo left Cornwall with his father to seek work in South Wales. He arrived in Barry. The town was a hive of industrial activity, similar enough to the Cornwall that he had left behind, but on a far larger scale. The docks had opened just six years earlier and export of goods from the town was growing rapidly, from one million tons in 1890 to nearly ten million by 1900. The Spargos, together with thousands of other people, flooded into Barry to make the most of the employment opportunities available. Unlike Cornwall, however, Barry had a strong labour movement focused on the docks and the railway. The town's trades' council had been established in May 1891.[13] Spargo joined the Navvies Union shortly after his arrival. At branch meetings he found himself, for the first time, in a body of like-minded individuals, not least the then chairman, Sam McCord, and his colleagues, Matthew Shepherd and Fred Walls. Each Sunday evening they organised a 'Navvies Church', held initially at the reading room in Cadoxton and later at the Regent Hall on Regent Street in Barry, where they invited speakers in to discuss matters such as Labour representation, socialism, commercial enterprise, land nationalisation, religion, and the SDF, with whom the Navvies Union maintained strong connections.[14]

The Barry branch of the Navvies Union, supplementing the one already established in adjacent Cadoxton, was formed on 7 March 1895 at a meeting held at the Barry Hotel on Broad Street and attended by Fred Walls, Matthew Shepherd, and John Ward, the president and founder of the Navvies Union, who had been in Barry for several weeks agitating for the establishment of branches across South Wales. Encouragement given to would-be members to join the union was entirely based on economic grounds. 'The least paid workers in London', remarked John Ward in his speech, for example, 'received more than the best paid in South Wales, and yet, if the price of provisions and house rent was taken into consideration, they would find but very little difference in them. They have never yet seen a body of men get good wages unless they were thoroughly organised'.[15] Within a few months, the Barry branch of the Navvies Union had gained around two hundred members, which compared favourably with the older Cadoxton branch's three hundred, and between sixty and seventy attended weekly meetings. By the summer, branch membership accounted for three in every four navvies employed at Barry dock – or eight hundred people.[16]

Such strength in numbers gave the Navvies Union considerable leverage in negotiating for the payment of trade union wage rates to workers, and indeed in exceeding them. Before the establishment of the union, wages were lower than elsewhere, the result of competition amongst workers and the refusal of companies to pay trade union rates. With union agitation it exceeded five pence per hour – amongst the highest wage rate for navvies in South Wales, but still a relatively poor rate of pay. Substantial membership also provided the opportunity to apply pressure for a range of other social and cultural benefits for workers and their families, such as an orphan's home, legal representation, medical care, and concerts and athletic tournaments. Of note was the establishment of an institute in Cadoxton. The brainchild of George Garnett, a tailor, the institute was opened on 26 September 1896 and spread over two floors providing a refreshment room, library, and meeting hall. Speaking at the opening, Councillor J. H. Jose, a Labour member of the urban district council, declared it 'a club on a new scale ... calculated to raise and not lower the well-being of the navvies ... This institution is a clarion call to the workers of Barry to leave degrading influences and realise their duties to themselves and their fellows. ... None are too bad to be uplifted and none are too good to aid in the work of uplifting'.[17]

The Trade Union Coffee Bar and Reading Room provided for the educational improvement of the workers, as well as a non-alcoholic place of entertainment in the evenings. It was a place of refuge and a soup kitchen during periods of unemployment or short working, such as the wet winter of 1897, when hunger was assuaged through the provision of a hearty breakfast and tea.[18] Sustaining the building, however, proved difficult and it closed within a year – an experiment in social activity that nevertheless helped to foster closer relations amongst the disparate navvies of Barry and Cadoxton. This was to prove crucial during the navvies' lockout, which erupted following a pay dispute in the summer of 1897 and paralysed construction work on the east dock for nearly three months.

The lockout took place at a time when Barry was the national centre of union organisation amongst navvies. Towards the end of 1896, a dispute had broken out in the Navvies Union, throwing the Barry and Cadoxton branches to the forefront of national activity. With John Ward, the union president, spending much of his time agitating amongst South Walian navvies, the London branches sought to assert their authority over the union by holding out against his re-election as president. This action, which ran contrary to the overwhelming support for Ward outside London, led to the resignation of Ward and the general secretary, Arthur Humphrey. Their parting shot was levelled against the 'narrow-mindedness and selfishness of the members of the London branches'.[19] Within a few months, the union had relocated to Holton Road, Barry, and John Ward became an active member of the town's labour movement, eventually joining the TLC. The union headquarters did not return to London until the end of 1899.[20]

At the heart of the Navvies' Union were members of the Barry SDF. The branch was founded in 1895.[21] Membership was relatively small, between thirty and forty members, but engagement with the navvies union amplified the branch's influence considerably.[22] As the *Barry Herald* commented in May 1896: 'whatever may be said of socialism or socialistic organisation it must be admitted that it would be difficult to find a more determined go-ahead set of fellows than those who comprise the local branch of the Social Democratic Federation'.[23] Within a few months, the Barry SDF were meeting on a weekly basis at Rosser's Coffee Tavern on Holton Road and involved themselves in the 1896 municipal elections by distributing leaflets and addressing crowds on the need for labour representation.[24]

In 1897, the branch ran two candidates at the municipal elections: John Spargo in the West Ward and Samuel McCord in the North Ward. In his election material, Spargo committed himself to adopting the Artisans' Dwellings Act, which provided for the construction of council housing, the construction of public baths and toilets, the municipalisation of the tramways, and a universal minimum wage for the district to be negotiated by the TLC.[25] Speaking in St Mary's Street, Cardiff, later that year, Spargo also reflected on the rise of racism in port-towns, which was, he said, 'the direct result of economic conditions'. In conjunction with the speaker, Mr Smidt 'a rather pleasant young gentleman with a foreign accent', he insisted that racial hatreds were unreasonable and that socialism would help to unite workers all over the world.[26] This principle was put to the test during the Boer War when Spargo was one of the most high profile critics and anti-war activists in South Wales, both through the SDF and the National Stop the War Committee.[27] Although such a stance was not without danger. Speaking in Gloucester at an official Stop the War meeting, Spargo was mobbed by a 'patriotic crowd' and had to be escorted from the Co-operative Hall by police.[28] He wrote angrily to the *Barry Dock News* to complain of the intimidation of 'organised gangs who deny ... the right of expressing opinions' about the war. He continued:

The very fact of gangs of ruffians deliberately planning to do violence to any citizen whose only offence is that he has the courage to express a profound conviction that, in this conflict, which is reddening the South African Veldt with the best blood of the two nations, England is in the wrong, ought to call forth the righteous indignation of a people whose fathers fought for, and obtained at fearful cost, the right of free speech and a free press.[29]

Following this letter, the press – and local Conservatives – eyed an opportunity to defeat Spargo in open debate and arrangements were made to hold a town-hall meeting in Ferndale featuring Spargo and John Littlejohns, the Conservative Agent in Glamorgan.[30] In a packed Tudor Hall, Ferndale, at the end of October 1900, Spargo made the case against the imperialist war and the origins of that conflict in capitalism. For his part, Littlejohns claimed that the British objective was to counter the Boers who intended to 'drive the British into the sea'.[31] Despite some debate in the newspapers in the weeks that followed, it was largely agreed by the press that Spargo had got the better of Littlejohns.[32]

A few months later, on 6 February 1901, John Spargo emigrated to the United States with his new wife, Prudence Edwards.[33] Shortly before they left, the pair were guests of honour at a farewell banquet organised by the Barry SDF, held at the town's Regent Hall on 1 February. He received the best wishes of the Bristol Socialist Society and an illuminated address signed by leading socialist figures such as Harry Quelch, Keir Hardie, and Henry Hyndman, and by his local comrades J. H. Jose and Samuel McCord.[34] Spargo's final speech was made on 3 February at Rosser's Coffee Tavern where he addressed his party comrades on the necessity of social democracy from a moral point of view. In a speech infused with religious observations, Spargo touched on themes of imperialism and industrial capitalism sketching out a critical history of political economy in doing so.[35] It was a characteristic speech that showed Spargo's not inconsiderable talents as a thinker. As *Justice* recognised in saying farewell, 'the socialist movement in this country will thus lose an active worker and a capable propagandist. However, what will be our loss will be America's gain'.[36]

Spargo's first few months in New York were difficult. He struggled to find work and joined the breadlines to survive the winter, relying on the goodwill of fellow socialists to provide shelter.[37] Corresponding with Henry Hyndman, Spargo reflected on a personal 'economic crisis' and his regret at leaving Britain. Replying, Hyndman enthused that 'you are there at a stirring time'.[38] He was right and Spargo had already thrown himself into the socialist movement in the eastern United States by the time Hyndman's letter arrived. The previous month the Socialist Party of America had been formed and Spargo became one of its organisers and lecturers, building on his work (and reputation) as an itinerant lecturer.[39] He was also gaining notability as a writer and was heavily involved (both as editor and on the editorial board) with *The Comrade*, the New York socialist journal, from its inception in September 1901, and the Chicago-based *Social Crusader* and its successor, *Socialist Spirit*.[40]

The *Social Crusader* had been established by J. Stitt Wilson in 1898 as part of the public activities of the Social Crusade movement. Having trained in the Methodist ministry, Wilson navigated towards the Social Democratic Party of America as a response to the poverty he witnessed in Chicago in the mid-1890s. The Social Crusade aimed at turning 'men from commercial barbarism, greed and mammon worship to social and common good and wealth; from social injustice to social justice; from industrial despotism to industrial democracy'.

They also ran a co-operative shop.[41] One of those heavily involved in the Crusade was George Davis Herron, a key exponent of the Social Gospel in the Great Lakes region of the United States, a close friend of Eugene Debs, and a founding member, in 1901, of the Socialist Party of America. Herron met John Spargo in June 1901 during the former's visit to New York to attend the opening of the Workingmen's Headquarters (the American equivalent of a Labour Hall) on the East Side of Manhattan.[42] The *Social Crusader* takes up the encounter:

> When the Crusaders arrived, about nine o'clock, they found the rooms filled to overflowing with fathers, mothers, and children: even babes in arms. Under the direction of Comrade J[ohn] Spargo, an English socialist who has done much to promote development of this character, a programme of entertainment was underway.

This meeting proved to be the start of a flourishing friendship – so much so that when Spargo's son was born in October, he was named George Herron – and Herron even arranged for a monthly stipend of one hundred and twenty dollars to be paid to Spargo by his own benefactor Carrie Rand.[43]

By the time Spargo returned to South Wales on a speaking tour in 1910, he had developed a prominent role in American socialist circles – making a name for himself both as a Christian Socialist thinker and as a muckraking journalist: his 1906 book *The Bitter Cry of Children* exposed the impact of child labour in coal mines and was one of the most successful exposés of poverty and exploitation of early twentieth century America.[44] He was also heavily engaged in his work on a biography of Karl Marx, which would appear in 1911.[45] The tour of South Wales was largely at the invitation of the ILP, which by then had eclipsed the SDF, and Spargo spoke at meetings in Merthyr, Ferndale, and, of course, Barry, where he was greeted as a returned prodigal son and as a figure 'from the early days' who could remind party members of the struggles (and heroics) of the past.[46] He reflected at Barry, 'in the old days – glorious days they were – when they stood defiantly with their backs against the wall, then there was a splendid sense of devotion to a great ideal'. It was, still, 'a time of sowing'. He noted, too, the transatlantic milieu of socialist activists of which he was very much a part:

> Sometimes ... traversing it [America] from coast to coast, he found men coming to him introducing themselves to him, and referring to meetings on Cadoxton Common, meetings on the Hayes in Cardiff, at the London Dock Gates, Southampton, and the Sheep Market in Bristol.[47]

Barry SDF were fortunate to have been possessed of a figure such as John Spargo and as a result they gained a prominence in local politics. This was denied the SDF elsewhere in South Wales, where it was a fleeting presence and one that had more impact on ideas than organisation. The earliest branch was established at Waun Afon near Brynmawr in the spring of 1885. It was the work of one man: John Price. He endeavoured to distribute propaganda in the Monmouthshire hills and maintained local contact in the pages of *Justice*. When Price died, the branch dissolved.[48] Then, in January 1887, prominent socialist speaker and secularist Annie Besant arrived in Cardiff to deliver a series of lectures on religion and socialism. Encouraging her audience in the necessity of socialist action and co-operation, Besant was greeted with applause and 'the audience appeared to fully appreciate and sympathise with her views'.[49] In an interview given to the *South Wales Echo*, Besant noted the emergence of movements across Britain that spoke to the evolution of socialism:

They are to be seen on every hand. Trades Unionism is a great step in that direction, whilst the co-operative system goes still further. This latter is a remarkable development, and is the outcome of an innate Socialistic movement which was created in the minds of the working classes by the pressure of sheer necessity.[50]

Besant was followed a few months later by John Fielding, a member of the SDF's executive council.[51] The local press gave not inconsiderable coverage to Fielding's lectures, not least because they exulted in the fact that the lectures struggled to gain an audience. Held on a Sunday morning, the first lecture (of three) was abandoned when only six people turned up.[52] Despite the poor attendance at the subsequent meetings, Fielding's talks caught the imagination of a handful of activists who endeavoured to establish a local branch of the SDF.[53] In the event, this group, led by Dr Arthur Parr, formed the Cardiff Socialist Union and aligned themselves with William Morris's Socialist League. Arthur Samuel Mead, a local entertainer and ventriloquist, was elected as secretary.[54] Post Office worker R. E. Thomas, later secretary of the Cardiff Impartial Society, and a member of the Cardiff Junior Liberal Association, was also an active participant. In a letter to William Morris, he enthused that 'the movement is in its incipient stage here in Cardiff but it is I am pleased to say, gradually but slowly gaining ground'.[55] In Merthyr too, there was a feeling that visiting lecturers were having an effect. 'I believe it [socialism] has taken deep root in some of the listeners' hearts', enthused one local activist.[56]

But it was an optimistic appraisal. The handful of activists in Merthyr found it difficult to expand their number and they sold very little in the way of newspapers or pamphlet literature. One activist wrote to the Socialist League to ask them to stop sending copies of *The Commonweal*, the League's newspaper, because it was 'impossible to get anybody here to take them'.[57] This may have been due, at least in part, to otherwise sympathetic individuals not wanting to be victimised or marginalised by the wider community or employers. As one Dowlais worker explained, 'if I signed I thought I might be a marked man'.[58] It was no better in Swansea, where the SDF went to the trouble of establishing a central meeting hall and circulating library in February 1894 – the branch had been formed a few months earlier.[59] Activists despaired at its failure. As Sam Mainwaring, the most prominent SDF member in Swansea, wrote:

> Wales, I fear, is past redemption. The hall in which comrade [Edmund A.] Cleeves and I have been trying to educate the workmen of Swansea has such a name that we find it next to impossible to get an audience at all now. You must have seen that we have been taking part in SDF work here, thinking they would not object to the propaganda of mild measures such as *Justice* contains but we find that the politicians and preachers have such a hold on them that they fear even to come to hear anything not approved of by them; still we mean to continue the fight – and if possible break down the prejudices now existing in this politician and priest ridden country.[60]

Although socialist literature and newspapers were placed in Swansea public library in the summer of 1894, the circumstances described by Mainwaring led to the folding of the SDF branch at around the same time.[61] He was probably not surprised, however, having written privately in 1893 that 'The people are so full of the idea that they are to be emancipated by political means that to teach communism just now is simply a waste of time'.[62] Socialist activity eventually coalesced around the Swansea Socialist Society, a body closer to the ILP, which was established in April 1897.[63] Mainwaring, by then, had returned to live in London.

The second half of the 1890s offered the SDF, albeit briefly, a period of possibility particularly in the coalfield. Aberdare SDF formed in 1896 and during the 1898 lockout, SDF branches sprang up in the Rhondda, Mountain Ash, and Pontypridd.[64] At Ynysybwl, the SDF drew on fertile ground. In 1893, a group of miners led by John Williams, later MP for Gower, but at the time secretary of the works committee, formed the Ynysybwl Labour Union, to press for workers' rights and protection from victimisation.[65] The following year, the miners played host to Beatrice and Sidney Webb, who had been invited to the village to talk on the necessity of trades unionism.[66] Early on in the 1898 strike, Enid Stacey, suffragette, Fabian, and ILP activist, visited to speak on free trade and socialism. She returned in August 1899, at the invitation of the Lady Windsor Lodge to discuss 'Freedom, Equality and Brotherhood', and 'The Social Teaching of the Lord's Prayer'.[67] Given this enthusiasm it is perhaps not a surprise that the Ynysybwl branch of the SDF enjoyed a sizeable membership – around one hundred and fifty, according to *Justice* – and alongside Pontypridd was the most active branch on the coalfield.[68] Whilst ultimately overshadowed by the miners' lodge, the SDF helped to lay the ideological groundwork for socialism in Ynysybwl and several of its adherents, including Abel Morgan, would dominate lodge committees for decades.[69] Morgan would go on to form the local branch of the ILP a few years later.

SDF activists were significant in Pontypridd, too, with Moses Severn, the president of the Pontypridd branch, serving as checkweigher at the Maritime Colliery and later as secretary of the Pontypridd and Rhondda District of the South Wales Miners' Federation.[70] Severn was joined by John Rhys Morgan who was active in the Abercynon SDF branch. Checkweigher at Abercynon Colliery and lodge secretary, Morgan was elected chair of the Pontypridd and Rhondda District in 1908.[71]

Elsewhere in the Cynon Valley and in the lower Taff valley, SDF activists rose through the SWMF and other trade unions to positions of local influence. The Mountain Ash branch, formed in 1901, dissolved in 1902, and revived on a somewhat surer footing in November 1904 (initially as the Penrhiwceiber branch), was typical. With an initial membership of seven, the branch had expanded to sixty members by September 1905.[72] They met at Mill's Coffee Tavern in Mountain Ash, which was home to the Mountain Ash TLC (founded in 1902) and the local branch of the Shop Assistants' Union.[73] A key figure, and prominent local activist for the SDF in this period, was William Henry Powell, the branch secretary. Born in 1883, Powell was a grocer's assistant and active in the National Union of Shop Assistants, Warehousemen and Clerks, eventually becoming branch president in Mountain Ash.[74] He encouraged the re-formation of the SDF in Ynysybwl in 1905, advocated Ruskin College classes in Mountain Ash, and when the TLC was revived in 1907 he secured election as treasurer and subsequently secretary.[75]

Symptomatic of the significance of the SDF in the Cynon Valley was the occasion in November 1906 when the Mountain Ash branch held their first major demonstration at the town's pavilion. On the platform was H. M. Hyndman, the guest of honour, who had been narrowly defeated at Burnley in the general election at the start of the year.[76] The room was decorated with banners and flags encouraging 'success to the SDF' and declaring 'workers of the world unite'. At the centre of it all was the chairman for the day: Charles Stanton, the local miners' agent.[77] Stanton liked to present himself as more militant and radical than Keir Hardie, the ILP figurehead, and it may be that the language of revolutionary socialism, more typical of the SDF, which was certainly expressed on the platform in Mountain Ash, provided him with a useful outlet.

The SDF's greatest legacy was intellectual rather than organisational. It came from Noah Rees. Lodge secretary during the Cambrian Combine Dispute, checkweigher, leading figure (and in 1906, chair[78]) of Mid Rhondda TLC, Ruskin College student, and one of the primary authors of the *Miners' Next Step*, Rees had little love for the Liberal Party or of Mabon's 'con-sillyation' and was firm in his belief that trade unions should be 'active political organisations'.[79] His experience was vast: he had been elected lodge secretary of the Ogmore Vale branch of the Amalgamated Association of Miners in the 1870s when he was just sixteen and was secretary of the Mid Rhondda Miners' Association before the establishment of the South Wales Miners' Federation.[80] In 1904, Rees joined with James Colton (president) and W. T. Lewis (treasurer) to form the Blaenclydach branch of the SDF, serving as its secretary. Until his departure for Oxford in 1907, he was its leading influence.[81] Colton had previously been the president of the Cardiff branch of the SDF and, as a baker by profession, had even run its socialist bakery from premises in Comet Street, Roath.[82]

Alongside his activities with the SDF, Rees was heavily involved in the National Democratic League, an attempt by the editor of the radical *Reynold's Newspaper*, W. M. Thompson, to forge an alliance of all the forces on the British Left. The NDL was founded in October 1901 and had the support of several leading figures, including Tom Mann, who became its full-time organiser.[83] It failed, however, to gain significant support outside London and most advocates of labour representation 'looked somewhat askance [...] regarding it as a diversion of effort'. Only in South Wales did the NDL develop any strength. Charles Stanton acted as regional adviser, and by the end of 1901 fifteen branches (of around seventy nationally) had been established accounting for several hundred members.[84] Half of them were in the Rhondda.[85] Noah Rees was secretary of the Blaenclydach branch, and conceived of the NDL as a platform to 'rouse the working classes from the apathy that now possesses them, and to try to get the young miners of the Rhondda to take a real interest in politics'.[86] This was to be achieved, in part, through the establishment of the National Democratic Club in Blaenclydach, which opened early in 1903.[87]

Later known as the Marxian Club, the club was a drinking den, had its own billiards tables, and football team, but was also a site of genuine – and significant – intellectual fervent.[88] In March 1903, for example, a paper was read on 'The Miners' Leaders and the Present Aspect of Affairs' in which the current leadership of the SWMF were criticised for having been 'outclassed by the employers' committee every time they meet'. The speaker complained further that 'the only policy they have originated is "leave everything to your leaders, boys"'.[89] Here, in embryonic form, was the syndicalist critique that would grow into the *Miners' Next Step* nearly ten years later. One of those who engaged and debated topics of this kind in the Marxian Club was William Henry Mainwaring, who arrived in Blaenclydach in 1903 to take a job at the Cambrian Colliery. He quickly became involved in the SDF, refining his politics under the tutelage of Noah Rees and replacing him as secretary of the Blaenclydach SDF when Rees was studying at Ruskin College.[90] Mainwaring too, was a major participant in the writing of the *Miners' Next Step*, although in his later years, as MP for Rhondda East, he tended to minimise the influence of the SDF and of syndicalism on its composition.[91]

For the most part, the SDF forces in South Wales weathered the factional crises that undermined the national party in the first decade of the twentieth century, and which led to the split in Scotland led by James Connolly and Neil MacLean in 1903, and in London by the Battersea branch the following year. Neither the Socialist Labour Party (formed in 1903) nor the

Socialist Party of Great Britain (formed in 1904), which resulted from the split, had much influence. When the SDF became the Social Democratic Party in 1907, the local branches followed suit, with members at Bargoed, Blaenclydach, and Merthyr Vale, sending delegates to the annual conference in Manchester. New branches emerged, or were reformed, at Abercynon, New Tredegar, and Treorchy. But the financial weakness of the SDF/SDP, particularly in contrast to the growing strength of the ILP, was apparent. In a resolution moved at the 1908 annual conference, James Patrick Lloyd of the Marxian Club in Blaenclydach urged financial support to enable the party to carry out its work in South Wales. 'I am', Lloyd suggested, 'the only speaker in the district' whereas the ILP had employed three district organisers. If the aim was to get '"gallant little Wales" on the side of Socialism they must send speakers and propagandists into the district'.[92] His plea was not listened to, and the resolution defeated on the grounds that South Wales did not deserve special treatment.

Lloyd's inferred isolation was a slight exaggeration. The poet Huw Menai, a key figure in the Merthyr Vale SDF/SDP, was a regular speaker in the Rhondda and the Cynon Valley, speaking to meetings in Mountain Ash, Abercynon, and Treorchy, between 1908 and 1909. Likewise, branches attracted national speakers to their events: the Mid Rhondda branch, which held public meetings at the Tonypandy Hippodrome, drew Harry Quelch and the future Burnley MP Dan Irving in 1907, and Abercynon drew the socialist writer and commentator E. E. Hunter in 1908.[93] And when the Cardiff SDP was established in 1910, the first speaker was the former Colne Valley MP, Victor Grayson, who told his audience that they should join the socialist movement before their children forced them to. 'The microbe of Socialism [is] now in the schools', he said, 'in the teaching profession, in the universities, everywhere; and the day [is] dawning when it would be the accepted creed of the human race'.[94] The following year, the SDP, in an effort to bring harmony to the Left, arranged a unity conference, which was held in Salford. Four branches from South Wales sent delegates – Barry, Merthyr Vale, Clydach Vale, and the Marxian Club – together with a representative of the South Wales Council, W. A. Wilkinson from Blaenclydach. At the end of the conference, delegates agreed to establish the British Socialist Party, which for a period was, as Victor Grayson predicted, a continuation of the SDP and so dominated by H. M. Hyndman.[95]

By the time of the so-called Great Unrest, which shook Britain after 1910, the non-ILP socialist forces in South Wales had reached a point of relative stability and geographic concentration. Half of the thirteen BSP branches in Wales were to be found in the Rhondda-Cynon-Taff area of the coalfield, with the others scattered in places as distant as Pembroke Dock, Barry, Llanelli, Newport, and Cardiff.[96] Despite several branches operating social clubs, which one BSPer from Aberfan thought 'had been the greatest help securing influence, enthusiasm, and organisation', the party struggled to expand.[97] In contrast to the North of England, where the BSP proved successful, for a time, in attracting grassroots members from the ILP, in South Wales it appears that the BSP inherited the existing membership of the SDF/SDP and the existing branch network and that was it. Certainly, the estimated twenty percent of West Yorkshire ILPers who defected, or the twenty five per cent in Lancashire, was not matched.[98] Given the contemporary development of the SDF and the ILP in the 1890s and 1900s, as well as a degree of overlap in branches and locations of early strength, there was always the slight possibility that the SDF rather than the ILP might have come to dominate, but this proved not to be the case. The organised political forces of the labour movement coalesced under the banner of the Independent Labour Party, rather than that of the Social Democratic Federation.

Independent Labour

In April 1890, delegates and interested parties from across Britain gathered at the Gladstone Hall of the Working Men's Liberal Club in Cardiff to discuss the feasibility of gaining more labour members of parliament and local authorities. The conference convenor, Walter H. Hughes, was the Liberal registration agent in the Monmouthshire valleys, and the conference chair, Isaac Evans, the miners' agent for Neath.[99] It was the clearest signal yet that working men desired to have their voice heard in the governance of the country. Evans, in his opening address, stated that 'the day [has] arrived when the working men of this country should lift their voices higher in the future than they had done in the past. They had been for a long time too silent'. In his address, Walter Hughes drew inspiration from the independent action by workers in the cultural sphere:

> If the working men of Blaenavon by a subscription of a halfpenny per week could maintain a fine institute, with excellent library and billiard-room, and could in a few years save £1,100 towards the erection of a building of their own, what could not be done by the working-classes of the country, working hand in hand, and contributing their halfpence regularly?

The conference exposed the tensions within the Liberal Party: should Labour go its own way, should it remain within the Liberal Party but form a distinct group to bring pressure to bear, or should it remain silent? Alfred Onions, later Labour MP for

Caerphilly, announced himself opposed to the formation of a separate labour party which was likely to be 'influenced by either political party'. In the event, the British Labour League came into being as a body determined to gain independent labour representation on local authorities and in parliament. Its executive committee consisted of Isaac Evans, President, Walter H. Hughes, secretary, and R. A. Lewis, of the Bristol and West of England Bank, Pontypridd, the treasurer. Amongst the advertised vice presidents were Alfred Onions and Mabon. Those on the council included John Williams of Ynysybwl, later MP for Gower, Edward Thomas (Cochfarf) of Cardiff, and David Morgan of Aberdare (Dai o'r Nant). Keir Hardie likewise appears to have been a supporter.[100]

Branches of the British Labour League were soon established, with a marked concentration in the Monmouthshire valleys.[101] The Abertillery branch, christened the 'Gladstone branch', tellingly, was formed at a meeting held near the town's Catholic church in June 1890. When almost four hundred people turned up to the meeting, branch members resolved to canvass the entire town to secure a large enrolment.[102] There was more muted reception in Glamorgan, with branches formed in Gilfach Goch and Ynysybwl, together with votes of support by miners in Aberdare and the Rhondda house coal district.[103] Support was also given by the trades councils of Cardiff and Newport in South Wales, and Bristol and Glasgow elsewhere in Britain.[104] However, following a canvass of lodges, the British Labour League was rejected by the Swansea and Neath District Miners' Association – demonstrating the limits of the League's appeal in that part of the coalfield.[105] There were similar difficulties in appealing to labour organisations in London.[106] Beyond these details, almost nothing is known of the British Labour League and it does not otherwise appear in histories of the labour movement.[107] It was related to the Labour Electoral Association, founded three years earlier in 1887, which had a similar purpose – to press for independent labour representation in parliament. Neither had a great deal of impact on the electoral fortunes of labour and are now long forgotten.

Yet their very existence signalled the growing political voice of the labour movement at the same time that its industrial voice was growing in strength because of the 'new unionism'. Walter Hughes, the secretary of the British Labour League, who had for many years been the secretary of the Welsh National Liberal Council (a post he left only in 1911[108]), saw a clear need to articulate the 'rights of labour' and established the links between revitalised trade unionism and political organisation in his own speeches at League meetings. 'Capitalists', he said in one such meeting, 'were combined everywhere by their common interests, and it appeared to him that society – that was to say, the society compound [sic] of the capitalist and privileged class – was an elaborate conspiracy against the workers, their principal aim being to keep down the standard of living [...] hence their relentless opposition to the new unionism'.[109] It was the substantial growth in trade union activity in the late 1880s and early 1890s, and the industrial strength of labour, on the other hand, which gave rise to the term 'new unionism' – it was widely used in the contemporary press – and reflected the repurposing of trade unions away from bodies representative of artisanal trades (craft unions) and towards a more general trade unionism which recruited skilled, semi-skilled, and unskilled workers through low membership fees.[110]

The leaders of these new unions, most notably Ben Tillett of the Dock, Wharf, Riverside and General Labourers' Union, which he founded in 1889, were self-declared socialists and less disposed to the more conciliatory approach that had been a feature of the earlier craft unions.[111] New unionism had several lasting effects: in parts of South Wales chapel ministers and some traditional Liberal Party activists recoiled at what they regarded as a dangerous new phenomenon. In Barry, the town's Young Wales Society debated the issue vociferously with John Rees, the secretary of the Barry Trades Council, taking the lead in advocating new unionism.[112] New unionism nevertheless drew South Walian labour more fully into the British trade union movement, with most of the trade union branches formed in the late-1880s and 1890s clearly part of unions that operated nationally.[113] This was not so much about 'anglicisation', or its 'dangers', but about a recognition of the terms of industrial conflict, the organisation of capital in Britain, and the need for a more concerted labour response.[114] Unsurprisingly, The emerging, pan-British model of trade union activity had a clear – inevitable – influence on the political organisation of labour in South Wales.

In 1892, the TUC issued its call for a meeting of delegates to discuss independent labour representation. Delegates met in Bradford in January 1893 and resolved to form the Independent Labour Party (ILP). Keir Hardie, the independent MP for West Ham South, was elected chairman.[115] The only Welsh delegate scheduled to attend the conference, Samuel G. Hobson, actually missed the train at Cardiff and did not make it.[116] Six months before the Bradford Conference, there had been a major rally in Cardiff addressed by Ben Tillett and Keir Hardie with the intention of generating support for an Independent Labour Party.[117] Hardie returned to South Wales a few months later, in October 1892, to address meetings in Cardiff and Neath to press the case for a national party ahead of the Bradford Conference; he also gave a major interview to the *South Wales Daily News*. Both meetings had the support of the local trades council, as well as other socialist organisations, such as local branches of the Fabian Society.[118] That autumn, Cardiff Trades Council established its own 'Labour Party' to fight elections to the city council and Board of Guardians.[119] Newport Trades Council followed with its own labour association, known as the Newport and District Independent Labour Party, in January 1893.[120]

The formation of the ILP in Bradford was a major event both galvanising existing labour organisation and acting as a fillip to new activity.[121] Writing in the *South Wales Daily News*, Samuel G. Hobson, enthused that the ILP was a 'healthy influence on our social and political life' and insisted that 'there is nothing revolutionary' in the party's programme of social, political, and economic reform.[122] A few weeks later, Cardiff Trades Council launched its new penny newspaper, the *South Wales Labour Times*, as the voice of the Labour Party in South Wales.[123] The first edition appeared on 4 March 1893.[124] Such was the apparent strength of the labour movement in Cardiff that a local branch of the ILP was not actually formed until 1894.[125] There was an active Fabian Society, a Labour Progressive League, and the Trades Council, together with a Labour Church. It was at a meeting of the Labour Church in July 1893 that Samuel G. Hobson first proposed the formation of a Cardiff ILP branch and the dissolution of the locally-focused Progressive Labour League and affiliation of Cardiff socialists with the national party.[126] Keir Hardie returned in March 1894 one again to 'preach the gospel' of socialism, focusing his attention on Cardiff, Swansea, Neath, Blaina and Abertillery.[127] Hardie's meeting at the Drill Hall in Swansea led to the formation of an ILP branch in the town and to efforts to form a 'Welsh Independent Labour Party'.[128] It was under this banner that the Cwmavon ILP was formed that May.[129]

The 'Wales' that the ILP perceived was, in actual fact, South Wales and Monmouthshire, as reflected in the reporting of meetings in Neath in May 1894.[130] By then, the ILP were active in Neath, Swansea, Morriston, and Cardiff, with efforts to form branches in the Rhondda and Barry ongoing.[131] Keir Hardie was confident enough in the political potential of the people of South Wales that he wrote in the *Labour Leader* that 'the people are very advanced not only politically but socially'.[132] He was not alone, the Swansea-based *South Wales Daily Post* similarly declared that 'it is expected that the movement will receive the support of a large number of the working population of the town'.[133] Cardiff ILP members were confident enough of the support of working people that they proposed to stand Samuel G. Hobson as their parliamentary candidate in the forthcoming general election; although in the event Hobson stood for parliament for the ILP in Bristol East.[134] By the time of the 1895 general election, held in July and August, the ILP had established a presence in South Wales, albeit primarily along the coast, with activists working hard to proselytise. Their focus was increasingly fixed on the South Wales Coalfield: the area of Wales most like the mill towns of northern England and Scotland where the ILP was at its strongest.[135]

It was in the Taff Valley that this activism had its most immediate impact. The Treharris branch of the ILP was formed in August 1895.[136] By the spring of 1896, the branch had grown to around thirty members and its leading members helped in the formation of the Merthyr Tydfil branch, which was established initially in December 1895 but reformed in September 1896.[137] The branches in Merthyr and Treharris invited well-known speakers to address meetings, discussed a range of local, national, and international affairs, and took part in elections to Merthyr Urban District Council.[138] By September 1896, the *Merthyr Times* could record justifiably that 'socialism seems to be making headway in our district'. At the same time, the paper recorded the imminent formation of an SDF branch at Aberdare, stating that 'judging from the crowd who gathered ... social democratic principles will find good congenial soil in

Aberdare'. [139] Within a few years of the formation of the ILP, there were around ten branches in existence across Glamorgan and Monmouthshire.[140] The party had made some impact on local politics, and branches continued to attract high profile speakers, notably Keir Hardie and Ben Tillett, but branches had also fallen by the wayside, particularly in western areas of Glamorgan such as Swansea and Neath.

The following year, 1898, which was marked by a lengthy coal lockout, and the formation of the South Wales Miners' Federation towards the end of the year, sharpened members' critique of local politics and led to a mushrooming effect on the ILP's presence in the South Wales Coalfield. The Merthyr branch claimed a membership of nearly three hundred by August 1898 and nearly thirty branches sent delegates to the South Wales District meeting that September, with several others offering apologies.[141] Willie Wright, the ILP organiser, similarly reported to Head Office in London that there had been a rapid proliferation of branches in South Wales.[142] At its annual meeting in December 1898, the Cardiff branch cheered the news and heard that the 'strike in the coal trade had resulted in a decided advancement all along the line'.[143] Such optimism was, particularly in the coalfield, somewhat misplaced and as the fervour of the lockout receded and workers began to count the financial costs, membership fees (which had been waived during the lockout) were one burden easily forgotten about. By the end of 1899, only nine branches of the ILP were still in existence.[144] Even the Treharris branch, which had been so prominent before the lockout, was disbanded in March 1899.[145]

But the situation was far from gloomy. Once the dust had settled on the coalfield, it was clear that the ILP had, in fact, consolidated its position in certain areas, notably in Cardiff, Newport, Abertillery, Aberdare, and Merthyr Tydfil.[146] A second ILP branch had opened in Cardiff in September 1898, for example.[147] According to Ernie Gough, a long-standing member of the ILP (and later the Labour Party), this branch, situated in Splott, was founded on the initiative of J. H. Thomas, later General Secretary of the NUR, Labour MP for Derby, and secretary of state for the colonies in the Labour government of 1924. Splott ILP met in an old loft above a bakery in Pearl Street.[148] In March 1899, the ILP branches in Cardiff merged with the Cardiff SDF and created the Cardiff Socialist Party – they had already been working together for a number of months.[149] This new organisation had its own socialist club in the Castle Arcade, organised lectures and talks on socialist topics, and published the *Labour Pioneer* between February 1900 and September 1902.[150] And following a revival in activity in western areas of Glamorgan, the ILP secured election to local councils in Swansea in 1898 and in Gwaun-Cae-Gurwen and Ystalyfera in 1899.[151]

Beyond these areas of initial strength, the ILP enjoyed something of a sustained growth spurt in the early years of the twentieth century – providing that the long-term trajectory was one of growth across the region rather than continued expansion and contraction in a limited number of areas. There were, for example, branches established in Aberdare, Ferndale and Hopkinstown in 1902; Mountain Ash and Cwmbwrla by 1903; Nantymoel, Maesteg, Gwaun-Cae-Gurwen, and Briton Ferry by 1904; and at Tondu and Barry by 1905.[152] Ynysybwl followed in 1906 and Abercynon in 1907.[153] When the South Wales ILP Federation met for their annual conference in Merthyr at the end of 1905, the annual report noted the existence of thirty four branches (up from seven in 1901) and declared that 'the outlook ... was never brighter ... It was evident that Socialism was looking up in South Wales'. A report published in the *Labour Leader* in November 1908, confirmed the rapid growth of the ILP in South Wales with as many as ninety five branches of the party in existence.[154] These branches undertook a number of electoral contests across a range of administrative bodies, including the Boards of Guardians, district and county councils, and parliament. By 1916, they had succeeded in securing the election of around four hundred members of these bodies, more than three quarters of them drawn from the ranks of the South Wales Miners' Federation.[155]

ILP branches were assisted in those municipal contests, and in parliamentary elections, by the decision of many trades and labour councils to affiliate to the Labour Representation Committee between its formation in 1900 and the formal establishment of the Labour Party in 1906. Newport TLC debated the topic of affiliation as early as the spring of 1900, but did not resolve to do so until 1902.[156] Aberdare considered its position in the same period.[157] As did Cardiff.[158] And Llanelli.[159] In Swansea, the decision to affiliate was taken in the autumn of 1901 but in a letter to the LRC's headquarters in London, the Swansea secretary, Matt Giles, warned that the trades and labour council contained 'some strong Lib-Lab members'.[160] A further affiliation decision was made the following year, albeit once again in the affirmative.[161] Neath Trades and Labour Council joined in September 1903.[162] In industrial areas, there was concerted effort to induce miners, railwaymen, and other workers, to switch allegiance from the Liberal Party and thereby tip the balance on trades and labour councils in favour of the Labour Representation Committee.[163] Affiliation gave trades and labour councils access to standardised platforms and policies on housing, pensions, education, and how to organise and run local branches, bringing uniformity at the local and national level. This was to prove formative in the steady professionalisation of the Labour Party in the first quarter of the twentieth century.[164]

Local idiosyncrasy was maintained, on the other hand, by a vibrant print culture. Indeed, growth in ILP and trades and labour council organisation was mirrored in the emergence of Labour-supporting newspapers across South Wales. These included *Llais Llafur* which was founded by Ebenezer Rees in 1898; the *Swansea and District Workers' Journal* which was established by the Swansea Trades and Labour Council in August 1899; the Aberavon *Labour Journal* which was established by the Aberavon Trades and Labour Council in 1901; and the *South Wales Worker* which was established by the Swansea ILP in 1902 following the closure of the *Swansea and District Workers' Journal* in December 1901.[165] These were followed in turn by the *Labour Pioneer* in Merthyr Tydfil founded in 1904[166], the *Labourite* in Newport in 1905[167], and the *Western Valleys Labour Journal* in 1906.[168] In addition to the emergence of a Labour press, there was the *South Wales Labour Annual*, first issued in 1902 and in existence until at least 1905.[169] Published by H. B. Davies from his offices in Short Street, Swansea, the *Annual* provided pen portraits of leading figures in the South Walian labour movement together with information about socialist organisations, trade unions, trades and labour councils, and ILP branches. These local developments sat comfortably within the much wider national and international socialist and labour press providing information sufficient to grow the labour movement at all levels.

Parallel to these initiatives was the growth of women's Labour politics, which fused together demands for equal rights and suffrage with municipal policy in areas such as birth control, maternity and child welfare, healthcare, early years' education, and care for the elderly.[170] In the view of Emmeline Pankhurst, speaking in November 1905, the ILP were thus the only party to properly champion women's rights.[171] The Women's Labour League was founded in London in 1906 to organise amongst women and ensure their election to positions of authority, and was associated with figures such as Margaret MacDonald,

Marion Phillips, Katherine Bruce Glasier, and Margaret Bondfield, who was to serve as Britain's first female cabinet minister in the 1929-31 Labour government. Although its earliest centres of activity were in London, Leicester, Preston, and Hull, by 1911 the League could claim more than one hundred branches all over Britain. Several of these were in South Wales.[172] Initially centred on Cardiff and Swansea, by 1908 a third branch had been established at Aberdare, with Barry and Merthyr Tydfil following in 1909, and Newport, Abertillery, Nantyffyllon, Tondu, and Ogmore Vale by 1911.[173] Regional conferences were also held by this time, branches sent delegates to a women's district committee akin to the South Wales ILP Federation, and in Swansea and the Rhondda women's activists wrote columns for the local Labour newspapers.[174] Elsie King, the branch secretary in Ystalyfera, wrote occasionally for *Llais Llafur*.[175]

Cardiff has long been identified as the centre of the Women's Labour League in South Wales.[176] Certainly, the most prominent women's activists in the region were resident in the city, including Mary Keating Hill, the first Welsh suffragette to be imprisoned for her campaigning, and Grace Scholefield, the branch president who served on the national executive of the League after 1913.[177] Members also supported the Cardiff shop assistants' union during their industrial dispute in 1913-14.[178] However, the branches in Aberdare, Barry, Newport, Swansea, and Ystalyfera were at least as active, as strongly integrated into Labour circles in their respective towns often through family connections, and were, in some respects, more successful (particularly electorally). In Abertillery, the Women's Labour League was linked to wider ILP circles through the Barker family – the branch secretary was Ethel Barker, daughter of George Barker, the town's future MP. The president of the Barry branch, Elizabeth Henson, was elected unopposed to the Cardiff Board of Guardians in 1910 and served until her resignation in 1917.[179] And in Swansea, the women's branch confidently declared that 'We are really waking the Labour members on the council up, and we are doing work that ought to have been done by the men years ago'.[180] They signalled that although the suffrage campaign was an important part of women's political activity, it was by no means the only facet.

ILP branches, the Women's Labour League, and trades and labour councils functioned, of course, because of the work of dozens of individuals, but the talismanic figure was Keir Hardie. His election as the junior member of parliament for Merthyr Boroughs in 1900 ensured an especially strong connection – more rhetorical than physical reality – between the rise of Labour and changing circumstances in the South Wales Coalfield. As K. O. Morgan recorded half a century ago, this was 'a facet of the radicalization of the political structure within the Merthyr Boroughs, the consequences of which set up a chain reaction far beyond the confines of the constituency'.[181] Hardie's election in Merthyr was hardly accidental and the processes of political change had been in train long before his selection at a stormy meeting in Aberdare in September 1900 and subsequent victory, and it seems likely that they would have continued regardless. It was the pace of change that Hardie's association with Merthyr altered. The circumstances that led to Hardie's selection are well-known.[182] As are the limits that might be placed on the extent of his 'independence'. As K. O. Fox wrote of Hardie's re-election in 1906, it 'seemed to reflect the extension and solidity of the Labour Movement in the area [but] was stultified by its dependence on Liberal goodwill'. Hardie benefited directly from the electoral pact between the Liberal Party and the Labour Party at the 1906 general election and his own arrangement with D. A. Thomas, his erstwhile Liberal 'opponent'.[183] Even in 1903, he had been accused of colluding with the Liberals three years before.[184]

More indicative of the emergence of the ILP as a political force separate from the Liberal Party, and a more indicative local figure, was James Winstone, the miners' agent for the Eastern Valley District and ILP activist who broke rank with the Liberal consensus of the SWMF to stand as ILP candidate for Monmouth Boroughs in 1906.[185] Born near Risca in 1863, Winstone had been active in successive miners' associations located at Risca Colliery in the 1880s and 1890s and, as chair of the workmen's joint committee for Risca and Abercarn in 1898, was a leading figure during the miners' lockout that year. He was one of the key individuals active in the formation of the South Wales Miners' Federation. In 1896 he was elected as Labour member for the north ward of Risca UDC, rising to be chair of that council, and in 1904, having moved to Pontnewynydd, he was elected to Abersychan UDC for the ILP. Three years later he was elected onto Monmouthshire County Council becoming chairman in 1921 and he also served on the Pontypool Board of Guardians.[186] In his own words he was an advocate of independent labour representation and an opponent of the electoral 'compromise' with the Liberal Party.[187]

Winstone's selection as parliamentary candidate ought to have been uncontroversial. The initial idea came from the National Amalgamated Labourer's Union via the Newport Trades Council in a process that began in 1903.[188] They then approached the South Wales Miners' Federation for support. As an indication of the nature of Newport's labour movement, the three delegates chosen to seek the Federation's support represented the NALU, the Seamen and Firemen's Union, and the Postmen's Union. Although the Federation refused to sanction Winstone as an official candidate, they did agree to provide half of Winstone's expenses 'to show their sympathy with the desire of Newport Trade Unionists for Labour representation'.[189] The conditions were accepted by the trades council a few weeks later.[190] In the event, however, under pressure from the Liberal Party, the Federation reneged on its decision and Winstone faced considerable abuse – including alleged death threats.[191] In the first major rally of the campaign, Winstone promised to work with existing miners' MPs to build a Labour Party in the House of Commons and to campaign for free trade, Irish Home Rule, for the abolition of poverty, and ensure that no child went hungry.[192] His campaign was funded by a 'shilling appeal' and the *Labourite* developed a clear, marketable image of Winstone the trade unionist and working-class representative. The Christmas 1905 issue of the *Labourite*, for example, stressed Winstone's sporting prowess and his leadership capabilities.[193]

In contrast with Hardie's campaign in Merthyr in 1900 and 1906, Winstone undertook an exhaustive series of campaign meetings, focusing his attention on electors in Newport, rather than Monmouth and Usk, which together formed the Monmouth Boroughs constituency. There was also a much stronger antagonism between the Labour Representation Committee in Newport and the local Liberal Party and the election was carried along by the rhetoric of class conflict. Winstone's childhood poverty was contrasted with the wealth of Lewis Haslam, the Liberal candidate, and there was a consistent emphasis on the slavery imposed by capital on labour. With business interests in the cotton mills of his native Lancashire, Haslam was one of the wealthiest candidates to stand in the 1906 general election, a fact which the Newport LRC sought to use to its advantage.[194] As it did the ironic coincidence that the Conservative candidate, Edward Emmanuel Micholls, was also a wealthy Lancastrian mill owner.[195] 'Don't be mis-led', remarked the *Labourite* early in 1906, 'this fight is between the wealthy plutocrat and the struggling working man, between the capitalists' association and the trade unionists'.[196] No distinction was drawn between the Liberal Party and the Conservative Party.

When the results of the poll were announced at the end of January 1906, Winstone came a respectable, but distant, third, drawing more than sixteen hundred votes and sixteen percent of the vote. Haslam, in the end, defeated Micholls by five hundred and ninety two. Both spent two pounds for every one spent on Winstone's campaign. At the close of poll rally at the Temperance Hall in Newport, Winstone was welcomed onto the platform by a rendition of the *Worker's Marseillaise*, a Russian version of the French national anthem made popular during the Russian Revolution in 1905. In his speech Winstone insisted – in the event correctly – that by the end of the parliamentary session the compromises of Lib-Labism would be found wanting and that the Labour Party would stand independent and that until then, the labour movement should organise, educate, and agitate. Winstone's reputation as an independently-minded socialist was made, and in press observations about the growing socialist influence in the South Wales Miners' Federation his name was regularly set alongside Keir Hardie and Charles Stanton's as one to watch. As the *Aberdare Leader* wrote in typical vein a few months after the 1906 general election:

As far as the Merthyr Boroughs are concerned the Miners' Federation and the ILP are, practically, one and the same thing. Why not be honest and go the whole 'hog' by electing Mr Keir Hardie as President ... They might keep Mr James Winstone to carry the red flag and Mr C. B. Stanton to beat the big drum.[197]

Had Winstone proven victorious in 1906, in a three-way contest for a single seat, he would now be remembered as the most important ILP figure to emerge from South Wales in the early part of the twentieth century. But that is what he was. Indeed, Winstone was indicative of what was going on in the South Wales Miners' Federation, industrially and politically, as it shifted its allegiance from the Liberal Party to the Labour Party, and amongst the most indicative of the impact of the ILP on South Wales generally.[198] Winstone's emergence as the identifiable successor to the first generation of Federation leaders after 1906 was apparent each year at the Federation's annual conference when he was nominated as the principal rival to William Brace for the vice presidency. When Brace succeeded Mabon as President in 1912, Winstone was duly elected – the first socialist to hold an officership of the South Wales Miners' Federation. Three years later, following Brace's decision to enter the wartime coalition government as Under-Secretary of State at the Home Office, Winstone became Federation President. By 1914, the South Wales Miners' Federation had almost one hundred and sixty thousand members, a population larger than any town in Wales besides Cardiff. To be its president was easily the most important office a socialist in South Wales could then hold and – Ramsay Macdonald's brief period as Prime Minister whilst MP for Aberavon in 1924, and Vernon Hartshorn's service in Macdonald's cabinets of 1924 and 1929-31 aside – remained so until after 1945.

Faith of the People?

The growth of the ILP in the first decade of the twentieth century, and its triumph over alternative left-wing political forms such as the Social Democratic Federation and its successors the British Socialist Party and the Social Democratic Party, was not accidental. It was the product of a great deal of hard work, intense campaigning, and newspaper publishing, as has been shown, but it was supported by a 'culture' that harnessed traditional working-class outlets such as sport, music, and religion to encourage independence of thought and action. A useful example of the growing relationship between political action and popular culture is the Barry branch of the ILP which was formed in November 1905.[199] The guest speaker at the founding meeting was Emmeline Pankhurst whose wide-ranging address touched on unemployment, education, and women's rights – on later visits Mrs Pankhurst referred to herself as the 'mother of Independent Labour at Barry'.[200] In its meetings thereafter the branch discussed matters such as 'Socialism', 'The Life of a Sailor', 'Housing and Public Health', 'Prison Reform', and 'Social Salvation'.[201] By the time Mrs Pankhurst returned to Barry the following year, the branch had secured premises for itself – christened the ILP Institute.[202]

The scale of ILP activity in Barry was recorded at the branch meeting held at the end of March 1906. Delivering his report, the secretary, E. J. Taylor, explained to members that the branch had organised twelve public meetings, four branch meetings, and six executive committee meetings.[203] Over the next six months, the branch held a further thirty eight public meetings, twenty three of them in the open air, and had held eighteen meetings of the branch (including executive). The sixth months thereafter consisted of twenty six public meetings and seventeen branch meetings. Indeed, between November 1905 and September 1908, the Barry ILP held nearly one hundred and fifty public meetings and nearly one hundred branch meetings.[204] Interspersing these meetings were whist drives and dances to build branch finances, the running of social groups including an amateur dramatic society which put on plays such as Henrik Ibsen's *The Enemy of the People* and Bernard Shaw's *Widower's Houses* and organised musical skits and revues, and the distribution of literature and pamphlets to members of the public.[205] Nor was Barry especially unusual: the Briton Ferry

ILP published their own hymn book, Neath ILP had its own male voice choir, as did Swansea ILP and Cardiff ILP, which had an orchestra and brass band as well.[206]

The cultural activities of the ILP were particularly strong in the Cynon Valley. The Aberdare branch appointed its own pianist – Lily Treharne – in February 1901 and even went to the trouble of purchasing a brand new piano in 1907.[207] A Band of Hope was formed that year for the children of ILP members and it was typically these children, accompanied by Treharne, who sang socialist songs at major ILP events in the district, notably the rally held in December 1907 addressed by Victor Grayson, the Labour MP for Colne Valley, and that of April 1908 addressed by Keir Hardie and Charles Stanton.[208] Their repertoire included *We'll Keep the Red Flag Flying*, *The People's Anthem*, *Lift Up the People's Banner*, *Sons of Labour*, *Men of Harlech*, and the *Marseillaise*.[209] In November 1908, seeking to replicate the success of the children's choir, the branch formed a male voice choir under the conductorship of David Evans, Robertstown. They sang the well-known classic, *Comrades in Arms*, ahead of a speech by James Parker the Labour MP for Halifax.[210] Down the valley at Mountain Ash, the ILP branch organised its own eisteddfod in March 1909, held at the workmen's institute. Drawing entries from across the local area for competitions that included the best rendition of an election song, the event even prompted a prize *englyn* on the life of Keir Hardie.[211] Hardie himself participated in these activities composing the song *Banner of Freedom* for an ILP demonstration in Porthcawl in 1908.[212]

Not every activity that emerged out of the labour movement in this period can be described as 'rational recreation', of course.[213] For there to be an effective appeal to the mass of the working class – particularly male workers – there had to be some attempt at including physical recreation in the ILP programme as well. Aberdare ILP, for example, had its own football team. The Clarion Cycle Club, founded in 1894, was the most significant step in this direction before the interwar years.[214] Cardiff Clarion Cycle Club, which was formed in 1898, was probably the first section in Wales. It enjoyed considerable success through the early part of the twentieth century.[215] A few years later, a section was formed in the Rhondda and in Newport – however the latter was to be the only club in existence in Wales on the eve of the First World War.[216] More prosperous were the Clarion Scouts, an offshoot of the Clarion Cycle Club intended more overtly for propaganda purposes, as Robert Blatchford explained in *The Scout*, the society's journal:

> In each town and in each district of a large town, let Scouting parties be formed. These Scouts are to be provided with tracts and leaflets, which they are to leave at the houses of the workers. Let one street be taken at one time, a tract being left for a week, to be called for the week after and left in the next street. The Penny Edition of *Merrie England* is specially designed for this purpose. Scouts should also be enlisted in all large factories, mines, and other works, in the regiments of the army, and amongst the police, their duty being to permeate their companions with Socialism.[217]

Branches of the scouts appeared in the Rhondda, Cardiff, Swansea, and Aberdare, between 1908 and 1909.[218]

Distribution of literature and pamphlets as well as 'permeation' of would-be comrades with socialism was not merely left to the scouts and willing activists pounding the streets. By the first decade of the twentieth century, the ILP had taken a leaf out of the co-operative book and set up its own shops, bookstalls, and cafés – the Merthyr shop in Pontmorlais being the best known. In Ton Pentre, for example, there was by 1908 an ILP shop which sold socialist literature and a variety of refreshments. It was, claimed the local newspaper, 'one of the novel features of Ton to-day'.[219] Swansea had its 'Bomb Shop' in Alexandra Road.[220] The literature secretary of Llanelli ILP ran a bookstall at which a wide number of works on Christian Socialism were available, including books by J. Stitt Wilson of Berkeley, California.[221] More prominently located were the bookstalls of the Cardiff, Maesteg, Pontypool, Abertillery, and Aberdare ILP branches, all of which were located in the towns' market halls.[222] The Aberdare stall opened on 26 May 1906, selling copies of the *Labour Leader* and socialist pamphlets. It proved remarkably successful, as the *Aberdare Leader* recorded: 'not only were the *Labour Leaders* sold and a considerable quantity of pamphlets and books disposed of, but as a result of this advertisement six new members were received'. The following week, having increased their order of the *Labour Leader* by fifty percent, the stall still sold out. It surprised no-one in the party, therefore, that the first quarter of 1907 saw over £15 worth of sales of the *Labour Leader* as compared to just under £4 in the corresponding quarter of 1906 (the last before the stall opened).[223]

The flow of pamphlets, hymn books, newspapers, and journals, together with outlets for physical recreation and mental improvement, and mission vans, are all indicative of labour's existence as an alternative to existing forms of education, leisure, and proselytising. The movement also presented itself as an alternative faith to that presented in the chapels and churches. It was an opposition that took two different forms: Socialist Sunday Schools and Labour Churches on the one hand and Christian Socialism on the other. Neither has been adequately explored in the South Wales context and yet they both provided a powerful means of communicating a socialist message to a population still vehemently attached to chapel culture with ever more radical political and industrial solutions.[224] The transformation of Labour into a form of religion, rather than merely a vehicle for its most radical expression, was the brainchild of John Trevor. Born in Liverpool in 1855, Trevor grew up in a strict Baptist family but was later converted to Unitarianism, becoming a minister in the Unitarian Church in the late-1880s. In 1890, he moved to Manchester to conduct his ministry, and it was here that his growing Unitarian faith began to fuse with an interest in labour politics. In April 1891, he attended a conference in London addressed by Ben Tillett, who attacked the profound alienation of the churches from working-class needs and interests, and Trevor returned to Manchester convinced of the need for a Labour Church. This was founded on 4 October 1891 in a meeting at Chorlton Town Hall. Little more than three months later, Trevor resigned his Unitarian ministry after a dispute and devoted himself full-time to the Labour Church movement.[225]

In his first sermon to the Labour Church, at that opening session on 4 October 1891, Trevor preached on what he saw as the failure of existing religious institutions to support the rights of labour and therefore workers needed their own church to embody both their religious faith and the belief in the rights of labour. That, he declared was the Labour Church.[226] The Labour Church quickly spread throughout much of industrial Lancashire, notably at Bolton, where the town's oldest congregational church transformed itself into a Labour Church, and the West Riding of Yorkshire, including Bradford where the ILP foundation conference in January 1893 was accompanied by a Labour Church service attended by as many as five thousand people.[227] The Church has typically been regarded as a 'half-way house between orthodox political liberal-radicalism and the ILP' and a clear stage in the 'transfer of social energy from religion to politics'.[228] In other words, it is presented as part of the inevitable process of secularisation that was taking place amidst the modernisation of British society in the late-Victorian and Edwardian period. This was also apparent in the growth of the secularist Ethical Society in areas such as Cardiff,[229] Aberdare,[230] Neath,[231] and Merthyr Tydfil.[232] The Society had close links with the emergent Labour Party – Keir Hardie spoke to the Merthyr branch, for instance[233] – and went further in its commitment to secularism than the Labour Church.[234]

Neither the Ethical Society nor the Labour Church movement had a significant presence in South Wales and the number of branches was small compared to both England and Scotland, as was also the case with Socialist Sunday Schools.[235] In those communities where they did develop, however, they had an important role to play particularly as a means of bringing together different aspects of socialist thought and activity. The first Labour Church in South Wales, founded in January 1893 after several months of agitation, was at Cardiff.[236] Led by Samuel G. Hobson and other members of the Cardiff Fabian Society, those who gathered each Sunday at the church hall sang socialist hymns, read pamphlets, and listened to sermons delivered by Hobson and others – including a number of national figures.[237] At their first meeting, held at St John's Hall, on 29 January 1893, the Cardiff Labour Church was addressed by Henry Halliday Sparling, a member of the Hammersmith Socialist Society and the Fabians. As Hobson later recalled, Philip Snowden was the most popular speaker alongside Keir Hardie (although he spoke less frequently than Snowden), whilst Enid Stacey and Katherine Conway attracted smaller audiences.[238] Ben Tillett, who spoke at the inauguration of the Swansea Labour Church in September 1893, also 'preached' in Cardiff on several occasions.[239]

Not content with speaking to their own members, the members of the Cardiff Labour Church endeavoured to evangelise their movement (and socialism) through the holding of meetings at the 'Hotel de Marl' – a notorious open-air shebeen in Grangetown that aroused the ire of nonconformity and Liberal councillors alike but was enormously popular with local workers – and the establishment of a Cinderella Society to provide material relief to poor children and form a band and choir to enable the children to take part in some form of meaningful recreation. Both are demonstrative of the socialist focus on poverty and the efforts both to ameliorate it and to explain its materialist underpinnings.[240] This active intervention in the economic circumstances of the poor and needy was also in evidence in the autumn of 1893 when the Labour Church raised money for the miners' strike, and in the following year when they raised money for the Albion Colliery Relief Fund and striking fuel workers in Swansea, and again in 1895 when distress was widespread and soup kitchens present in numerous communities across the whole region.[241] It may, in fact, reflect the strong role played by women in the church. In November 1893, for example, the Cardiff Labour Church was put in their charge and throughout its existence women and men were regarded as equals.[242]

Within a couple of years, the Cardiff Labour Church had fallen into abeyance, as had that at Swansea, and the mooted churches at Abertillery and Neath had never materialised – only the Barry Labour Church (in practice the name given to SDF Sunday meetings held there) had any significant presence before 1898.[243] For Arthur E. Ellery, a young theology student from Birmingham who arrived in Cardiff in 1898 having been rejected from the ministry because of his radical politics (and membership of the Labour Church), the absence of a Labour Church was something that needed to be rectified – he succeeded in bringing John Trevor to Cardiff in October 1898 to assist his efforts.[244] At this meeting, held at Ellery's house in Grangetown, there were supporters from the ILP, the SDF, and the Carlylian Club, a moral debating society based in Roath. E. T. Robinson, the old secretary of the Cardiff Labour Church, was appointed treasurer to assist Ellery.[245] Hereafter, Ellery slipped into the role previously played by Samuel G. Hobson and proved himself the foremost advocate of the Labour Church movement in South Wales agitating, in Barry and Swansea for the re-formation of branches. This failed at Barry, but in Swansea a successful Cinderella Club was set up.[246]

It is notable that none of the moves to set up labour churches in the 1890s took place in the coalfield – indeed, the coalfield was considerably behind equivalent industrial areas of Britain in establishing a labour church of any kind, particularly the north of England. Only in the aftermath of the religious revival of 1904-5 did the connection between the labour movement and religion become overt, beginning in the Cynon Valley and spreading later to parts of Merthyr Tydfil and to the Rhondda.[247] In Aberdare, the ILP developed a labour church in 1906.[248] The following year, Rev George Neighbour, a Baptist minister at Mountain Ash, set up a labour church there.[249] In 1908, the ILP in Pentre in the Rhondda heard a 'sermon' by Thomas Isaac 'Mardy' Jones outside the Zion Chapel which, coupled with frustration at antagonistic remarks made by chapel ministers towards the labour movement, resulted in efforts to establish a branch there.[250] Subsequent efforts by activists in Penygraig, however, ran into difficulties when Rhondda Education Committee refused to allow meetings to take place in school halls.[251]

This developing network was greatly aided by a number of high-profile Christian Socialist speakers who travelled regularly to address open-air meetings, rallies, and Labour Church or

Socialist Sunday School sessions, among them George Lansbury, the Rev Reginald John Campbell, and the American preachers J. Stitt Wilson and his brother Ben. Campbell's activities are the best known, certainly in the Welsh context, and have been subject to some academic scrutiny.[252] In 1907, it was rumoured that Campbell would be invited to contest Cardiff at the next general election on behalf of the ILP.[253] Although the rumour was denied by Campbell himself in an interview with *The Times*, his presence in South Wales at the same time as the rumour was being recorded in the press added to the speculation that he would agree if asked.[254] In an interview with the *Cardiff Times*, a leading member of the Cardiff ILP observed that 'were he to come forward he could win the seat comfortably ... we have no doubt that the working men as a body are in sympathy with us, and in a fight they would be on our side'.[255] Upon being asked by a delegation of Cardiff ILPers, Campbell stated that he could neither agree nor disagree with the offer. The matter was left to lie on the table and the ILP never did contest the single-member Cardiff constituency.[256]

Campbell's message to those who attended his meetings in Cardiff, Barry, Tredegar, Merthyr, Aberdare, and the Amman Valley, was both socialist and Christian in form. As he declared in Cardiff, 'socialism was the practical expression of Christianity as he understood it'.[257] A few months earlier, Campbell had set down his vision of how the two could be combined into a single movement and begin the process of overcoming the 'distrust which at present exists between many of the leaders of the Socialist movement and the advanced representatives of the Christian religion'.[258] One of those upon whom Campbell's new theology had considerable impact was James Griffiths, elected in the 1930s to be president of the South Wales Miners' Federation, then MP for Llanelli, and a Labour Cabinet Minister in the postwar government. As Griffiths explained in his autobiography, as a young miner in Ammanford his introduction to Campbell's ideas came initially in the form of columns in *The Christian Commonwealth* and *The Examiner*. 'These [...] suddenly threw two bombs into our family circle, the New Theology and Socialism. This set us all arguing at home, at chapel, and in the mine and mill [...] The journals and their sermons, and the visits of preacher and politician [Keir Hardie], were to lead me to "The Movement" which ever after was to be my life'.[259]

In order to formalise the connections between the new theology and the political socialist movement Campbell, together with F. R. Swan a congregational minister and ILP member, founded the League of Progressive Thought and Social Service in January 1907.[260] The League had a strong connection with Wales – its first summer school was held at Penmaenmawr in August 1907 and the following year it was held in Aberystwyth – and by 1909 there were as many as ten branches in South Wales alone, accounting for three hundred paid-up members. There was also a district committee.[261] The strongest branches were in the coalfield. The Treorchy branch was founded in November 1907 on the initiative of W. T. Owen who became the organising secretary.[262] A second branch came into existence in Tonypandy in April 1908, meeting at Llwynypia Workmen's Institute, and by the end of the year branches were also in existence in Ferndale and Gilfach Goch.[263] In the Cynon Valley, similarly, strong branches were formed in Mountain Ash and Abercwmboi, with efforts to engage interest in Abercynon and Aberdare as well.[264] And in Pontardulais, the league branch came into existence in June 1909 following a visit by W. T. Owen.[265]

The Progressive League (as it was popularly known) provided an organisational framework through which a leftward shift could be encouraged amongst chapel ministers, deacons, and members of the congregation. The Abercwmboi branch serves as a useful example. Founded in January 1909 when fifteen men, mostly miners resident in John Street, were expelled from the Bethlehem congregational chapel for holding 'new theological' beliefs; or, as the chapel's annual report put it denying 'the faith which was once delivered unto the saints'.[266] The minister at Bethlehem was J. Bowen Davies, who had been the pastor at the chapel since 1897 and overseen a period of considerable growth.[267] During the revival of 1904-5, in particular, Bethlehem saw a large increase in membership.[268] The rise of the new theology, however, unsettled this period of growth and went hand in hand with the rise of the ILP in the area. In an interview with the *Aberdare Leader*, Bowen Davies complained of those expelled from the chapel that 'most of them have adopted the political views of Mr Campbell and are ILPers. They are a very cantankerous lot, and the church will go on better without them'. Amongst those expelled were Samuel Davies, one of the chapel deacons, and Roderick Rhydderch, whose father remained 'a most faithful member of Bethlehem'.[269] Perhaps not surprisingly, the Rev Bowen Davies was a public advocate of the Liberal Party.

Events in Abercwmboi coincided with the resignation of the Rev George Neighbour in Mountain Ash; his active support for the ILP had earned the scorn of the deacons at Mount Pisgah Baptist Chapel and effectively forced him out of his ministry there. Instead of taking up offers to work for the ILP full-time, including one to become a regional organiser in North Wales, Neighbour remained in Mountain Ash and founded a branch of the Brotherhood Church.[270] It was immediately successful drawing worshipers from across the district, including those expelled from the Bethlehem chapel in Abercwmboi and others persecuted (as he put it) owing to their socialist views, and by early 1908 had a membership roll of eighty. A Sunday School and a Band of Hope were also set up, thereby providing the framework of typical chapel activity – an alternative culture of religion familiar enough in form but with a much more open communion.[271] By 1910, the church had grown sufficiently large to merit the purchase of two houses in Napier Street, which were then converted into meeting rooms and a library. By this time, members had also joined the South East Wales district of the Unitarian Church.[272]

With the security of the Brotherhood Church and its congregation behind him, George Neighbour found himself increasingly in demand as a speaker on socialist and religious matters. Taking the opportunity afforded by those meetings he frequently expressed his belief that socialism was on the rise 'in spite of the prejudice displayed by the churches and others'. It was, he said, 'the only means of uplifting humanity from the present deplorable and demoralising condition'.[273] He lectured across South Wales on the unfairness of capitalism and the concentration of wealth in the hands of the few, rather than those of the many who toiled to produce it. But perhaps his most frequent 'sermon' was on the intolerance of existing churches and chapels and on the Christian validity of socialism.[274] In Abercwmboi, similarly, the members of the Progressive League took to heart the growing enthusiasm for their movement and spoke out in favour of Christianity as a faith of action to overcome inequality and unfairness, rather than a mere profession of belief.[275] As one visitor to a Progressive League meeting noted in the press, 'it was impressed upon me that they had come together not so much for worship as for social intercourse and mutual aid and inspiration'.[276] There was, then, an atmosphere of change evident in the Cynon Valley, with a younger, more progressive element opening up within the wider field of nonconformity and so mirroring the trend visible in local politics.

Neither South Wales, nor Britain, were alone, of course, in debating the possibilities of Christian Socialism. In the United States, Canada, and Australia, the labour and socialist movements grappled with the question, partly through the influence of a small network of activists who travelled back and forth to spread the gospel of the religion of socialism.[277] Amongst the most interesting are J. Stitt Wilson and Ben Wilson. J. Stitt Wilson was born in Canada in 1868 but spent most of his life in the United States. A supporter of Eugene Debs's presidential campaigns and candidate for governor of California himself – he was elected mayor of Berkeley, California, in 1911, on a socialist ticket – he was one of the most prominent socialists in America in the early part of the twentieth century. He grew up in a strict Wesleyan Methodist family and trained for the ministry alongside his undergraduate studies at Northwestern University in Illinois. The most important of the church posts that he held during those four years was at Erie Street Methodist Church, located in a poor, working-class district of Chicago. He was also involved in the Northwestern University social settlement. The experience transformed J. Stitt Wilson's political beliefs and by the time he graduated in 1897, he was a self-professed socialist.[278]

From 1897 until his move to California in 1901, J. Stitt Wilson, together with his brother Ben, was heavily involved in the social crusade, a group of Methodists and Congregationalists based in Chicago who aimed at awakening workers in the United States to the evils of capitalism and transforming Christianity into a socialist movement.[279] The group published a journal, *The Social Crusader* between 1898 and 1901, and were based at the university settlement house.[280] In 1899, J. Stitt Wilson, together with two other members of the social crusade, William H. Wise and Dr James H. Hollingsworth, travelled to Britain on a mission to study the social conditions of industrial slums with regard to the bearing of those conditions on the development of progressive Christianity. Their initial base was Mansfield House, the prominent social settlement in the East End of London.[281] During this trip the men engaged with the ILP and with the Brotherhood Church, both of which impressed them.[282] Family illness cut short Wilson's involvement in the trip but he returned to Britain in January 1900. Not long after he arrived back, Wilson preached at the Brotherhood Church in London.[283] Thereafter he spent a small amount of time in Birmingham, Scarborough, and Tunbridge Wells before travelling to Bradford, where much of his visit was conducted. According to the *Chicago Daily Tribune*, Wilson made over one hundred addresses and in Bradford addressed open-air meetings attended by as many as five thousand people.[284] Plans were also put in place to return in 1901, but these were scrapped when Wilson moved to California.[285]

J. Stitt Wilson made a brief return to Britain in 1907, when he addressed the Progressive League's summer school in Penmaenmawr and declared that 'the present capitalist social structure fostered every feeling and sentiment which was contrary to the mind of Jesus of Nazareth'.[286] But it was in 1908 that his first major social crusade took place, with a large number of meetings held in South Wales, as well as in the North of England (notably in West Yorkshire) and in the Midlands. The first of the South Wales meetings was held in Cardiff on 27 June. Starting out from Cathays Park, a large procession travelled through the main streets of the city centre led by a local brass band and the Clarion Scouts. Banners declared that 'socialism [is] the hope of the world' and 'socialism demand[s] justice not charity'. The next day, Wilson addressed meetings in Llandaff Fields and Roath Park, the latter in front of around five thousand people as in Bradford. Throughout all of the meetings socialist songs resounded on the air.[287] A few weeks later, Wilson arrived in Barry and was again paraded through the streets of the town and presided over a number of meetings at St Mary's Hall.[288] In all, J. Stitt Wilson spent six weeks in Cardiff and Barry preaching the socialist gospel before moving on to address meetings in Swansea (under the auspices of the Swansea Socialist Society) and the Progressive League's summer school in Aberystwyth. Present at the Swansea meetings was George Neighbour, who served as chairman.[289]

Wilson arrived in the coalfield itself in September 1908 – although this phase of his trip was cut short. Eugene Debs had announced his candidacy for the presidency of the United States and Wilson raced home to join in the final stages of the election campaign. He returned, however, in early December picking up his coalfield tour in the Cynon Valley.[290] Wilson took to the stage at the drill hall in Mountain Ash and declared that 'socialism was not anti-religious'. His message drew heavily on the Bible, linking left-wing thought to wider religious faith. 'Socialism' he added in an address at Penrhiwceiber, 'did not commence with Blatchford or Karl Marx' but with Moses (whom he regarded as 'the great Labour leader'[291]) and Jesus and Buddha. 'The spirit of socialism was to reorganise and readjust the social conditions until the world was made a garden of God, presentable to Him who created them'.[292] Just a few years after the religious revival that had gripped many parts of the coalfield, this was the ideal message of hope and change. He repeated it at the Theatre Royal in Cardiff a few days after Christmas, at an ILP meeting chaired by J. H. Thomas.[293]

In the new year, Wilson turned his attention once more to the coalfield.[294] At Penygraig he appealed for more critical reading of the daily press, telling audiences that a socialist faith was inevitable if one looked at the world for what it was. On the dais he held aloft a copy of the New Testament, which he called 'the most deadly instrument in the world against tyranny, injustice, mammonism, and the cruelty and brutality of the present social order'.[295] In a variant on this theme, he addressed a meeting at Clydach Vale with a lecture explaining that socialism was the fulfilment of Christian teaching.[296] And at the English Congregational Chapel in Ton Pentre, he told audiences that he had 'come to make socialists'.[297] Drawing on Jesus's motif of explaining his ethics through parables, Wilson returned to his theme of the world as a garden and told large audiences at the Theatre Royal, Shiloh chapel, and Penydarren school, that 'socialism is the gardener who comes to guarantee every flower the full freedom of life'.[298] His last speech was at Swansea in April.[299] The departure of J. Stitt Wilson did not bring the social crusade to an end, the ILP enjoyed the support of his brother, Ben, who arrived in the coalfield in March 1909 and carried on the work of preaching the socialist gospel for several months.[300] In July, to mark Ben Wilson's visit, the Cardiff ILP even marched through the streets of the city centre headed by the ILP band and carrying banners declaring that 'socialism will abolish poverty'.[301]

In September, J. Stitt Wilson returned to South Wales once more, joining his brother on their social crusade. This time, the brothers travelled further west addressing meetings in Gwaun-Cae-Gurwen and Brynamman, as well as in Cardiff, Barry, Merthyr, Abercynon, and the Rhondda.[302] One of those who heard the Wilson brothers preach in the west on this tour was William Morgan Davies of Cwmgors.[303] He recalled many years later that having read J. Stitt Wilson's pamphlet 'The Messiah Cometh: Riding Upon the Ass of Economics' he did not share the belief espoused by the Wilson brothers that the teachings of Christ were political in nature, they were, Davies felt, grounded in faith. However, Davies reflected that upon hearing J. Stitt Wilson's sermon to Carmel chapel in Gaun-Cae-Gurwen, which contained hardly any political rhetoric, instead being firmly couched in religious language, he began to agree.

Let there be many windows in your soul
That all the glory of the universe may beautify it
Not the narrow pane of one poor creed
Can catch the radiant rays that shine from countless sources.

Another of those who was much influenced by the Wilsons' social crusade through the coalfield between 1908 and 1910 was the writer Dorothy Edwards, who was born in Ogmore Vale in 1903. Her father, Edward, was the local headmaster and a key figure in the ILP and co-operative society in the town, as well as a vegetarian. He organised camps on the mountainside which were attended by Keir Hardie, George Lansbury, Robert Smilie, and J. Stitt Wilson, and involved his daughter at a young age. As Claire Flay notes, this was to be a lifelong commitment to ethical socialism and in her diary, Edwards dedicated one passage to the memory of J. Stitt Wilson himself.[304]

Why did American missionaries spend so much time in the South Wales Coalfield in the first decade of the twentieth century? They were part of a general movement of progressive ideas back and forth across the Atlantic, a movement which had considerable influence on the intellectual development of political radicalism and social democracy in the 1890s and 1900s, but which also drew on the long tradition of moral responses to economic questions.[305] The dramatic economic and demographic transformation of the South Wales Coalfield at the end of the nineteenth century exposed both the possibilities and the iniquities of capitalism and the coalfield was recognised as a place where a sharp moral critique would find an audience. Several existing leaders of the labour movement and their successors, including Alfred Onions, James Winstone, A. J. Cook,

John Hopla, S. O. Davies, and Arthur Horner, all shared a religious background which they drew on in their secular attacks on unfairness and inequality. Writing in the *Merthyr Pioneer* in 1915, for instance, J. Stitt Wilson stated that 'I impeach capitalism as the supreme anti-Christ of modern times. I take my stand on the life and spirit and teaching of Jesus, and declare that capitalism is a menace to every purpose and programme of the Christ'.[306] Sentiments that even the most radical miners' leader in the early part of the twentieth century would have agreed with.[307]

The ebbing and flowing of the labour movement's engagement with Christian teaching and religious faith was symptomatic of the many socialisms that were emerging in South Wales in the period before 1910. The ethics of reasoning otherwise were multifaceted and engaged many different, but often mutually sympathetic, voices. Politics, of course, had always had certain religious leanings: the Conservative Party were willingly identified with the Anglican Church, the Liberal Party with nonconformity, but the labour movement could rely on neither in its progression from ideas to fully fledged organisations. The political pillars of the labour movement, then, were never simply about winning elections, and in part they did owe more to Methodism than to Marx; they were about looking at the world in more moral and ethical ways, and always with the belief that 'it doesn't have to be this way'. Symptomatic of the ethical socialism pursued by J. Stitt Wilson and those who shared his vision of Christianity was a desire to think about innovative solutions to contemporary crises. One such innovation was advocating the adoption of a vegetarian diet during the 1898 miners' lockout because it would improve the quality of food that miners and their families could afford. The same idea re-emerged during the 1910-11 Cambrian Combine dispute.[308]

Both dates – 1898 and 1910 – signify change within the industrial attitudes of the South Wales miners. To look at a list of when each miners' union in the British coalfields formed is to look at something quite surprising: Northumberland in 1864, Durham in 1869, Somerset and Cumberland in 1872, Derbyshire in 1880, Lancashire, Nottinghamshire and Yorkshire in 1881, South Derbyshire in 1883, the Midlands in 1886, Leicestershire in 1887, Bristol in 1889, North Wales in 1891, South Wales in 1898. Given the region's history of radicalism, the fact that it was the last coalfield to organise might seem, on the surface, to be remarkable. Eric Evans, in his assessment published in the early 1960s, thought it symptomatic of the relatively harmonious relationship between employer and employee in the coalfield until the last decade of the nineteenth century.[309] But this is to miss the importance of geography, with communications running down valleys, rather than across; and the economic and demographic pace of change which was rather different from the other coalfields. The rapid expansion of the South Wales Coalfield came in the 1890s and 1900s – precisely the period when the most concerted efforts at forming a regional trade union were successful. Moreover, if the formation of the South Wales Miners' Federation in 1898 is also placed in the longer-term trend that includes the rise of the co-operative societies, the persistence at finding an independent political path for the representation of labour, and the constellation of socialist organisations, then it can be seen not as a 'belated catch up' but as the culmination of changing attitudes to industrial and political activity. Its formation also heralded the beginning of a new era, one in which the miners took the lead in articulating social democracy and making *Labour Country*.

The Fed

In 1927, in the aftermath of the general strike and miners' lockout, the South Wales Miners' Federation published a short pamphlet setting out its own idea of its own history. It was, understandably, given this was part of the Federation's rebuilding of itself, a congratulatory History:

> There is probably no organisation in the world which has such close relationship to the community it serves as the South Wales Miners' Federation has to the people of the mining areas of South Wales. For the last twenty or thirty years it has become so much a part of the life of the people of this Coalfield that every man and woman living in this area turn instinctively to it for advice and protection in almost every kind of difficulty or trouble they meet from time to time.[310]

Of course, the Federation was never fully accepted by every miner on the coalfield, but from the moment of its establishment on 11 October 1898, it provided industrial cohesion to the miners and the singular (articulate, working-class) voice necessary to unify the South Wales Coalfield in a way that political parties could not.[311] Like earlier unions and miners' associations in the coalfield, the Federation was a confederal body composed of twenty districts (each with their own committee, agent, sub-agent, treasurer, and secretary) and colliery lodges that were at the heart of its democratic structure. The districts had considerable autonomy and it is not surprising that, as historians have often discerned when examining the mosaic of South Wales politics, no two were quite the same, even when they were neighbours. There were differences, for instance, between the west (that is, the anthracite coalfield) and the east. Into this structure were fed ideas articulated by members inside and outside the lodge environment. The democratic structure of the Federation provided a considerable platform for the socialist thought articulated by men such as Noah Rees and John Rhys Morgan, and they knew they could use its institutions to further their cause. The same was true of syndicalists such as Noah Ablett and A. J. Cook, labourites such as Aneurin Bevan and James Griffiths, and communists such as Arthur Horner, Bill Paynter, Dai Francis, and Dai Dan Evans. In this way, the Federation was never just an industrial organisation, it was always guided by the politics and aspirations of its members.

The most quixotic figure of all was Mabon, who endeavoured to stand with one foot in each camp to give the impression that he, and he alone, could hold the miners and the masters together in peace. The sliding scale, which precipitated the conflict in 1898, was his invention and he fought to keep it in place, even to the frustration of miners themselves. As *Justice* recorded in May 1898, 'Abraham is perhaps the most unpopular man in this district to-day, and the miners are not loathe to point out that they pay him about £700 per annum for doing nothing at all'.[312] *Justice*, the newspaper of the Social Democratic Federation, was hardly a neutral observer, but its interest in the coalfield pointed to the presence of socialists who spoke to mass meetings, organised branches, distributed newspapers and pamphlets, raised funds that were sent into the coalfield from outside to support soup kitchens and boot repair centres, condemned the use of troops by the government, and agitated as though the new dawn was just upon the horizon.[313] Mabon could hardly corral this spirit for his own ends and the failure of his efforts during 1898 led to 'even the most cautious, peaceful and conciliatory amongst the men [being] driven into bitterness by the tactics employed by the owners'.[314] Uniform anger, exacerbated by defeat in a rising market when economic conditions should have favoured the worker, not the employer, led to the overcoming of traditional divisions. To defeat the unity of the Monmouthshire and South Wales Coal Owners' Association, the miners realised, they needed a single body of their own and it was not the already sizeable one of William Abraham.

The 1898 strike began on 1 April and lasted until 1 September, when, after the announcement was made that the strike was over, the bells of Cardiff's churches pealed in jubilation.[315] The American consul in the city struck a more sombre tone in correspondence with the US State Department. 'Nothing', he remarked, 'appears to have been gained by it [the strike] beyond what might have been derived four months earlier'. Nevertheless, he concluded, 'peace is practically assured throughout the entire coalfield'. The irony was that the establishment of the South Wales Miners' Federation, and the struggle to bring about full membership within communities, assured that peace was very often the last thing available to miners. In Ynysybwl, for instance, tension over making the Lady Windsor Colliery a fully unionised workplace was such that the village constantly teetered on the edge. At one meeting of the lodge, held in Trerobart school in September 1899, members passed a resolution stating simply that 'non-unionists are not to be tolerated'.[316] Then in August 1900, the lodge presented the Ocean Coal Company with notice of strike action.[317] This was delayed to 'give more time' to the non-unionists to join up, but eventually, on 1 October 1900, the strike began.[318] It concluded that afternoon when the remaining non-unionists joined the Federation.[319]

One hundred percent union membership at the Lady Windsor did not last for very long and there were regular notices of intent to strike given by the unionised workers to apply pressure to those that consistently waivered. Indeed, an examination of the local press reveals a nearly annual effort to maintain full unionisation. In 1905 and again in 1908, for instance, the pattern established in 1900 prevailed. Full unionisation was achieved, either with a brief stoppage or none, only for it to drift away again slowly. In 1906, however, a strike on the issue lasted for several days.[320] The Lady Windsor Lodge was not alone in applying pressure in this fashion, nor was it unique in never being quite able to maintain full membership: nearly seventy stoppages took place between 1898 and 1904 on this issue.[321] The most frequent cause of non-membership was financial difficulty and the struggle to keep up payments. John E. Morgan, the lodge secretary, reflected half a century later that:

> Generally, non-payment of dues was not caused by hostility to the organisation, but rather from a faulty disbursement of the family income. That this is true is surely proved by the fact that since the dues have been kept at the colliery office there has been no protest whatever against the union contributions.[322]

This was the Federation at the local level learning from experience, altering its practices to suit circumstances, and thereby introducing into the union a range of idiosyncrasies that strengthened its cohesiveness.

From the outset, the Federation was always more than a trade union, since miners exercised considerable and often singular political power at the local level. Although somewhat mediated by other interests – not least the chapel – this provided lodges with a clear degree of influence over the affairs of mining communities. But this power and influence was not always exercised, or took several years to come into its own, with the growth of the lodge as the arbiter of local politics a longer process in certain areas than others. In the case of Ynysybwl, for instance, which had already experienced a flourish of radical political activity in the 1890s, the emphasis placed on building up the Federation in the colliery workforce seems to have resulted in the relative absence of political activity by the lodge until around 1910, and although the lodge ensured that David Smith was elected to the local school board in 1901 as Labour candidate, and Hugh Price was similarly elected to the urban district council in 1902, these were singular occurrences.[323] For the most part, Ynysybwl was represented by David Rhys Morgan, the local GP, and David Rogers, a bookseller and newsagent and, although a Liberal, generally a man considered to hold 'advanced views and as "not far from the kingdom" (of Labour)'.[324] Rogers was nearly unseated in 1912 by William H. May, an Unofficial Reform Committee activist and later miners' agent in Pontypridd, during the lodge's campaign for a public park in the village. May lost by just thirty six votes.[325]

The 1902 urban district council election, which provided the Lady Windsor Lodge with its first electoral victory, was also indicative of some of the challenges that faced the Federation as it became directly involved in grassroots politics. Two potential candidates emerged: Silas Williams, checkweigher and lodge committeeman, who was a committed Liberal, and Hugh Price, an engineman who was a Labour member.[326] In the lodge's selection ballot, Price won four hundred and sixty votes to Williams's three hundred and thirty five, and in the absence of a Liberal or Conservative opponent was assured of victory.[327] Until, that is, the sudden intervention of another collier, James H. James, led to a contested election.[328] Those who voted for James did so, insofar as they explained their actions publicly, because 'he was prepared to contest the seat and serve the ratepayers at his own expense, whereas the other candidate's expenses would be borne by his fellow-workmen through the local lodge'.[329] In the event, James's intervention, encouraged as it was by local businessmen, nearly scuppered the lodge's electoral ambitions: Price won narrowly two hundred and ninety two votes to two hundred and fifty six.[330] Fractures of this kind, informed clearly by antagonism towards the intervention of trade unions into the political sphere, and placed in the context of annual struggles to build Federation membership, point to a coalfield that was not characterised (as was once thought) by a 'Liberal consensus'.[331]

Nor was it quite the case that, as Cliff Prothero, born in Ynysybwl in 1898, recalled years later, there were 'very few socialists in the village and those who were in sympathy with this new doctrine were considered to be very queer people'.[332] As early as 1905, when the miners were still officially affiliated to the Liberal Party, the lodge in Ynysybwl was actively agitating on behalf of Keir Hardie and pressing compatriots in Pontypridd to 'secure' a labour candidate to fight the 1906 General Election against the long-serving Alfred Thomas. Many of those who were influential in the lodge in this period were founder members of the ILP branch established in the village in February 1906.[333] During the affiliation campaigns in 1906 and 1908, the colliery voted clearly in favour of joining the Labour Party – in 1908 this was a majority of two to one. They also supported the publication of a dedicated labour newspaper for the district – possibly the Merthyr Borough *Labour Pioneer*.[334] And they were responsible for inviting a litany of socialist celebrities to the village to speak.[335]

Not all lodges acted in the same way, either in the early years of the Federation, or towards the very end of its long existence, but the intervention of miners' lodges into political affairs on behalf of independent labour transformed the coalfield. With more substantial financial resources than fledgling branches of the ILP, this intervention enabled Labour to better compete with Liberal and Conservative opponents, eventually establishing a hegemony of its own. It was to be a symbiotic relationship, for the lodge not only intervened in politics through political parties, it was a political organisation. To return to the campaign for recreational amenities in Ynysybwl, which nearly toppled David Rodgers in 1912. This began with a resolution tabled in 1901 by Morgan Walters, founding member of the lodge and the Ynysybwl ILP.[336] It drew on popular support within the community and correspondence was passed to local landowners asking for a piece of land for a park. When the request was rebuffed, the lodge tried again, albeit with the same response.[337] Eventually, the local authority intervened, secured the ground, paid the lease, and fenced the site in.[338] But the impetus had come from the lodge and its ILP membership, it was they who organised mass meetings and they who maintained popular demand. Had landlords been willing to negotiate directly with the lodge, as they were subsequently with Liberal councillors, the park would have been recognised as an early example of Federation welfare.[339] The principle of the lodge as a transformative body for the community had nevertheless been established.

The capacity of the Federation to absorb new ideas, to develop strong community links, and to act as a political focus, was substantial. But its efficacy between 1898 and the transformations which came after 1910 was somewhat limited by the political and industrial instincts of William Abraham and his moderate colleagues in the Federation and in parliament. Inevitably this led to conflict, just as Abraham had courted a certain degree of conflict in the 1870s and 1880s to advance the position of labour (and, in retrospect, his own career). It was to be an intellectual battle between cautious labourism, which sought the advancement of labour whatever contradictions were entailed, and stood its ground within the umbrella of the Liberal Party and socialism, direct and overt, to which the younger generations were increasingly attached. It meant different choices from those made in the past. Indicative of the new way was James Winstone, who stood for the ILP in the general election of 1906. Although he lost, his candidacy encouraged his rise through the ranks of the Federation until, in 1915, he reached the top – the first president of the Federation to be a declared socialist. It was clear that the future of the South Wales Miners' Federation was socialist, but the revolution inside the union needed a jolt. That was Tonypandy.

Notes

[1] The 'progressive age' is more commonly evoked in American and Canadian historiography but its transatlantic meaning merits application to Wales. For American historians, the Progressive Era was marked by the coming together of a coalition of interests which sought to provide improvements for the urban poor and for society generally. This was also the period in which the labour movement in Canada and the United States began to coalesce around social and cultural matters as well as politics and industrial relations. See, for instance, Daniel T. Rodgers, *Atlantic Crossings: Social Politics in a Progressive Age* (Cambridge, 1998); Roy Rosenzweig, *Eight Hours for What We Will*; Ian McKay, *Reasoning Otherwise: Leftists and the People's Enlightenment in Canada, 1890-1920* (Toronto, 2008).

[2] *PC*, 28 September 1888; *CT*, 29 September 1888.

[3] *CT*, 17 November 1888.

[4] Not for everyone, however. Swansea's elites saw Cardiff as 'a combination of hell and harlots'. EEx, 8 April 1899. 'There are more women of bad fame in the streets and drinking shops of Cardiff in one twenty-four hours than in all the other parts of Wales put together ... Cardiff prides herself on being the Chicago of Wales. Both begin with the letter C; both are cheeky, churlish, and given to cock-crowing and self-adulation. You can "bet your bottom dollar" on that!'

[5] *EEx*, 30 September 1893.

[6] Henry Hyndman, *The Record of an Adventurous Life* (New York, 1911), 184.

[7] As above, 192.

[8] As above, 205.

[9] The biographical details in this paragraph draw on Kenneth Howard Hilton, 'A Well-Marked Course: The Life and Works of John Spargo' (Unpublished PhD Dissertation: Syracuse University, 1991) and Markku Ruotsila, *John Spargo and American Socialism* (London, 2006).

[10] John Spargo, *The Spiritual Significance of Modern Socialism* (New York, 1908), 18-19.

[11] Hilton, 'A Well-Marked Course', 19.

[12] University of Vermont, Special Collections, John Spargo Papers, 3/41: 'Confessions of an Old Fogy', I, 19.

[13] *BDN*, 8 May, 22 May 1891. Initial moves had been undertaken in the summer of 1890. *BDN*, 15 August 1895.

[14] For instance, *BH*, 1 May 1896, which describes a Navvies Church meeting at Cadoxton Common.

[15] *BDN*, 8 March 1895.

[16] *BDN*, 9 August 1895, 23 August 1895.

[17] *BD*, 2 October 1896; *BH*, 2 October 1896.

[18] *BDN*, 12 February 1897.

[19] *EEx*, 8 October 1896.

[20] *BDN*, 3 November 1899.

[21] *BDN*, 13 December 1895.

[22] *Justice*, 25 May, 6 June 1896.

[23] *BH*, 29 May 1896.

[24] *BH*, 21 February, 28 February, 6 March, 13 March, 20 March, 3 April 1896; *BDN*, 24 April 1896.

[25] *BDN*, 27 November 1896; *BH*, 26 March 1897. The minimum wage debate is considered in James Thompson, 'Political economy, the labour movement and the minimum wage, 1880-1914', in E. H. H. Green and Duncan Tanner (eds.), *The Strange Survival of Liberal England: Political Leaders, Moral Values and the Reception of Economic Debate* (Cambridge, 2007), 62-88; James Thompson, *British Political Culture and the Idea of 'Public Opinion', 1867-1914* (Cambridge, 2013).

[26] *SWDN*, 14 September 1897.

[27] He maintained a firmly pro-Boer stance. *BH*, 13 October 1899; *BDN*, 25 August 1899.

[28] *SWDN*, 13 March 1900.

[29] *BDN*, 6 April 1900.

[30] *RL*, 21 July, 18 August, 29 September, 20 October 1900.

[31] *RL*, 3 November 1900.

[32] *RL*, 17 November, 24 November 1900.

[33] The pair married in Cardiff on 24 January 1901. *BDN*, 1 February 1901. Prudence died in 1904 aged 28. *BDN*, 8 April 1904.

[34] Hardie also wrote separately to Spargo to offer his best wishes. 'Letter from Keir Hardie to John Spargo, 12 January 1901', Spargo Papers, Box 12, Folder 42. Spargo had been a regular speaker at Bristol Socialist Society meetings. See the scrapbooks (containing programmes of events) compiled by Samuel Bale, the society's secretary, held at Bristol Central Library. B19560 covers the years 1910-1933; B19561 covers the years 1886-1933.

[35] *BDN*, 8 February 1901. He published the lecture the following year in the United States. John Spargo, *Where We Stand* (New York, 1902).

[36] *Justice*, 19 January 1901.

[37] The couple eventually settled at 324, East 56th Street.

[38] 'Letter from H. M. Hyndman to John Spargo, 26 August 1901', University of Vermont Special Collections, John Spargo Papers, Box 14, Folder 6.

[39] *BDN*, 24 May, 21 June, 19 July 1901.

[40] *BDN*, 28 June, 6 September, 18 October 1901.

[41] *Social Crusader* 1, no. 1 (September 1898), 3-10, 15.

[42] *Social Crusader* 3, no. 7 (July 1901), 4-5. The Workingmen's Headquarters was situated at 312, East 52nd Street, a few streets away from Spargo's tenement flat.

[43] *BDN*, 25 October 1901; Hilton, *Spargo*, 119.

[44] John Spargo, *The Bitter Cry of the Children* (New York, 1906).

[45] Early fruits of which appeared as John Spargo, 'The Influence of Karl Marx on Contemporary Socialism', *American Journal of Sociology* 16, no. 1 (July 1910), 21-40.

[46] *BH*, 9 September 1910; *EEx*, 12 September 1910; *MEx*, 10 September 1910; *BDN*, 16 September 1910; *Tarian y Gweithiwr*, 22 September 1910.

[47] *BH*, 16 September 1910.

[48] *Justice*, 10 January, 7 March, 16 May, 25 July, 8 August 1885.

[49] *SWDN*, 17 January, 18 January 1887.

[50] *SWE*, 17 January 1887.

[51] *SWE*, 19 March 1887.

[52] *WM*, 21 March 1887.

[53] *Justice*, 26 March 1887.

[54] IISH, Socialist League Archives, 2225: 'Letter from A. S. Mead to Socialist League, 9 April 1888'. For a sense of Mead's activities with the League see: *The Commonweal*, 16 June 1888. Here he is reported as speaking to the Guildford Street Improvement Class on socialism.

[55] IISH, Socialist League Archives, 2968: 'Letter from Richard E. Thomas to William Morris'.

[56] IISH, Socialist League Archives, 2531: 'Letter from John Rees, Dowlais, 28 August 1887'.

[57] IISH, Socialist League Archives, 2174: 'Letter from Robert R. Mainwaring to H. A. Barker, 23 October 1887', 'Letter from Robert R. Mainwaring to H. A. Barker, 7 February 1888'.

[58] IISH, John Rees Letter.

[59] *The Cambrian*, 8 September 1893; *Justice*, 3 December, 17 December 1892, 16 September, 23 September 1893; *SWDP*, 4 September 1893. The latter also had outreach meetings in Landore coffee tavern. *Liberty* 4 (April 1894), 32; *SWDP*, 9 February 1894; *The Cambrian*, 9 February 1894; *Justice*, 30 September 1893; *Liberty* 4 (April 1894), 28.

[60] IISH, Max Nettlau Papers, 782: 'Letter from Sam Mainwaring to Max Nettlau', 10 May 1894.

[61] *SWDP*, 14 August 1894; *WM*, 6 August 1894.

[62] IISH, Max Nettlau Papers, 782: 'Letter from Sam Mainwaring to Max Nettlau', 14 February 1893'.

[63] *SWE*, 13 April 1897; *SWDN*, 23 November 1897.

[64] ALS, Aberdare Socialist Party, Minute Book, 1901-1906; ALS, Aberdare ILP, Cash Book, 1902-1908; GA, DXHJ/2-7, Aberdare Socialist Society Collection; *Justice*, 23 October 1897, 30 July 1898, 6 August 1898, 24 September 1898, 1 June 1901, 20 July 1901; *GFP*, 3 September 1898.

[65] TNA, FS 7/10/879, Ynysybwl Labour Union. The organisation is mischaracterised in the Registrar of Friendly Societies Reports as a quarrymen's union. The rulebook of the society, however, explicitly states that it is for employees of the Lady Windsor Colliery. I am grateful to Dr Ben Roberts for this information.

[66] *CT*, 14 September 1895; *TG*, 12 September 1895. The meeting is

mentioned by John E. Morgan, albeit he records as taking place in 1896. John E. Morgan, *A Village Workers' Council: A Short History of the Lady Windsor Lodge South Wales Miners' Federation* (Pontypridd, 1950), 45.

[67] *PC,* 29 April 1898; *GFP,* 14 May 1898, 9 September 1899.

[68] *Justice,* 24 September 1898.

[69] SWML, AUD/310: 'Interview with Abel Morgan conducted by Dave Egan, 1972'; AUD/311: 'Interview with Abel Morgan conducted by Dave Egan, 1972'. The SDF branch chair was Samuel J. Lewis. The secretary William Gibby, was the librarian at the workmen's library in Augustus Street. A revival of the SDF branch in June 1905 eventually gave way to the ILP in February 1906. *SWDN,* 1 August 1898; *GFP,* 28 May 1898, 5 August 1898, 4 February 1899, 11 February 1899. *Justice,* 11 June 1898; *AL,* 24 June 1905; John E. Morgan, 'Unpublished account of the setting up of the ILP in Ynysybwl', John E. Morgan Papers, SWML, Swansea cited in Burge, *Gleaming Vision,* 29.

[70] *GFP,* 12 November 1898.

[71] *AL,* 22 August 1908.

[72] *AL,* 5 November 1904. A useful description of the founding of the Mountain Ash branch 'in a little room at Miskin' is given by Thomas Bennett, the vice chairman, in a letter to the *AL,* 2 September 1905. For the initial Penrhiwceiber branch see, *Report of the Twenty-Fourth Annual Conference of the Social Democratic Federation* (London, 1904), 6. The Treharris branch was also in existence by then.

[73] *AL,* 20 December 1902, 18 February, 4 March 1905.

[74] *AL,* 5 November 1904, 14 January 1905.

[75] *AL,* 24 June 1905, 25 November 1905, 14 December 1907, 15 February 1908, 15 August 1908.

[76] Adams was born in Maesycwmmer in 1855. She grew up in Newcastle and trained as a teacher. In 1897, she was elected to the London School Board as a socialist candidate, gaining re-election in 1900. Jane Martin, 'Mary Bridges Adams and Education Reform, 1890-1920: an ethics of care?' *Women's History Review* 13, no. 3 (2004), 467-488.

[77] *AL,* 10 November 1906. Stanton was a member of the ILP, and an

ILP member of Aberdare UDC for the Aberaman ward. David Howell, *British Workers and the Independent Labour Party, 1888-1906* (Manchester, 1983), 29.

[78] *RL*, 21 July 1906.

[79] *RL*, 15 August, 26 September 1903. The subsequent activities of the Mid Rhondda TLC are documented in the 1909-1922 minute book. This is at the NLW: MS 18148E. A copy is held at Treorchy Library.

[80] RPA, U DAR/x1/2/52: 'Interview with W. H. Mainwaring, 5 October 1966'.

[81] *RL*, 10 September 1904, 19 January 1907. The *RL* suggests about thirty members joined at the inaugural meeting.

[82] *SWDN*, 14 September 1897, 8 September 1898. He later moved to the Amman valley and married the Russian-American anarchist Emma Goldman in 1925.

[83] *Reynold's News*, 28 October 1900.

[84] Frank Bealey and Henry Pelling, *Labour and Politics, 1900-1906: A History of the Labour Representation Committee* (London, 1958), 51; Tom Mann, *Why I Joined the National Democratic League* (London, 1901), 7, 12. The South Wales branches were at Aberavon, Abercarn, Aberdare, Barry, Coedpenmaen (Pontypridd), Cwmparc, Dinas, Mid Rhondda (Blaenclydach), Mountain Ash, Nantymoel, Penarth, Pentre, Penygraig, Porth, Trecynon, and Treorchy.

[85] Williams, *Democratic Rhondda*, 67.

[86] *RL*, 15 December 1900, 5 January 1901.

[87] *AL*, 28 February, 28 March 1903.

[88] *RL*, 29 September 1906. A second club opened at 45 Penygraig Road, Penygraig, in 1906. A branch of the ILP was formed here shortly afterwards but eventually collapsed when a rival branch refused to merge. *RL*, 31 March 1906; *AL*, 10 August 1907.

[89] *AL*, 7 March 1903.

[90] RPA, U DAR/x1/2/52: 'Interview with W. H. Mainwaring, 12 September 1966'; 'Interview with W.H. Mainwaring, 5 October 1966'.

[91] A point underlined in W. H. Mainwaring's contributions to Vincent

Kane's 1965 documentary, *The Long Street*, which makes no
mention of either. See especially *The Road to Pandy Square*.

[92] *Report of the 28th Annual Conference of the Social Democratic Party*
(London, 1908), 9-10.

[93] *RL*, 5 October, 2 November, 9 November 1907, 13 June 1908;
AL, 4 July, 26 September, 10 October 1908; *MEx*, 22 May 1909.

[94] *EEx*, 7 November 1910.

[95] *Report of the Socialist Unity Conference* (London, 1911); *Clarion*,
11 August 1911.

[96] *Report of the First Annual Conference of the British Socialist Party*
(London, 1912).

[97] *First Annual Conference BSP*, 12.

[98] Keith Laybourn, 'The Failure of Socialist Unity in Britain, c.1893-
1914', *Transactions of the Royal Historical Society* 6ser, no. 4
(1994), 170.

[99] *CT*, 12 April 1890.

[100] *Ardrossan and Saltcoats Herald*, 10 October 1890.

[101] *CT*, 16 August, 8 November 1890; *PFP*, 27 February, 6 March
1891; *PC*, 22 May 1891; *TG*, 13 November 1890; *SWDN*, 6 May
1890.

[102] *PFP*, 27 June 1890.

[103] *AT*, 12 July 1890; *PC*, 24 October 1890; *TG*, 21 August 1890;
SWDN, 9 January 1891.

[104] *SWDN*, 30 October 1890, 10 January 1891; *SWE*, 31 January
1891; *WM*, 5 December 1890.

[105] *CT*, 28 June 1890.

[106] *Reynolds News*, 3 August 1890. Although by this date the
League claimed a membership of ten thousand, primarily based in
South Wales.

[107] It is absent from Martin Wright, *Wales and Socialism: Political
Culture and National Identity Before the Great War* (Cardiff, 2016),
for instance, although it does make a brief appearance in David A.
Pretty, 'David Morgan ('Dai O'r Nant'), Miners' Agent: A Portrait of
Leadership in the South Wales Coalfield', *WHR* 20, no. 3 (2001),
495-531.

[108] By which time he appears to have been an enthusiast of Keir

Hardie. LSE, Francis Johnson Correspondence, ILP/4/1906/102. Letter from Walter Hughes to Keir Hardie, 17 February 1906.

[109] *PFP*, 27 February 1891.

[110] L. J. Williams, 'The New Unionism in South Wales, 1889-92', *WHR* 1, no. 4 (1963), 413-430; Deian Hopkin and John Williams, 'New Light on the New Unionism in South Wales, 1889-1912', *Llafur* 4 No. 3 (1986),67-79; Alastair J. Reid, *United We Stand: A History of Britain's Trade Unions* (London, 2004).

[111] Jonathan Schneer, *Ben Tillett: Portrait of a Labour* Leader (London, 1983). The Miners' Federation of Great Britain was also formed in 1889, at the Temperance Hall in Newport.

[112] *BDN*, 25 November 1892; *South Wales Star*, 18 November 1892.

[113] Williams 'New Unionism', 428-9; Joe England, 'Notes on a Neglected Topic: General Unionism in Wales', *Llafur* 9, no. 1 (2004), 45-58.

[114] For instance, Wright, *Wales and Socialism*, 38. Wright follows Williams in stressing Anglicisation.

[115] The full details of this formation are laid out in Howell, *British Workers*.

[116] ILP, *Report of the First General Conference, Bradford, 14th January 1893* (Glasgow, 1893), 8.

[117] *South Wales Star*, 15 July 1892.

[118] *SWDN*, 15 October, 18 October 1892.

[119] *SWDN*, 16 September 1892.

[120] *SWE*, 13 January 1893; *WM*, 13 January 1893. The branch president was G. Vickery, the vice-president C. Bradshaw, the secretary E. J. Davies, and the treasurer a Mr Gibbs. One of their first acts was to settle on meeting at premises that were not licensed. This was also the desire of the Dowlais ILP a decade later, see Dowlais ILP, Minute Book, 1901-1904, RBA, SWCC: MNA/PP/69/1.

[121] K. O. Fox, 'The Emergence of the Political Labour Movement in the Eastern Section of the South Wales Coalfield, 1894-1910' (Unpublished MA Thesis: University of Wales, 1965).

[122] *SWDN*, 27 January 1893.

[123] *SWDN*, 3 February 1893. Deian Hopkin has shown that there

were as many as two hundred and fifty socialist and labour
newspapers and journals published in Britain between 1880 and
1900. Deian Hopkin, 'The Socialist Press in Britain, 1890-1910', in
George Boyce, James Curran and Pauline Wingate (eds.), *Newspaper
History from the Seventeenth Century to the Present Day* (London:
Constable, 1978), 294-306. See also his 'The Newspapers of the
Independent Labour Party, 1893-1906' (Unpublished PhD Thesis:
University of Wales, Aberystwyth, 1991).

[124] *South Wales Labour Times*, 4 March 1893. The paper survived
until May 1893.

[125] *WM*, 1 August 1893.

[126] *SWDN*, 31 August 1893.

[127] *WM*, 21 February 1894.

[128] *SWDN*, 7 March 1894; *WM*, 7 March 1894.

[129] *GG*, 11 May 1894.

[130] *EEx*, 28 May 1894.

[131] *EEx*, 28 May, 31 May 1894; *BDN*, 15 June 1894, 15 February
1895; *South Wales Star*, 15 June 1894. The leading figure in
Swansea was Sam Mainwaring. *SWDP*, 7 March 1894.

[132] *LL*, 26 May 1894.

[133] *SWDP*, 10 February 1894.

[134] *SWDN*, 26 April 1895; *WM*, 10 May 1895; *SWE*, 8 July 1895.

[135] Keith Laybourn and Jack Reynolds, *Liberalism and the Rise of
Labour* (London, 1986); Keith Laybourn and David James, *The
Rising Sun of Socialism: The ILP in West Yorkshire* (Wakefield, 1991);
J. A. Jowitt and R. K. S. Taylor (eds.), *Bradford, 1890-1914: The
Cradle of the ILP* (Bradford, 1980).

[136] *MT*, 29 August 1895. The branch president was William Harvey
Marcombe, who had previously been active in the town's debating
society. Marcombe subsequently moved to Cardiff and became
secretary of the Cardiff ILP. By 1901, he was resident in the
Rhondda and working at the Naval Colliery in Penygraig. Active in
the Mid-Rhondda Trades and Labour Council, he was elected
president in 1910. *SWDN*, 12 October 1894; *Merthyr Times*, 9
January 1896; *RL*, 5 March 1910. The secretary was S. Jenkins.
Merthyr Times, 12 September 1895.

[137] *Merthyr Times*, 5 December 1895, 9 July, 3 September 1896; *LL*, 7 December 1895.

[138] *Merthyr Times*, 21 November 1895, 9 July, 13 August, 20 August, 3 September 1896; *LL*, 1 February, 15 February 1896.

[139] *Merthyr Times*, 17 September 1896.

[140] *ILP News*, December 1897. These were: Abertillery, Cardiff, Dowlais, Ebbw Vale, Maerdy, Maesycwmmer, Merthyr Tydfil, Newport, and Treharris.

[141] *SWDN*, 6 September 1898.

[142] Howell, *British Workers*, 245.

[143] *EEx*, 6 December 1898.

[144] Howell, *British Workers*, 245.

[145] *GFP*, 25 March 1899.

[146] The example of Merthyr is discussed in detail in Howell, *British Workers*, 246-253.

[147] *EEx*, 12 September 1898.

[148] SCOLAR, Dave Simpson Collection, Coal Trimmers File, 'W. Campbell Balfour notes from interview with Ernie Gough, undated'. In later years, following Thomas's return to South Wales from Swindon, he mortgaged his house to be able to purchase a meeting hall for the ILP in Neath Street, Splott.

[149] *EEx*, 16 March 1899; *SWDN*, 30 December 1898.

[150] *Labour Pioneer: The Organ of the Cardiff Socialist Party*. This is held at Cardiff Local Studies. For the institute see the November 1901 edition. The paper was edited by A. E. Ellery, the former secretary of the Cardiff SDF and Labour Church organiser, and T. J. Hart, President of Cardiff Trades Council and ILP activist. It followed an attempt to organise a socialist newspaper in Cardiff the previous year. The *South Wales Democrat*, which launched in January 1899 but had ceased to exist by the end of the year. *GFP*, 21 January 1899. One copy, for July 1899, has survived at CLS.

[151] *The Times*, 23 January 1941; ILP, *Annual Conference Report, 1900*, 12. The branches in these communities had been formed the previous year, *ILP News*, September 1898.

[152] *AL*, 7 June 1902, 20 December 1902, 16 May (Cwmaman), 23 May 1903 (Mountain Ash). The paper recorded of the Mountain Ash

branch 'evidently the ILP is popular here, and we have reason to believe that in time to come the young branch will grow and develop into a firm stem'. *RL*, 26 November 1904; *The Cambrian*, 18 December 1903 (Cwmbwrla), 22 July 1904 (Gwaun-Cae-Gurwen), 2 September 1904; *CT*, 3 September 1904 (Briton Ferry), 3 June, 19 August 1905 (Maesteg); *BDN*, 17 November 1905; *GG*, 26 October 1906; *Pontypridd Chronicle*, 22 March 1902 (Hopkinstown); *EEx*, 11 July 1904 (Tondu).

[153] *AL*, 31 August 1907.

[154] *LL*, 20 November 1908.

[155] SWML, SWMF, Minute Book, 1916: entry for 9 October.

[156] LHASC, Labour Party Archive, LP/LRC/2/224-226, Letters from F. H. Heath, 24 May 1900-23 April 1901; LP/LRC/2/22-23, Letter from F. H. Heath, 11 April 1901; LP/LRC/1/306-7, Letter from F. H. Heath, May 1900; LP/LRC/5/276, Letter from F. H. Heath, 3 November 1903.

[157] LHASC, LP/LRC/3/281-3, Letters from F. H. Heath, July 1901-January 1902.

[158] LHASC, LP/LRC/5/9-30, Replies from Trades Councils Re Affiliation, October-November 1902.

[159] LHASC, LP/LRC/6/250-1, Letters from D. A. Edwards, 6-22 November 1902; LP/LRC/LB/1/136-7, Letter from D. A. Edwards, 8 November 1902.

[160] LHASC, , LP/LRC/3/362, Letter from Matt Giles, 28 November 1901; LP/LRC/3/363-5, Letters from W. Davies, November 1901-January 1902.

[161] LHASC, LP/LRC/5/371-2, Letters from Llew. Hopkins, October 1902.

[162] LHASC, LP/LRC/10/311, Letter from Thomas Church, 23 September 1903.

[163] For examples from Abertillery and Blaina, see LHASC, Labour Party Archive, LP/LRC/20/11, Letter from T. Emberly, 2 January 1905; LP/LRC/25/3-4, Letters from Emlyn Evans, 30 September-9 October 1905; LP/LRC/27/225, Letter from James Pitman, 20 November 1905. Similarly, Bedlinog: LP/LRC/7/245-6, Letter from David Jones, Secretary of Bedlinog ILP, March 1903. And Merthyr

Tydfil: LP/GC/19/73-4, Letters from William Harvard, 25 September-1 October 1907.

[164] LHASC, LP/GC/12/3, Letter from E. Stonelake, 24 February 1907; LP/GC/20/250, Letter from J. D. Kinsey, 21 October 1907; LP/LRC/22/2, Letter from T. Ll. Francis, 11 April 1905; LP/GC/18/133, Letter from E. Williams, 1 August 1907; LP/LRC/24/430-431, Letters from Dafydd J. Thomas, 8-15 June 1905.

[165] Robert Smith, *In the Direct and Homely Speech of the Workers: Llais Llafur, 1898-1915* (Aberystwyth, 2000); Deian Hopkin, 'The Labour Party Press', in K. D. Brown (ed.), *The First Labour Party, 1906-1914* (London, 1985); David Cleaver, 'Swansea and District's Labour Press, 1888-1914', *Llafur* 4, no. 1 (1975), 35-42. The Aberavon *Labour Journal*'s formation is discussed in *The Cambrian*, 11 October 1901. It was edited by George T. Owen, a leading figure in the Aberavon Labour Party, and carried the motto 'devoted to the moral and intellectual advancement of the workers'.

[166] *MEx*, 15 July 1904. This paper is not to be confused with the more famous *Pioneer* established in 1911 on the initiative of Keir Hardie. The earlier *Labour Pioneer* was established by the Merthyr and Dowlais TLC with support from the ILP and the Labour Representation Committees in the Taff Valley.

[167] The *Labourite* was established by the Newport Labour Representation Committee in 1905, ostensibly to support the parliamentary candidacy of James Winstone at the 1906 General Election. *EEx*, 3 November 1905. Copies survive at Newport Central Library. See also, LHASC, LP/LRC/25/222-225, Letters from E. A. Williams, 25-28 September 1905; LP/LRC/27/209, Letter from E. A. Williams, 1 November 1905.

[168] The *Western Valleys Labour Journal* was edited by Albert Charles Willis, who worked underground at the Arrael-Griffin Colliery in Six Bells. Willis was elected to Abertillery UDC and Monmouthshire CC under the ILP banner. He emigrated to Australia in 1911 and quickly involved himself in the Australian Labor Party in New South Wales. He served in the New South Wales parliament between 1925 and 1933, serving for three years as secretary of mines.

[169] Copies of the *South Wales Labour Annual* survive in Swansea Central Library (1902, 1904, 1905), CLS (1903), and the LSE

(1903, 1904). H. B. Davies was president of the Swansea Typographical Association and at the start of the twentieth century also served as president of Swansea TLC.

[170] Speaking in Roath Park, Cardiff, in 1914, Katherine Bruce Glasier called for old people's homes whilst speaking at a Women's Labour League Rally. *WM*, 21 September 1914.

[171] *Labour Leader*, 17 November 1905. This contrasts with the existing historiography which has tended to stress the importance of the Liberal Party and women's liberalism. Ursula Masson, *For Women, For Wales and For Liberalism: Women in Liberal Politics in Wales, 1880-1914* (Cardiff, 2010); eadem, 'Political Conditions in Wales are quite different…,' Party Politics and Votes for Women in Wales, 1912-15', *Women's History Review* 9, no. 2 (2000), 369-388.

[172] Neil Evans and Dot Jones, '"To Help Forward the Great Work of Humanity": Women in the Labour Party in Wales', in Duncan Tanner, Chris Williams and Deian Hopkin (eds.), *The Labour Party in Wales, 1900-2000* (Cardiff, 2000), 215-216.

[173] *CT*, 4 November 1905, 18 April 1908; *AL*, 15 February, 21 March 1908; *BH*, 17 September 1909; *MEx*, 25 September, 2 October 1909; *EEx*, 29 January 1910; *DH*, 12 July 1912.

[174] *BDN*, 30 September 1910; *Llais Llafur*, 30 May 1914. The articles are collected in Jane Aaron and Ursula Masson (eds.), *The Very Salt of Life: Welsh Women's Political Writings from Chartism to Suffrage* (Dinas Powys, 2007). The women's column in the *Swansea and District Worker's Journal* was written by Ruth Chalk (née Thomas), the Swansea branch secretary. She had worked to form the branch with Elizabeth Williams, wife of David Williams, the town's first ILP councillor, and was a key influence in the establishment of the Ystalyfera branch of the Women's Labour League in December 1913. *Llais Llafur*, 3 January 1914. Mrs Chalk stood, unsuccessfully, several times before the First World War as a Labour candidate for the Swansea Board of Guardians.

[175] Elsie Muriel King (1891-1980) was a school teacher and served as headmistress of Gurnos Infants School from 1924-1953. See a profile piece to mark her retirement in *South Wales Voice*, 18 December 1953. She was active on the constituency executive for

Brecon and Radnor. Her father, Thomas King, a wagon repairer, was chair of the Ystalyfera branch of the ILP in 1914. *Llais Llafur*, 7 March 1914.

[176] Evans and Jones, 'Women', 219.

[177] Grace Scholefield (1873-1951) was born in Halifax, West Yorkshire, and settled in South Wales with her husband Nathan William Scholefield (1862-1915) in the late-1890s, initially in Merthyr Tydfil and subsequently in Cardiff. Both had been active in ILP circles in Keighley, Mrs Scholefield even stood for election to the local council, and were involved in the establishment of the first ILP branch in Merthyr. Nathan Scholefield served as secretary of the South Wales ILP Federation in the early 1900s. See his obituary in the *Merthyr Pioneer*, 4 December 1915. For Keighley politics see David James, *Class Politics in a Northern Industrial Town: Keighley, 1880-1914* (Keele, 1995). Mary Keating Hill (1881-1962) was born in Mountain Ash, the sister of novelist and Labour councillor Joseph Keating (1871-1934) and Irish MP Matthew Keating (1869-1937), and married into a middle-class family in Cardiff. Initially involved in the Women's Social and Political Union, she subsequently served as the local secretary of the Women's Freedom League and was very active in the ILP in Cardiff and across the wider region. For her role in the suffrage movement see Ryland Wallace, *The Women's Suffrage Movement in Wales, 1866-1928* (Cardiff, 2009).

[178] *WM*, 20 January 1914.

[179] *BH*, 25 March 1910; *BDN*, 7 September 1917. She was re-elected unopposed in 1913, also. *BDN*, 14 March 1913. Elizabeth Henson (1870-1962) was born in Jarrow and was the wife of James Henson, the Bristol Channel secretary of the National Sailors' and Firemen's Union.

[180] Evans and Jones, 'Women', 218.

[181] K. O. Morgan, 'The Merthyr of Keir Hardie', in Glanmor Williams (ed.), *Merthyr Politics*, 58.

[182] K. O. Fox, 'Labour and Merthyr's Khaki Election of 1900', *WHR* 2, no. 4 (1965); K. O. Morgan, *Keir Hardie*.

[183] K. O. Fox, 'The Merthyr Election of 1906', *National Library of Wales Journal* 14, no. 2 (1965). The previous year, Merthyr's

Labour Representation Committee had resolved not to run two candidates in the 1906 election to concentrate on securing Hardie's re-election, even going as far as to oppose the determination of the local SWMF lodges to run a candidate of their own. LHASC, Labour Party Archive, LP/LRC/22/49-50, Letters from Dai Davies, 18-19 April 1905; LP/LRC/23/66, Letter from Dai Davies, 23 May 1905.

[184] LSE, Francis Johnson Correspondence, ILP/4/1903/67.

[185] *EEx*, 20 August 1901; *GG*, 1 May 1908. Hartshorn ironically also succeeded James Winstone as President of the South Wales Miners' Federation in 1922 following the latter's death in 1921. Hartshorn's career is discussed by Peter Stead in his 'Vernon Hartshorn: Miners' Agent and Cabinet Minister', *Glamorgan Historian* 6 (1969), 83-94.

[186] *County Observer and Monmouthshire Central Advertiser*, 2 April 1904; *EEx*, 26 February 1907; *Colliery Guardian*, 6 May 1921.

[187] LSE, Francis Johnson Correspondence, ILP/4/1909/544: Telegram from James Winstone to Keir Hardie, 26 November 1909.

[188] *The Labourite*, Number 1, November 1905; LHASC, LP/LRC/29/337-441, Letters from F. H. Heath, December 1905-January 1906; LP/LRC/28/295-298, Letters from F. H. Heath, 6-16 December 1905.

[189] *CT*, 8 April 1905.

[190] *County Observer and Monmouthshire Central Advertiser*, 22 April 1905.

[191] *EEx*, 23 June 1906. Certainly some felt that Labour candidates should not stand for non-mining seats since that split the Liberal vote. LHASC, Labour Party Archive, LP/LRC/23/244-5, Letters from John Twomey, Newport, 3-8 May 1905; LP/LRC/30/171-2, Letters from F. H. Brown, 12-27 January 1906; LP/LRC/30/170/1-2, Letter from F. H. Heath, 8 January 1906.

[192] *The Labourite*, Number 2, December 1905.

[193] *The Labourite*, Xmas Special, December 1905; Peter Stead, 'Working-Class Leadership in South Wales, 1900-1920', *WHR* 6, no. 3 (1973), 329-353.

[194] The strong relationship between the Liberal Party and business interests in this period is considered in G. R. Searle, 'The Edwardian

Liberal Party and Business', *English Historical Review* 98 (1983), 28-60.

[195] Micholls was Jewish and had previously stood for election to London County Council. Geoffrey Alderman, *London Jewry and London Politics, 1889-1986* (London, 1989), 44-45.

[196] *The Labourite*, Number 4 (January 1906).

[197] *AL*, 29 September 1906.

[198] It should not be surprising that Winstone – and Vernon Hartshorn – were convinced that affiliation of the South Wales Miners' Federation to the Labour Representation Committee was highly likely, even as early as the Spring of 1903. LHASC, Labour Party Archives, LP/LRC/7/414, Letter from James Winstone, 21 March 1903; LP/LRC/LB/1/345, Letter from James Winstone, 24 March 1903; LP/LRC/LB/2/31, Letter from James Winstone, 19 May 1903; LP/LRC/14/232, Letter from Vernon Hartshorn, 24 April 1904; LP/LRC/14/163-4, Letters from Vernon Hartshorn, 10 and 25 April 1904; LP/LRC/24/275, Letter from James Winstone, 2 July 1905; LP/LRC/24/509-10, Letters from James Winstone, 8-10 July 1905.

[199] Details from other branches in this period can be gleaned from extant records. See, Dowlais ILP, Minute Book, 1901-1904, RBA, SWCC: MNA/PP/69/1; Bedlinog ILP, Account Book and Press Cuttings, 1901-1921, RBA, SWCC: MNA/POL/5/1; Briton Ferry ILP, Letter Book, 1908-1909, RBA. SWCC: MNC/PP/20; Aberdare Socialist Party, Minute Book 1901-1906, ALS; Aberdare ILP Papers, GA, DXHJ; Merthyr Tydfil ILP, Cash Book, 1910-1954, LSE, ILP/Section 9/61;

[200] *BDN*, 17 November 1905; *BH*, 4 May, 17 August, 7 September 1906.

[201] *BDN*, 19 January, 26 January, 2 February, 16 March, 30 March 1906.

[202] *BH*, 12 October 1906.

[203] *BDN*, 23 March 1906.

[204] *BDN*, 28 September 1906, 8 March 1907, 4 October 1907, 20 March 1908, 25 September 1908. This may usefully be compared to the Rhondda district committee (which included Pontypridd and

Ynysybwl) which recorded nearly three hundred meetings organised in 1909. *RL* (Maesteg edition), 22 January 1910.

205 *BDN*, 22 April 1910.

206 A copy of the Briton Ferry hymn book is at the SWML. A photograph of the Neath ILP choir dated to around 1910, originally owned by W. S. Watkins, is at RBA, MNA/PP/124/2/2. For activity in Cardiff see: *Clarion*, 27 January 1904, *CT*, 10 July 1909, 'Labour and May Day Festival, Theatre Royal, Cardiff, 6 May 1908'. CLS, Cochfarf Papers, Box 5. Thanks to Martin Wright for this information. For Swansea: *The Cambrian*, 12 February, 2 April, 7 May 1909, 8 October 1909, 18 March 1910.

207 Aberdare Socialist Society, Minutes, 21 February 1901; GA, DXHJ/2.

208 *AL*, 16 November 1907.

209 *AL*, 15 February, 18 April 1908; *CT*, 18 April 1908.

210 *AL*, 14 November, 21 November, 28 November 1908, 10 April, 10 July 1909.

211 *AL*, 27 March 1909. The *MEx*, 5 June 1909 provides a full English translation of the poem. The Mountain Ash eisteddfod was not the only one held that summer. A few days later, there was an eisteddfod at Pontycymmer. *GG*, 11 June 1909.

212 *EEx*, 6 June 1908. The song was set to the tune of Hen Wlad Fy Nhadau. It became Hardie's signature theme alongside his election campaign hymn 'Vote Vote Vote for Keir Hardie' and was included in the song book of Sylvia Pankhurst's East London Federation of Suffragettes. See, *MEx*, 3 April 1909. It was one of the 'hymns' sung at A. J. Cook's funeral in 1931. *Western Daily Press* (Bristol), 6 November 1931.

213 For more on this sporting phenomenon see: Daryl Leeworthy, 'Partisan Players: Sport, Working-Class Culture and the Labour Movement in South Wales, 1920-1939', *Labor History* 55, no. 5 (2014), 580-593. The wider relationship between sporting activity and working-class community is discussed in David Smith and Gareth Williams, *Fields of Praise: The Official History of the Welsh Rugby Union, 1881-1981* (Cardiff, 1980); Dai Smith, 'Focal Heroes: A Welsh Fighting Class', in Richard Holt (ed.), *Sport and the Working*

Class in Britain (Manchester, 1990), 198-217; Martin Johnes, *Soccer and Society: South Wales, 1900-1939* (Cardiff, 2002); Gareth Williams and Peter Stead (eds.), *Wales and its Boxers: The Fighting Tradition* (Cardiff, 2008).

[214] Dennis Pye, *Fellowship is Life: The National Clarion Cycling Club, 1895-1995* (Bolton, 1995).

[215] *SWLP* (Cardiff), May 1901. This edition refers to the club entering its third season. For further details see: *SWLP*, June 1901, March 1902, May 1902; *Clarion*, 26 August 1904.

[216] Greater Manchester County Record Office, Records of the Clarion Cycling Club, O16/39: 'Scrapbook containing List of Sections for 1912, 1913, and 1914'; *Clarion*, 14 October, 21 October, 28 October 1904.

[217] *The Scout*, March 1895. It is pertinent to the argument in the present chapter that Blatchford saw no distinction between the ILP or SDF and instead encouraged scouts to enlist all converts to either organisation.

[218] *Clarion*, 18 December 1908, 1 January 29 January 1909; *LL*, 10 July, 16 October 1908; *Llais Llafur*, 11 July 1908; *AL*, 19 September 1908.

[219] *RL*, 14 March 1908.

[220] *DH*, 11 September 1913.

[221] *Llanelli Mercury*, 4 March 1909.

[222] *CT*, 5 January 1907; *TG*, 9 May 1907. The Cardiff stall was eventually run by Ernest Lewis Gillett, a long standing member of the ILP and a member of a radical family of atheists, suffragists, and socialists. By the time of the Great War, the stall was also selling anarchist literature. *Solidarity*, October 1913, May 1914; *EEx*, 18 March 1910. The Pontypool stall is noted in the *Labourite*, Number 8, May 1906. The Abertillery stall in the *Labourite*, Number 9, June 1906.

[223] *AL*, 9 June 1906, 20 April 1907, 12 October 1907.

[224] An attempt is made in Robert Pope, *Building Jerusalem: Nonconformity, Labour and the Social Question in Wales, 1906-1939* (Cardiff, 1999) and in his 'Facing the Dawn: Socialists, Nonconformists, and Llais Llafur', *Llafur* 7, no. 3-4 (1999), 77-88. However, objections may be raised of the argument presented in this

reading not the least of which is its presentation of the old 'adage' that Labour owed more to Methodism than to Marx. Better insights, focusing on the 1904-5 religious revival, can be gleaned from John Harvey, 'Spiritual Emblems: Visions of the 1904-05 Religious Revival', *Llafur* 6, no. 2 (1993), 75-93.

[225] *Manchester Times*, 9 October 1891; *Leeds Times*, 21 November 1891; *Manchester Courier*, 12 December 1891. Biographical details are taken from Trevor's autobiography. John Trevor, *My Quest for God* (London, 1897). For the influence of Tillett's speech, see: 239-240.

[226] *Workman's Times*, 9 October 1891.

[227] *Labour Prophet*, May 1892, February 1893. For a broader sense of the context into which the Bradford Labour Church was created see: Jack Reynolds and Keith Laybourn, 'The Emergence of the Independent Labour Party in Bradford', *IRSH* 20, no. 3 (1975), 313-346.

[228] Eric Hobsbawm, 'Labour Traditions', in his *Labouring Men*, 376; Henry Pelling, *The Origins of the Labour Party, 1880-1900* (London, 1954), 139; Stanley Pierson, 'John Trevor and the Labour Church Movement in England, 1891-1900', *Church History* 29 (1960), 445-460. For a contrary view, which stresses the intellectual basis of the Labour Church see: Mark Bevir, 'The Labour Church Movement, 1891-1902', *Journal of British Studies* 38, no. 2 (1999). Neil Johnson, *The Labour Church: The Movement and Its Message* (London, 2017) is the most recent analysis of the initiative and lays emphasis on its theological message.

[229] *EEx*, 29 December 1903. The Cardiff Ethical Society had its origins in the Ruskin Institute, the headquarters of the city's ILP. It opened in St Mary's Street in 1903 and ran classes in trade unionism, the works of John Ruskin, economics, and public speaking. *EEx*, 11 October 1904. CLS, Ruskin Institute, *Annual Report, 31 March 1904*. Later it moved to Paradise Place and subsequently the Royal Arcade. Similar relations were evident in Merthyr Tydfil where the town's Ruskin Institute and the local ILP were closely associated. *EEx*, 31 October 1905. The Merthyr Ruskin Institute was in Post Office Lane. See: *MEx*, 16 January 1909. A third Ruskin Institute was established in Newport. *Merthyr Pioneer*, 11 March 1916.

[230] *AL*, 23 January 1904.

[231] *The Cambrian*, 17 November 1905. The secretary of the Neath

Ethical Society was J. H. Murrin, an active member of Neath TLC.
Later he moved to Blackwood where he ran a bookshop. He
established Blackwood Ethical Society, soon to be rechristened the
Blackwood New Era Society, in 1918. Although it struggled to
develop through lack of access to meeting spaces. *The Humanist:
Organ of the Ethical Movement*, 1 August, 1 November 1918.

[232] *AL*, 16 January 1904.

[233] *CT*, 24 September 1904.

[234] I. D. MacKillop, *The British Ethical Societies* (Cambridge, 1986).

[235] This is especially true of Yorkshire. As Cyril Pearce noted the
Socialist Sunday School played a considerable role in the making of
conscientious objection during the First World War. Cyril Pearce,
Comrades in Conscience (London, 2001).

[236] *EEx*, 30 January 1893; *Labour Prophet*, November 1894. A
second Labour Church, opened by Ben Tillett in Swansea in
September 1893, appears to have been of limited existence. *The
Cambrian*, 22 September 1893; *SWDP*, 18 September 1893.

[237] *Labour Prophet*, May, June, July 1893, May, August 1894, June
1895; John Trevor (ed.), *The Labour Church Hymn Book* (London,
1895). A copy of the 1906 edition, published in Manchester,
survives in the Brinley Griffiths (Crynant) collection, SWML. Hobson
sat on the executive of the Labour Church Union.

[238] Samuel G. Hobson, *Pilgrim to the Left: Memoirs of a Modern
Revolutionist* (London, 1938), 41.

[239] *SWDP*, 18 September 1893; *SWDN*, 12 August 1893; *EEx*, 4
December 1893; *CT*, 2 February 1895.

[240] *EEx*, 7 June 1893; *CT*, 10 June 1893.

[241] *WM*, 12 October 1893; *EEx*, 7 July 1894; *CT*, 23 February
1895; *Labour Prophet*, May 1894.

[242] *Labour Prophet*, December 1893; *CT*, 15 December 1894.

[243] *BDN*, 1 May, 7 August, 11 September 1896; *Labour Annual*,
1895, p. 43.

[244] *EEx*, 18 January 1898; *WM*, 11 October 1898. Ellery quickly
involved himself in the Cardiff socialist movement, becoming
secretary of the SDF. *CT*, 8 April 1899.

[245] *CT*, 15 October 1898.

[246] *BDN*, 17 November 1899; *WM*, 17 January 1900.

[247] *MEx*, 10 April 1909.

[248] *AL*, 12 May 1906; *London Welshman*, 12 May 1906.

[249] *Y Brython*, 17 October 1907; *AL*, 12 October 1907.

[250] *RL*, 5 September 1908.

[251] *RL*, 13 January 1912.

[252] The fullest study is Jacqueline David's unpublished doctoral thesis. *A Spiritual Pilgrimage: A Biographical Study of R.J. Campbell* (Durham University, 1991). For his own views see R. J. Campbell, *A Spiritual Pilgrimage* (London, 1916).

[253] *GG*, 26 July 1907.

[254] *The Times*, 25 July 1907.

[255] *CT, 27 July 1907.*

[256] *Weekly Mail*, 3 August 1907.

[257] *CT*, 3 August 1907.

[258] R. J. Campbell, *Christianity and the Social Order* (New York, 1907), viii.

[259] James Griffiths, *Pages from Memory* (London, 1969), 12.

[260] *The Christian World*, 17 January 1907; Keith Robbins, 'The Spiritual Pilgrimage of the Rev. R. J. Campbell', *Journal of Ecclesiastical History* 30, no. 2 (1979), 272.

[261] *AL*, 10 April 1909; *CT*, 10 April 1909.

[262] *RL*, 16 November 1907.

[263] *RL*, 9 May, 10 October 1908.

[264] *AL*, 18 July, 1 August, 17 October 1908, 23 January 1909.

[265] *The Cambrian*, 2 July 1909.

[266] *AL*, 24 April 1909.

[267] *CT*, 29 May 1897. He came to Abercwmboi from the Presbyterian College in Carmarthen but was a native Cardiganshire. *AL*, 19 May 1917.

[268] *SWDN*, 30 November 1904.

[269] *AL*, 7 November, 12 December 1908.

[270] *Weekly Mail*, 26 October 1907; *AL*, 12 October 1907.

[271] *Al*, 26 October, 16 November 1907, 25 January, 4 July, 7 November 1908.

[272] *MEx*, 14 May, 17 September 1910.

[273] *AL*, 8 February 1908.

[274] *GG*, 28 February, 27 March, 29 May, 17 July 1908; *RL*, 29 February 1908; *The Cambrian*, 21 August 1908.

[275] *AL*, 3 July, 17 July 1909.

[276] *AL*, 26 June 1909.

[277] Frank Bongiorno, *The People's Party: Victorian Labor and the Radical Tradition, 1875-1914* (Melbourne, 1996), 149-152; McKay, *Reasoning Otherwise*, ch. 4. An interesting intervention on the subject in the United States was made by John Spargo. 'Christian Socialism in America', *American Journal of Sociology* 15, no. 1 (1909), 16-20.

[278] J. Stitt Wilson, *How I Became a Socialist* (Berkeley, 1912).

[279] Ben Wilson had previously been Methodist minister at a church in Spring Valley, Illinois, a mining area.

[280] Northwestern University, *The '99 Syllabus* (Evanston, Il, 1898), 109. J. Stitt Wilson had also joined the faculty as an assistant professor of English. As above, 2.

[281] *Chicago Daily Tribune*, 9 February 1899; *Chicago Sunday Tribune*, 14 May 1899.

[282] *Social Crusader* (15 March 1899), 3-10; (June 1899), 3-7; (March 1900), 3-8; (April 1900), 3-6. The three men attended at the ILP annual conference held in Leeds, where J. Stitt Wilson addressed delegates. *The Times*, 5 April 1899.

[283] *The Observer*, 14 January 1900.

[284] *Chicago Sunday Tribune*, 15 April 1900.

[285] *Social Crusader* (January 1901), 27.

[286] *Weekly News and Visitors' Chronicle for Colwyn Bay*, 9 August 1907.

[287] *CT*, 4 July 1908.

[288] *BDN*, 17 July 1908; *BH*, 24 July 1908.

[289] *The Cambrian*, 21 August 1908.

[290] *AL*, 5 December 1908; *TG*, 17 December 1908.

[291] *RL*, 16 January 1909.

[292] *AL*, 12 December 1908.

[293] *Weekly Mail*, 2 January 1909.

[294] *GG*, 12 February, 19 February 1909; *MEx*, 23 January, 27 February 1909.

[295] *RL*, 9 January 1909.

[296] *RL*, 23 January 1909.

[297] *RL*, 16 January 1909.

[298] *MEx*, 16 January 1909.

[299] *Llanelly Mercury*, 22 April 1909.

[300] *RL*, 27 March, 15 May 1909.

[301] *CT*, 10 July 1909.

[302] *RL*, 18 September, 23 October, 30 October, 13 November 1909; *GG*, 24 September 1909; *MEx*, 18 September 1909; *BH*, 1 October, 8 October 1909; *AL*, 23 October 1909; *BDN*, 15 October 1909; *CarmJ*, 29 October 1909.

[303] SWML, AUD/273: Interview with William Morgan Davies, conducted by Hywel Francis, 1972.

[304] Claire Flay, *Dorothy Edwards* (Cardiff, 2011).

[305] Rodger, *Atlantic Crossings*; Hilton, *Age of Atonement*; Green and Tanner, 'Introduction'.

[306] *Merthyr Pioneer*, 15 May 1915.

[307] Including Noah Ablett, who stressed his departure from the chapel aged fifteen in his autobiographical writing. See Noah Ablett, 'What We Want and Why', in J. H. Thomas et al, *What We Want and Why* (London: Collins, 1922).

[308] *SWE*, 19 September 1898; *SWDN*, 12 October 1898; *RL*, 4 February 1911.

[309] Evans, *Miners*, 227.

[310] South Wales Miners' Federation, *An Outline of the Work Accomplished on behalf of the South Wales Colliery Workers* (Cardiff, 1927), 3.

[311] *SWDN*, 12 October 1898. The description of the South Wales Miners' Federation in this section draws in part on David Burton Smith, 'The Re-Building of the South Wales Miners' Federation, 1927-1939: A Trade Union in its Society' (Unpublished PhD Thesis: University of Wales, 1976), 1-50.

[312] *Justice*, 7 May 1898. It was a point echoed by Hardie a few weeks later. *LL*, 2 July 1898.

[313] *SWE*, 21 June 1898 – records the resolutions passed at mass meetings organised by Bristol Socialist Society; Keir Hardie appealed in the *LL* for funds to support the soup kitchens. *LL*, 25 June 1898. The SDF passed a resolution expressing its 'heartiest sympathies' at its annual conference in Edinburgh. *SWDN*, 8 August 1898.

[314] L. J. Williams, 'The Strike of 1898', *Morgannwg* 9 (1965), 77.

[315] 'Letter and Supplementary Report from United States Consul, Cardiff, to J. B. Moore, Assistant Secretary of State, Washington D.C., 2 September 1898'. Consulted on microfilm at SCOLAR.

[316] *Weekly Mail*, 2 September 1899.

[317] *Weekly Mail*, 4 August 1900.

[318] *Weekly Mail*, 6 October 1900.

[319] *CT*, 6 October 1900.

[320] *Weekly Mail*, 31 May 1902, 7 November 1903, 16 September 1905; *CT*, 7 April 1906, 14 April 1906; *AL*, 6 June 1908.

[321] Williams, *Capitalism, Community and Conflict*, 41.

[322] Morgan, *VWC*, 16.

[323] *PC*, 9 March 1901, 8 March, 12 April 1902. Smith was founding chairman of the Ynysybwl ILP in 1906.

[324] Morgan, *VWC*, 47. Rodgers was considered 'Labour member for Ynysybwl'. *AL*, 25 November 1905.

[325] *Rhondda Socialist*, 11 April 1912.

[326] *PC*, 15 February 1902.

[327] *PC*, 8 March 1902.

[328] *PC*, 15 March 1902.

[329] *PC*, 22 March 1902.

[330] *PC*, 29 March 1902, 12 April 1902.

[331] David Gilbert, *Class, Community and Collective Action: Social Change in Two British Coalfields, 1850-1926* (Oxford, 1992), 117.

[332] Cliff Prothero, *Recount* (Ormskirk, 1982), 1. This was also the view of Tom Watkins when interviewed by the Coalfield History Project in the 1970s. See: SWML, AUD/335, 'Interview with Tom Watkins, 23 October 1972'.

[333] Morgan, *VWC*, 45.

[334] Copies of which are extremely rare. No. 2 (August 1905) is at NLW; No. 5 (January 1906) is at ALS.

[335] Morgan, *VWC*, 45-6; SWCC, Lady Windsor Lodge, Minutes, 26 April, 10 May, 27 September 1905, 16 August 1906, 25 July 1908; *EEx*, 3 August 1906.

[336] Newspaper reports indicate that a letter was sent to Lord Windsor, the landowner, by community representatives in 1898, although it is not clear who they were. Given later initiatives it seems reasonable to suggest the work committee at the colliery, of which Morgan Walters was a member. *GFP*, 21 May 1898.

[337] SWCC, Lady Windsor Lodge, Minutes, 7 November, 5 December 1906, 2 January 1907. Morgan, *VWC*, 66.

[338] Mountain Ash UDC, Minutes of Council, April 1910-September 1910: 12 July 1910.

[339] Morgan, *VWC*, 66.

PART II
Remaking South Wales

CHAPTER THREE

On The Brink

In June 1907, Thomas Isaac Jones, a twenty-eight year old former Ruskin College student from Ferndale, was elected to the post of checkweigher for the No. 3 Pit at Maerdy ahead of more than seventy rivals.[1] A month earlier, he had been elected to the executive council of the South Wales Miners' Federation.[2] Jones had gone up to Ruskin College in 1902 and quickly established himself as one of the ablest of all Welsh students there.[3] He had a particular interest in economics and undertook research on the question of mining royalties – work that was published in the *Economic Review* in July 1905. Together with a further article published in January 1906, this research earned him a fellowship of the Royal Economic Society.[4] His 1905 article, 'The Riddle of Mining Royalties', began in a characteristically forceful tone:

> Social evils are apt to arise unobserved, and to continue undisturbed, till they become a permanent drag on society, or are only uprooted by strenuous effort. The effects of such evils may be discerned before their causes are clearly defined and long before any adequate remedies have been found. So complex, indeed, are the issues at times that the very attempt to uproot long-continued abuses may introduce conditions more serious than those it is proposed to abolish.[5]

It can be read as a prognosis of the mining industry in general in the early twentieth century but also of the very particular circumstances found in South Wales.[6] It was an accurate prediction of the brutal rupture that the region was about to face, and in which Jones was to take full part.

Thomas Isaac Jones returned to the Rhondda in 1905 and quickly established himself as a leading light in the ILP in Ferndale – by the end of the year he was branch chairman and in the various mock parliaments held in the Rhondda Fach frequently took on the guise of Keir Hardie.[7] By the Spring of 1906, he was chairman of the Ferndale Lodge.[8] His reputation was made through his advocacy of a scholarship fund to send students to Ruskin College. As he explained to a meeting in Blaenclydach in June 1906, 'the object ... [is] to give them a sound knowledge of social and economic questions, so that they shall return to the factory or mine and use their knowledge for the uplifting of their fellow men'. His own years at Ruskin College, he said, had made him a 'far wiser man'. He repeated the message a few weeks later in Penrhiwceiber.[9] In fact, Jones zig-zagged across the coalfield throughout 1906 addressing more than one hundred meetings; as Richard Lewis notes, 'it was a campaign of which he was so proud that he still made reference to it ... many years later'.[10] It was a deserved sense of pride, since the Rhondda No. 1 District agreed to support two scholarships worth sixty five pounds each in October 1906.[11] These went, in the first year, to Noah Rees of Blaenclydach, Noah Ablett of Porth, and to Tom and Jack Evans of Cwmparc.[12]

Jones's abilities as a teacher were also recognised and when Glamorgan County Council established an evening continuation class in economics in the Rhondda in 1906, he was appointed as the tutor.[13] When the classes were cancelled in 1908, one councillor complained of Jones's teaching that 'all the students who have attended those classes have become socialists and infidels'. The *Rhondda Leader* added that 'in certain quarters ... those classes are held responsible for the revival of the working class at the district council elections'.[14] In addition to economics,

Jones gave public lectures on key figures in labour movement history such as the co-operator Robert Owen. On Labour Day, 1907, for instance, he declared Robert Owen to be 'Wales's Greatest Welshman'. Using Owen's example, he warned that 'the labour movement inaugurated by Robert Owen had divided itself into three streams' but concluded that 'those three streams were destined to unite in one great river of progress'. He repeated the message to a meeting of Pentre ILP on Christmas Day.[15]

As checkweigher for Maerdy No. 3 Pit, Thomas Isaac Jones proved influential and laid much of the groundwork for the village's later reputation as a hotbed of socialist radicalism. As the Agent of Locket's Merthyr, Taliesin Richards, observed in July 1909, 'the men are entirely dominated by the socialistic doctrines given out by "Mardy Jones", checkweigher'.[16] This enabled Jones to take a belligerent stance on matters such as the implementation of the eight hours act and non-unionism. Richards reflected, 'it has been, to say the least, humiliating to have your employees coming to the office, practically dictating to your management what shall be permitted, altered or refused'.[17] There was considerable scope for antagonism in a village where, as the common saying at the time went, the beds did not have time to cool. Richards himself reflected on this in a letter to the Cardiff offices of Locket's Merthyr in 1910.[18] One haulier living in Oxford Street, he noted, resided in a house consisting of five rooms – two down, three up – in which fifteen people lived. Of the around eight hundred houses in Maerdy at the time, there was an average of three workmen living in each one, in addition to wives and children. The pressure within Maerdy, on bread and butter issues, was considerable and Thomas Isaac Jones, who had by now adopted the moniker 'Mardy', knew precisely how to manipulate and foster it. He was by no means alone, particularly in the Rhondda.

Across the mountain from Maerdy and Ferndale, in Llwynypia, John Hopla experienced a similarly rapid rise to prominence because of his ability to marshal growing discontent and to lead it somewhere meaningful.[19] Hopla was born in Pembroke in 1882 and migrated, with his family, to the Rhondda as a young man. In less than a decade, before his death, from an underlying heart condition exacerbated by gaol and hard labour, at the age of thirty two in 1914, Hopla moved through the ranks as checkweigher and lodge chairman at the Glamorgan Colliery, just to the north of Tonypandy. His leadership, as well as his wider work as chair of the local medical aid society and the Llwynypia Workmen's Institute committee, was commemorated in a plaque unveiled at the Institute in February 1916.[20] It summed up Hopla's role in the community and pointed to the growing influence of ILP activists at the local level. The turning point in Hopla's life was the 1908 strike in Llwynypia. As so often in the coalfield, the dispute was about wages and the decline in wage levels following the absorption of the Glamorgan Colliery into the Cambrian Combine that year. As one newspaper noted, 'some of the workmen submit that the prices paid for their labour give them a certain amount of indifference as to whether they cut coal or not'. Arrayed against the workmen were managers who complained that wages were too high; the miners regarded that as a figment of their imagination.[21]

Four thousand miners at the Glamorgan Colliery struck at the end of the day shift on 23 November 1908. The next day, a mass meeting, held under the presidency of John Hopla, took place at Llwynypia. Thomas Richards, the SWMF general secretary, and the local miners' agent, D. Watts Morgan, spoke calling on the men not to escalate the situation. In a clear echo of events two years later, the miners warned their leaders that if they were not paid a living wage, they would call on comrades from other pits in the Cambrian Combine to come out in solidarity with them.[22] A dispute of a few thousand could quickly become one of tens of thousands and a potential touchpaper for coalfield-wide industrial action. Or something else entirely: when the coal owners' Combine offered to provide food to schools to feed children affected by the strike, the lodge issued notice that its members would withdraw their children from school if it happened.[23] The established leadership of the miners, Richards, Watts Morgan, and William Abraham, seemed to have lost control of – or at least any kind of influence over – the lodge.[24] They listened instead to the new men, to ILP men such as Hopla and James Winstone.

Winstone's intervention was a signal of looming political change and one that called for a distinct shift away from the established tenets of the Liberal Party both in rhetoric and purpose. As one correspondent of the *Rhondda Leader* noted during the 1908 strike:

> Your [the paper's] grave concern that whoever would be the future Labour candidate should be of the type of the sitting member – Labour tinctured by Liberal Welsh Nationalism – leads me to ask whether this is a new party. What does it mean to the Llwynypia workmen now out on strike to know that they have a Welsh Nationalist in Parliament? We have too long submitted to such sentiment, and it ill becomes anyone, considering the present position of our people in the twentieth century to put forward such a plea ... The orthodox parties have made these things [the bondage of capitalism and landlordism] of small concern; hence the uprisings of the Labour and Socialist movement as a protest against the wrongs endured so long.[25]

Such clear-voiced dissent targeted both Liberalism, Lib-Labism, and nationalism, and had consequences on several fronts, not merely in terms of parliamentary representation but also within miners' lodges and amongst officials at the collieries. John Hopla, Thomas Isaac 'Mardy' Jones, James Winstone, and other ILPers were direct beneficiaries of this upsurge in radical behaviour – Hopla was elected checkweigher and then lodge chairman in quick succession – and crucially they also knew how to guide it.

In October 1909, Mardy Jones was elected as registration agent for the B Area of the South Wales Coalfield (consisting of the parliamentary constituencies of Merthyr, Rhondda, and East and South Glamorgan), defeating Thomas Andrews of Treharris, a Labour member of Merthyr Board of Guardians.[26] The post prompted Jones's resignation from his job with Locket's Merthyr and the election of a new checkweigher at the No. 3 Pit. The man elected was Noah Ablett. Taliesin Richards, the company agent, watched the ballot carefully reporting to head office that 'I regret to say that Noah Ablett ... is a greater demagogue than Jones ... [but] he is not so cunning as his predecessor'.[27] Ablett was able, nonetheless, to lead a strike against non-unionism in early October 1910, with as many as two thousand setting down tools, but failed, narrowly, to bring his men out in support of the Cambrian Combine dispute.[28] The ballot was lost by a mere five votes and Locket's Merthyr – and William Abraham, no doubt – breathed a sigh of relief, as Richards reported 'in spite of continued efforts by the socialistic section ... the men have remained firm'.[29] The defeat kept Ablett on the margins of what happened next.

By the time of Ablett's election as checkweigher at Maerdy No. 3 Pit in the summer of 1910, the Rhondda was alive with industrial confrontation. In the first week of October, over seventeen thousand miners struck on the issue of non-unionism and notices on nearly eight thousand others were fast expiring. A demonstration of strength amongst miners at Ocean Coal

Company pits took place on the morning of Wednesday 5 October, with thousands marching through the streets of Cwmparc, Treorchy, and Pentre, behind the symbolic white shirt. As the march went past the houses of non-unionists it came to a halt and a deputation of lodge officials sought to induce those inside into taking membership. The *Western Mail* complained of 'aggressive measures', although all sides noted a lack of violence.[30] Further processions, all of them featuring the white shirt, were held over the weekend drawing large crowds and proving somewhat successful in bringing non-unionists into the fold.[31] When the dispute spread to the Cynon Valley later in the month, similar tactics were employed. A large procession marched from Penrhiwceiber to Abercynon, for instance, headed by the town crier 'lustily ringing his bell' and three colliers carried a white shirt, an infant's vest, and a 'feminine nether garment' (as the *Merthyr Express* had it).[32]

Non-unionism was a perennial problem affecting mining communities across the coalfield with considerable frequency. Localised strikes were common – Chris Williams has noted nearly seventy stoppages on this issue between 1898 and 1904 alone.[33] In Ynysybwl, the Lady Windsor Lodge insisted from the outset that 'non-unionists are not to be tolerated' and went on to press the issue through almost annual strike action.[34] In Maesteg, which saw some of the most serious white shirting activity of all, non-unionists were greeted with a variety of forms of ritual humiliation. One miner was 'belaboured with brooms, splashed with pigs'-wash, painted with black lead, and deprived of his shirt by the Amazons of Maesteg'.[35] At Caerau, as many as five hundred people marched through the streets shouting – 'Pay the Federation' – at a man being led by the arm at the head of the line. Nine miners were brought before magistrates in Maesteg after that demonstration on charges of intimidation.[36] Similar scenes were witnessed at Bryncethin, near Bridgend, two years later.[37] What made the Rhondda different in 1910 was the perfect storm of a widespread non-unionism dispute and the wage dispute that engulfed the Cambrian Combine. One some level or other, almost every miner and mining family in the Rhondda was impacted – and by consequence so was the entire local economy.

A Place Called Tonypandy

It was at the Ely Pit in Penygraig, rather than the Glamorgan Colliery in Llwynypia, as many had expected since 1908, that the issue of poor wages, work in unproductive seams, and the intransigence of the new coal combine came to a head.[38] Originally operated by the Naval Colliery Company, the Ely Pit was a fairly recent acquisition for D. A. Thomas, made as a consequence of the Cambrian Combine's formation. In 1909, the mine managers sought to develop a new seam: it came to be known as the Bute Seam, a notably rocky and difficult-to-work part of the coalfield. The men were offered 1s 9d a ton, whereas the workmen sought a wage of 2s 6d a ton to reflect the difficulty of working. The differential, and the insistence on both sides of the veracity of their demands, proved the catalyst for the Cambrian Combine dispute. When the dispute failed to be resolved at the Joint Consolidation Board in July 1910, industrial action became an inevitability. The owners of the Ely Pit posted lockout notices on 1 August, to take effect one month later. The seam in question affected seventy men, the lockout notices left another thousand men potentially idle.[39] In throwing down the gauntlet, the Cambrian Combine managers unwittingly sparked a conflict they could not, in the end, control. In less than a week after the lockout took effect, the number of men out had trebled, with both the Naval and Pandy pits striking in sympathy on 5 September. John Hopla and Will John, senior miners' officials at the Llwynypia Colliery, indicated that they believed in solidarity action and that their workmen would likely vote to join the dispute when balloted.[40]

On the ground, miners were remarkably organised, quickly countering any threats to shut shops, and so starve them quickly back to work. They sent diagrams of the seams in question to local religious leaders and arranged for their display in prominent public places to prove their case. The same diagram was published in the press in mid-September, with a contrary diagram provided by Leonard Llewelyn, the general manager of the Combine, provided shortly afterwards. As Tom Smith, one of the miners' leaders, explained at a public meeting in Trealaw, the men 'organised a band of ... workers to go round from house to house to educate the people ... so that they all might know that what [we] were fighting for was bread and cheese and a decent living'. There was a cost of living crisis. In an interview with the *Rhondda Leader*, one elderly miner explained that although 'the miner to-day earns more money than he did ... I don't think he is much better off ... because the cost of living has gone up. Rents have gone up, food prices have gone up'. He concluded, 'I would not care to say that he has much more money left than he had in the eighties'.[41] Without a living wage, miners and their families faced penury even if in full employment.

This situation meant that some were prepared to work in drift mines typically boycotted by the lodges, and others to renounce their Federation membership on the Combine's promise of better wages.[42] It was all a measure of the evident economic pressure. But such action was bitterly opposed by the majority and prompted visible protests: at Blaenclydach and Clydach Vale a procession of four thousand cheered on by women marched down the hill towards Tonypandy. 'At each of the houses of the workmen in respect of whom the demonstration was held', reported the local press, 'a halt was made and slight booing indulged in'. When these tactics failed, the local lodges canvassed landladies in the area asking them to get non-unionist lodgers to either sign up or to seek lodgings elsewhere.[43] The Naval Lodge also issued a manifesto declaring to 'our fellow workmen of South Wales and Monmouthshire' the facts of the dispute and calling on their comrades to stand in solidarity with the 'despotic policy' of the Cambrian Combine.[44] Amidst public demonstrations and debate, and to regain control of the situation, the SWMF leadership held an emergency conference at the Cory Hall in Cardiff to discuss its own response. At the end of seven hours of debate, it was resolved to ballot the membership on whether to levy a sum to support the miners of the Cambrian Combine in their own dispute or to hold a general strike of the nearly one hundred and fifty thousand Federation members.

The results were published a week later and showed a majority in favour of the levy, which had, in any case, been the Federation executive's own recommendation. On closer inspection of the district results, however, there were several areas in favour of strike action. In the Aberdare district, for example, over four thousand voted for a strike compared with two thousand seven hundred for the levy. There was a majority in favour of industrial action in the Maesteg district and in the small Pembrokeshire coalfield. There were slight majorities in favour of the levy, by contrast, in Merthyr and in Ogmore and Gilfach. Perhaps most surprisingly – and undoubtedly frustrating to the miners of the Cambrian Combine lodges – the Rhondda No. 1 District voted sixteen thousand to eight thousand two hundred in favour of the levy.[45] The figures for Maesteg and Aberdare no doubt reflect the fact that thousands were already out because of the Powell Duffryn dispute in the Cynon Valley and the looming strike notices, due to expire on 1 November, for several thousand miners in Maesteg and

Coegnant. 'All efforts at securing peace', the *Rhondda Leader* reported solemnly a few days after that deadline had 'proved abortive'.[46]

The 1 November 1910 was relatively quiet, although additional police were moved into the strike affected areas.[47] The next day was not. Rioting broke out in the Cynon Valley and the windows of various minor colliery officials resident in Aberaman and Abercwmboi were smashed. One official was stripped of his coat and waistcoat in another form of white shirting. Matters came to a head at nine o'clock in the morning when a workmen's train carrying around one hundred men reached the Tonllwyd Crossing. Rocks were hurled at the carriages and windows were smashed. The working miners who tried to escape the train were trailed by a crowd hooting and hollering abuse.[48] Within a few days, only five hundred of the ten thousand miners employed in the valley were working, all of them at the Blaenant Colliery in Abernant, east of Aberdare town centre. They had resolved not to come out unless the whole of the coalfield agreed to strike and so continued to work. The men were guarded by foot and mounted police as they went down at five o'clock in the morning and came up in the evening.[49] Like their comrades in the Rhondda, the Aberdare miners published a manifesto stating their purpose. It declared:

> We should fight now for a living wage ... The workers in the coal mines are being screwed down more and more, the employers are combining and piling up huge funds to enable them to make the oppression greater. Humanity does not count – profit is the god. If we continue dumb and submissive things will become worse. Arise, then, in your might, and assert your manhood. ... Rise before you are completely crushed. Fight for the sake of your manhood, fight for the sake of humanity.[50]

The Aberdare miners called themselves in that manifesto 'slaves of the lamp', a deliberate reference to a Rudyard Kipling story published in 1897 which featured a group of young school boys who decide to take their revenge on an oppressive and humiliating schoolmaster.[51] In the face of the consolidated power of the coal combines and the rising cost of living, miners experienced a sharp decline in the value of wages with one pound falling in value from twenty shillings in 1905 to fourteen shillings and seven pence in 1914.[52] It was against this economic situation that they took aim. The *Cambrian* newspaper captured the mood in the coalfield at the end of the first tumultuous week of November 1910:

> With the prospect of a general strike ... opening up... [there is] a bitterness of temper which has been foreign to industrial disputes as a rule. There is a serious reason to apprehend bloodshed if matters continue to worsen as they have been steadily doing for the past few months.[53]

By the time of the following week's issue, that Rubicon had been crossed.

'Exactly what will happen in the coalfield of South Wales in the near future', observed the newspaper *Justice*, the organ of the Social Democratic Party (as the SDF was now known), 'would puzzle a prophet'.[54] A few days later, on the eve of the riots, the noted syndicalist Tom Mann arrived in the Rhondda to see for himself what was going on. His reports, published in *Justice*, offer a clear sense of the efforts on the ground the Monday before rioting broke out in Tonypandy. Those efforts were focused on bringing out all the men from the mines including the one thousand enginemen, craftsmen, ostlers, and stokers, all of whom were still at work. The demonstrators rose from bed and were on the march at ten to five in the morning to ensure they were picketing their respective pits at five o'clock sharp. There were ten squads of fifty men who took to the main routes and to the mountain roads to talk with those coming off the night shift or onto the day shift. As the rain fell, choruses rang out in English and Welsh, with women's voices as common as men's. For it was the women, Mann notes, who made the most impassioned pleas to the officials, enginemen, ostlers, and craftsmen, pleas that were often 'in pretty emphatic Welsh, which I could not understand'.[55]

At nine o'clock in the evening, some four thousand gathered outside the Glamorgan Colliery, just north of Tonypandy, to picket. A small group of younger miners broke off and attempted to rush the colliery gates. As the crowd swelled, and with rain falling steadily, relations between the miners and the police soured. One eyewitness recalled:

> When we got down to the colliery we stood in row with the policemen who were in two rows across the colliery entrance. The miners were up on the bank where they had gathered piles of stones – it was a prepared thing. There was lots of shouting from up on the bank but you couldn't understand what was being said because there was so much noise. The miners shouted to me, 'get from here with that baby missus'. As we left … the stones began to fly, we could hear them as we made our way home.[56]

The volleys and fighting lasted for hours before order was restored. Severe damage was done to the colliery pay office. There were injuries to both sides: the *South Wales Daily Post* reported, for instance, that five Swansea policemen had suffered injuries during the combat, as had a Bristol policeman drafted into the area.[57] At one in the morning, uncertain that the police would be able to maintain order in Mid Rhondda despite reinforcements, the Chief Constable, Lionel Lindsay, telegrammed for troops to be sent in.

As dawn broke, shattered glass, wood, blood, and rocks, lay strewn across the colliery site and in the nearby streets. This was the detritus left at the end of the first skirmish of the battle. Mounted police patrolled Mid Rhondda and nervous residents went about their day-to-day business. The headmaster at Llwynypia Boys' School noted that morning that 'attendance has been low – owing to disturbances last night'.[58] At noon, a mass meeting was held at the Mid Rhondda Athletic Ground in Tonypandy where a telegram was read out from Winston Churchill, the Home Secretary. 'Rioting must cease', he insisted, 'confiding in the good sense of the Cambrian Combine workmen we are holding back the soldiers for the present and sending only police'.[59] By now the Rhondda was already occupied: as many as eleven hundred police were on the scene and a further contingent of two hundred Metropolitan Police had been sent up from London.[60] The meeting at the Athletic Ground dispersed and several thousand proceeded to the gates of the Glamorgan Colliery once again. Events took a similar course as the previous evening. One miner recalled:

> We congregated again next night but were prepared for them now … we had barrelled stones ready there, we took them off the colliery there … well we pre-arranged this and sent the boys up now to irritate the police.[61]

Shortly after five o'clock in the evening the boys began their attack throwing stones at the windows of the colliery powerhouse preventing proper (and safe) operation of the machinery inside. Lindsay ordered his men to clear away those responsible, but miners stationed outside the colliery gates armed with iron bars, wooden poles, and pickaxes, fought back.

The entrance was eventually cleared but not without some exertion on the part of the police and several injuries. In all, the battle lasted two hours and resulted in the death of a miner – Samuel Rays, who was killed by blows to the head by a blunt instrument, almost certainly a police baton. One Swansea policeman, who was on the front line, reflected later that 'I have never seen anything like it in my life. There was blood everywhere, and injured men were lying about all over the place. Even the women had their aprons full of stones'.[62] Speaking at the inquest into the death of Rays in December 1910, Lionel Lindsay admitted that 'it was touch and go. The crowd retaliated blow for blow and it was a question whether the police would succeed or not'.[63]

At eight o'clock, the action shifted from the colliery to the shopping centre as the strikers, formed in procession, marched through Tonypandy towards Penygraig, smashing windows of shops and businesses and looting as they went.[64] The headmaster of Llwynypia Boys' School noted the following morning that 'about one hundred and twenty five tradesmen's premises were considerably damaged and many shops were completely looted'. One business owner complained of damage and loss of more than one thousand pounds.[65] Only with the arrival of the Metropolitan Police reinforcements at ten o'clock did the rioting cease. Not everyone caught up in the police baton charges and fighting was a miner. As the Boys' School log records, 'Mr Griffiths, one of our assistant masters, was truncheoned last night by the police in one of their charges along the thoroughfares. Many innocent pedestrians suffered severely'.[66] Indeed, despite the lurid headlines that followed in the press and which proclaimed the 'reign of terror' and a 'red revolution', the only individual that died was, as the correspondent for *Justice* put it 'a miner, whose head was smashed by the truncheon of a policeman'. This, he reflected, referring to the newspaper headlines elsewhere 'is the class that values the roof of a power-station or the shop window of a tradesman above the life of a Welsh miner'.[67]

Tonypandy duly gained its deserved notoriety but events in Aberaman were equally symptomatic of the confrontation between capital and labour. On 8 November, as the confrontation in Tonypandy and Llwynypia turned bloody, a crowd of men and women gathered outside Aberaman Miners' Institute and marched towards the coal washery located on the road between Cwmbach and Aberaman. The washery was guarded by thirty policemen, but when the first elements of the crowd reached their positions so unprepared were the police that some were still eating their dinner. There were soon as many as two thousand people at the washery. Sticks and stones were hurled and fires lit. Attempting to disperse the crowd, the outnumbered police turned the colliery water hoses onto their opponents but succeeded only in making the miners and assembled women very wet and angry. Next came a baton charge that sent the crowd into flight in all directions. In the morning, one hundred and fifty Metropolitan Police and one hundred and fifty cavalry arrived to assert civic authority. As night fell on the 9 November, now buoyed on by news of what had happened in Tonypandy the night before, another crowd gathered outside the miners' institute. Shop windows in the main street were smashed, contents looted, and there were numerous fights with mounted police.[68]

Messages of support for the miners flooded into the Rhondda and the Cynon Valley from expected quarters, just as much as condemnations appeared in the press. The students of Ruskin College, meeting on 9 November, passed a resolution setting out their appreciation of the efforts of the miners to obtain fair wages and working conditions. The London Trades Council, similarly, expressed 'its warmest sympathy with the miners' and issued a condemnation of the import of troops into the area.[69] Within a week the riots in Tonypandy had been turned into a film and was shown at the Drill Hall Picture Palace in Bridgend and at the Romilly Hall in Barry.[70] But why did the protest demonstration outside the Glamorgan Colliery turn its force onto the shopkeepers of Tonypandy? It seems clear from Dai Smith's analysis that the crowd had a deliberate purpose and targeted shops and business premises with local knowledge and a calculated insistence. This was to be revenge meted out to grocers who had refused lines of credit, or had called them in; to chemists who exploited the inability of the general population to enjoy the services of a doctor; and to landlords who had conspired to manipulate the rental market and squeeze ever more profit out of Rhondda's poor-quality housing stock.[71] At a time of acute distress, the economic separation of the business class of the Rhondda and Cynon Valley from the colliery workforce was both obvious and harmful, as was their self-appointed role as leaders in their fragmented community. A letter from the Aberdare Valley Workmen's Central Relief Fund put the matter succinctly:

> When it is remembered that there are no other industries of any importance in the Valley, the position of the wage-earners and dependents will soon be acutely felt, whilst those who were previously on the brink of destitution are now reduced to dire necessity. Further, the wages of those previously earning were so low that no provision could be made to withstand a period of acute depression.[72]

Soup kitchens and school canteens provided the necessary lifeline. By the end of November, the canteen committee for Aberdare, which provided school meals, had fed over two and a half thousand children a total of thirty five thousand meals.

There were soup kitchens run by the Workmen's Relief Fund in Llwydcoed, Trecynon and Cwmdare.[73] Its funds were supported by William Haggar, the cinema owner, the students of Ruskin College, the Social Democratic Club in Mountain Ash, the miners' institute in Aberaman, local publicans, and Mr Bracchi, the Italian café proprietor in Aberdare.[74] An equivalent kitchen operated at the school hall in Llwynypia.[75] In the week that followed the riots, it was the business of organising this relief that took precedence. It was an uneasy pause and did not last.

On 21 November, further confrontations took place at Tonypandy railway station as rumours circulated of blacklegs being imported by train that evening. The strikers demanded the right to scrutinise passengers but were refused. Stones were hurled at the train instead and windows smashed. By late evening, tensions had reached fever pitch once more and the police were subjected to a hail of missiles. Reinforcements were hastily dispatched to quell the violence. Baton charge after baton charge pushed the crowds, by now comprising both men and women, into the steep side streets of Penygraig and further into the dark. As the police entered terraced streets they were pelted with buckets of hot water from bedroom windows, household utensils such as cutlery, and even the contents of chamber pots. Amidst newspaper reports of intimidation of railway workers, there were also accusations of further police brutality. One of the most heavily beaten was Noah Morgan, the chairman of the Naval Lodge, who had endeavoured to calm tensions. On retreating from the Glamorgan Colliery, Morgan had encountered a woman crying on the side of the road. She had been knocked out by a police baton. He offered to walk her home. On that journey they encountered a group of Metropolitan Police who proceeded to beat him with their truncheons and shouted abuse at him. 'I have never been subjected to such cruel treatment in all my life', he told one journalist, 'I don't feel like doing anything more in the interests of peace'.[76]

As 1910 gave way to 1911, the press reflected on a tumultuous year. Even Christmas in the Rhondda seemed grey and dour – a feeling added to by the heavy rain. Three months of industrial dispute had taken their toll and were it not for the special arrangements made by the local education committee and co-operative societies to host parties in schools, many might have wondered whether Santa Claus had gone on strike too. 'Christmas Day', remarked the *Rhondda Leader*, 'could easily have been mistaken for an ordinary Sunday'.[77] In the Cynon Valley, shops had special 'strike sales' to try and get rid of excess stock and the soup kitchens maintained their service over the Christmas period. There too, it was much less of a holiday than usual.[78] The grim picture of soup kitchens and a muted Christmas was added to by the failure of the executive council of the South Wales Miners' Federation to act in solidarity. Early in the new year, Tom Mann, writing in the pages of *Justice*, reflected on this ongoing struggle of twelve thousand miners in the Rhondda and Cynon valleys, and turned his fire on those still working and the Federation leadership. 'When their own immediate neighbours and fellow workers are being humiliated by the owners', he wrote, 'they do stand by and do nothing to help their mates, they actually supply the dominating, bullying owners with the only possible means of beating their own workmates and fellow-unionists by supplying coals for the same customers'.[79]

In the second week of January, the workmen of the Cambrian Combine held further mass meetings in Tonypandy at which resolutions were passed committing the men to renewed picketing and the firm insistence that they would only deal with working abnormal places once a minimum wage had been secured. That week, pickets headed to the Britannic Colliery in

Gilfach Goch. The chief constable, Lionel Lindsay, by now extremely jittery in his approach to the dispute, wrote exaggeratingly in his diary of 'disquieting news from Gilfach Goch'.[80] He hastily arranged for fifty police and thirty soldiers to accompany him, in military fashion, to head off the pickets and for a cohort of fifty police to travel to Llwynypia in case any trouble arose there. His senior police colleagues and the military commanders on the ground persuaded him to curtail this course of action, believing, justifiably, that it would be antagonistic. In the event, the existing garrison of police and soldiers from the Royal Munster Fusiliers guarded the Britannic Colliery and picketing passed off without disturbance. There were some broken windows and rough handling of colliery officials in Tonypandy and Llwynypia but otherwise the district remained calm. The departure of the Metropolitan Police a few days later and their replacement by members of the Monmouthshire Constabulary added to the sense that the worst of the trouble was over.[81]

That is, until a tactical error on the part of the authorities at the end of February. From the moment that the Llwynypia lodge joined the Cambrian Combine dispute on 1 November 1910, the strike had been organised by a small group of men who formed the Joint Strike Committee. These were Will John, Mark Harcombe, Tom Smith, Noah Rees, and John Hopla. As the dispute dragged on into 1911, and with little prospect of conciliated resolution, the authorities tried to weaken the capacity of the Joint Strike Committee through targeted arrests, having otherwise failed to weaken their resolve. Hopla was one of the early victims. In February 1911, he was summoned to appear before Pontypridd Police Court on a charge of intimidation of colliery officials. The attempt backfired, although Hopla left the court £20 poorer. Hundreds of strikers, headed by the Llwynypia Fife and Drum band and the town crier, had marched to the court to protest and to stand in solidarity with him – they also packed the public gallery. 'Every batch of police met', the *Rhondda Leader*'s correspondent noted, 'was hooted and booed vigorously'.[82] A few months later, following a disastrous train crash near Pontypridd, which claimed the lives of several members of the Federation executive, Hopla and his comrades from the Joint Strike Committee, notably Tom Smith and Noah Rees, were elected in their place (Hopla at the head of the ballot) radicalising it almost immediately. Noah Ablett joined them.[83]

It was probable that some of these men would have found their way to the front rank of the Federation at some point, but the Cambrian Combine dispute, the changing nature of collective politics in the Rhondda, and the coincidence of the railway crash, accelerated their rise. The next step was to find a way to harness the new context, to encourage and develop the politics to which they had been dedicated for many years, and to make the most of their new platform. The first indication of this new mood was a manifesto published in 1911 and signed by Noah Rees, Will John, Tom Smith, Mark Harcombe, and John Hopla. It made for powerful reading:

A ballot vote decided that Mid Rhondda was to be the cockpit of the fight, and that having accepted the position with misgivings, the Combine workmen entered the fight, and were still not beaten. We have been deliberately and foully misrepresented by a large section of the public press. We have been bludgeoned by the police. One of our comrades lost his life in contending with the police. Two comrades, in the stress of the struggle through illness and privation, committed suicide ... We ask you to say, friends, that the time has arrived when the surrender policy of our apologetic leaders must stop. They have not realised what it means to us in suffering.[84]

What began as a bread and butter dispute put the wind behind the sails of a brand of radical politics that had previously only existed on the margins: industrial syndicalism.[85] On 20 November, the editor of *Justice*, Harry Quelch, spoke to a large crowd at the Theatre Royal in Tonypandy on the theme of 'Death to the Coal Owners' Monopoly'. He turned his attention to capitalism and the alienation of workers from the rights of ownership, and remarked on the authorities' evident contempt for working people. 'The collier', he said, 'faced daily risk to keep body and soul together, but it did not matter to the owner ... The strike now going on was the outward sign of the class war'.[86] W. A. Wilkinson, a leading figure in the Marxian Club in Blaenclydach, went as far as to claim that demand for *Justice* was so high that 'we shall sell 1,000 copies this week' and that it was 'the most closely read and widely-discussed paper sold in the Rhondda'.[87] Whether this was actually true, it was symptomatic of a growing lack of faith in the political settlement and in Mabon's leadership. In a letter to the *Rhondda Leader*, published amidst the December 1910 general election, four ILP branches and two SDP branches issued an appeal 'to all Trade Unionists to abstain from voting and working ... for Mabon as a protest against his industrial and political action'. In twelve months Mabon's vote share and his majority, as well as overall turnout, fell by more than three thousand – and thus they did not turn into votes for his Conservative opponent, Harold Lloyd.[88]

The group of active syndicalists in the South Wales Coalfield before 1910 was very small. Within the SWMF itself there were Noah Ablett, George Dolling, W. H. Mainwaring, and William Ferris Hay. Other activists included George Jackson of the Sailor's and Firemen's Union, and Alfred and George Cox of the Docker's Union, all of them based in Newport; Jonah Charles, a Labour member of Margam Urban District Council, was active in the Docker's Union in Port Talbot; and James Rigg of Pontypridd was a member of the Brass Founder's Union.[89] Of these, the most significant were Hay and Ablett.[90] It was Ablett who attended the first British conference on industrial syndicalism, at the Coal Exchange in Manchester, on 26 November 1910. There he spoke on events engulfing the Rhondda and the potential of syndicalism. Another figure of growing significance, whom Ablett might well have met in Manchester, was the Irish trades union leader, James Larkin.[91] But it was Hay who provided the intellectual exposition of syndicalism in pamphlets and in the socialist press and was the most anti-politics figure in the South Walian syndicalist movement. Ablett, as D. K. Davies has shown convincingly, remained in comradely debate with Hay, but his own tinge of realism meant that he was never able to follow him entirely.[92]

The intellectualism of the Rhondda was not fully replicated in the Cynon Valley. Charles Butt Stanton, the leading figure in the latter, was not a natural theorist and moved with the advanced men of the Rhondda only when it suited him, and never very easily. Although a member of the Social Democratic Party, Stanton's reputation was as a firebrand and organiser of the miners he represented as district agent – a technique that earned him a position on the executive committee of the Miners' Federation of Great Britain in 1911. Unlike Noah Ablett, John Hopla, and the others of the new generation in the Rhondda, Stanton enjoyed an international reputation as well as a domestic one. In 1913, the *Encyclopédie Socialiste,* a French directory of leading members of the Socialist International, described Stanton as part of a 'very combative element ... amongst whom he manifests a somewhat parliamentary tendency, in the French fashion'.[93] He was also labelled the leader of the Welsh revolutionary socialist miners. Neither observation was particularly accurate.

Such intellectual radicalism as developed in the Cynon Valley in 1910 had far more to do with Tom Eynon, a name now largely forgotten, than with Stanton. Born in Aberaman in the mid-1870s, Eynon subsequently moved to the Rhymney Valley and was elected checkweigher at the New Tredegar Colliery in 1907.[94] By then regarded as an 'obstinate socialist', Eynon, like Stanton and the advanced men of the Rhondda, was a member of the Social Democratic Party and loathed Mabon and the old leadership of the SWMF.[95] In 1909 he stood, unsuccessfully, to become miners' agent for the Rhymney Valley, losing to the more traditional Walter Lewis.[96] Early in 1910, Eynon, together with William Scammells and George Jones, established a 'Federation Reform Committee' and through its auspices called for the formation of a single, national miners' union. At a meeting in New Tredegar held that May, Eynon declared that 'something should be done to try to stir up a revolutionary feeling. It was essential, for the contented slave was the worst enemy of liberty'.[97] Further meetings were held in New Tredegar and in Eynon's native Cynon Valley that summer which resulted in the formation of the South Wales Wage-Rate Association, a body hostile to the SWMF as led by Mabon.[98]

Speaking at a meeting held in Aberaman in late October 1910, a matter of days before the street violence there, Eynon launched a scathing attack on the SWMF president:

There was too much of the Mabonic idea in South Wales, and Mabon should be asked to resign, as he should not be an impediment to the progress of Labour. Labour leaders were doing very well. Mabon had a beautiful house in the heart of the Vale of Glamorgan. The present constitution of the Miners' Federation was rotten.[99]

The proposals of the Wage-Rate Association were not all that different, ideologically, from the framework offered by the Unofficial Reform Committee; Eynon's politics, after all, stemmed from the same Marxian worldview. But the Association which he helped to establish in 1910 was much less effective because it sought to press for change from the outside, and the Association existed as a rival to the SWMF not as a platform for debate and reform from within. Not surprisingly the endeavour met with considerable resistance and came to be regarded (and dismissed) as part of the wider problem of non-unionism and anti-Federationism, rather than the radical solution it purported to be. Although the Association temporarily absorbed several workers from the Cwmcynon Colliery in Mountain Ash at the end of 1910, it soon fizzled out. The Rhondda method, of reform from within, was recognised as the most effective approach.[100] On his death in 1915, Tom Eynon was lionised as a committed advocate of social democracy and the alternatives of 1910 were forgotten.[101]

The debates on reform within the South Wales Miners' Federation took place alongside the gradual winding down of the Cambrian Combine dispute. And it sat alongside new ideas about industrial production and its relationship to class being woven into the political arguments about the 'worker as consumer' then being made by the Labour Party's leading national figures, notably Ramsay Macdonald and Philip Snowden.[102] The ILP's *Labour Leader* told readers that 'we are all consumers'.[103] The SWMF, of course, were focused on the economic relations of production rather than on consumption, but both recognised the need to move activity beyond the local level. As Vernon Hartshorn, then miners' agent for Maesteg, declared at a May Day rally in Pontypridd in 1911, the Cambrian Combine dispute had demonstrated that whenever localised conflicts 'called for the cessation of work by twelve thousand men, it was a case where seven hundred thousand ought to join hands with them'. He continued:

> A national stoppage would teach the community at large what the real value of the colliery was, and what was still more important, it would teach the latter his own value. Once the whole of the miners came out in one body the whole trade of the country would be brought to a standstill before the men had been out a fortnight.[104]

The Powell Duffryn dispute in the Cynon Valley and the Cambrian Combine dispute in the Rhondda highlighted the need to secure a minimum wage to guard against the rising cost of living (and in that sense, it was about both production and consumption). The two districts were at the vanguard of a debate that was soon to take place in every coalfield and amongst every miners' association in Britain, as well as in the Labour Party. In July 1911, in a sign that the South Wales Coalfield were willing to act as a single unit, the Federation adopted a manifesto penned by Noah Ablett and Ted Gill (Abertillery), which set out the case for a minimum wage. They appealed directly to the 'sympathetic comradeship of their English and Scottish fellow-workmen ... Do not let the Welshmen lose that precious faith – the one most essential to solidarity and the most formidable weapon against our oppressors'.[105] They hoped for the manifesto to be discussed at the Miners' Federation of Great Britain conference on 28 July, but their appeal was rejected.[106]

Conciliation – which the miners of the Cambrian Combine took as capitulation – was finally reached in August 1911, after ten months of dispute, but the war of ideas, and the antagonism evident between the workmen of the Cambrian Combine and those of Powell Duffryn in the Cynon Valley and the older leadership of the SWMF, was evident.[107] Noah Rees wrote in the aftermath of the Miners' Federation of Great Britain decision not to hear the South Wales appeal that 'the members of this body who are, and have been for many years, professed Socialists are as reactionary as the most hidebound Lib-Lab among them. To them it seems that no improvement in conditions, no raised standard of comfort is possible, until the mines are nationalised'.[108] And such an outcome, startlingly enough, was thought, by the 'advanced men', to be inadequate. They desired more complete transformation, namely the implementation of industrial democracy and the socialisation of the mining industry with power vested in the hands of the workforce. But there was a more general anger, too, focused at William Abraham. Little wonder that rumours abounded in the aftermath of the combine disputes that Mabon intended to retire as SWMF president.[109] He did so the following year.

Despite the resolution of the conflicts in Mid Rhondda and the Cynon Valley, essentially a defeat for the men in either case, it took several weeks for the mines to reopen after such a lengthy stoppage. Arrangements had been made to resume work at the Cambrian, Glamorgan, and Britannic collieries, but the Naval Colliery remained closed.[110] At a mass meeting held on the Mid Rhondda Athletic Ground on August Bank Holiday, the workmen of the Combine resolved to go back together or not at all. As they waited the return to work, the 'advanced men' pondered their next steps.[111] On 27 May 1911, before the resolution of the strike, the group met in Cardiff to discuss their strategy. Two days later, on the motion of Charlie Gibbons, a miner from Maerdy, the group formed themselves into a 'party for the purpose of propagating advanced thought': the Unofficial Reform Committee.[112] Then, on 19 August 1911, the group launched the *Rhondda Socialist*, a halfpenny newspaper that labelled itself 'the "bomb" of the South Wales workers'.[113] For the next three years, the *Rhondda Socialist* (from May 1913, when printing shifted to Merthyr Tydfil, the *South Wales Worker*) was the public mouthpiece of unofficial reformers and printed the debates and ideas that were emerging from the group.

Those ideas coalesced in the *Miners' Next Step*, a pamphlet-length manifesto that encapsulated the principles of the Unofficial Reform Movement and of radical reform of the South Wales Miners' Federation from within. The pamphlet was drawn up in a series of meetings held in Tonypandy in the summer of 1911, with the final draft finalised in November. It was a cooperative effort: the preamble was written by Noah Ablett and Charlie Gibbons, the programme by George Dolling and David Richards, the constitution by Noah Rees and W. H. Mainwaring, the policy statements by William Ferris Hay, and the remainder by Hay and Tom Smith.[114] The *Miners' Next Step* was published by the Tonypandy printer, Robert Davies, a few months later.[115] It had a remarkable, and immediate, impact on the South Wales Coalfield – the title was even used as an advertising slogan for an emigration company based in Tonypandy within a few months.[116] Calling for a minimum wage of eight shillings, a seven hour working day, and for workers' control of the mines, the document was at once an attempt to locate the next phase of the industrial struggle in the circumstances of the Cambrian Combine dispute, but also to go beyond the strategy that had already failed to bring victory and meaningful change. Power was to be vested in the rank and file, leaders reined in, and an industrial 'democracy' developed which would allow for a better future for the miners and their families.

Crucially, the *Miners' Next Step* carried the ideas that had been discussed and debated in the Rhondda into the wider coalfield. Rhondda-based activists such as Charlie Gibbons and George Dolling sold hundreds of copies, but so too did lodge activists in other communities including W. H. May and

John E. Morgan of Ynysybwl.[117] One reader, who called himself 'Marxian' remarked, 'what more conviction do we want than that contained in the "Miners' Next Step"'?[118] But it was controversial, too, especially in the aftermath of the victorious national minimum wage strike (March-April 1912). Charles Stanton was one of those who used the *Miners' Next Step* as an excuse to break with the advanced men whom he had courted during the 1910-11 dispute. In an interview with French journalist Jean Longuet, published in the French socialist newspaper *L'Humanité*, Stanton signalled his split. Longuet began:

> Are there not in Wales some comrades who have adopted a thesis about which the London Press and Conservative politicians are making a great deal of fuss?

Stanton replied:

> It is true that some very young and active propagandists, who are quite inexperienced, have been led away by some translations of French pamphlets, and have taken part in movements of which the Tory Press has made much. They have also published a pamphlet, *The Next Step*, in which they ask the miners to 'ca canny' in order to ruin the owners. In that way, the miners would own the mines. This is detestable and childish. This has done us a great deal of harm, and has been of great use to D. A. Thomas, the truculent coal owner, who has persuaded all his co-owners to resist the miners' demands. This pamphlet is also anti-socialist, for our aim is not to give the mines to the miners, but to socialise all the means of production, of distribution, and of exchange, in order that they may belong to all the community.[119]

Whilst Stanton may have taken political objections to the stance on industrial democracy contained in the pamphlet, it is almost certainly the case that he also objected to the attacks on miners' leaders contained in it. Having been unleashed during the dispute of 1910-11, he was not willing to be reined in himself, even by his erstwhile friends. It escaped few people's notice that Stanton had his eye on a parliamentary seat.[120]

Stanton was not alone in stepping back from the radicalism of the 1910-11 period and looking at reform within the SWMF in a different way. Vernon Hartshorn from Maesteg, and Ted Gill and George Barker from Abertillery, refused to follow the Unofficial Reform Committee.[121] Hartshorn, the most moderate of the three, was dismissed by the advanced men as being part of the 'old school'.[122] 'Chief among these traitors occupying this despicable prominence', insisted the unofficial reformers, 'stands Vernon Hartshorn! Puffed into rapid and underserved prominence, trading on the ideas and efforts of abler men'.[123] He was regarded by the Liberals in a rather more positive light: Lloyd George privately championed Hartshorn's appointment as a magistrate in Maesteg in 1913, for example, despite local concern about Hartshorn's socialism.[124] The divergence of Ted Gill and George Barker from the Unofficial Reform Committee was subtler in nature and reflected their commitment to nationalisation.[125] Indeed, Barker, the miners' agent at Abertillery, whose personal papers record subscriptions to the *South Wales Worker*, the *Socialist Review*, *Plebs*, the anarchist newspaper *Freedom*, and the Vegetarian Society, was undoubtedly on the left of the SWMF.[126]

At a public debate at the Judge's Hall, Trealaw, in November 1912, Barker and Gill spoke in favour of nationalisation whilst Noah Ablett and Frank Hodges, the miners' agent at Tondu, argued against it. In his opening statement, Barker called nationalisation of industry 'the greatest proposal the labour world has ever yet evolved' and insisted that only nationalisation would bring the full fruits of labour. Ablett then attacked Barker's position by noting the relationship between the state and the interests of capital. As he put it:

> You will have to face another thing after nationalisation. In all future strikes and organisation, you will be faced with a far more formidable organisation of capitalists than the Cambrian Combine and the Coal Owners association of Great Britain. You will be faced by the state, and you know how much force and power is behind that to force through any matter they may desire. If you want another strike, you must strike against practically the whole of society, against the state. This is a much bigger job than striking against the coal owners.[127]

The same points had been made in the *Syndicalist*, the newspaper of the 'industrial democrats' in Britain, in April 1912 by a correspondent calling himself a 'South Wales miner'. It read: 'this strike has taught us that any conflict of this magnitude must not reckon only on direct employers as the enemy, but also the forces of the government'.[128]

This was a powerful argument against the intrinsic value of nationalisation and one borne out of direct experience of the combine disputes in South Wales in 1910-11, when the Rhondda, Pontypridd, and the Cynon Valley had been occupied by the police and the army. It was also borne out of the experiences of raids undertaken by the police on radical working men's clubs in Abercynon, Mountain Ash, Tonypandy, Blaenllechau, and Ystrad, in the second half of 1912.[129] These raids were ostensibly to prevent drunkenness and the excessive sale of alcohol but given the practical use of the clubs as meeting places and sites for lectures, the action of the authorities was undoubtedly politically motivated. As *Justice* noted of one club, 'the average consumption [of beer] for twelve months averaged £5 14s per member. This is only an average of slightly over one pint of beer per day'.[130] Hardly excessive. Whereas, in the months running up to the raid on the William Morris club in Abercynon the main attraction had in fact been a series of lectures on socialism delivered by Owen Hughes of Pontypridd.[131] He had also spoken at the Hyndman Club in Mountain Ash.[132] Both were linked to the left-wing British Socialist Party.

The William Morris Club was struck off the register of licensed clubs in November 1912 for a period of six months because of 'poor record keeping' and after-hours drinking. The attempt by the prosecution to describe, as subversive, sales of 'Red Flag Toffee' and 'Marseillaise Chocolate' were dismissed, even by the *Western Mail*, as overly comedic.[133] The premises reopened as the Abercynon Workingmen's Socialist Club in May 1913, but was again subject to police raids and fines for the illegal sale of alcohol.[134] The Hyndman Club in Mountain Ash was struck off for twelve months on the same basis. As was the Blaenllechau Workmen's Radical Club and Institute (ironically, a Liberal venue rather than a social democratic or Marxist one).[135] This was, as W. A. Wilkinson, secretary of the South Wales Council of the Social Democratic Party, and a leading member of the Marxian Club in Blaenclydach, reflected, a convenient way of closing down the environments in which the advanced men met and debated.[136] So much, Ablett could point out, for the good nature of the British state. As could Tom Mann, who lectured an audience in Trealaw on 'the Fallacy of Political Action' in November 1912.[137]

No sooner had the authorities seemingly closed one meeting place than others cropped up elsewhere. Nor were the police and courts the only ones antagonised by such mushroom growth. In June 1913, D. Watts Morgan complained at a meeting of the Rhondda No. 1 District, of which he was agent, that speakers from the syndicalist Industrial Democracy League, such as Tom Mann, were travelling around the region and spreading disunion within the SWMF. Watts Morgan noted, too, that 'he was sorry that one of his own colleagues on the executive council of the Federation was involved [that is, Noah Ablett]. He had hoped that they had had enough of disunion'.[138] The Industrial Democracy League was founded early in 1913 and had its origins in the Industrial Syndicalist Education League founded by Tom Mann in November 1910.[139] Mann was much influenced by a visit to France in May 1910, where he had seen first-hand the politics of the French trade union the *Confédération Générale du Travail*. The ISEL, as its name suggests, was intended primarily as a means of spreading syndicalist ideas throughout the British labour movement and it used public speaking, lecture tours, pamphlets, as well its own newspaper, *The Industrial Syndicalist* (later simply *The Syndicalist*), as a means of doing so.[140]

The leading figures in South Wales were those from the Rhondda who were involved in the writing of the *Miners' Next Step*, particularly W. H. Mainwaring, Noah Ablett, Noah Rees, and William Ferris Hay, although syndicalist influence spread across the region from Swansea in the west to Newport in the east.[141] The group held their first local conference under the auspices of the Industrial Democracy League in Barry. Forty miners attended[142] Alongside the Unofficial Reform Committee within the SWMF, the group established a more general association, the Trades Union Reform League, with Mainwaring as its chief point of contact, to press for the adoption of syndicalist methods in other trade unions. Its platform was as follows:

1 That we stand for the principle of one union for the whole workers in a given industry.
2 That any proposal that tends to remove the basis of power from the officials to the rank and file must be supported.

3   That an education policy be carried on so as to enable the
    workers to control and administer the industry in which they
    are engaged.[143]

The TURL was regarded with outright hostility amongst some
in the Rhondda No. 1 District of the Federation, with one lodge
declaring it 'conceived for the purpose of destroying our present
Federation' and demanding that those involved resign their
membership because 'in our opinion, it is quite inconsistent for
them to hold a position in both organisations'.[144] The same
attitude had been apparent during the earlier phase of
attempted external reform led by Tom Eynon. And yet it
represented a steady focus of attention away from the battle
against poor union leadership and 'respectable' Labour MPs
towards other ways of extending workers' control, not least the
great democratic potential of the local council. William Ferris
Hay, writing in the *South Wales Worker* in the summer of 1913
put it in the following terms:

> Here it is possible to have Labour representatives who are much
> more under the control of organised Labour than a
> parliamentary representative would ever be. Strong Trades and
> Labour Councils to select, return and instruct such local
> administratives would shift the basis of power from the Council
> Chamber to the Trade and Labour Council.[145]

This reads as something of a compromise from Hay's earlier
statements published in the *Rhondda Socialist* at the end of
1912:

> The political action of the working class consists in those
> conscious acts by which it seeks to achieve its own
> emancipation. Such acts must be ... exercised through its own

institutions, and cannot, by their very nature, be performed by "representatives" sent to the council chamber of our enemies.[146]

Although Hay had certainly not abandoned his anti-political and anti-parliamentary worldview, the embrace of the democratic potential of very deliberate political activity drew him onto the same broad territory as others in the SWMF and other unions (who were not aligned with the industrial syndicalists) who regarded winning council chambers as an essential step forward for the extension of democratic control.[147] As T. I. Mardy Jones put it in 1912:

> The colliery villages could be better planned, better lighted and kept, be made more ornamental with trees; they could have more parks, libraries, gymnasiums, play-grounds, and very much else if the Council so decided. But the local Council does not so decide, because the workmen permit the Council to be manned by rate-savers; that is, persons whose concern seem to be the saving of the rates instead of using their powers for the public advantage.[148]

In the period leading up to the outbreak of the First World War, this position of gaining municipal electoral strength, together with the political and parliamentary road to socialism, was asserted by the national Labour Party leadership and leading trades unionists.[149] Ablett, too, cut a more pragmatic figure. He lambasted Hay and his allies in the pages of the *South Wales Worker* for what he regarded as their impossibilism (and they retorted against his "moderation"), and he kept visibly aloof from the South Wales Worker League – the militant faction of the Unofficial Reform Committee led by Hay, Charles Gibbons, A. J. Cook, and James B. Grant, which emerged early in 1914.[150] They tried to keep the anti-parliamentary enthusiasms of 1910-1912 alive, but with relatively little success. In January 1914, the *South Wales Worker* lamented that 'the Rhondda during the past year has been a place of the dead'.[151] By the summer, the *South Wales Worker* itself had ceased to exist. With the minimum wage won and the coal industry at its productive peak – fifty seven million tons of coal across more than six hundred mines by nearly a quarter of a million miners – the economic conditions that had encouraged radicalism and militancy seemed, in the Rhondda at least, to have passed.

Socialism with a Spanish Accent

Twenty miles to the north east of Tonypandy, in Dowlais, there were similar debates being held about the future of socialism and democratic organisation. They too were sustained by an equal commitment to socialist organisation, industrial democracy, and radical trade unionism, but they also drew on ideas that were prevalent in Spain and the wider Spanish-speaking world and they were conducted in Spanish.

In 1900, the first Spanish workers arrived in the town as employees of the Dowlais Iron Company.[152] They quickly established themselves as active trades unionists, joining the local unions and maintaining their membership of their Spanish federation – one of those initially employed was Fermin Urlezaga (1870-1912) vice president of the *Sociedad de Obreros de la Región Vizcaya*.[153] The arrival of a group of radical Spaniards attracted the attention of Sam Mainwaring, the veteran socialist and anarchist from Swansea whose activism on the left had its origins in the Socialist League founded by William Morris in the 1880s. Mainwaring travelled to Dowlais (alongside the Cuban-Catalonian Fernando Tarrida del Marmol) to attend a conference held on 5 August 1901 which had been organised by anarchists in the Spanish community by then resident in the town.[154] Mainwaring attacked the existing state of trade union organisation locally and nationally, offering an anarchist solution to the 'problem'.[155]

Following the conference, anarchists in Dowlais resolved to form a new trade union branch of their own, which was chaired by Melchor Bustamante, and to affiliate to the anarchist labour federation formed in Spain the previous year. The leading figure amongst the anarchists was the journalist and writer Vicente Garcia.[156] Exiled from the Basque Country by state repression of the labour movement, he arrived in Dowlais in 1900 and found a job at the steelworks. There he remained for five years before leaving for Bordeaux to resume his career as a journalist. Garcia was already well-known amongst Spanish anarchists in Europe and the Americas by the time he moved to Dowlais and used his experiences of agitating amongst workers in Spain to organise anarchist movements in South Wales. In the autumn of 1901, in addition to organising a trade union organisation, Garcia and other like-minded individuals, including Bustamante, met at the Holly Bush Inn to form an anarchist group ostensibly to organise a commemoration for the Chicago Martyrs, the four men hanged by the State of Illinois for their alleged participation in the Haymarket Affair of 1886.[157] They hoped to involve others in Dowlais and Merthyr but found the Welsh workers to be 'more backward than those of Vizcaya. They have a complete disregard for their rights. They are content just to relax and have a beer'.[158]

Such division was equally apparent in Abercraf, albeit with far more overt xenophobia on the part of the Welsh population. Like the Dowlais Steel Works, the International Anthracite Colliery in Abercraf had a reputation for employing international (albeit chiefly French) workers. For a village typically regarded as almost entirely Welsh-speaking, and with a political culture derived from rigid nonconformity and Lib-Labism, this resulted in what one journalist described 'cosmopolitan Abercrave', with residents moving there from France, Spain, Portugal, Germany, and Belgium, as well as from elsewhere in Wales.[159] The international workforce was regarded by the native population as having 'special privileges', especially not having to work abnormal places underground from which it was difficult to make a living.[160] Objections were also raised about the fact that they could speak neither Welsh nor English – potentially dangerous in working underground.[161] In July 1914, a 'racial feud' broke out on precisely this issue, with Welsh miners refusing to work underground with their Spanish counterparts. Mass meetings were organised and the local miners' agent, Johnny James, directed to interview the colliery management with a view to ending the practice of employing foreigners and sacking those already working at the pit.[162] In 1915, James Winstone and Thomas Richards met with the chief inspector of mines to submit a protest against the employment of workers from Spain and Portugal at the International Colliery. They pointed to the unknown political sympathies of the migrant workers which was, in their view, 'an exceedingly dangerous proceeding'.[163]

Throughout 1914 and 1915, *Llais Llafur*, sought to ferment conflict between the Spanish community and the local Welsh population. In xenophobic terms it remarked that the Spaniards had 'enjoyed the freedom of Welsh citizens' and ought to desist from seeking and taking jobs at the International Colliery because 'ingratitude is not to be tolerated'.[164] It claimed, outrageously, that 'the foreign element is ousting the native ... Abercrave will be a Spanish town in reality, and ... our children will be obliged to leave the home of their fathers to seek a livelihood elsewhere'.[165] It readily reported meetings held at chapels and outside which called for the deliberate removal of the Spaniards and promoted the agreement reached with the coal companies in the wider region that Spaniards sacked from the International Colliery would be refused work in other pits.[166] Although this was soon broken when several Abercraf Spaniards were employed at the Ystrad Fawr Colliery in Bedwas.[167] One of the paper's journalists remarked caustically, 'are the managers going to take steps to print the Mines Act in Spanish to enable the migrants to understand its clauses?'[168] Even as late as 1917 the issue was not quite settled, with Winstone again tasked with mediating.[169] Despite attempts at forcing the Spanish community out of Abercraf, most of the more than two hundred migrants remained and continued to work at the International Colliery with the full support of the SWMF Executive.[170] Indeed, the Executive issued instructions to the local lodge in March 1918 stating that 'we recommend the Abercrave Workmen to offer no opposition to the Aliens formerly employed at the Collieries to return thereto'.[171]

The irony of this flare up of xenophobic tension and the questions posed by the SWMF leadership about the political allegiance of the Spaniards is that most had travelled to Abercraf from Dowlais and Merthyr. They brought with them political allegiances to anarchism on the one hand, and to PSOE on the other. They were also keen members of the South Wales Miners' Federation. As one Spaniard observed, 'one might claim that there has been greater loyalty to the Federation on the part of the "foreigners"'.[172] Although there does not seem to have been a branch of PSOE formed in Abercraf, the anarchist cell was known as the *Ferrer Group,* named for the Catalan anarchist Francisco Ferrer, which appears to have been established in around 1911. Certainly, it was already sending money to the Americas for the purchase of newspapers and magazines by the end of that year.[173] Its main point of contact was Melchor Esteban, who had previously been resident in Dowlais.[174] An article in *A Comuna*, a Portuguese anarchist journal, published in 1923, records that the *Ferrer Group* helped to develop a strong understanding of libertarian and anarchist activity in Abercraf and worked intensively propagandising the cause elsewhere in South Wales.[175] Their main contacts were with anarchists in Neath and Swansea, such as Sam Mainwaring, and with their Spanish brethren in Dowlais and Merthyr, and only belatedly with the wider population in Abercraf.[176]

Appeals for 'the Welsh people to practice the spirit of international solidarity of the workers' initially fell on deaf ears, as they had in Dowlais a decade before, and there were calls from within the Spanish community in South Wales to form a distinct trade union separate from the South Wales Miners' Federation or the steelworkers' union to protect their own interests.[177] Although that did not occur, a Spanish Culture Society was formed in Abercraf to protect the community from xenophobic attacks and to encourage greater understanding of Spanish culture, and links with the ILP in Merthyr were strengthened. As the *Merthyr Pioneer* recorded in 1916:

> Comrades were escorted back by several young immigrants, who avowed themselves adherents of the International. The impression left on the ILPers was that the opposition to the Spaniards, recently shown in the locality, is due solely to the fact that their point of view has not been ascertained. If the miners decided to better their conditions, they would find the Spaniards amongst the first to co-operate.[178]

The Spanish workers were consistent in their adherence to the international workers' cause and to local solidarity, and were taken aback by attempts, in their view, 'to fan the flames of racial hatred'.[179] Their response to the accusations of pro-German sentiment during the war was to reject them by using the language of solidarity and socialism. 'Our greatest enemy as workmen the world over', they wrote, 'is militarist autocracy. It is our most earnest and sincere desire as Spaniards that Great Britain will triumph, because you have right and justice on your side, and it will mean more freedom and liberty for the workers all the world over'.[180] But in both Dowlais and Abercraf such appeals to internationalism and solidarity had failed to win an audience. Socialism with a Spanish accent seemed to be unwelcome.

At least, that was the impression to be gained from the anarchists in both places, who kept their distance from the 'natives' as a result. A different view was held by those whose allegiance was to the Spanish Socialist Workers' Party (PSOE), which also had a Dowlais branch.[181] The PSOE worked closely, and effectively, with the Merthyr and Dowlais ILP branches and several Spaniards were members of both.[182] Writing in PSOE's newspaper, *El Socialista*, in May 1902, Fermin Urlezaga noted that the Spanish socialists there celebrated May Day together with the local ILP branches. They sang Spanish socialist hymns, British socialist hymns, and the Internationale. 'I believe', Urlezaga wrote, 'that in a few years' time all British workers will celebrate May Day in this way'. The Dowlais PSOE branch communicated regularly with *El Socialista*, going as far as to form a group to buy shares in the newspaper, as well as with regional socialist newspapers and journals.[183] This predated the ILP's efforts at setting up a newspaper in Merthyr and may well have informed the process. Certainly, the links between the PSOE branch and the ILP in Merthyr and Dowlais encouraged intellectual debates around evolution, collectivism, revolution, poverty and social justice, and internationalism. And it ensured that ideas formulated abroad percolated the labour movement in Merthyr and Dowlais.[184]

This came to fruition in October 1909 when the Merthyr and Dowlais ILP branches protested the execution of the Catalan activist Francisco Ferrer and again in the autumn of 1917 in response to the heavy-handed manner in which the Spanish government in Madrid reacted to a general strike in Barcelona.[185] Regarded subsequently by historians of Spain as a 'quasi-revolutionary' moment, the general strike 'demonstrated the growing co-ordination of the working-class Left'.[186] Repression brought international outrage, but it was not an event that caught the widespread attention of the labour movement in South Wales, except in those areas where Spaniards had organisational links. At a meeting of the Merthyr ILP branch in September 1917, a circular was read from the Spanish communities at Dowlais and Abercraf pointing to the use of the military on the streets of Barcelona and government repression. In response, a letter of protest was sent to the Spanish Ambassador in London.[187] The same circular was read at a meeting of the Aberdare ILP branch the following month, with much the same response.[188] And in early November, the Neath Socialist Society passed what it called a 'strong resolution' condemning government action in Spain when the circular was read at its meeting.[189] The Merthyr Trades and Labour Council also held a lengthy discussion on the Spanish crisis, pledging to work for the release of the leaders of the general strike and to lead a petition of the TUC to respond on behalf of the British labour movement.[190]

Although the anarchists in Dowlais had little to do with either the PSOE branch or the ILP, they similarly kept themselves informed through their own newspapers and through their proximity with each other. They also made occasional use of the British anarchist newspaper, *Freedom*.[191] Of those identified as being part of the anarchist groups in Dowlais and Merthyr, three lived in one boarding house on Union Street, two in another boarding house close by; and the rest lived in neighbouring streets: the 'Spain within Wales' that one second-generation Welsh-Spaniard later recalled.[192] This was a close-knit community of relatively few people – the 1901 census recorded around one hundred and twenty Spanish-born residents in Dowlais and not every Spaniard was an anarchist – that felt itself to be, and acted accordingly, part of a global movement. In 1907, for instance, responding to the International Anarchist Congress, held in Amsterdam in August that year, a group called *Obra y Silencio* was established in Dowlais to advance the interests of the newly formed Anarchist International. Another of the groups established in Dowlais, *Ni Dogmas, Ni Sistemas*, which formed in 1915, was connected to anarchist networks in the Americas.[193]

There is also some indication that the Dowlais anarchists connected with political movements drawn from Italy and Eastern Europe, as well as with further Spanish anarchist cells in Cardiff.[194] An anarchist group in Blaina, known as a 'society of resistance', was established by the area's Italian immigrant community and was led by Giuseppe Sestili, a miner who moved into the area in around 1902.[195] The group seems to have been active until 1907 and was sending money across to Dowlais for transmission to the continent to support a number of anarchist causes, including providing financial support to imprisoned anarchists in Italy and Spain.[196] Yet another group called *Reivindicacion* in Dowlais was led by Marcus Harris (probably Marks Harris, a Jewish immigrant from Poland) and was formed in late-1909 and remained in existence for at least the next decade.[197] Although these groups were tiny, far smaller than the average branch membership of the ILP, and miniscule compared to SWMF lodge memberships, their existence, and persistence, served as a reminder that because South Wales absorbed immigrants on a substantial scale in the early part of the twentieth century, it was also exposed to ideas conducted in a range of different languages with connections all over the world.[198] For them at least, Edwardian South Wales was not, as K. O. Morgan once described it, bound together by the 'beguiling appeal of the Liberal past' which encouraged a 'common sense of tradition and destiny', the very essence of complacent Liberal nationalism, but by a far more radical approach to politics. In this they found common cause with the ILP.

Voice of the People

When news reached Ynysybwl that war had been declared in August 1914, John E. Morgan, the lodge secretary, his brother Abel, and fellow ILP member W. H. May, later miners' agent for Pontypridd, immediately began to organise the anti-war movement. Abel, as Alun Burge records, was active in the No Conscription Fellowship and the National Council for Civil Liberties and his home in Thompson Street was thrown open to those seeking a haven for their anti-war stance.[199] W. H. May was likewise a member of the NCF. As lodge secretary, John E. Morgan often attended the county tribunals to prevent weeding out of the workforce at the Lady Windsor Colliery and kept a regular log of men liable to be called up for active service, particularly following the introduction of conscription in 1916.[200] The two brothers also attended the peace conference in Cardiff organised by the ILP and the NCCL in September 1916, and found themselves pelted with rotten tomatoes and flour bombs as they made to escape in the company of James Winstone, the South Wales Miners' Federation president, and by 1915 ILP candidate for Merthyr Boroughs (of which Ynysybwl was part). 'I remember', John E. Morgan wrote many years later, 'wiping the paste off Winstone's profuse curls and from his shoulders as we marched along ... When I reached St Mary Street and saw the people so calm and collected, I felt like asking myself, had I been dreaming, or had I had a nightmare'.[201]

The third of the Morgan brothers, Bethuel William, was preparing to begin his studies at Bangor Normal College as war broke out. Born in Ynysybwl on 7 June 1892, for the three years prior to the war he had been working as an uncertified assistant teacher, initially at Miskin Mixed School in Mountain Ash and then at Carnetown Mixed School in Abercynon. In 1913, he sat the matriculation exam for the University of Wales. He remained at Bangor Normal until December 1915, but did not return to complete his studies until 1919. For the first fifteen months of the war, Bethuel Morgan was just one of many who refused to volunteer or attest on religious or political grounds and instead attempted to carry on with their lives as normal. But in adopting an anti-war stance, he faced considerable challenges and his refusal to join either the territorial corps or the college officer training corps left him outcast from his peers. Leaving Bangor for the Christmas vacation of 1915-16, he had resolved to suspend his studies and not return in the new year. He felt he could not go back.[202]

Three months later, on 2 March 1916, the Military Service Act came into force, bringing with it conscription. At the age of 24, Bethuel Morgan knew he would be one of those called up. And so it proved. He refused, however, and appealed to the district tribunal in Mountain Ash on the grounds of conscience. At that tribunal, he claimed absolute exemption from military service because 'he believed in the sanctity of human life'. Subjected to leading questions about German atrocities, his resolute stance drew the ire of one of the tribunal members who barked 'you are trying to save your skin'. Bethuel replied calmly, 'I have a soul, if that man hasn't'.[203] His appeal for exemption was denied, albeit with leave to apply to the county tribunal. Those hearings were held in Pontypridd the following month. Bethuel Morgan again declared that 'war was contrary to Christianity' and therefore he would 'obey the dictates of his conscience and refuse all military orders'. He was awarded non-combatant status, but his was an absolutist position and he turned it down.[204]

Bethuel Morgan's case was heard alongside those of several of his friends and colleagues, each a member of the ILP: Gwilym Smith, Percy Kendall, and Emrys Hughes.[205] They were all sent to Cardiff Barracks where they refused to obey military orders such as refusing to get changed into uniform and to submit to medical examination.[206] Together the group were subjected to torrents of abuse from the soldiers present at the barracks. Threats such as 'before God, if there were no one else present I would tear you limb from limb', or 'you will have hell at the depot, and be fed on bread and water', or 'I hope you will be shot', or, finally, 'you're bloody well in the Army now and will have to say "Sir"'.[207] This collective refusal to cooperate led to a court martial at the end of May, the first of its kind held in Wales during the war. The hearing exposed the abuse that the group had been subject to, language that Bethuel referred to as violent in his statements to the court. 'The whole atmosphere of the recruiting office', he insisted, 'was one of bullying and cowardice'.[208] A military court was having none of this and the imposition of a harsh sentence was inevitable. The group were all sentenced to two years' hard labour, with a remission of eighteen months. To emphasise precisely who was in charge, and to humiliate the men, the sentence was promulgated at Cardiff Barracks in front of three hundred soldiers, ninety per cent of whom had already seen active service.[209]

The men were transferred from Cardiff to Devizes Military Prison on 31 May 1916 having been seconded, together with Idwal Williams of Tonyrefail, to the Wiltshire Regiment.[210] They were escorted to Cardiff's Great Western station (now Cardiff Central) by seven armed soldiers and were handcuffed together in pairs. Given their continued refusal to accept military protocol, the serving soldiers had to carry the prisoners' kit since they refused to touch it. Hughes's sister, Agnes, wrote later 'how ludicrous it seems that so many soldiers were required to accompany five Conscientious Objectors, well handcuffed, on a railway journey'.[211] At Devizes, the men were placed on a meagre diet of bread and water. Agnes Hughes travelled down a week later to visit her brother and his comrades. She was appalled at what she saw:

> After much pleading, I was allowed special permission to see my brother. I could easily see by the change in his physical condition that all the stories we hear of Conscientious Objectors are not exaggerated. He was looking haggard and thin – the inevitable results of not living on the luxuries enjoyed by the military officers, but for the most part on a bread and water diet, and not much of that. He said that they had all been treated in a similar manner, and had received a very bad time. Khaki had been forced on him six times – after this forcing his hands had been handcuffed to prevent him from removing it.[212]

The men went on hunger strike for the first time shortly afterwards: Idwal Williams ended up in hospital as a result of his twenty-one day fast. Hunger strikes and continued refusal to accept military orders led to the five men being court martialed for a second time on 11 July 1916, this time with a Major Hawkes of the Wiltshire Regiment presiding.[213] One by one, they reiterated their stance. Percy Kendall: 'I am a socialist, and believe in the brotherhood of man and the sanctity of human life'. Idwal Williams stated that he too was a socialist. Emrys Hughes stated that he was a socialist and a pacifist. Bethuel Morgan gave the following impassioned speech, which merits quoting in full:

> I am guilty of the facts, but do not admit that I am a soldier. I am a follower of Jesus Christ, and as such I am a Conscientious Objector to all war and to all kinds of military service. Christ

was and is a Prince of Peace and I, like my Master, am an advocate for Peace. I contend that all war influences thoughts [that] are in direct conflict with those of a true Christian. I was nurtured on a religious hearth, and from my youth I have been susceptible to religious impressions. From the age of twelve years, I have been a member of the Baptist Denomination of the Christian faith. At all times I have been unswerving in my sincerity to the principles of Christ. The omnipotent alone knows my sincerity in my convictions and the struggles that I have made to remain loyal to Christ's teachings.

I have suffered and sacrificed in the past. During my first year at the Normal College of Bangor I refused to join the Territorial Corps. During the second year I refused to join the Officers' Training Corps. I have also suffered confinement for three months and, if needs be, I am prepared to sacrifice my life, in order to prove to the Government, and to my nation, my loyalty to Christ.[214]

Given a further sentence of twenty one months' hard labour, commuted to eight months, Morgan was removed to Somerset County Gaol at Shepton Mallet and placed in the hands of the civilian authorities.[215] After serving a short period at the Gaol, Morgan and his comrades were transferred 'in chains' to Cardiff Gaol where they remained until 3 October 1916. They were then released onto the Home Office Scheme and set to Weston-Super-Mare (or, in Idwal Williams's case, to Llanelli), where they carried out the hard labour to which they had originally been sentenced. Only Emrys Hughes, considered the most militant of the five, was kept behind bars. The work in Weston took place on Milton Hill, a little outside the town centre, where men were engaged in work for the Home-Grown Timber Committee. That is, chopping down trees. Conditions in Weston were considerably better than those the men had been used to in prison and they were able to form a democratically-elected committee to organise provisions and form a drama society to entertain themselves.[216] There was a fine line of tolerance from the authorities, however, as Idwal Williams discovered when he tried to agitate for improved conditions at the camp in Llanelli. He was sent to the work centre at Wakefield Prison instead.[217]

The case of Bethuel Morgan and his comrades was not uniquely harsh, indeed its severity is markedly similar to the experiences of many other conscientious objectors across Britain.[218] And it had a galvanising effect on the anti-war sections of the labour movement. As Burge notes, the treatment of Bethuel Morgan and the others embittered his older brother Abel Morgan, whose anti-war fervour only increased.[219] And it had an impact on the community of Ynysybwl as well. The workmen at the Lady Windsor Colliery passed a unanimous resolution against the Military Service Act and anti-war campaigners were a regular feature in Ynysybwl's social life.[220] It's easy to think of Ynysybwl as out of step with the rest of South Wales, with the exception of ILP-pacifist strongholds such as Briton Ferry, Tumble, or Merthyr Tydfil.[221] But that would be to misrepresent the dynamics of change and the cracks that were already apparent in the old way of doing things. Goronwy Jones, later lodge chairman in Ynysybwl, reflected in an oral history interview in 1972 that whereas 'there was nothing against the war', at the beginning at least, and that 'the youngsters were proud to march behind the flag', there was hardly a 'great rush' to join up.[222]

Events in 1915, particularly the miners' strike which began on 15 July and ended ten days later with David Lloyd George, then munitions minister, agreeing to demands for improved pay and conditions, have typically been portrayed as marking a revival in militancy and radicalism. Although some have argued that the 1915 strike was a 'patriotic' act, in contrast to accusations made at the time that it was a traitorous action to take in the middle of a war, neither conclusion is accurate.[223] The 1915 strike was a further example of the industrial rules established by the rank-and-file of the South Wales Miners' Federation as a result of the combine disputes of 1910-11: in the face of exploitation by unscrupulous coal owners profiteering from the output demands of war, the results of those earlier disputes had to be reasserted. The quick succession of Keir Hardie's death in September 1915, the selection of James Winstone, the acting President of the SWMF, as the official ILP candidate in place of Charles Stanton (who expected the seat to be his), and Stanton's victory at the by-election at the end of November can easily be misinterpreted. Whilst it was true, as K. O. Morgan, has written that Stanton's 'uninhibitedly pro-war campaign ... easily carried the day', we should perhaps be more cautious about its implications. It was not really the case that, as Morgan concluded, 'in Hardie's own mining stronghold, the seat of Henry Richard and the shrine of Dic Penderyn, the appeal of patriotic jingoism and of establishment attitudes was overwhelming'.[224]

In fact, Stanton won in 1915 because the finances and powers of the establishment, from the upper echelons of government to the media, were focused on defeating the ILP. This coalition of power proved overwhelming and were enough to mobilise anti-Labour and anti-socialist sentiments in the constituency.[225] As the *Spectator* tellingly put it, 'to say that it is as good as a substantial victory at the front is no exaggeration'.[226] Technically, there was a political truce for the duration of the war, but privately Liberals and Conservatives regarded the situation in Merthyr Boroughs as an exception: 'the truce presupposed a condition of unanimity in wishing to prosecute the War to a conclusion', as the Conservative Party chair, Arthur Steel-Maitland, wrote in a letter to the party leader Andrew Bonar Law.[227] Since they could not make the charge of pacifism stick to Winstone, although it was clear he was anti-conscription, the Conservatives did not entertain a more overt challenge to the truce. That did not preclude significant private involvement in Stanton's favour, however. As Barry Doyle has demonstrated, Conservative Party funding of one hundred and fifty pounds was provided to Stanton in the election (the equivalent of one pound in every five he spent), with additional funds coming from Conservative-aligned organisations and newspapers such as the *Morning Post*.[228] Without such resources, Stanton would not have succeeded.

Not much more than a month after Stanton's election, miners in Aberdare elected their new agent. In the last rounds of that election process, the remaining candidates were Noah Ablett, Idwal Thomas, and Owen Powell. Ablett advocated a revolution to overthrow the capitalist system in Britain and was an opponent of the war. Owen Powell, checkweigher at the Fforchwen Colliery, Cwmaman, and the then chairman of Aberdare Urban District Council, was a member of the 'moderate' wing of the Labour Party. Idwal Thomas, on the other hand, was an absolute pacifist, peace campaigner, member of the No Conscription Fellowship and the Union of Democratic Control, and the youngest member of Aberdare Urban District Council representing the Gadlys ward. His views were the opposite of Stanton's. Speaking in April 1916, for example, Thomas denounced the introduction of conscription as the 'most dangerous act the democracy of this country ever had to face ... Trade Unionists were gradually getting the reins of power into their hands and the upper classes saw in conscription a means of crushing the workers'.[229] In a closely fought contest, Powell topped the penultimate poll just twenty two votes ahead of Idwal Thomas. Owen Powell won the final round by just one hundred and sixteen votes over his opponent, the absolutist Idwal Thomas. The jingoism that apparently carried Stanton to parliament had not lasted very long. If, indeed, it was ever there at all.

One of those who experienced the shock of anti-war sentiments in the South Wales Coalfield was Emmeline Pankhurst, who travelled to the region in September 1915 for a pro-war lecture tour. Arriving in Bargoed, she encountered 'a distinct hostile and difficult element' who heckled her.[230] On investigation, she discovered several sources of anger, including antagonism towards the mine owners and towards the absentee Liberal MPs who 'had not been in [their] constituency since war broke out'. As she maintained her speaking engagements, Mrs Pankhurst grew ever more concerned. 'The situation is very serious', she wrote directly to Lloyd George, 'if vigorous action is taken to grow patriotic and national feeling much can be done to counteract the pernicious influence of the UDC [Union of Democratic Control]. Strikes and rumours of strikes fill the air. We are working night and day and have huge meetings but we came into the fold very late'.[231] Both eventually came to the same conclusion: the organisational efficacy of the radicals was far in advance of their numbers.[232] But it was not merely a question of organisation and propaganda, there was also the matter of economics. As Merthyr Borough Labour Party argued in March 1915, there was a fundamental need to tackle the cost of living crisis brought about by the war.[233]

Rising prices had already given the activists of the Unofficial Reform Committee, such as William Ferris Hay and A. J. Cook, a renewed sense of purpose. Cook arranged a public meeting in Porth in mid-August 1914, in the face of pressure from the police to cancel it, to protest the rising cost of food. He insisted later that:

Seeing the wives and children are deprived of their rightful defenders and can make no organised protest we must do our duty as trade unionists and as citizens to force the Government, who in one night could vote £100 millions for destruction of human life, to see that justice is meted out to these unfortunates. Remember our first duty is to those at home.

Cook took a leading role in the organisation of relief in the lower Rhondda and in the campaign against price exploitation. It was a campaign taken up by trades and labour councils across South Wales. In Carmarthen, for instance, the trades and labour council demanded that 'the government acquire immediate powers to arrest and reduce the inflated prices now charged for all commodities'.[234] Cwmbach Co-operative Society passed resolutions to the same effect. As did Swansea Labour Association.[235] As did the Welsh ILP Divisional Council.[236] By 1916, with no action from the government, the Merthyr *Pioneer* began to talk of a 'food prices crusade' with the campaign led directly by the trades and labour councils and the South Wales Miners' Federation.[237] In parts of the coalfield there was also a milk strike, or boycott, the first action being taken by the Lady Windsor Lodge in Ynysybwl.[238] There followed a range of similar boycotts of milk supplies in Pontardawe, the Cynon Valley, and in parts of Merthyr.[239] What followed was a concerted push by the Labour Party for the establishment of municipal milk supplies, although this proved difficult to undertake in practice. As the Merthyr town clerk, T. Aneuryn Rees, noted, such action would require an act of parliament to provide local authorities with the relevant powers.[240] Nevertheless, the chairman of Bedwellty Food Control Committee, Isaac Jones, suggested in an interview with the *Pioneer* that 'municipalisation of milk is inevitable as well as other commodities. Local industrial opinion demands municipalisation on a wide scale, the trend of events seeming to prove the ILP logic in the past'.[241]

Systematic food control was eventually established by the government in the summer of 1917 and food control committees set up across the country. Rationing followed in 1918. Before that time, food and milk prices fluctuated, eroding living standards, and workers looked on aghast at the soaring profits of those who controlled the flow of essential goods. It was certainly the case that labour's effective response to this cost of living crisis bolstered its support.[242] New branches of the ILP, often formed by those who were anti-conscription, even if their anti-war stance was more muted, began to appear in communities that had previously not seen political activity by the labour movement or where it had declined. The Bedlinog ILP branch was reported to be in a 'flourishing condition'; in Aberdare, the local branch was in a strong enough condition to take charge of new meeting rooms in a prominent town centre location and arranged to form a sub-branch in Aberaman.[243] In Blackwood, Syd Jones, checkweigher at the Llanover Colliery, alongside thirty other comrades formed a branch.[244] A branch was formed at Pengam, too, at the beginning of May 1916.[245] A. J. Cook, encouraged by the growing strength of the ILP, wrote of 'the awakening' in the Merthyr *Pioneer*:

> Daily I see signs amongst the working class with whom I move and work of a mighty awakening. The chloroforming pill of patriotism is failing in its power to drug the mind and consciousness of the worker. He is beginning to shudder at his stupidity in allowing himself to become a party to such a catastrophe as we see today.[246]

To capitalise on this awakening, the *Pioneer* encouraged the setting up of the Pioneer League ostensibly to bolster its readership but also, in practice, to provide an avenue for debate and discussion on the war and on socialist ideas.[247] Branches often provided moral and financial support to conscientious objectors, as well. In the Rhondda, the branch committee comprised many of those who had previously been involved in the Unofficial Reform Committee, such as Cook, W. H. Mainwaring, and Noah Ablett, but there were new, increasingly significant faces too including William Phippen and Arthur Horner.[248] In Mountain Ash came the support of Rev George Neighbour and Noah Tromans, ILP member of the Board of Guardians.[249] The trades and labour councils in Aberdare, Merthyr, and Mountain Ash lent their support, as did the Dowlais District of the South Wales Miners' Federation, several ILP branches including those at Brithdir, Glais, Mountain Ash, and Cwmbach, and the Aberfan Social Democratic Club.[250] By 1916, there were branches of the league in Abercwmboi, Bargoed, Tonyrefail, and Ystradgynlais as well.[251] Pontypridd followed, perhaps belatedly, in 1918.[252]

Alongside the new, there was a revival and repurposing of the old. The Rhondda Socialist Society, which had been fairly dormant (but not extinct) since the outbreak of the war, quickly grew in strength after 1916 and expanded its remit to cover Pontypridd and parts of the Ely Valley, such as Tonyrefail. The Rhondda and Pontypridd Districts Socialist Society, as it eventually became known[253], was launched in the autumn of 1916 and attracted key figures such as James Winstone to its meetings.[254] The society also held their own eisteddfodau. In Abertillery, the New Era Union, which had been established by J. Morris Evans, a former Baptist minister, along with Ted Gill, in July 1909, now provided a platform for a range of left-leaning speakers.[255] Before the war, Frank Hodges had spoken on 'The Religion of Social Democracy', for instance, but by 1915 it was the turn of more radical men such as John Scurr, the Australian-born socialist activist and post-war mayor of Poplar.[256] In 1916, together with the Abertillery ILP, the society held a welcome home rally for local conscientious objectors.[257] The society's minute book, extant from June 1916 to December 1919, records discussions on contemporary politics, on the validity of rejecting the parliamentary route to socialism, the Bolshevik Revolution, and the activities of the Rhondda Socialist Society. The minutes, which also cover meetings of the ILP and the Socialist Labour Party branches in Abertillery, reflect the political radicalisation of some after 1916.[258]

What was going on in the coalfield in the latter years of the First World War hardly escaped the notice of the authorities. Symptomatic of the growing power and influence of the labour movement and the ILP was the extent to which the coalition government regarded it as an existential threat to its own interests. A. J. Cook was targeted by the intelligence services, the police, and the Home Office because of his political activities. As Paul Davies describes: 'The police engaged shorthand writers and plainclothes officers to record his meetings', these were then transcribed and sent to London where they were maintained in files that traced Cook's movements during the last years of the war.[259] He was not alone in being followed and discussed in the secretive transmissions between police headquarters in Cardiff and the intelligence services in London. In fact, by December 1916 the intelligence services had compiled a list of almost two hundred people in whom it had an interest. This included obvious names such as Noah Ablett, George Barker, A. J. Cook, W. H. Mainwaring, Idwal Thomas, Noah Rees, and James Winstone, but also included a range of individuals whose politics ranged considerably. On the one hand there were MPs and senior South Wales Miners' Federation officials such as Mabon, Alfred Onions, and Thomas Richards; and on the other individuals such as Noah Tromans, the conscientious objector and future Caerphilly MP Morgan Jones, the writer Mark Starr, Monmouthshire ILP organiser Minnie Pallister, the future Abertillery MP George Daggar, and Enoch Morrell.[260]

The authorities were primarily concerned with the influence of the peace movement and anti-conscription campaigners, but the revolution in Russia in March 1917 transformed the situation completely.[261] Russia's participation in the war was thrown into doubt, and the provisional government's adoption of universal suffrage and freedom of speech and the demands made by the Bolsheviks for the war to end bolstered the left's peace campaigning across Europe.[262] Moreover, it fuelled a more determined response to the industrial and political situation. At the Federation rules conference organised in June that year, the proposal of the Cwmaman lodge to revise Clause B was adopted. This gave the South Wales Miners' Federation the expressed duty – in practice a long-term objective – to:

> Secure the complete organisation of all workers employed in and about the collieries situated in the South Wales coalfield with a view to the abolition of capital.[263]

The previous month, at the annual conference of the Federation at the Cory Hall in Cardiff, James Winstone struck an ebullient tone:

> All hail to the Russian Revolution – the government might well release our own political prisoners. Let us hope it is the beginning of a much desired consummation – Workers of the world unite – not kings, not thrones, but men. Give us no more giants, but elevate the race, inspired and sustained by no other motive than the complete emancipation of the workers from the system of wage slavery throughout the world and the building

up of a Co-operative Commonwealth wherein each person shall live a free, full and natural life.[264]

It was hard to imagine a more different atmosphere to that which apparent in the aftermath of his defeat to Charles Stanton eighteen months earlier. Suddenly momentum lay with the labour movement and there was fresh wind in the sails of radical political perspectives. The Unofficial Reform Committee came back to life, this time with a branch structure – Cook had previously called for an end to the 'industrial truce' which 'opened the way for any encroachment upon our rights and liberties'.[265] This allowed for considerable discussion around the implementation of the terms of the *Miners' Next Step* and even, as occurred in Aberdare, whether it could be improved. The debate was carried into workers' education classes which, by the time of the Bolshevik Revolution in November 1917, had more than twelve hundred people attending and imbibing a Marxist view of the past and present. If many of the leading figures were the same as before the war, the wider circle involved around two hundred activists representing the coalfield outside of the Rhondda and Cynon Valley. They were all united by a desire to effect a 'class-conscious awakening among the proletariat' and with the international example of Russia to draw on, this was no longer an abstract theory but a seemingly practical reality. Little more than two years later, in early February 1920, the Welsh Divisional Council of the ILP adopted a resolution calling on the national party to affiliation to the fledgling Communist International (Comintern). Like the Federation rule changes in 1917, it was a sign that Moscow, rather than London, Berlin, or Paris, let alone Chicago or New York, was the key inspiration. The implications were to be profound.

A Turning Point?

In the final stages of the First World War, there was an acceleration in the political development of the labour movement, partly because of inspiration from events in Russia in 1917, partly because of political developments in Britain in the wake of conscription in 1916, and partly because of the steady transfer of allegiance of the Irish nationalists from the Liberal Party to the Labour Party in protest at the government's handling of the Irish situation.[266] The Conservative Party reacted to this rise by attempting to attract support from organised labour, launching the Unionist Labour Movement in 1919. Originating in Lancashire, the ULM enjoyed not insignificant support in South Wales with branches formed in places such as Stanleytown and Ynysybwl. The most prominent figure was Gwilym Rowlands, a district councillor in the Rhondda (his father was manager of Penygraig Colliery) and chair of the Dunraven Conservative Club in Penygraig.[267] Rowlands would go on to be elected chairman of the Conservative Party's national sub-committee on labour in 1925, presiding over the party's attempt to reach out to working-class male voters with a message that appealed to them as workers and as organised labour.[268] The Conservatives also invested heavily in developing their women's organisations, with some success: the Neath Conservative Association claimed six hundred women members by 1925 with seven branches formed across the constituency[269]; a similar situation was evident in the Cynon Valley.[270] The Penrhiwceiber branch alone claimed a membership of more than one hundred by the mid-1920s.[271]

This was, very clearly, a reaction to the rise of Labour and one that recognised the grassroots organisational strength of that movement and the way it was constructed out of both trades unionism and political activity. In other words, it recognised the need to counter the trades and labour council, the deciding factor in Labour's ultimate success after the First World War. In 1903, there were eleven trades and labour councils in existence in South Wales, mostly in those areas, such as Merthyr Tydfil, where the electoral success of the labour movement was increasingly strong – twelve of the fourteen Labour councillors elected to the new Merthyr Borough Council in 1905 were sponsored by the trades and labour council.[272] Amongst them was Enoch Morrell, checkweigher and future president of the South Wales Miners' Federation, who was elected mayor, and John Davies, miners' agent for Dowlais, who was unanimously elected to be mayor of the then County Borough of Merthyr ten years later. The number of trades and labour councils rose slowly to nineteen by 1914, but rapidly during the war years with over fifty in existence covering all parts of South Wales by 1919. Although councils were formed throughout the period after 1914, most were established (or re-established in some cases) after 1916, the turning point in political activity during the war.[273] Not only did they campaign on political and industrial matters traditional to the labour movement, they expanded their political message in line with developments within the Labour Party nationally (culminating in the 1918 programme), provided advice locally on a range of topics including establishing trade unions and on pensions and welfare, and campaigned for the introduction of a more democratic system of government. This inevitably gave Labour a more universal appeal at the ballot box.

The example of the Ynysybwl TLC, which formed in the summer of 1916, was indicative, both of the electoral ambition of the trades and labour councils and the local nature of their complexion. The meeting to form the body was organised by the joint committee of the three colliery lodges in the village, Mynachdy, Darren Ddu, and the Lady Windsor. Their aim was to use industrial strength to effect political change and they were 'unanimously decided in favour of contesting seats on the Guardians and on the District Council' seeking the support of shop assistants and teachers in doing so.[274] This was equally true of the Ammanford and Llandybie TLC formed in April 1917 and the Cwmamman TLC formed in October that year.[275] Both were formed, together with the Burry Port and Gwendraeth Valley TLC on the initiative of the Anthracite miners.[276] Speaking at the meeting to form the Ammanford Council, Jim Griffiths, later MP for Llanelli (1936-1970) and President of the SWMF (1934-36), remarked that they 'would not rest content until every seat they could claim on the urban, rural and county councils were won for Labour'.[277] In other words, it was no longer sufficient to keep industrial activity and political activity separate – they were part of the same struggle.

In the coalfield, the trades and labour councils were largely dominated by the miners' lodges, but, significantly, were not exclusive to them. As Chris Williams has written of the Rhondda councils, 'the existence of a broader organization spread their influence and provided some for the weaker trade unions'.[278] Sue Demont has observed the same phenomenon in Tredegar.[279] The first meeting of the Monmouthshire Federation of Trades and Labour Councils which was held in Newport in September 1915, for example, had more than two hundred delegates representing more than fifty five thousand members across a range of trade unions.[280] In Mountain Ash, the trades and labour council had members from the painters' union, municipal employees, insurance agents, and shop assistants, in addition to the miners' lodges.[281] At Skewen, the trades and labour council was described as 'representative of the bulk of the workers in the constituency' including miners and dockers.[282] And at the end of 1917, the Ynysybwl Co-operative Society took the decision to affiliate to trades and labour councils in each of the areas where it had business interests.[283]

In this way, the trades and labour councils provided a mediated but uniform voice for organised labour at the local level, particularly as a political organisation. Financially, too, it removed the entire burden of support for Labour Party representatives on local authorities from the SWMF districts and placed it in the hands of the trades and labour councils – their breadth made for more inclusive political activity.[284]

Of course, this process of development was not straightforward and initially made the relationship between the various elements of the Labour Party more complex, with the ostensibly industrially-focused trades and labour councils sitting alongside electorally-focused Labour Representation Associations. The existence of trades and labour councils at ward level, too, further added to this organisational complexity, although in some parts of the coalfield, such as the Rhymney Valley, there were joint committees established which co-ordinated activity within district council areas.[285] The model eventually adopted, notably in the Rhondda, was that piloted in Merthyr Tydfil. In October 1914, the annual conference of the Merthyr Labour Representation Association voted to concentrate forces by merging with the various trades and labour councils to create a single body 'responsible for the organisation and financing of the local Labour movement'.[286] It was christened the Merthyr Borough Labour Party.[287] Progress towards the formation of the Rhondda Borough Labour Party took rather longer and was not completed, in practice, until 1923 when, as Chris Williams noted, 'an orthodox Labour Party structure' was established, although the name was adopted in 1918.[288] In Newport, the Labour Party (formed in February 1913) and the trades council merged on 4 April 1918 to form the Labour Representation Committee of the Newport Trades and Labour Council, albeit that the model was the same as in Merthyr and the Rhondda.

This network of trades and labour councils was matched by improved constituency organisation, aided, by the redistribution of parliamentary seats in 1918. At the 1910 general elections, with constituencies based largely on the geographical divisions of counties and amalgamated seats linking together municipal boroughs, Labour had a much greater challenge to win than in the smaller, and more geographically focused seats, which followed in 1918. It was easier for them to win Pontypool, with its overwhelmingly industrial electorate, than to win North Monmouthshire, which had a more mixed demographic. Boundary changes in Llanelli 'worked to Labour's advantage, integrating the industrial areas into one constituency and ensuring that the forces of the trade union movement were not divided, as they had been'.[289] The creation of individual membership of the Labour Party in 1918, following the party's new constitution, also demanded a stronger party structure since membership was no longer solely based on affiliated organisations. The result was the formation of the Divisional Labour Party (DLP), subsequently the Constituency Labour Party (CLP), which brought together delegates from across council boundaries and affiliated organisations and the membership to coordinate campaigns. Aberdare DLP, formed in January 1918, is a typical example. It comprised (and it was hardly unusual in such composition) twenty trades union branches, two trades councils, three women's co-operative guilds, two co-operative societies, three ILP branches, and a net membership of nearly twenty five thousand. Its aim, 'to present a united front politically as well as industrially to the common enemy' – capital.[290]

With a growing cohort of councillors and aldermen, Labour became more professional in its political organisation: party whips were established amongst councillors and co-ordinating groups formed so as, in the words of Labour's cohort on Ebbw

Vale Urban District Council, 'to take united action upon important questions'.[291] In Aberdare, a group was formed in 1903 after a string of splits in the Labour vote in the council chamber proved embarrassing to the trades and labour council and led to questions as to the meaning of 'Labour' as a political force.[292] It mirrored the formation of a Labour group on the Merthyr Board of Guardians, at the behest of Merthyr TLC, in 1902, to avoid the same fate, and the later formation of a group on Monmouthshire County Council in 1908.[293] The groups, akin to the Parliamentary Labour Party, sat as separate entities from the trades and labour councils and, as such, although responsible to them, could act independently when it mattered. Labour in government was never identical, either in composition or ideology, to the membership of the Labour Party. Ted Stonelake, secretary of Aberdare TLC, and a district councillor himself, noted in this vein that 'the Council could not dictate to their representatives on all matters. The group should decide certain matters among themselves'.[294] Nevertheless, from this point onwards, Labour councillors presented (for the most part) a united front within the council chamber – it gave them a significant advantage over their less well-organised rivals.

The formation of Labour groups on local authorities culminated in 1914 in the establishment of the South Wales Association of Labour Members.[295] Spearheaded by T. I. Mardy Jones and strongly supported by the South Wales Miners' Federation and its districts, the new association was, in the words of James Winstone, 'a new era for the forces of Labour in Wales'.[296] It was intended to bring uniformity of action to the Labour Party in local government and provided a strong platform for debate and discussion on a range of issues including housing, education, and rating reform. As Mardy Jones explained in 1920, the association 'endeavours to influence ... on definite lines of policy for the whole area'.[297] Thus in 1917, the association published Mardy Jones's pamphlet on rating reform, *Colliery Rating Exposed*, which was welcomed by the Labour press as 'the charter of rating reform in South Wales' and the likely basis for local government platforms at the next round of elections.[298] It debated Mardy Jones's proposals to abolish Glamorgan County Council together with the urban and rural district councils and to split the county into eleven county boroughs (including Cardiff, Swansea, and Merthyr, which were already so designated).[299] And it provided a uniform voice when combating local government cuts, welfare cuts, and attacks on the trade union political fund in the early 1920s.[300]

The consequent effects of electoral professionalisation were profound, as even a cursory glance at the chronology of Labour's capture of local government – and long-term sustainability of Labour rule – demonstrates. Both Glamorgan and Monmouthshire county councils were won in 1919, together with fourteen urban and rural district councils, and several Boards of Guardians.[301] Over the course of the early 1920s, a further eight local authorities were added to the list, which continued to expand into the 1930s. As Chris Williams put it in the year 2000, in parts of South Wales '1919 was the beginning of an – as yet – unbroken sway over the local state'.[302] Moreover, Labour prided itself on being an inclusive movement representative of the whole of the working class, one which brought the entire community together. The Monmouthshire County Council Labour group boasted in 1928, for instance, that:

The present County Council consists of forty nine Labour members ... drawn from miners, ministers of religion, schoolmasters, engineers, miners' agents, checkweighers, insurance agents, welfare and institute secretaries, co-operators and businessmen. There is one Labour woman councillor. One is the general secretary of the South Wales Miners' Federation – the Right. Hon. Thomas Richards. All the Labour members have had good practical training for public affairs, either in the trade unions, the co-operative movement, or business.

In urban district councils in mining areas, such a list of backgrounds might be less broad, but those elected to council positions from the Labour Party generally shared the characteristics of effective 'training for public affairs' gained from the labour movement itself and, in the words of one South Walian, were people 'who have lived our lives, known poverty, and should be able to represent our interests best'. Labour's electoral success suggests this was hardly an unusual judgement.

Nor was the appeal to women's political activity a cynical one. Following the advent of limited parliamentary suffrage in 1918 and the establishment of individual membership of the Labour Party in the same year, the entire basis of women's organisation was remodelled with the Women's Labour League disbanded and women's sections established in its place. A full-time organiser, Elizabeth Andrews, was appointed to oversee developments and she often assisted with the establishment of sections in areas where the Women's Labour League had not been present, such as Tredegar and Treherbert.[303] Following a visit by Elizabeth Andrews in May 1919, when she urged those present to get involved in local government, women in Tredegar signalled their intention to form a women's section. This was in place by early 1920, affiliated to the Trades and Labour Council, and had as many as sixty members.[304] Regional advisory councils took up the work formerly done by the district committee. Those in East Glamorgan and Monmouthshire were particularly effective campaigning on maternity and child welfare, pensions for widows, birth control, healthcare, and nursery schools.[305] The women's sections organised women's days, mass demonstrations, and a range of cultural and social activities, as well as being firmly part of the electoral machinery of the Labour Party. In a signal of their confidence in the early 1920s, mass demonstrations of women's sections on women's days in Newport saw banners declare 'the day is dawning'.[306] By the end of the decade there were nearly one hundred sections in East Glamorgan alone, with scores elsewhere in Glamorgan and in Monmouthshire.[307]

Of course, the period when Labour came into local office, 1918-1921, was marked by the emergence of a boisterous, left-wing, would-be alternative in the form of the CPGB, and by the degradation of the economic settlement hard-won by the coal miners before the First World War. Both forced the Labour Party to consider its response carefully, searching for ways of mediating away through the turbulence of the interwar economy and of countering the more left-wing message by implementing practical and effective policies. The post-war temper, after all, was framed by Lloyd George's (ultimately failed) offer of a land fit for heroes. In the words of one ILP member in conversation with the future novelist Jack Jones: 'You ex-service men came home expecting to have everything on the plate, didn't you? And here you are without bread in the house'. Jones had returned home to Merthyr in 1919 from active service on the Western Front. In the summer of 1920, with the economy still reasonably buoyant, he treated his family to what he described as a blissful holiday in Weston-Super-Mare complete with a banquet. 'Beef, tender and plenty of it, potatoes and greens and pudding to follow – oh, a grand dinner'. Six months later, there was a slump in the coal trade which 'had us wanting food … three shifts a week was all the pit was working, and there were days when there was not even bread in the house … Talk about hard times'.

For Jack Jones, 'bitter as gall, and ready for anything', a speech given by Noah Ablett, by then the miners' agent for Merthyr

Tydfil, convinced him that there needed to be a more radical solution than that offered by the coalition government led by Lloyd George or by the Labour Party. He joined the South Wales Socialist Society. 'In less than a month after joining I was on the stump telling all within sound of my voice what I thought of a Government which had treated us ex-service men the way I said it had'.[308] The South Wales Socialist Society had been formed in Cardiff in 1919 out of the revitalised Unofficial Reform Committee and Rhondda and Pontypridd Districts Socialist Society, ostensibly to bring unity to the labour movement in South Wales but nevertheless directly opposed to the Independent Labour Party. Its chair was William Ferris Hay and its most significant achievement was the publication of a sequel to the *Miners' Next Step* – *Industrial Democracy for Miners: A Plan for the Democratic Control of the Mining Industry* published in 1919. Guided by a theory of class warfare, it was soon part of the constellation of left-wing societies that responded to the formation of the Communist International in Moscow in March 1919 by setting out to form a communist party in Britain.[309] The first wave of negotiations began in June 1919 and were attended by D. A. Davies, secretary of the South Wales Socialist Society.[310] Eventually Davies was replaced by Frank and George Phippen and Ness Edwards, since they were resident in London – as students at the Central Labour College – on the basis that this would save the South Wales Socialist Society money in train fares back and forth to the meetings.[311]

In the spring of 1920, amidst protracted negotiations that became increasingly fraught over the issue of affiliation to the Labour Party, a key demand of the British Socialist Party, the largest body involved in the negotiations, the South Wales Socialist Society ceased to exist with most branches reforming under the banner of the Socialist Labour Party. The SLP's policy was non-affiliation. Previously almost non-existent in South

Wales, save for individual activists such as the Cardiff-based conscientious objector, A. E. Cook, this gave the SLP a much more significant presence in the coalfield, particularly in Abertillery, Aberdare, Barry, Cardiff, the Rhondda, and Gwaun-Cae-Gurwen near Ammanford.[312] Although not every South Walian participant followed the same path to non-affiliation, most were committed to the idea and it was evidently the position of the South Wales Communist Council which came into being in the summer of 1920 as the new South Wales umbrella group. Some followed the lead of Sylvia Pankhurst, the most prominent voice in favour of an anti-parliamentary, anti-affiliation stance for the Communist Party, and joined her rival Communist Party (British Section of the Third International) when it was formed in London in June 1920.[313] The chair at the CP (BSTI)'s inaugural conference was, indicatively, D. A. Davies.[314] This was unsurprising since he had previously sought to position the South Wales Socialist Society in support of Pankhurst in 1919.[315]

Others joined the Communist Unity Group, an initiative organised from within the SLP that sought to achieve a single communist party by offering an affiliation vote after a year – on the basis the BSP branches would recognise in that year that joining the Labour Party would not work.[316] The attempt led the SLP executive to repudiate those involved and most stepped away from the SLP. In Cardiff, for example, this led to the reformation of the SLP branch as the nominally independent Cardiff Socialist Labour Party as a protest at the heavy-handed response of the SLP executive. It is perhaps telling that the Welsh contribution to the unity convention which formed the Communist Party of Great Britain in London in July 1920 was largely drawn from the ranks of the Communist Unity Group, rather than any other body. Indeed, the contribution was fragmentary and did not speak with a single voice. There were representatives of the British Socialist Party (namely the Merthyr Vale branch), members of the Caerphilly Central Labour College class, Ferndale Socialist Society (the representative was Charlie Gibbons of the Unofficial Reform Committee), and the CUG branches from Aberdare, Abertillery, Cardiff, and Trethomas. The leading figure amongst them was William Hewlett of the Abertillery CUG, who was elected onto the CPGB's provisional committee.

But who exactly was William Hewlett? Hewlett had been involved in radical politics prior to the First World War and was a member of the anarchist workers' freedom group established in the town at that time. During the war, he was active in anti-war campaigns and in the no-conscription movement, helping to smuggle individuals (including Arthur Horner) out of South Wales to Ireland. He also developed networks to smuggle bomb-making equipment and gunpowder to Ireland via Liverpool.[317] Following the formation of the South Wales Socialist Society, he was active in the Abertillery branch, and the key figure in the Communist Unity Group in Monmouthshire. Together with checkweigher Syd Jones of Blackwood, he established the Workers' Democratic Education League in July 1916 with support from Bargoed, Oakdale, Wattsville, Blackwood, and Abertillery. Jones was elected chairman and Hewlett secretary.[318] Hewlett willingly described his politics as revolutionary and determined, reflecting on the formation of the CPGB that 'I have looked forward, worked, and waited for the day when the British workers would assemble for an honest effort to form a real, live revolutionary Communist Party'.[319] He was, in effect, entirely typical of those who had developed politically in the non-Labour left before the First World War and who moved into the CPGB in the war's aftermath.

Hewlett's death in a railway accident in Russia in July 1921 provided the fledgling CPGB with its first martyr.[320] He was afforded a hero's funeral in Moscow and buried in the Kremlin Wall Necropolis. Hewlett had been in Russia as part of the British delegation to the World Trade Union Congress, a communist initiative to counter the social democratic International Federation of Trade Unions launched in Amsterdam in July 1919. Alongside him were Harry Pollitt, Robin Page Arnot, and Ellen Wilkinson, who was later Labour MP for Middlesbrough East (1924-1931) and Jarrow (1935-1947) but at this time was an active member of the CPGB. Hewlett's prominence in communist circles was evident when he, rather than others of the party, was asked to give the fraternal address on behalf of the CPGB to Comintern delegates at the Bolshoi Theatre in Moscow. Hewlett was introduced by Congress chair, Grigory Zinoviev. 'He recently arrived from the field of battle', Zinoviev remarked enthusiastically, 'where the coal miners' strike is raging'. Hewlett then rose to speak. His comments were indicative of the divisions between Labour and the CPGB:

> In the name of the British miners, I thank you with all my heart for the outstanding support that you and especially the Russian miners, have sent during their strike. [...Some] comrades, who had been honoured last year in Russia, betrayed us. I will name only [Jimmy] Thomas, [Robert] Williams, and [Ramsay] MacDonald. I am ashamed to say that they abandoned the miners, leaving them to struggle alone in a losing battle. The latest reports tell us that the miners are still struggling and will continue to struggle. [...] We vow that the British Communist Party will work without respite until the battle is won and the proletarian revolution reaps its harvest around the world.[321]

This division was underlined in the Caerphilly by-election held in August 1921 following the death of Alfred Onions, the

SWMF treasurer and the town's MP since 1918. The by-election set the CPGB against the Labour Party for the first time. The Labour candidate, Morgan Jones, was a controversial choice – a teacher in a mining constituency, as well as a conscientious objector imprisoned during the war, he had had to stress his own mining credentials during the selection process.[322] The communist candidate, Bob Stewart, a Scottish trade union organiser and conscientious objector, was still in prison as the campaign began.[323] Both men had been members of the No Conscription Fellowship. In standing against the Labour Party, the CPGB had sought to, in their words, 'demonstrate just how far and in what way revolutionary political action differs from the creeping thing the worker has learned to know and hate as parliamentarian'.[324] The division rested on the communist belief in revolutionary potential, theory and ideas, and Labour's belief in democratic socialism and action enacted through parliament and local government. Morgan Jones won comfortably, defeating his coalition rival by nearly five thousand votes and Stewart by more than eleven thousand. He became the first conscientious objector elected to parliament after the First World War. Most voters had favoured ballots over barricades.

For his part, Lloyd George, the coalition prime minister, believed that the rising tide of Labour could be halted if only the right message could be found to win South Walians back to the Liberal cause.[325] As one Liberal Party 'spy' wrote, 'a sustained attack on these South Wales Labour Constituencies would undoubtedly produce good results'.[326] This also proved to be a false assessment. Labour's position continued to be consolidated and the party proved easily able to defeat rivals to the left and right – it did so again at the Pontypridd by-election in 1922 and in that year's general election won every seat in South Wales except Monmouth, Newport, Swansea West, Llandaff and Barry, and the three Cardiff constituencies. But why?

The traditional lineaments of Labour's rise point not to the fringe activities of communists, anarchists, syndicalists, and Marxists of differing hues, but to the coming together of growing parliamentary representation, growing local government strength, the consolidated position of the ILP, co-operative societies, non-mining trade unions, trades and labour councils, and, above all, the radicalising position of the South Wales Miners' Federation. There is no reason to doubt this narrative. Certainly, as an organisation the CPGB, the strongest of Labour's rivals on the left, was very small: at the outset of the 1920s the party could claim no more than fifteen branches almost all of which were concentrated in the central part of the coalfield.[327] But this imbalance of numbers and relative organisational strength differed little from the earlier experience of the ILP when faced with the dominant position of the Liberal Party in the 1890s. The difference in the 1920s was that the CPGB branches focused not on political outcomes, which had been the hallmarks of Keir Hardie's ambitions for independent labour representation, but on the raising of a revolutionary consciousness. Thus, communists stressed, in the words of Charlie Gibbons, 'the vital work of the educational and industrial field'.[328] And for all that branches, such as Cardiff, could report 'very successful meetings' and 'good literature sales', or even that 'our Welsh comrades are out for efficiency and realise their responsibilities to the revolutionary movement', its influence and presence was limited by a lack of institutional representation.[329]

Those consciousness-raising activities are what justify a continued interest in what might otherwise be regarded as the 'froth' on the surface of mainstream political radicalism. After all, in the era of the Lib-Labs, men like James Winstone and Vernon Hartshorn, who were at the centre of mainstream Labour politics in South Wales by the beginning of the 1920s, were themselves regarded as the socialist froth atop the sensibleness of Mabonism. This serves as a reminder that Labour's rise was neither pre-ordained in its 'final' form, nor linear, in the traditionally-argued sense. That linearity too readily flattens out the many divergences that Labour as a consolidating force might have taken and which are reflected in the alternatives made peripheral by the priorities Labour set and took advantage of. It might have remained a willing annexe to the Liberal Party; it might have become a bombastic, 'patriotic' force along with Charles Stanton; it might have travelled down the road of rejecting parliament as the some on the far left urged, particularly the industrial syndicalists like William Ferris Hay. But it did not. Instead Labour adopted, through experience and because the social, economic, and cultural circumstances of the period allowed for (and demanded) it, a middle ground: pragmatic, plural, reflexive, rather than utopian, absolute, or revolutionary. In prioritising the ballot box and the institutional framework of democratic government, locally and nationally, it could translate radical political ideas such as Noah Ablett's industrial unionism into social democratic action.

The emergence of the CPGB coincided with the steady downturn in the mining industry, growing industrial unrest, and a willingness amongst mainstream figures to adopt and adapt some of the militant language of the new communist left. To speak forcefully the language of class consciousness rather than national identity (as had been the hallmark of the Liberal Party). In April 1921, on the cusp of the miners' lockout and renewed hostilities within the coal mining industry, James Winstone, SWMF President, issued a statement. Widely published, and equally widely read, it declared that the SWMF provided the 'shock troops of the proletarian army whose weapons are not guns or bayonets but basic human rights'.[330] Winstone died three months later and was therefore never able to guide his union towards the winning of those rights, but his tone was indicative of the direction that organised labour and the Labour Party were to take in the interwar years. The battle they were to fight was not grounded in communist ideology or the principles of revolutionary activity, of course, but in the long democratic struggle to establish fair working conditions, to secure a living wage, to construct decent, affordable housing, to provide effective healthcare and life-long education. To 'universalize the consumption of the best that society can afford', as Aneurin Bevan was to write many years later.[331] That was to be the principle on which Labour Country was constructed.

Notes

[1] *RL*, 29 June 1907.

[2] *RL*, 2 February 1907.

[3] *RL*, 3 May 1902.

[4] *RL*, 2 June 1906.

[5] T. I. Jones, 'The Riddle of Mining Royalties', *Economic Review* 15, no. 3 (July 1905), 271.

[6] Points reiterated in T. I. Jones, 'The South Wales Coal Trade', *Economic Review* 16, no. 1 (January 1906), 15-31.

[7] *RL*, 4 November 1905, 24 March 1906.

[8] *RL*, 21 April 1906.

[9] *RL*, 16 June 1906; *AL*, 23 June 1906.

[10] Richard Lewis, *Leaders and Teachers: Adult Education and the Challenge of Labour in Wales, 1906-40* (Cardiff, 1993), 54.

[11] Rhondda No. 1 District, *Minutes*, 15 October 1906.

[12] Robin Page Arnot, *South Wales Miners: A History of the South Wales Miners' Federation, 1898-1914* (London, 1967), 168.

[13] *RL*, 7 April 1906.

[14] *RL*, 26 September 1908.

[15] *RL*, 11 May, 14 December 1907. The three streams were, of course, co-operation, trades unionism, and political socialism.

[16] GA, DNCB/16/35, Locket's Merthyr Coal Company, Agent's Letter Book, 1906-1911: letter dated 31 July 1909.

[17] As above, letter dated 8 July 1909.

[18] As above, letter dated 8 January 1910.

[19] For a fuller analysis of John Hopla see my, 'Tonypandy 1910: Foundations of Welsh Social Democracy', in Quentin Outram and Keith Laybourn (eds.), *Secular Martyrdom in Britain and Ireland: From Peterloo to the Present* (London, 2018) and Dai Smith, *The World John Hopla Turned Around* (Treorchy, 2014).

[20] *RL*, 19 February 1916.

[21] *EEx*, 25 November 1908.

[22] *EEx*, 26 November 1908.

[23] *RL*, 12 December 1908.

[24] *EEx*, 30 November 1908.

[25] *RL*, 19 December 1908.

[26] *AL*, 16 October 1909.

[27] Locket's Merthyr Agent's Letter Book, letter dated 12 September 1910.

[28] *RL*, 8 October, 15 October 1910.

[29] Locket's Merthyr Agent's Letter Book, letter dated 11 December 1910.

[30] *Weekly Mail*, 8 October 1910.

[31] *CT*, 8 October 1910.

[32] *CT*, 15 October 1910; *MEx*, 5 November 1910; *AL*, 12 November 1910.

[33] Williams, *Capitalism, Community and Conflict*, 41.

[34] *Weekly Mail*, 4 August 1900. These strikes are discussed in Daryl Leeworthy, 'A Workers' Village: John E. Morgan, the Labour Movement and the Politics of the Past in Ynysybwl, 1880-1920', *North American Journal of Welsh Studies* (2014). See *Weekly Mail*, 3 September 1910 for the spread of the non-unionism issue to the village in that year as well.

[35] *WM*, 5 October 1906.

[36] *GG*, 5 October 1906.

[37] *GG*, 25 September 1908; *Weekly Mail*, 19 September 1908.

[38] What follows draws on Dai Smith, 'Tonypandy 1910: Definitions of Community', *Past and Present* 87 (1980), 158-184, and my own, 'Foundations of Social Democracy'. See also, Dai Smith, *In the Frame: Memory in Society, Wales 1910 to 2010* (Cardigan, 2010).

[39] *RL*, 3 September 1910; *SWDP*, 8 September 1910.

[40] *CT*, 10 September 1910.

[41] *RL*, 10 September 1910. Tom Smith's speech is also reported in this edition.

[42] This may be compared with the observation by Morgan James John, the manager at the Lady Windsor Colliery, in 1913, that miners in Ynysybwl took jobs at the valley's drift mines where 'they are paid higher wages than by the Lady Windsor Colliery. Our colliers are much keener on looking out for their own money'. RHP, RHOHP.2015.3, Lady Windsor Colliery Copy Letter Book, 1913-1914: letter dated 14 July 1913.

[43] *RL*, 6 August 1910.

[44] *RL*, 17 September, 24 September 1910.

[45] *CT*, 1 October 1910.

[46] *CT*, 29 October 1910. The Aberdare dispute began unofficially on 20 October. *AL*, 5 November 1910.

[47] For instance, *BH*, 4 November 1910 which reported that sergeant Dan Griffiths and several constables from Barry had been 'hurried off to Aberaman'.

[48] *AL*, 5 November 1910; *SWDP*, 4 November 1910.

[49] *SWDP*, 5 November 1910.

[50] SCOLAR: *Coal War Bulletin: Manifesto by Aberdare Miners* (1910); This was also published in *Justice*, 3 December 1910.

[51] Martin Barclay, 'The Slaves of the Lamp: The Aberdare Miners' Strike, 1910', *Llafur* 2, no. 3 (1978), 24-42; Rudyard Kipling, 'Slaves of the Lamp, Part I', *Cosmopolis: A Literary Review* (April 1897).

[52] D. K. Davies, 'The Influence of Syndicalism and Industrial Unionism on the South Wales Coalfield, 1898-1922: A Study in Ideology and Practice' (Unpublished PhD Thesis, 1994), 42.

[53] *The Cambrian*, 4 November 1910.

[54] *Justice*, 19 November 1910.

[55] *Justice*, 12 November 1910. This is based on a report sent by Mann on 7 November.

[56] Interview with Sarah Ann Jones and Margaret Williams, cited in Gwyn Evans and David Maddox, *The Tonypandy Riots, 1910-1911* (Plymouth, 2010), 65.

[57] *SWDN*, 8 November 1910.

[58] GA, ER22/4, Llwynypia Boys' School Log Book, 1892-1915: entry for 8 November 1910.

[59] *SWDP*, 9 November 1910.

[60] *SWDN*, 9 November 1910.

[61] Interview with John Wannell cited in Evans and Maddox, 68.

[62] Interview with PC Davies, cited in Evans and Maddox, *Tonypandy*, 73; this is based on an interview in the *Cambrian*. 11 November 1910.

[63] *RL*, 24 December 1910.

[64] *GG*, 11 November 1910.

[65] *CarmJ*, 11 November 1910.

[66] Llwynypia Boys' School, Log Book, entry for 9 November 1910.

[67] *Justice, 19 November 1910.*

[68] *AL*, 12 November 1910.

[69] As above.

[70] *GG*, 11 November 1910; *BH*, 11 November 1910.

[71] Two years earlier, as Smith shows in 'Tonypandy 1910', Mid Rhondda TLC affiliated to the workers' housing committee to press for reform of the sector. *RL*, 3 November 1908. In Swansea, newspapers reported that it was the policy of the town's Labour Party to drive private capital out of this form of investment. *The Cambrian*, 16 April 1909. And in Merthyr Tydfil, housing reform was placed at the forefront of municipal campaigns culminating in 1910 in an independent survey produced by Merthyr TLC. *Housing Conditions in the County Borough of Merthyr Tydfil: The Results of Investigations by the Merthyr Tydfil Trades and Labour Council* (Merthyr, 1910); *EEx*, 29 May 1905. The report was published in early July 1910. *AL*, 9 July 1910.

[72] *AL*, 12 November 1910.

[73] *AL*, 26 November, 3 December, 17 December, 24 December 1910.

[74] *AL*, 19 November 1910.

[75] Llwynypia Boys' School, Log Book, entry for 22 November, 25 November, 28 November 1910.

[76] *CT*, 26 November 1910.

[77] *RL*, 31 December 1910.

[78] *AL*, 31 December 1910.

[79] *Justice*, 14 January 1911.

[80] GA, DCON/78, Lionel Lindsay Diary, 1911: entry for 10 January 1911; *RL*, 14 January 1911.

[81] *RL*, 21 January 1911.

[82] *RL*, 25 February 1911.

[83] *RL*, 28 January, 29 April 1911; *Justice*, 6 May 1911.

[84] *RL*, 27 May 1911.

[85] Davies, 'Syndicalism and Industrial Unionism', 44.

[86] *RL*, 26 November 1910.

[87] *Justice*, 3 December 1910.

[88] *RL*, 17 December 1910.

[89] *The Industrial Syndicalist* 1, no. 3 (September 1910).

[90] D. K. Davies, 'William Ferris Hay, Noah Ablett and the Debate Over Working-Class Political Action in the south Wales coalfield, 1910-1914', *Llafur* 3&4 (1999), 89-100.

[91] *The Industrial Syndicalist* 1, no. 6 (December 1910). James Connolly was also present in the coalfield in this period, appearing as the guest of the ILP in Pontypridd and Cardiff in the summer of 1911. *Labour Leader*, 18 August, 25 August 1911.

[92] Davies, 'Syndicalism and Industrial Unionism', *passim*.

[93] *Encylcopédie Socialist* (Paris, 1913), 165. The translation is my own.

[94] *EEx*, 28 March 1907.

[95] *EEx*, 26 August 1907; *EEx*, 27 September 1905.

[96] *Weekly Mail*, 15 May 1909.

[97] *EEx*, 6 May 1910; Davies, 'Syndicalism and Industrial Unionism', 118.

[98] *EEx*, 18 June, 30 June 1910; *AL*, 4 June, 18 June, 25 June. 23 July, 27 August 1910.

[99] *Weekly Mail*, 29 October 1910.

[100] *AL*, 5 November 1910.

[101] *Monmouth Guardian*, 20 August 1915; *AL*, 4 September 1915

[102] Thompson, *British Political Culture*, 234-236; Philip Snowden, *The Living Wage* (London, 1912).

[103] *LL*, 13 February 1913.

[104] *RL*, 6 May 1911.

[105] *RL*, 15 July 1911.

[106] *Manchester Guardian*, 15 July 1911.

[107] *RL*, 19 August 1911.

[108] *Justice*, 26 August 1911.

[109] *RL*, 14 October 1911.

[110] *RL*, 2 September 1911.

[111] By this point the group of advanced men included Noah Ablett, W. H. Mainwaring, Noah Rees, George Dolling, William Ferris Hay, and A. J. Cook.

[112] NLW, W. H. Mainwaring Papers, 4, Notebook, 27 May-17 December 1911: Entries for 27 May, 29 May 1911. Gibbons had entered the orbit of Ablett and others in 1909 when 'quite by accident I happened to attend a debate at the Lewis Merthyr lodge room ... between Noah Ablett and Mardy Jones on the question of the relative merits of the Central Labour College as against Ruskin College'. Gibbons reached out to Ablett and 'my real education on trade unionism was begun'. *South Wales Worker*, 5 July 1913. Several debates on this theme took place between Jones and Ablett. The meeting described by Gibbons was likely that which took place in May 1909. *RL*, 29 May 1909. A further debate took place at the Queen's Hotel in Tylorstown on 24 August. *RL*, 2 September 1909.

[113] It was published by the Rhondda Socialist Newspaper Committee from the offices of the Welsh Democracy Printing Company at 31 Mill Street, Pontypridd. See the company registration file: TNA, BT 31/11560/89164 – Welsh Democracy Printing Company, 1906-c.1916. By 1913, the *South Wales Worker*'s offices were at 27 Upton Street, Porth.

[114] RPA, U DAR/x1/2/52, Correspondence 1965-1966: 'Notes of Interview with W. H. Mainwaring, 6 and 12 September 1966'. See also the draft copies of the *Miners' Next Step* in W. H. Mainwaring's papers held at the NLW. For a detailed discussion see David Egan, 'The Unofficial Reform Committee and the Miners' Next Step', *Llafur* 2, no. 3 (1978), 64-80.

[115] Unofficial Reform Committee, *The Miners' Next Step: Being a Suggested Scheme for the Reorganisation of the Federation* (Tonypandy: Robert Davies & Co, 1912)

[116] *RL*, 20 July 1912.

[117] See the appendix of documents in Egan, 'Unofficial Reform', 77.

[118] *RL*, 6 April 1912.

[119] *Justice*, 13 April 1912; *L'Humanité*, 25 March 1912. A similar interview, conducted with Vernon Hartshorn and George Barker, was published on 30 March 1912. Note also the material on the three

men in the *Encylcopédie Socialiste, Syndicale et Coopérative de L'Internationale Ouvrière* (Paris, 1913) which discusses the shifting formulations of the emerging radical left in Britain, particularly pages 189-191.

[120] Stanton first stood as Labour candidate for the East Glamorgan constituency in December 1910 and regarded himself as the rightful successor to Keir Hardie in Merthyr.

[121] T. I. Mardy Jones, likewise, stepped back from the radicalism he had displayed in the previously decade.

[122] That is William Brace (the veteran Lib-Lab MP for South Glamorgan and Mabon's successor as Federation president), Thomas Richards (Lib-Lab MP for West Monmouthshire and Federation secretary), and Alfred Onions (Federation treasurer).

[123] *RL*, 20 April 1912.

[124] Parliamentary Archives, David Lloyd George Papers, LG/C/10/2/29, 'Letters to and from David Lloyd George and H. Read, 13-14 November 1913'. D. A. Thomas likewise proposed to Lloyd George that Hartshorn be appointed to the Local Government Board in 1916, 'if appointments [are] made from outside civil service'. LG/F/43/5/2, letter from D. A. Thomas (Lord Rhondda) to David Lloyd George, 14 December 1916.

[125] Although K. O. Morgan suggested of Gill that 'there was ... a profound strain of patriotism in his makeup' and this prompted his 'rejection of ideas from abroad'. K. O. Morgan, 'Socialism and Syndicalism: The Welsh Miners' Debate, 1912', *Bulletin of the Society for the Study of Labour History* 30 (1975), 22-37. Compare this with the remark made by Ramsay MacDonald that 'in South Wales [...] racial temperament and economic hardship offered special promise for the Syndicalist propaganda'. *Syndicalism: A Critical Examination* (London, 1912), 43. A wider discussion of anti-British accusations made of syndicalism can be found in Paul Ward, *Red Flag and Union Jack: Englishness, Patriotism, and the British Left, 1881-1914* (Woodbridge, 1998), 90-93.

[126] SCOLAR, George Barker Scrapbooks.

[127] Morgan, 'Socialism and Syndicalism', 29.

[128] *The Syndicalist* 1, no. 3 (April 1912).

[129] *DH*, 12 December 1912.

[130] *Justice*, 9 November 1912.

[131] *Justice*, 26 July, 7 September 1912.

[132] *Justice*, 10 August 1912.

[133] *Justice*, 16 November, 7 December 1912.

[134] *AL*, 2 May, 23 May, 30 May 1914; *Justice*, 23 August 1913.

[135] For Blaenllechau see also the lengthy report in the *RL*, 12 October 1912. The Blaenllechau Workmen's Radical Club and Institute had a membership of three hundred and seventy eight and had been in existence roughly two years. Situated at 7 Commercial Street, it was ostensibly designed to disseminate Radical (i.e. Liberal) principles and to advance 'the cause of the Radical Party, for social intercourse, mental and moral improvement, and rational recreation'. It was raided because of drunkenness. Allegedly.

[136] *Justice*, 14 December 1912.

[137] *RL*, 9 November 1912.

[138] *RL*, 14 June 1913. The two men clashed at a further meeting a few weeks later. *RL*, 16 August 1913.

[139] The ISEL held its first annual general meeting, tellingly, at the Communist Club in Charlotte Street, West London, in February 1913. *The Syndicalist*, March-April 1913, 5.

[140] Lewis H. Mates, *The Great Labour Unrest: Rank-and-File Movements and Political Change in the Durham Coalfield* (Manchester, 2016), 149, 195. Mates records lecture tours to Durham conducted by Noah Rees in 1911 and W. F. Hay in 1912.

[141] For Swansea, see *Cambria Daily Leader*, 15 February 1913, which describes the Swansea Socialist Society as the 'Syndicalist split in the local Labour Party'. The Swansea Socialist Society was paralleled in the more well-known Rhondda Socialist Society, established by members of the Unofficial Reform Committee in 1911. According to one observer, 'the Rhondda Socialist Society emanated from the meetings in Tonypandy in the Aberystwyth Restaurant'. SWML, AUD/396: 'Interview of J. L. Williams conducted by David Egan, 24 April 1973'. A. J. Cook led an IDL branch in Porth. Paul Davies, *A. J. Cook* (Manchester, 1987), 18-19.

[142] *BDN*, 11 July 1913.

[143] *The Syndicalist*, February 1913, 4.

[144] *Cambria Daily Leader*, 12 May 1913.

[145] *South Wales Worker*, 19 July 1913. Cited Davies, 'Syndicalism', 60.

[146] *Rhondda Socialist*, 28 September 1912.

[147] See the comments made by J. H. Thomas in Carmarthen in 1909. 'Unless [Labour] were represented on public bodies, these permissive acts [e.g. on housing] would never be put into form'. *Weekly Mail*, 17 April 1909.

[148] *GFP*, 1 March 1912.

[149] *Abergavenny Chronicle*, 6 February 1914; *Cambria Daily Leader*, 28 March 1914.

[150] *South Wales Worker*, 13 June 1914; Robert Pitt, 'Educator and Agitator: Charlie Gibbons, 1881-1967', *Llafur* 5, no. 2 (1988), 72-83.

[151] *South Wales Worker*, 10 January 1914.

[152] The experience of growing up amongst the Dowlais Spaniards was relayed by Maria Fernandez in an interview with Hywel Francis. See: SWML, AUD/439, 'Interview with Maria Fernandez, 16 May 1974'. See also, SWML, AUD/200, 'Interview with Nicolas and Casimira Duenos (née Esteban), 11 December 1972'; Hywel Francis and Dai Smith, *The Fed: A History of the South Wales Miners in the Twentieth Century* (London, 1980), 11.

[153] *WM*, 2 June 1900.

[154] *Freedom* 15, 158 (June 1901), 23; *Freedom* 41, no. 440 (February 1927), 8. Mainwaring and del Marmol subsequently established the anarchist newspaper *The General Strike*, with its slogan 'watch your leaders' in October 1903.

[155] F. Manubens, 'Desde Londres', *Suplemento a la Revista Blanca*, 24 August 1901. Cited in James Yeoman, '*Salud y Anarquía desde Dowlais:* The Translocal Experience of Spanish Anarchists in South Wales, 1900-1915' in *International Journal of Iberian Studies* 29, no. 3 (2016), 278.

[156] As Sam Mainwaring discovered on his visit to Dowlais a few months earlier: the Spaniards were 'devoted to trade union principles, and strong in the belief that the worker's first duty is to

combine'. *Freedom* 15, no. 161 (September 1901), 48. Notice of Mainwaring's visit is reported in *Freedom* 15, no. 158 (June 1901), 23.

[157] *La Protesta* (Cadiz), 14 November 1901, 1 ; 5 December 1901, 2. In addition to Garcia and Bustamante, those involved were Francisco Puerta, Ponciano Gracia, Ábila Calpe, Manuel Rey, Florentino San Martin, José Arguelles, Constantino Bada, Pedro San Martin, Leon Serrano, Francisco Cruz, Edmundo Kaminski, and Juan del Mazo.

[158] *La Protesta*, 26 September 1901, 2-3.

[159] *Brecon and Radnor Express*, 23 July 1914.

[160] Hywel Francis, *Miners Against Fascism: Wales and the Spanish Civil War* (London, 1984), 35-6.

[161] *Brecon County Times*, 2 September 1915.

[162] *South Wales Weekly Post*, 25 July 1914; *Brecon County Times*, 23 July 1914; *Amman Valley Chronicle*, 23 July 1914.

[163] *Llais Llafur*, 6 November 1915; South Wales Miners' Federation, *Minutes*, 20 September, 18 December 1915.

[164] *Llais Llafur*, 12 June 1915.

[165] *Llais Llafur*, 25 August 1914.

[166] *Llais Llafur*, 28 August, 9 September,11 September 1915, 16 October.

[167] *Llais Llafur*, 28 October 1916; *Monmouth Guardian*, 27 October 1916.

[168] *Merthyr Pioneer*, 12 February 1916.

[169] *Llais Llafur*, 21 April 1917; South Wales Miners' Federation, *Minutes*, 12 May 1917.

[170] Although initially the SWMF Executive had authorised a district strike if the Spanish workers were not sacked. South Wales Miners' Federation, *Minutes*, 25 March 1916.

[171] South Wales Miners' Federation, *Minutes*, 25 March, 20 April 1918.

[172] *Llais Llafur*, 18 July 1914.

[173] *Tierra y Libertad*, 13 September 1911.

[174] *Tierra y Libertad*, 20 January 1915.

[175] *A Comuna* (Porto), 28 October 1923.

[176] Francis and Smith, *The Fed*, 13.

[177] *Brecon County Times*, 23 July 1914; *Llais Llafur*, 11 September 1915; *Tierra y Libertad*, 18 November 1914.

[178] *Merthyr Pioneer*, 8 July 1916.

[179] *Llais Llafur*, 1 August 1914.

[180] *Llais Llafur*, 26 June 1915.

[181] Francis and Smith, *The Fed*, 12.

[182] I am grateful to Maria Williams (née Fernandez) for her observations on the branch and for showing me her father's party membership cards, which included both the Dowlais ILP and Dowlais PSOE. Her father was member number three of the PSOE branch.

[183] *El Socialista* (Madrid), 20 June 1902, 11 March 1917. Maria Williams recalled copies of *El Socialista* being passed around the Spanish of Dowlais into the 1920s and 1930s. The range of connections to the regional left press in Spain was impressive and included: *La Voz Del Pueblo* (Santander), *La Lucha de Clases* (Bilbao), *La Guerra Social* (Barcelona), and *El Aurora Social* (Oviedo).

[184] *El Socialista*, 16 May, 20 June, 14 November 1902, 5 June 1903.

[185] *MEx*, 23 October 1909. The branches passed a resolution stating that 'we do desire to express our horror at the murder of Señor Ferrer by the Spanish authorities. We also express our sincere hope that our Comrades of Freedom in Spain will not be deterred from further fighting for their glorious cause'.

[186] Gerald H. Meaker, 'Civil War of Words: The Ideological Impact of the First World War on Spain, 1914-18', in Hans A. Schmitt (ed.), *Neutral Europe between War and Revolution, 1917-23* (Charlottesville, 1988), 2; Angel Smith 'From subordination to contestation: the rise of labour in Barcelona, 1898-1918', in idem (ed.), *Red Barcelona: Social Protest and Labour Mobilization in the Twentieth Century* (London, 2002), 38.-39.

[187] *Merthyr Pioneer*, 22 September 1917.

[188] As above, 20 October 1917.

[189] As above, 10 November 1917. This was undoubtedly encouraged by Sam Mainwaring Jr, the nephew of the Swansea-born Anarchist of

the same name (1841-1907), who was a prominent figure in the Neath Socialist Society and had previously been Secretary of the Briton Ferry ILP.

[190] *Merthyr Pioneer*, 27 October 1917, 4 May 1918.

[191] For instance, the appeal made by Abercraf and Dowlais Spaniards to act on the 1917 general strike in Barcelona. *Freedom* (London) 31, no. 341 (October 1917), 51.

[192] South Wales Miners' Library, AUD/251: 'Growing Up in Spanish Abercrave, lecture by Leandro Macho, 27 September 1976'; VID/38: 'Interview with Leandro Macho, 1985'.

[193] Torres was a donor to the Mexican-American anarchist newspaper, *Regeneracion*, from at least 1913. *Regeneracion* (Los Angeles), 8 November 1913. He was also sending money to the Cuban newspaper *Tierra* at around this time. *Tierra*, 10 August 1913. *Tierra y Libertad*, 10 February 1915, 25 December 1918.

[194] For Cardiff see: *Tierra y Libertad*, 8 September 1915. Maria Williams also recalled having Spanish family in Cardiff although not their political leanings.

[195] *La Protesta*, 8 February 1902. Albeit he is recorded on the census as Joseph, taking the anglicised form of his name, and in the Spanish press occasionally as José.

[196] *Tierra y Libertad*, 2 February 1905, 31 January 1907; *La Revista Blanca*, 3 November 1904.

[197] *Tierra*, 10 January 1910. Harris was then living at 14 Union Street, Dowlais. The branch went through several different names including *La Voz del Obrero* and *Pro Prensa*. *Tierra y Libertad*, 13 January, 28 April 1915, 10 April 1918.

[198] South Wales may be usefully compared with anarchist connections in London. See, for instance, Piettra di Paola, *The Knights Errant of Anarchy: London and the Italian Anarchist Diaspora (1880-1917)* (Liverpool, 2013); Constance Bantman, *The French Anarchists in London, 1880-1914: Exiles and Transnationalism in the First Globalisation* (Liverpool, 2013). For the instructive transatlantic context see: Travis Tomchuk, *Transnational Radicals: Italian Anarchists in Canada and the U.S., 1915-1940* (Winnipeg, 2015).

[199] Burge, *Gleaming Vision*, 42; *GFP*, 4 May 1916.

[200] See the table in John E. Morgan's handwriting setting out likely call-ups to the war effort from the Lady Windsor Colliery, c.1918. The original is held as part of the SWCC. Available online: http://cymru1914.org/en/view/archive_file/4032126/1 [Accessed 21 December 2017] Also Morgan's interventions on behalf of Edward Lloyd made to the Mountain Ash Tribunal in 1918. Available online: http://cymru1914.org/en/view/archive_file/4032053/.

[201] Morgan, *VWC*, 37-8.

[202] Bethuel eventually graduated from Bangor Normal College in 1920. Thereafter he taught at Abercynon Mixed School until his sudden death on 24 October 1925.

[203] *Merthyr Pioneer*, 11 March 1916.

[204] As above, 29 April 1916.

[205] Gwilym Smith (then aged 22) was a school teacher and a member of the English Congregational Church on New Road, Ynysybwl. His father, David Smith, was chairman of the Mynachdy Colliery Lodge and had been a Labour member on the Mountain Ash School Board before its abolition in 1904. Percy Kendall (then aged 23) was a platelayer from Abercynon then working on the Taff Vale Railway. Emrys Hughes (then aged 21) was a school teacher from Abercynon and had worked with Bethuel Morgan at Carnetown, he subsequently worked as a journalist and was a biographer of Keir Hardie (his father in law); he was elected Labour MP for South Ayrshire in 1946. Hughes held the seat until his death in 1969.

[206] *AL*, 20 May 1916.

[207] *Llais Llafur*, 20 May 1916.

[208] *Merthyr Pioneer*, 20 May 1916.

[209] *Abergavenny Chronicle*, 26 May 1916; *AL*, 27 May 1916.

[210] *Merthyr Pioneer*, 4 November 1916. Williams was a miner, a member of the NCF, and Secretary of the Llantrisant and Llantwit Fardre TLC. He was arrested on 26 April 1916. *Merthyr Pioneer*, 6 May, 27 May 1916.

[211] *Merthyr Pioneer*, 17 June 1916.

[212] As above, 1 July 1916. This impression was remarkably common. See, for instance, the report relative to Aneurin Parker and

Harry Morgan, both of Tonyrefail, whose health had been 'severely tested in prison, and has left its mark on them'. *Merthyr Pioneer*, 14 October 1916.

[213] *Western Daily Press*, 12 July 1916.

[214] *Merthyr Pioneer*, 22 July 1916.

[215] As above, 29 July 1916.

[216] As above, 21 October 1916.

[217] As above, 4 November 1916.

[218] For instance, the case of ILP organiser Rev. George Neighbour of Mountain Ash who was sent to Abergele and was subjected to weeks of field punishment for refusing to yield. *Merthyr Pioneer*, 20 May 1916.

[219] Burge, *Gleaming Vision*, 42.

[220] Echoing John Davies's observation that 'military conscription was a shattering blow to Liberal values'. John Davies, *A History of Wales* (London, 1994), 515.

[221] SWML, Interview with Len Williams by Dave Egan and Richard Lewis, 21 May 1974', AUD/282; 'Interview with George Protheroe by Alun Morgan, October 1972', AUD/309. Protheroe notes tellingly that 'Aberdare was more for war than Merthyr'. For Tumble see the interview with Jack John conducted by Merfyn Jones, 1 February 1973. John recalled that there were 'a lot of them'.

[222] SWML, AUD/314, 'Interview with Goronwy Jones by David Egan, 1 October 1972'.

[223] Anthony Mor-O'Brien, 'Patriotism on Trial: The Strike of South Wales Miners, July 1915', *WHR* 12 (1984), 76-104.

[224] Morgan, *Rebirth*, 173.

[225] Barry M. Doyle, 'Who Paid the Price of Patriotism? The Funding of Charles Stanton during the Merthyr Boroughs By-Election of 1915', *English Historical Review* 109, no. 434 (1994), 1215-1222.

[226] *The Spectator*, 4 December 1915.

[227] Cited in J. O. Stubbs, 'Lord Milner and Patriotic Labour, 1914-1918', *English Historical Review* 87, no. 345 (1972), 724.

[228] Doyle, 'Patriotism', 1219.

[229] *AL*, 22 April 1916.

[230] Parliamentary Archives, Lloyd George Papers, LG/11/2/21: Letter

from Emmeline Pankhurst, 30 September 1915. Other strong branches of the Union of Democratic Control existed in Merthyr and Ystalyfera; Aberdare ILP affiliated to the organisation in the aftermath of Stanton's by-election victory. *Merthyr Pioneer*, 6 February, 6 November, 4 December 1915; *Llais Llafur*, 21 November 1914.

[231] Parliamentary Archives, LG/D/11/2/24: Letter from Emmeline Pankhurst, 14 October 1915.

[232] As above, LG/D/11/2/25: Letter from Emmeline Pankhurst, 15 October 1915.

[233] *Merthyr Pioneer*, 3 April 1915.

[234] *Cambria Daily Leader*, 19 February 1915.

[235] *South Wales Weekly Post*, 6 February 1915.

[236] *Merthyr Pioneer*, 6 February 1915.

[237] As above, 25 November 1916.

[238] *AL*, 14 October 1916.

[239] *Merthyr Pioneer*, 11 November, 25 November 1916; *Cambria Daily Leader*, 10 November 1916.

[240] *Merthyr Pioneer*, 9 December 1916. A similar attitude was expressed by the clerk of Maesteg Urban District Council in 1916 and by Swansea's town clerk in 1919. *Glamorgan Gazette*, 10 November 1916; *South Wales Weekly Post*, 6 December 1919.

[241] *Merthyr Pioneer*, 17 November 1917.

[242] At the Welsh Divisional Conference in Merthyr in January 1916, as many as fifty branches were in attendance. *The Observer*, 23 January 1916.

[243] *Merthyr Pioneer*, 15 May 1915, 1 January 1916. The club rooms were at 2 Cardiff Road.

[244] As above, 15 January 1916. Syd Jones attended the Central Labour College and, in addition to his lodge duties, became an adult education tutor for the Blackwood and Abertillery districts. See: Lewis, *Leaders and Teachers*, 96.

[245] *Merthyr Pioneer*, 6 May 1916.

[246] As above, 15 April 1916.

[247] For a wider sense of the *Merthyr Pioneer* in this period see: Deian Hopkin, 'The Merthyr Pioneer, 1911-22', *Llafur* 2, no. 4 (1979), 54-64. See also, Labour Pioneer Press Ltd, *Registered Rules of the*

Labour Pioneer Press Ltd., Merthyr Tydfil (Merthyr Tydfil, 1915). A copy is held at the Bodleian Library, Oxford.

[248] *Merthyr Pioneer*, 11 September, 18 December 1915. William Phippen was also secretary, alongside W. H. Mainwaring, of the Rhondda Valleys' Anti-Conscription Committee. *Merthyr Pioneer*, 1 January 1916.

[249] As above, 9 October 1915.

[250] As above, 8 May, 15 22 May 1915; 24 June, 22 July 1916.

[251] As above, 16 January, 4 March, 24 June, 19 August 1916. The Tonyrefail branch had its own meeting rooms situated on Pretoria Road, Tonyrefail. *Merthyr Pioneer*, 26 August 1916.

[252] *Merthyr Pioneer*, 6 July 1918.

[253] It was initially relaunched as the Rhondda and District Socialist Society in 1916. *Merthyr Pioneer*, 14 October 1916.

[254] *Merthyr Pioneer*, 24 March 1917, 9 November 1918.

[255] *South Wales Weekly Argus*, 10 July 1909. The group also ran education classes based on readings from the works of Engels and the German socialist Ernest Untermann. *Plebs*, v. 1, no. 12 (December 1909), 250. Morris Evans was the minister of Memorial Baptist Church, Abertillery, between 1904 and 1906. Although born in Wales, Evans grew up in the United States and attended Bucknell University in Pennsylvania. *The Christian Register*, 19 October 1916.

[256] *South Wales Weekly Argus*, 18 June 1910; *DH*, 16 October 1915. Hodges had also been a tutor for the New Era Union in 1910. Lewis, *Leaders and Teachers*, 96.

[257] *Merthyr Pioneer*, 23 December 1916.

[258] For instance, William Hutchings, whose funeral in 1921 was entirely secular and featured 'hymns' such as the *Red Flag*. The *SWA* went so far as to call it a 'communist's interment'. *SWA*, 15 November 1921; *South Wales Gazette*, 18 November 1921.

[259] Davies, *Cook*, 26. Many of the documents from the file – TNA, HO 45/10743/263275 – were published in Deian Hopkin, 'A. J. Cook in 1916-18', *Llafur* 2, no. 3 (1978), 81-88.

[260] BodL, Milner Papers, MS Milner Dep 377, leaves 168-178; published in Aled Eirug, 'Spies and Troublemakers in South Wales', *Llafur* 12, no. 1 (2016).

[261] Francis and Smith, *The Fed*, 22.

[262] *Merthyr Pioneer*, 31 March, 16 June 1917.

[263] *Herald of Wales*, 16 June 1917. The resolution was moved by W. J. Edwards (1888-1962), a former Ruskin College student (1908-9) and at that time checkweigher at the River Level Colliery, Aberdare. In 1920 he was elected a county councillor for Labour, serving until 1946. See, W. J. Edwards, *From The Valley I Came* (London, 1956), 234. For Edwards' career see also a profile published in *AL*, 12 May 1956, to coincide with the release of the memoir.

[264] *Merthyr Pioneer*, 5 May 1917.

[265] As above, 15 April 1916.

[266] The transfer of the Irish allegiance being a key theme of Paul O'Leary, *Immigration and Integration: The Irish in Wales, 1798-1922* (Cardiff, 1998).

[267] *Glamorgan County Times*, 17 February 1923. The minute book for the Glamorgan Unionist Labour Committee is held at the National Library of Wales. NLW, GB 0210 CARCON/31, City of Cardiff Conservative Associations Records, Glamorgan Unionist Labour Committee, Minute Book, 1918-1930. Rowlands was elected to parliament as MP for Flintshire in 1935.

[268] Stuart Ball, *Portrait of a Party: The Conservative Party in Britain, 1918-1945* (Oxford, 2013), 269.

[269] *Home and Politics*, August 1925, 21.

[270] As above, November 1925, 16; December 1925, 16.

[271] As above, March 1926.

[272] See the account given to the national Labour Representation Committee by Dai Davies of the Merthyr and Dowlais TLC that September. LHASC, Labour Party Archive, LP/LRC/25/91-2, Letters from Dai Davies, 22-25 September 1905.

[273] For instance: the Dulais Valley in 1915, *Llais Llafur*, 10 July 1915; Garnant early in 1917, *Amman Valley Chronicle*, 1 March 1917; Ystalyfera in April 1917, *Merthyr Pioneer*, 7 April 1917; Gowerton in December 1917, *Herald of Wales*, 8 December 1917; Hirwaun early in 1918, *Merthyr Pioneer*, 19 January 1918; and Dunvant in October 1918, *Cambria Daily Leader*, 7 October 1918.

[274] *Merthyr Pioneer*, 24 June 1916. An attempt to affiliate to the

Mountain Ash TLC, which had reformed in 1914, was defeated. *Merthyr Pioneer*, 22 July 1916. For the Mountain Ash organisation see *AL*, 23 May 1914. The Ynysybwl TLC's secretary was F. J. Priday, a checkweigher at the Lady Windsor Colliery. *AL*, 2 March 1918. He had previously been chairman of the first formation of the Mountain Ash TLC and served as secretary of the Ynysybwl Medical Aid Society. *DH*, 7 July 1921.

[275] *Amman Valley Chronicle*, 11 October 1917.

[276] As above, 23 November 1916.

[277] *Cambria Daily Leader*, 30 April 1917. Griffiths served the council as secretary. A separate council for the Amman Valley had been formed previously. *Amman Valley Chronicle*, 22 March 1917.

[278] Williams, *Democratic Rhondda*, 76.

[279] Susan Demont, 'Tredegar and Aneurin Bevan: A Society and its Political Articulation, 1880-1929', (Unpublished PhD Thesis, 1990).

[280] *Merthyr Pioneer*, 25 September 1915.

[281] *AL*, 20 June 1914.

[282] *Cambria Daily Leader*, 30 August 1917.

[283] *Merthyr Pioneer*, 22 December 1917.

[284] *Herald of Wales*, 25 November 1916.

[285] *Merthyr Pioneer*, 14 October 1916. Williams, *Democratic Rhondda*, 102. This process was also apparent in the South Glamorgan Labour Party, which drew members from Llantrisant, Llantwit Fardre, and Tonyrefail, at its northern extent and from Barry at its southern extent, and in the Swansea Valley. *Merthyr Pioneer*, 11 March 1916, 31 March 1917. The South Glamorgan Labour Party had been formed in 1913. *Barry Dock News*, 8 May 1914. For the 'united action' in the Rhymney Valley see *Merthyr Pioneer*, 26 February, 29 April 1916.

[286] *Merthyr Pioneer*, 31 October 1914; *Aberdare Leader*, 20 June 1914.

[287] *Merthyr Pioneer*, 3 April 1915.

[288] Williams, *Democratic Rhondda*, 103.

[289] Deian Hopkin, 'The Rise of Labour: Llanelli, 1890-1922', in Geraint H. Jenkins and J. Beverley Smith (eds.), *Politics and Society in Wales, 1840-1922* (Cardiff, 1988), 172.

[290] *Merthyr Pioneer*, 19 January 1918.

[291] *EEx*, 19 April 1910.

[292] *AL*, 16 May 1903.

[293] *CT*, 7 March 1908; *AL*, 20 September 1902.

[294] *AL*, 13 March 1909.

[295] *Llais Llafur*, 6 June 1914; *Amman Valley Chronicle*, 11 June 1914; *Merthyr Pioneer*, 6 June 1914. It was initially called the Federation of Labour Representations for South Wales. The *Merthyr Pioneer*, proposed instead that it be called the South Wales Labour Council – prefiguring the later South Wales Regional Council of Labour.

[296] For district funding see, Williams, *Democratic Rhondda*, 104.

[297] Labour Party, *Report of the Twentieth Annual Conference* (London, 1920), 36.

[298] *Merthyr Pioneer*, 30 June 1917; T. I. Mardy Jones, *Colliery Rating Exposed* (Cardiff, 1917).

[299] *Glamorgan Gazette*, 26 December 1919; T. I. Mardy Jones, *The Good Government of Glamorgan: The Case for County Borough Areas* (Pontypridd, 1920).

[300] *DH*, 18 May 1921; *Yorkshire Post*, 18 May, 28 December 1921; *Northern Whig*, 23 February 1925; *Nottingham Journal*, 23 February 1925.

[301] Labour Party, *Annual Report* (London, 1920), 36; Williams, 'Challenge', 142.

[302] Williams, 'Challenge', 143.

[303] The minute book of the Treherbert Women's Labour Section for 1920-1921 is held, together with the minute books and other records of the Tynewydd Women's Labour Section for 1924-1934, at the Rhondda Heritage Park, Trehafod. RHO 2017.288-292. The Treherbert minutes record that the section was 'founded on Monday evening, 28 August 1920, inaugurated by Mrs Andrews, organiser in the Labour Party'. The branch affiliated to the local Trades and Labour Council in November 1920. The Tynewydd section was established in October 1924. I am grateful to Sara Brown and Kath Lewis for facilitating my access to these records.

[304] *DH*, 24 May 1919; *MEx*, 31 May 1919, 14 February, 24 April

1920. The section is considered by Demont, 'Tredegar', 65, 278, 347-8, whose discussion I have followed here. The branch president was Kathleen Vaughan, wife of D. J. Vaughan, Labour MP for the Forest of Dean, 1929-31. The branch secretary was Sarah Ann Moon (1876-1936), wife of Edward Henry 'Ted' Moon (1874-1932), vice president (1911-12) and president (1912-13) of Tredegar Trades and Labour Council and a member of the Bedwellty Board of Guardians and Tredegar Urban District Council. See Demont, 'Tredegar', 126, fn. 1. The branch treasurer was Mary Elizabeth Conway, wife of Walter Conway, secretary of Tredegar Medical Aid Society from 1915 and chairman of the Bedwellty Board of Guardians. Walter Conway was the 'first clearly identifiable socialist in Tredegar' and a Central Labour College tutor in the town. Demont, 'Tredegar', 90, fn. 1. Another of those active in the Tredegar women's section was a Mrs Edwards, a resident of the Sirhowy ward, who stood for election to Tredegar Urban District Council in 1931. *DH*, 12 February 1931.

[305] *DH*, 24 January 1922, 27 February 1925.

[306] *DH*, 11 June 1923.

[307] Evans and Jones, 'Women', 222.

[308] Jack Jones, *Unfinished Journey* (London, 1938), 187-191.

[309] *The Call*, 13 March 1919.

[310] *The Call*, 26 June, 21 August, 28 August, 10 November 1919.

[311] *Workers' Dreadnought*, 13 March, 15 May 1920; Walter Kendall, *The Revolutionary Movement in Britain, 1900-1920* (London, 1969) 385; LHASC, CP/CENT/COMM/10/03. Ness Edwards' involvement in the organisation of the Communist Party is not mentioned by Wayne David in his biography. Wayne David, *Remaining True: A Biography of Ness Edwards* (Caerphilly, 2006) Frank and George Phippen, the sons of William Phippen, had been conscientious objectors during the war and had escaped to Ireland to avoid conscription. George, the older of the two, had been kicked out of Pentre Labour Club for his anti-war views. SWML, AUD/394, 'Mr and Mrs D.J. Davies Interview, 1974'. George shared a room at the Central Labour College next door to Aneurin Bevan. Later in life he became an organiser for the CLC in London. Smith, *Aneurin Bevan*, 205; 'George Phippen', in J. Bellamy and J. Saville (eds.), *Dictionary of Labour Biography, Volume 5* (London, 1979), 179-181. For

Frank's CLC study see, Richard Lewis, 'The Central Labour College: Its Decline and Fall, 1919-1929', *Welsh History* Review 12, no. 2 (1984), 240-1. He was subsequently the first National Central Labour College organiser in Bristol.

[312] The experiences of the Socialist Labour Party in Gwaun-Cae-Gurwen are related by Glyn Evans in his oral testimony. See SWML, AUD/346, Interview with Glyn Evans, 5 March 1973. The most significant figure to emerge from the Socialist Labour Party in this area was D. J. Williams (1897-1972), later MP for Neath (1945-1964). Williams attended the Central Labour College (1919-1921) and Ruskin College (1923-24) and worked as a tutor for the National Council of Labour Colleges in Scotland in the 1920s before returning to Gwaun-Cae-Gurwen in 1931. He visited Moscow on a workers' delegation in 1934. See his, *Capitalist Combination in the Coal Industry* (London: Labour Publishing Company, 1924). My thanks to Hywel Francis for this information.

[313] Frank Phippen, for instance, was a regular correspondent of Pankhurst's *Workers' Dreadnought* (originally the *Woman's Dreadnought*) and for a period in 1919 wrote the paper's South Wales Notes. See, for an indicative flavour, the columns of 22 March and 29 March 1919.

[314] *Workers' Dreadnought*, 26 June 1920.

[315] *The Call*, 15 July 1920.

[316] The Communist Unity Group's manifesto was published in *The Call*, 29 July 1920. It dismissed the Labour Party as 'steeped to the neck in the respectabilities and conventions of the bourgeois democracy – a veritable rump of liberalism'. The CUG's Nottingham manifesto issued in April 1920 was signed by William Hewlett (Abertillery), J. W. Dyer (Aberdare), W. J. Edwards (Aberaman), D. R. Owen (Garnant), and A. E. Chappell (Cardiff).

[317] Francis and Smith, *The Fed*, 23; for details of the smuggling see: 'Max Goldberg interview, 1974', South Wales Miners' Library: AUD/347.

[318] *Merthyr Pioneer*, 22 July 1916. Not surprisingly the most effective branch was that based in Abertillery. *Merthyr Pioneer*, 5 August 1916. The group were renamed the Central Labour College League in November 1916 at the league's second major conference

held in Cardiff. *Merthyr Pioneer*, 9 December 1916. See also: Lewis, *Leaders and Teachers*, 114-115.

[319] *The Communist*, 5 August 1920.

[320] *The Communist*, 6 August 1921.

[321] John Riddell (ed.), To the Masses: Proceedings of the Third Congress of the Communist International, 1921 (New York, 2016), 89-91.

[322] His Federation opponent was William Harris, the SWMF Political Organiser. Morgan Jones's election literature, a copy of which is held in the Lloyd George Papers, stresses his links to mining and his time working underground. Parliamentary Archives, Lloyd George Papers, F/34/4/18. *Western Daily Press*, 8 August 1921.

[323] James Klugmann, *History of the Communist Party of Great Britain, Volume I: Formation and Early Years, 1919-1924* (London, 1969), 48. Bob Stewart (1877-1971). Born in Angus, Stewart grew up in Dundee and spent a period of time in South Africa at the start of the twentieth century. During the First World War he had been a member of the No Conscription Fellowship. A founder member of the CPGB, he became the party's spymaster and the British representative on the Comintern. He was described by the intelligence services as 'a secret agent for England on behalf of the Third International'. TNA, KV2/1180: Robert Stewart, 1920-1941. See also his, *Breaking the Fetters: The Memoirs of Bob Stewart* (London, 1967). See also the file of cuttings on the election held at the LHASC: CP/CENT/PL/08/02.

[324] *Communist*, 13 August 1921.

[325] Parliamentary Archives, Lloyd George Papers, F/167/2: 'Report on Caerphilly By-Election, 1921'.

[326] *Western Morning News* (Plymouth), 23 August 1921; 'Report on Caerphilly By-Election, 1921'.

[327] *The Communist*, 12 August 1920.

[328] *Communist Unity Convention: Official Report*, 12.

[329] *The Communist*, 26 August, 21 October, 28 October 1920. The secretary of the Cardiff branch was A. E. Chappell, 72 Salisbury Road, Cathays, formerly of the Socialist Labour Party.

[330] *DH*, 13 April 1921.

[331] Aneurin Bevan, *In Place of Fear* (London, [1952] 1962 edn), 200.

CHAPTER FOUR

And Quiet Flows the Taff

On Tuesday, 22 February 1921, a special conference of the Miners' Federation of Great Britain opened at Central Hall in Westminster. On its agenda was the question of unemployment. One by one, delegates from South Wales stood up to testify to the ravaging effects of the economic downturn on their communities. A. J. Cook got to his feet. 'The national federation', he complained, had a 'lack of fighting spirit'. He looked around the hall, perhaps hoping to catch the gaze of those on whom he turned his fire:

> I am told by many older men that we must try again constitutional methods, that is Parliament [...] That is why we are getting no further. If we cannot move Parliament to do something we ought to be able to do it ourselves. We have been talking about control of the industry. We have talked about national combination. We have, first of all, to destroy the system, if we have come to the conclusion that there is no solution under this present system.[1]

Some such as S. O. Davies, miners' agent for Dowlais, cheered. Others, such as Thomas Richards, the moderate, pragmatic secretary of the South Wales Miners' Federation, gave visible indication of their lack of enthusiasm for Cook's interpretation of current events. They understood, nevertheless, that unless action was taken to deal with unemployment, South Wales would continue to suffer. Addressing delegates directly, Richards stated 'you are not feeling it so acutely, your pits are working regularly, and there are not starving men, women and children – if you had you would begin to cry out yourself'. In the end, the South Wales delegates were defeated in their call for national action. Even armed with a special report compiled for the SWMF executive which showed a higher percentage of unemployment in South Wales compared with coalfields in England, they were unable to win the day.

Growing unemployment contrasted with the return of the coal industry to private hands after wartime control. Although the miners vehemently protested the rush to push re-privatisation through parliament, the Decontrol Act passed unhindered. The coal owners seized the opportunity to announce revised wage structures. In South Wales, there was to be a considerable downward revision from the highpoint of nearly twenty two shillings per shift reached just a few months earlier. Cook warned at mass meetings that the likely reduction would be as much as fifty percent, a prediction that proved accurate. A showdown was inevitable. On 31 March 1921, the government surrendered control of the industry; the wage revision notices issued by the coal owners became effective. The following day, on 1 April, the coal mines of Britain, together with over a million workers, stood idle.

Speaking in parliament on 5 April, Sir Robert Horne, the newly appointed Chancellor of the Exchequer (he had come into office on 1 April), questioned the legitimacy of the stoppage:

> The Miners' Federation does not contest, indeed it acknowledges the fact that the industry cannot pay today the wages they are asking, because the money is not there, and the prices will not yield proceeds sufficient to it, and that is why they are asking for a subsidy. Can you say that a reduction in wages which is involved in an economic system like that is a deliberate attack on wages? Is it to be said that in every case

you can construe it as a deliberate attack on wages if the government refuse to come forward to subsidise a particular industry in order to give them the wages they want? I leave that to the judgement of the House.

Speaking later in the debate, Vernon Hartshorn responded by drawing attention to the situation in South Wales:

We are offered our pre-war wages, plus forty six per cent, while the cost of living is one hundred and forty one per cent above pre-war times. We are asked to meet that additional cost with forty six per cent increase on our pre-war wages. That is an absolutely hopeless proposal. It is a wage on which people cannot make both ends meet in this high cost of living. ... The government can exert pressure and exert their authority, but they can only do it when they are helping to mould a fresh policy and that is what they should set about doing. We can all make fiery speeches but they are no good. The government should adopt an attitude of the kind of which I am certain is being adopted by everybody on our side because we are anxious to avoid a repetition of this kind of thing, and we are anxious to get a settlement at the present time.

His pragmatism went unheeded.

Speaking in Maesteg a week later, Hartshorn expressed disbelief that the situation had arisen. 'The people who are responsible for the government are going to see our civilisation swamped because the miners are asking for a reasonable standard of existence', he said. But he was also aware of the potential for dangerous splits in the SWMF's collective decision-making processes and warned that members should not allow individual lodges to 'imagine that they could run a better policy locally'.[2] It was a thinly veiled barb. Four months earlier,

Hartshorn had resigned from the SWMF executive after being subjected to abuse from the SWMF's left-wing, declaring that 'he was not going to surrender his own judgement, based on years of experience, at the behest of any "ginger group", and he refused to be dictated to by the extremist section'.[3] The division rested on the appropriate response to the economic situation in the mining industry, both aimed at avoiding sectional wage agreements that were damaging to South Walian living standards. By early 1921, South Wales coal was being mined at a loss of one pound per ton, whereas nationally the rate was seven shillings. Hartshorn was firm in his belief in the need to remove trade tariffs to grow exports and the pragmatic willingness of miners to meet output targets through increased working time, on the one hand, and the coal owners to reduce profits on the other; for the unofficial reform committee the response was a reduction of output and working time per head with a view to increasing employment.[4]

Hartshorn was not unduly reticent in his attacks on the government and the coal owners. He stressed his view that 'the policy of both ... is sinister ... That is, the desire to restore at all costs the power and prestige of private enterprise, which has been shaken and menaced during the war by the power of collectivism'. The moderate position was, in fact, taken by Frank Hodges, the general secretary of the Miners' Federation of Great Britain, and formerly miners' agent for the Garw district, who reflected that a reduction in wages was inevitable and that all steps should be taken to avoid industrial action since, 'if they approached the question after two or three weeks' lock-out, it would ... be a calamity of the first order to drift into such a lock-out, and then begin negotiating'. The coal owners' terms would be even more stringent. Hodges caused controversy when he appeared to suggest that the demand for a national wages board be temporarily dropped to enable further negotiations, but it was a position shared by the MFGB's president, Herbert Smith, as well.[5] Hodges and Smith were defeated at a national conference on 21 March, when delegates voted to campaign for a national wages board. It became the central demand of the South Wales miners during the three-month lockout. As Noah Ablett put it, 'we will fight till the last gasp'.[6]

Women too took up the political struggle. At a meeting of the Pontypridd Women's Labour section in April 1921, a resolution was passed demonstrating the effects of the lockout on all parts of the community. Their own stance on the lockout was readily apparent:

> This meeting of miner's wives held at Pontypridd stands firm by our husbands in this great struggle for the 'rights to live' realising as Chancellors of the Exchequers of the home that the wages offered to our families to exist upon with the present cost of living and would reduce our status below poverty line.

A few weeks later, the section organised a rally at the Park Cinema addressed by Hettie Jones, a councillor from Bargoed, at which women's views on the proposed wage revisions for mineworkers were presented and debated. They placed an advertisement in the newspaper inviting men along to hear the views of the assembled women.[7] There was even a demand in the aftermath of the lockout from the Monmouthshire Women's Labour Advisory Committee that women be permitted to attend lodge meetings.[8] This was not a debate that was discretely about the mining industry and its own concerns: strikes, lockouts, and living standards impacted on the entire community.

Indeed, the lockout had a tremendous impact, exacerbating the coalfield's postwar economic fragility, and there was widespread suffering by the end of the dispute. Strike pay amounted to little more than a few shillings a week. 'I do not think in the Welsh coalfield', Hartshorn stated in early June, 'any of the miners have received from the Federation payments amounting in the aggregate to £1'.[9] Families survived through meals from soup kitchens and school feeding programmes – by the end of April eleven thousand children were being fed in Rhondda's schools and nearly eight thousand in Merthyr.[10] Business fluctuated in shops and cinemas, as did wages. At Llanbradach Workmen's Hall staff were placed on day to day contracts and eventually had to take a thirty-five per cent pay cut to keep the hall open.[11] And teachers bore the burden of providing and supervising school meals once the School Feeding Acts had been implemented by local education committees.[12] As the lockout dragged on, teachers became increasingly concerned that they would be overwhelmed during the midsummer vacation and lose their holiday, as they had during Whitsun when it was suspended. The local head teachers' association and the NUT made representations to the education committee to begin feeding away from schools, particularly during the summer, but the lockout ended before resolutions were considered.[13]

When the lockout ended towards the end of June 1921, with the coal owners victorious, families were left to pick up the pieces, and the SWMF to face up to the challenges ahead. Speaking in the Rhondda, Vernon Hartshorn painted a stark future. 'A period of reaction had set in', he said, 'but the workmen had concentrated upon disagreement between each other, whereas one of the lessons they should have learned was the great need for unity in their ranks'. Lodges in the Eastern Valley District had called for the resignations of the entire SWMF and MFGB executives.[14] Hartshorn repeated the message in Aberdare, denouncing the attitude of the coal owners as 'the most dishonourable episode in the history of mining'. The consequence of the lockout was that the employers would get a greater profit in relation to wages than under any agreement that had ever been made for the Welsh coalfield; whilst the wages of the men would be so low as to compel them to adopt a standard of living lower than any obtained during the past fifty years.[15]

For the fifty or sixty thousand miners who were unemployed by the autumn of 1921, conditions were even worse. The SWMF set up a levy of seven shillings a week to help sustain those miners during their period of unemployment, but it struggled to afford it much beyond the end of October. Hartshorn could point, too, to the destitution of miners who were in employment because of the reduction in their wages. As he put it in parliament:

> Out of earnings they had four pence go to the doctor's fund, three pence to the library, four pence to the hospital, five pence to health insurance, seven pence to unemployment insurance, one shilling and four pence for coal, seven shillings and six pence for rent, and six pence to the Federation. That was eleven shillings and three pence per week continually deducted.[16]

A week's wage might only be twelve or fifteen shillings, oftentimes less – the minimum wage won in 1912 had ceased to exist.

Politically, the response to the failure of the 1921 lockout was fractious. The SWMF membership were pushing and pulling in multiple directions, some more radical than others, although most recognised, as A. J. Cook did, that 'it will be impossible to get peace with the mining industry under private ownership'.[17] The tensions were apparent at the SWMF's annual conference held in Cardiff in July when over two hundred delegates debated the lockout and the wage settlement that had been imposed on them by the coal owners. Famously, by a vote of one hundred and twenty to sixty three, the conference urged the MFGB to affiliate to the Red International of Labour Unions (the communist trade union organisation), although it was regarded by Vernon Hartshorn as a 'matter of little moment', one that was 'little more than the academic expression of opinion by the more ardent spirits'.[18] Certainly it was something of a headline distraction: other motions at the conference included one from Nile Mile Point and the Tredegar Combine lodges calling on the SWMF to withdraw its support for the Central Labour College because of its links to Marxian teaching.[19] And there was the wider question of what to do about rapidly falling membership and its attendant consequences: between 1920 and 1922, SWMF membership collapsed from one hundred and ninety seven thousand to just eighty seven thousand with influence on the MFGB executive consequently reduced as a result.[20]

The 1921 lockout set out the battle lines of the conflict that was to dominate the interwar years. Colliery owners, victorious at each stage, victimised those they wished to get rid of, with lodges forced to seek their own ways of taking the fight to the owners locally.[21] At Ynysybwl, the Lady Windsor lodge refused the company's terms on rent reductions and sought the assistance of the local council, by then dominated by Labour councillors, to prosecute for provision of poor quality housing.[22] In nearby Abercynon, Emrys Hughes, the wartime conscientious objector, stood for the ILP at the urban district council elections in the Spring of 1922 in order to dislodge Dr Isaac Morris, the chairman of the Joint Standing Committee, in protest at the heavy deployment of police during the lockout.[23] And Vernon Hartshorn urged faith in the possibilities of the Parliamentary Labour Party. 'Although Labour might not take over the reins of government', he said at a rally in Pontypridd, 'he had no doubt that the crowd at present in Parliament would be replaced by a sturdy body of labour men, in a position to dominate the policy of any government that might be in office. Then they would be able to shake off the iniquitous agreement'.[24]

Hartshorn's faith in the rising parliamentary position of Labour was no doubt encouraged by the series of by-election victories in the South Wales Coalfield in 1921 and 1922, notably Caerphilly and Pontypridd. The victory of Thomas Isaac Mardy Jones over the Liberal, and would-be government minister, T. A. Lewis, in Pontypridd in 1922 certainly helped to precipitate the Coalition's collapse. When the country went to the polls in November 1922, Labour increased its parliamentary representation by more than eighty seats, including many of the seats in Glamorgan that had been won by the Coalition government in 1918. Notable amongst the seats won were Aberdare and Merthyr, both lost in 1918. In the former, where the miners' official George Hall won, Labour stressed Charles Stanton's links to the Conservative Party and the coal owners. 'We notice', Labour remarked caustically in its election newspaper, 'that Mr Stanton commenced his campaign in the Conservative Club. We are not surprised'.[25] Stanton denounced his opponents as 'ILP cranks, communist lunatics, and the wild men of the woods'.[26] In the event, 'the flag-wagging Miners' Agent – the Britisher – who deserted his Party in 1915 was beaten to a frazzle'.[27] Stanton settled in Hampstead and ran a pub, taking occasional work as an actor. He died, in obscurity, in 1946. Merthyr was won by R. C. Wallhead (1869-1934), a conscientious objector, a city councillor in Manchester, and the then chairman of the ILP. He held the seat until his death.

Labour's electoral programme in Aberdare included new housing and the nationalisation of both the railways and the mines, policies that were overwhelmingly popular in that constituency, as they were across South Wales.[28] In Aberdare, Labour's majority nearly doubled between 1922 and 1924, and was almost four times as large by 1929. In Merthyr it rose from around two thousand to more than fourteen thousand over the same period. What the party offered at elections was increasingly visionary, emblematic of Labour's growing confidence and professionalism in the early 1920s. As the party's 1923 parliamentary manifesto stated:

> Labour policy is directed to the creation of a humane and civilised society. When Labour rules it will take care that little children shall not needlessly die; it will give to every child equality of opportunity in education; it will make generous provision for the aged people, the widowed mothers, the sick and disabled citizens. It will abolish slums, promptly build a supply of decent homes and resist decontrol till the shortage is satisfied. ... Labour stands for equality between men and women: equal political and legal rights, equal rights and privileges in parenthood, equal pay for equal work.

At a time when wages and living standards were falling and unemployment was rising, such a vision was attractive to voters. In 1924, Labour formed its first minority administration.[29] The same year, it appeared that the militants had gained momentum in the trade union movement, notably in the MFGB with the election of A. J. Cook as general secretary and the SWMF with the election of S. O. Davies as vice president. And the militants were hardly supportive of the Labour government itself, claiming that the MFGB had spent nearly seventy thousand pounds to get Labour elected and were being 'treated in the most contemptuous manner by Labour's figurehead'.[30] That was, by Ramsay Macdonald. Macdonald who, as prime minister and foreign secretary, was busy renegotiating the international reparations treaty with Germany and other international partners; and the militants charged that the new arrangements would flood the British market with cheap German coal to the detriment of the already vulnerable British coal industry, fears similarly expressed in cabinet by Vernon Hartshorn. In the event, this did occur under the Conservatives when they returned to power at the end of 1924 and was a contributory factor leading to the General Strike in 1926.

In Power, Not in Office

The early 1920s were a period of consolidation for the Labour Party, especially in areas where power had been secured at the local level. Despite swingeing budget cuts from central government and the turbulence of industrial unrest and steadily increasing unemployment, Labour looked to democratise society as far as possible, and to encourage an engaged model of citizenship. To make the most of being in power locally, but not in governmental office. Using grants available through the Miners' Welfare Fund, which was established by the post-war coalition government in 1920, Labour expanded local welfare on a colossal scale transforming the landscape of the coalfield. New playing fields, swimming pools, playgrounds, institutes, public halls, and libraries were all opened, with more than one and a quarter million pounds (around seventy five million pounds today) spent on amenities of this kind during the 1920s and 1930s. A further five hundred thousand pounds (or almost thirty million pounds today) was spent on expanding healthcare provision in addition to the existing medical aid societies. The welfare committees that were established to administer grant applications and to oversee the projects that were funded adopted structures migrated from trades union practice, instilling in this new model of public welfare the same democratic instinct found elsewhere in the labour movement.

The Miners' Welfare Fund was administered via a two-tier structure consisting of a national committee charged with overall responsibility for administering the Fund and twenty five district committees that oversaw and co-ordinated coalfield-specific schemes. There were always an even number of coal owners and miners' federation representatives. The South Wales area was organised by the South Wales and Monmouthshire Joint Committee which, until 1928, divided the coalfield into eight sub-districts and distributed sums of money proportionally according to population. Monmouthshire and the central coalfield did rather better than the western districts, with around a quarter of the investments made in the Rhondda and Pontypridd. After 1928, the system was centralised with money allocated directly to schemes upon submission of a grant form. Despite grievances within South Wales, particularly during the period of proportional investment, outside commentators often praised the way the Fund was administered. The industrial welfare activist Robert Hyde, writing in the *The Times*, argued that 'in South Wales the fund is administered with wisdom and foresight', adding that 'a rule has been made that whilst distress prevails only those schemes which enable unskilled work to be provided shall be accepted'.[31]

From an orthodox trades union perspective, this rule was dangerous because it effectively undermined the value of labour, but the number of voluntary welfare schemes which developed across the coalfield – accounting for nearly one hundred and twenty recreation grounds between 1922 and 1928 – suggests that such qualms were temporarily set aside and that laying out a playing field or recreation ground or open-air swimming pool was something that the unemployed took great pride in.[32] Even when, as was the case in Blaengarw, the scale of the project – carving out a playing field from the mountainside – practically exhausted the men of the village.[33] As Hywel Francis and Dai

Smith reflect, 'the welfare movement tapped the socialist enthusiasm of the mining valleys'.[34] This was especially true in areas on the fringes of local authorities or in the more far-flung reaches of the coalfield. Trehafod, the 'Cinderella of the Rhondda', used the money available through the Miners' Welfare Fund to correct what it perceived to be its long-standing neglect by the two local authorities which it straddled, Rhondda and Pontypridd. 'Trehafod is without an Institute, a recreation field, and even without a playground for children', lamented the *Rhondda Leader* in 1924. The Welfare Fund, it was hoped, would bring money to the village to provide those facilities with any additional expenditure raised through whist drives, carnivals, and sports competitions. This was also the aim at Resolven and at Cymmer in the Afan valley.[35]

A significant proportion of the Miners' Welfare Fund was also spent on a wave of institute and welfare hall construction, adding significantly to the Victorian and Edwardian inheritance. By 1926, more than sixty institutes had been financed in this way, either as new builds or, as was the case at Bedwas, the completion of pre-war schemes.[36] These included the welfare hall at Aberaman where a grant of four thousand pounds was spent converting a former billiard hall; the welfare complex at Beddau where the ambitious plans of the Llantwit Fardre, Tynant and Beddau Area Miners' Welfare Committee featured an indoor swimming pool, assembly rooms, institute library, and a concert hall for twelve hundred people; and the institutes at Nantyffyllon, Senghenydd, Caerphilly, Blaenycwm, Glyncorrwg, Bryncethin, and Deri.[37] At the opening of the Nantyffyllon institute in August 1926, Vernon Hartshorn declared that 'a bit of colour was coming into people's lives'. This was not merely spending for the sake of spending but, he pointed out, quoting Lloyd George, a way of getting 'rid of the drabness' that prevailed in the coalfield.[38] There was also the sense that, in stark contrast to industrial relations, the growth of welfare and community action was a way of healing the rifts in South Walian society. Enoch Morrell, the Federation president, expressed his gratitude at finding 'representatives of the employers and workmen labouring together for the common weal'.[39]

The decision to invest so heavily in recreational amenities, both indoor and outdoor, in the early 1920s, rather than in extending educational provision or further developing medical aid societies, as occurred elsewhere in Britain, was a conscious one and an indication that Labour's administration of the coalfield was to be holistic. Not merely content with being able administrators of capitalism, the ideological intent of the labour movement was to inculcate democracy as widely as possible and to extend the meaning of welfare from education and health to its broadest sense. As T. I. Mardy Jones put it a decade earlier:

> The colliery villages could be better planned, better lighted and kept, be made more ornamental with trees; they could have more parks, libraries, gymnasiums, play-grounds, and very much else if the Council so decided. But the local Council does not so decide, because the workmen permit the Council to be manned by rate-savers; that is, persons whose concern seems to be the saving of the rates instead of using their powers for the public advantage.[40]

Rather than replicate existing schemes, money from the Miners' Welfare Fund was used to enable social and cultural activity across the entire community. This vision encouraged orchestras, choirs, theatre groups, debating societies, educational classes in language, politics, history, economics, literature, and religion, and sports teams. In Merthyr, the Independent Labour Party sponsored Esperanto classes and arranged for free classical music concerts 'for the purpose of stimulating a proletarian interest in good music'; at Bargoed, Kenfig Hill, Neath, and Briton Ferry, choirs were established that quickly gave rise to musical evenings of their own; Tredegar and Bedwas had their labour orchestras; and sports teams were an important aspect of party life for party members, especially in Cardiff, Newport, and Barry.[41] The significance of this social and cultural activity to the movement was illustrated most effectively by Aneurin Bevan who remarked in 1924 that 'in Tredegar they could congratulate themselves upon organising a Labour movement [... with] every phase of the movement provided for'.[42]

Myra O'Brien of Pontypridd is a good example of just how this was achieved both within and without of the labour movement. As a teacher, O'Brien was especially active in the National Union of Teachers and National Association of Head Teachers and served on local and Welsh committees for both. An active co-operator, she was president of the Pontypridd Women's Co-operative Guild. She was a founding member, and long-term president, of the Pontypridd Labour women's section, and was the first woman to sit as chair of Pontypridd Trades and Labour Council (serving from 1922-1925) and as president of Pontypridd Divisional Labour Party. Before her death in November 1935, she had also been elected as both county and district councillor. Her public service was not limited to political and trade union activity, either. For twenty five years she served as secretary of the Pontypridd and District Institution for the Blind, and was prominent on the county and South Wales blind association committees as well. She was a co-opted member of the parks and maternity and child welfare committees for Pontypridd Urban District, a member of the town's Public Assistance Committee, of the After-Care committee for the Labour Exchange, and of the cottage homes committee for Church Village. Together with D. L. Davies, the town's MP between 1931 and 1937, she was especially active amongst the

Irish nationalist movement in Pontypridd and was a key influence in bringing them over to the Labour cause.[43]

But neither was Myra O'Brien unusual in having such a full diary of engagements every week. In each district of the coalfield, and in this regard South Wales was typical of other parts of Britain, there were similarly focused activists including Aneurin Bevan and Archie Lush in Tredegar, Abel Morgan and William Hazell in Ynysybwl, and organisers such as Minnie Pallister and Elizabeth Andrews, who understood that governance was not an either/or distinction between elected representatives on the one hand and non-governmental organisations on the other. They were part and parcel of the same thing, and if socialism was to be successfully developed both elements needed to be guided by the same principles. Labour's process of consolidation in the early 1920s was therefore not merely electoral. Had it been so, the party might well have faced a more severe test of its strength during the second half of the 1920s and in the early 1930s when Labour was forced into retreat at the ballot box elsewhere in Britain, and when the trade union movement was weakened. Instead, the economic and industrial tests to which South Wales was subjected during that period provided ample evidence of the successful inculcation of Labour's values across the social and cultural sphere. And it was a radical pragmatism that helped both to smother the idealised ambitions of those on the left who wished to overthrow existing institutions and those on the right who sought the removal of Labour from power entirely.

Whatever Labour could achieve in local government was always mediated by the economic circumstances of the early 1920s and by the determination of central government to make cuts to public expenditure. The former was exacerbated by falling revenues from the rates and demographic changes that meant the loss of thousands of young, economically active people, with those whose demands on public resources were greatest remaining behind. It was a situation shaped by the coal mining industry. For all Labour's aspirations to govern in a broad sense, and to represent workers and their families regardless of their connection to mining, being the party of local government in the early 1920s meant that it could not escape the administrative consequences of the ongoing coal war. Politics were polarised, with the labour movement pitched against a wide spectrum of opponents, external and, at times, internal. Respectability clashed with radicalism, militants with moderates, and the Labour Party with the Communist Party. What happened in 1926 was the ending of a phase of industrial organisation and militancy that had begun in the 1890s, triumphed in the period 1910-1915, and come to a shattering halt in the defeat of 1921. Without being the party of government, there was relatively little the Labour Party could do to prevent the general strike and miners' lockout, but it was still faced with the choice of what to do to ameliorate the situation in the South Wales Coalfield itself.

Showdown

On Saturday 1 May, 1926, the sergeant in charge of Hopkinstown police station near Pontypridd noted in his log the stillness prevailing over the Great Western Colliery. Nearly three and a half thousand men were idle. Two days later, on 3 May, he recorded that the horses were risen at five o'clock in the morning and taken to the nearby Cwm Farm, where they would be left to graze on the pasture for the duration of the strike. The ostlers, who had previously been working underground caring for the horses, were given three days a week to attend the farm; at the end of May that was reduced to a single day.[44] Seeing more than two hundred horses brought up was evidence enough to the local population that the industrial action was going to be severe, but few could have foreseen that the horses would not go back underground until the cold of winter. By 7 May, almost every colliery horse in Pontypridd had been brought to the surface.[45] The same sight was recorded in every colliery village and mining town across South Wales.

May Day was marked by the now traditional demonstrations. At Pontypridd this was held at the Palladium Cinema, the press recorded it as being 'crowded by miners', as was the Nixon's Workmen's Hall in Mountain Ash. At the Palladium in Aberdare the demonstration was thronged with people, notably a large contingent of women who had marched in procession from Aberaman (the demonstration had originally been intended for Aberdare Park but bad weather prompted the change of venue). Within the hall, banners heralded lodges, associations, and union branches. Amongst them was a 'particularly ominous' black banner which bore the inscription *Death Before Starvation* and had a skull and crossbones motif woven into it.[46] Edwin Greening, who was present at the rally, recalled many years later that it left him with a 'feeling of an impending grave crisis'.[47] And at the Pavilion Cinema in Abertillery, miners cheered when the meeting chairman declared that 'if any man was going to get [us] through the present crisis it was Mr A. J. Cook'.[48]

In the weeks leading up to the General Strike, Cook cut a publicly fierce but privately exhausted figure. He was caught in an uncompromising situation: on the one hand Federation policy, democratically voted upon, refused to countenance wage reductions, on the other the coal owners refused to negotiate away from their stated position of longer hours for lower wages. It fell to Cook to maintain solidarity amongst the miners even though there were just two possible courses of action left: capitulation or a pitched battle. The Conservative government sided with its friends, hoping to break union power once and for all. Tom Jones, acting Cabinet Secretary and confidant of the Prime Minister, Stanley Baldwin, recorded in his diary that 'it is impossible not to feel the contrast between the reception which Ministers give to a body of owners and a body of miners. Ministers are at ease at once with the former, they are friends jointly exploring a situation. [...] It was [...] a joint discussion of whether it were better to precipitate a strike or the unemployment which would result from continuing the present terms. The majority clearly wanted a strike'.[49] They got what they wanted in the end.

In South Wales, the coal owners were especially intransigent. On 22 April they issued a pamphlet warning that 'the collieries in South Wales cannot work regularly and the collieries which are at present temporarily closed cannot re-open unless they are in a position to compete successfully, not only with foreign countries, but with other Districts in the United Kingdom which at present have a much lower cost than South Wales'. Their hands, they argued, were tied by the necessities of the market and their wage revision offer could not be weakened without serious consequences to employment.

> Over 70% of the output is exported, and therefore comes into direct and constant competition with coals produced by other countries. Cost of production and consequently the price at which South Wales coals can be offered in foreign markets is the prime factor in determining the amount of employment which can be given.

> South Wales has a higher standard wages cost, and a lower output per workman per shift, than any other exporting district.[50]

This was a clear attempt at isolating South Wales. This tactic might have worked, had it not been for the prominence of South

Wales miners on the Miners' Federation of Great Britain committee during 1926: A. J. Cook and S. O. Davies, who had been elected onto the MFGB committee two years earlier, were intimately familiar with the habits of the coal owners and worked to counter them by maintaining pan-district unity.

The same day, Edward Loveluck, architect and district surveyor for Penybont Rural District Council, received a 'secret and confidential letter' from Illtyd Thomas, the chair of the Cardiff Area Volunteer Service Committee and a mining engineer by trade. The letter contained an invitation to Loveluck to become vice chair of the committee and take responsibility for organising volunteers in the Bridgend area in the event of a General Strike. The volunteers would be engaged in maintaining food supplies, ensuring that coal was delivered to businesses, and in general performing 'duties essential for the maintenance and well-being of the community but not for the purposes of acting as strike breakers'.[51] In the fortnight, or so, before the strike broke out, Loveluck was able to recruit one hundred and eighty seven volunteers in the Bridgend area, most of them were (or might be seen to be on their way to being) middle-class. They were solicitors, teachers, students, accountants, and so on.[52] Illtyd Thomas's committee in Cardiff was able to recruit as many as three hundred volunteers from the student population alone and there were five hundred special constables.[53] Of the volunteers in Bridgend, thirteen were women (including Loveluck's wife) and they tended (or were expected) to run kitchens – notably a lorry drivers' canteen – or do clerical work for the committee. As was the case across Britain, those participating in this 'lark for the sake of their country' were generally from middle- and upper-class backgrounds.[54]

Of course, strike breakers were not universally middle-class. In the list of volunteers compiled by Loveluck were those giving their traditional employment as lorry driver, bus conductor, tram driver, railwayman, docker, and collier. Five miners broke the strike, actively volunteering to do so. The youngest of them was twenty, a colliery labourer from Bridgend; the oldest a thirty-seven-year-old collier from Pontycymmer. Completing the list were a collier from Ogmore Vale, one from Maesteg, and another from Bridgend. What their motivations were is unrecorded, but at the age of twenty or twenty-one, or thirty, or thirty-seven, it is unlikely that they were all acting in the same way. Likewise, it is difficult to say what happened when the lockout took the industrial dispute into the autumn. Did they join in? Did they remain aloof from the struggle? Did they join the employers' union? It is possible that they were, as was the case with strikebreakers in Monmouthshire, alienated from the politics of the South Wales Miners' Federation and expressed this by not taking part in the industrial dispute.[55] What is clear is these men were not alone in refusing to take part in the strike and their number would grow.

From London it all looked very different. 'Tuesday, May 4th, started with the workers answering the call', recorded A. J. Cook in his chronicle, 'From John O'Groats to Land's End the workers answered the call to arms to defend us, to defend the brave miner in his fight for a living wage'.[56] He continued: 'Confidence, calm, and order prevailed everywhere, despite the irritation caused by the volunteers, blacklegs, and special constables. The workers acted as one. Splendid discipline! Splendid loyalty!' Cook's description of workers' solidarity was broadly true of South Wales, alongside the awareness of strike breakers and special constables. What he could not capture was the atmosphere which prevailed in Cardiff and Newport. In Newport, the first day of the General Strike was felt to be akin to 'Sunday with the shops open'.[57] Cardiffians too experienced a momentarily different way of life. 'Never have the streets of the Welsh metropolis been so filled with pedestrians in the early morning', reported the *Evening Express*, 'from all parts of the suburbs there were thousands of pedestrians and all were cheerfully optimistic and the better for rising an hour earlier and taking the best of all exercises on a bright, sharp morning'.[58] The same impression of crowded streets was carried in a letter from D. T. Salathiel, the secretary of the Welsh National Liberal Federation, sent from his office in Charles Street to A. J. Sylvester, Lloyd George's private secretary, on 6 May.[59]

A few days later, the *Western Mail* recorded that one prominent Cardiff resident had 'spent Monday morning taking joy rides between St Mary Street and the Pier Head in order to show his appreciation of the volunteer workers. He has not yet counted up his expenses'.[60] On 5 May, Cardiff Corporation had restarted their tram and bus services using voluntary labour, albeit not without some hostile response from those on strike. Salathiel described crowds booing as the buses and trams passed by, occasional attempts to blockade them, and 'one or two scrimmages between the strikers and volunteers'.[61] But he also described tensions within the crowds, with some seeking to drown out the booing, and even some of the strikers privately intimating that they were uncomfortable with a more radical line. This was hardly surprising. Prior to the strike the labour movement in the city had been in some disarray, with clear tensions emerging between the communists and the Labour Party.[62] One communist described the city's trades and labour council as 'one of the rottenest in Britain'; the trades and labour council itself had taken to expelling the South Ward for running a communist as a local council candidate in the municipal elections.[63] During the strike itself, the Central Strike Committee was careful to hold the communists at arm's length by providing them with administrative work only. This, in the opinion of the city police, ensured that they were only able to exercise influence where they already had it.[64]

In many parts of South Wales, the strike was more universal – symptomatic of the overwhelming dominance of railwaymen and miners in the trade union movement – and brought a halt to a wide range of activity. All railway services were stopped in the Taff, Cynon, and Rhondda valleys, with no train travelling north of Taff's Well for the duration of the strike. Officials in the Vale of Neath also reported complete shutdown of train services.[65] At Fishguard, food transport ships from Ireland were prevented from unloading their cargo by pickets.[66] In Chepstow, effort was focused on encouraging the railway clerks to join the strike and convincing the Building Trades Operatives to cease construction work on Chepstow Racecourse. The latter action caused 'considerable concern to promoters of this society sport', as the local strike committee reported to the TUC.[67] At Pontnewynydd near Pontypool pressure was applied by the strike committee on sports clubs not to hire buses and charabancs because their appearance on the roads 'has a demoralising effect and [gives] rise to rumours'.[68] And at Ynysybwl, the Joint Strike Committee prevented any form of transport entering or leaving the village without its permission: the local education committee even deferred to the strike committee to deal with the transport of school children from Ynysybwl to Abercynon, the specially labelled buses travelling only if the strike committee issued a permit.[69]

But there were some limitations. An hourly passenger rail service was restored between Cardiff and Caerphilly by 7 May, and the Great Western Railway (GWR) were also able to run services on the South Wales mainline between Cardiff and Swansea and on the mainline between Cardiff and London.[70] Despite all two hundred and fifty railwaymen based at Llantrisant station having struck on 4 May, the police sergeant at Pontyclun noted in his log, passenger services – albeit very limited – were restored on 6 May. Three days later, as many as eight passenger services were passing through Pontyclun between Cardiff and Swansea, rising to nearly twenty trains (predominantly passenger services) by 12 May.[71] Similarly, despite blockades in Fishguard, food stuffs continued to be delivered to the South Wales ports. Cheese, milk, butter, and eggs farmed in the West Country and destined to be sold in markets and shops in South Wales still arrived, but travelled by boat and road, rather than by rail. As one newspaper from Clevedon reported, in the first week of the strike paddle steamers in the Bristol Channel had carried over two thousand gallons of milk and fifty tons of eggs, butter and cheese, from Somerset to South Wales.[72] This was aided by the non-participation in the strike of the Cardiff dockers (in contrast with the dockers at Barry), and the presence of the cruiser HMS Cleopatra in the upper Bristol Channel to assist shipping.

The coherence of the strike in the coalfield – and to some extent in the coastal towns and cities – was due to the absorption by the labour movement of the vast majority of the functions of local government and the establishment of strike committees able to function in this way. They were themselves sophisticated and effective organisations. Where local authorities were already run by the Labour Party, this process was straightforward; where they were run by other parties, strike committees anticipated – and often met with – a degree of hostility or refusal. In the words of the Newport strike committee, 'we are anticipating trouble with our corporation departments owing to their attitude'.[73] Central Strike Committees (CSC) were formed in hub towns and cities, such as Merthyr Tydfil, Pontypridd, Cardiff, or Newport, with lines of communication to local strike committees in villages or outlying areas. The CSCs were broadly representative of the labour movement in each community with the functions – and bureaucratic machinery – of trades and labour councils utilised to full effect. Pontypridd CSC is an instructive example. Its officers were those of the Pontypridd TLC and it was based at the council's offices in Mill Street.[74]

By absorbing the bureaucratic machinery of the trades and labour councils, the CSCs could coordinate their activity in extremely effective ways – the relationships between organisations had already been established both at the local level and regionally through the East Glamorgan Federation of Trades Councils. Merthyr Tydfil CSC, for example, brought together fifty-two lodges and three unemployed organisations with over one hundred and forty delegates able to be present at its meetings. It had four districts representing outlying areas – Treharris, Merthyr Vale, Troedyrhiw, and Dowlais – with each district committee running four sub-committees dealing with sports and entertainments, permits, food, and finance. The central committee added communication and intelligence subcommittees to that list.[75] Such a level of co-operation and organisational sophistication would have been unthinkable had the CSCs been arranged *ad hoc* as a reaction to the strike call. In the colliery villages, the strike committees generally absorbed the functions of the Lodge, albeit with representation for railwaymen as well. In Ynysybwl, the strike committee was a version of the Lodge committee.[76]

Certain communities went further. The Bedlinog Council of Action, formed on 4 May, certainly had the colliery lodge at its centre, but also held a series of public meetings to decide democratically what to do about feeding the children of the village and set up a women's committee which had sole responsibility for the provision of food.[77] That committee liaised with teachers to arrange school feeding and on its recommendation the Council of Action sent a dispatch rider to

Maerdy to learn what methods had been adopted there to ensure children did not go hungry.[78] These multiple functions – which also included an entertainments committee and a decision to boycott the 'capitalist press' – ensured that the Bedlinog Council of Action continued to operate for several months after the strike, marshalling activity in its own area and applying pressure to maintain Federation unity in nearby communities. Its business was not formally wound up until 13 August.[79] In Llanelli, under the guidance of Enoch Collins, the communist chairman of the town's trades and labour council, the Council of Action even commandeered police stations, the police themselves receiving direct instructions from Council members, and took control of the food supply.[80] As the *British Worker* put it, 'everything [was] at a standstill in Llanelly'.[81]

With no work to occupy their time and the solidity of the strike ensuring that pickets were, in general, not required, miners and their families organised sports and entertainments. In Port Talbot, these included a range of games including baseball, football, and marbles. The local press considering them to be an important 'safety valve'.[82] In Monmouthshire, Arthur Jenkins, the miners' agent for the Eastern Valley, remarked at a mass meeting that if soldiers were sent into the area to maintain order, they would offer to play football matches against them.[83] In Pontypridd, the strike committee liaised with the town's YMCA to organise a concert.[84] In Swansea, a day of sports was held at Victoria Park, together with cricket and football matches throughout the strike.[85] And in Merthyr Tydfil, the strike committee consulted with the Chief Constable on a daily basis, gaining the support of the police in organising a range of sports events and concerts. These included at least a dozen concerts and a football competition featuring two matches a day, as well as cricket and bowls matches. This had the effect, as the town's chief constable remarked later, of 'keeping the strikers off the streets' but large audiences and participation in the sports suggested that the entertainment was nonetheless welcome.[86] Entertainments of this kind set the tone for maintaining community cohesion through the long months of the lockout, particularly the summer months when children were out of school.

Of significance was the widespread political activation of women during the strike, particularly as it moved into the second week of May, a momentum that was then carried into the lockout. For several months prior to the strike, Elizabeth Andrews, through her column in the *Colliery Workers' Magazine*, had sought to alert women readers to the necessity of being politically active in the struggles ahead. As she put it in April 1926, 'the most powerful weapons the miners can have in this struggle will be a one hundred percent trade unionism, one hundred percent support and co-operation of their womenfolk, and one hundred percent confidence in our leaders'. The article concluded with the assertion that special women's meetings would be held in the coalfield.[87] They were. In his diary, Stan Awbery noted that on the 10 May he had addressed a large meeting of women in Swansea.[88] Similar meetings were recorded in Ynysybwl, Ogmore Vale, Nantymoel, and Caerau. Likewise, that day's *British Worker* reported a sizeable gathering of around five hundred women at Gelli Park in the Rhondda, as well as a procession of two thousand women through the streets of Tonypandy. Led by Mrs John, the wife of the Rhondda West MP, Will John, they marched four abreast silently towards De Winton fields where, after a mass meeting, they then dispersed. A similar show of solidarity took place in Ferndale, where one thousand women marched, and in Treorchy (although the numbers present were not recorded).[89] And between 12 and 13 May, Elizabeth Andrews addressed twenty meetings, with as many as ten thousand women attending in total.[90]

Although women had previously been active in labour and liberal politics, as well as in the suffrage movement, and were a common sight in industrial disputes, this marked a new phase of militancy, one that had been anticipated during the 1921 lockout and now lasted into the 1930s.[91] Not only did women organise their own rallies and debate their own response to the industrial crisis, they took part – enthusiastically and, at times, aggressively – in picketing.[92] Symptomatic of this kind of participation were two events which took place in Cardiff, both of which involved attacks on strike volunteers. A sixteen-year-old girl was sentenced to fourteen days in gaol or fined twenty shillings for swearing at a volunteer on St Mary's Street, whilst forty nine year old Edna O'Brien was given one month's hard labour for attacking a tram and smashing its windows.[93] The press often reacted with surprise at the prominence of women in these events, the *Western Mail* calling it a 'strange feature'; the authorities were no less perturbed. One magistrate, imposing a two-month sentence on Elvira Bailey from Treorchy, in November 1926, explained his harshness as the result of finding that 'women have been taking too prominent a part in these disturbances'.[94]

Abuse directed towards strike breakers, volunteers, the police, and special constables, was typically verbal rather than physical. In Pontyclun, the police log recorded that on 14 May, there was an incident outside a fish and chip shop in the village. Late in the evening, the smell of vinegar, salt, and fat, filling the air, two miners stood leaning against a wall, eating their chips. A third man walks past and into the shop. 'There's the special, bloody shithouse', barked one of the miners, 'a traitor to the camp'. After a dressing down by the police, who were within earshot, the miner hurriedly suggests that 'he is a pal of mine, I was only joking'. The truth was perhaps a little different.[95] Certainly in Swansea, the presence of strikebreakers was not tolerated. The town's joint strike committee issued a statement on 9 May, which included this ominous, biblical warning: 'Judas sold Jesus for some pieces of silver and then went and hung himself. The Joint Strike Committee would be delighted to supply the rope necessary for the worms that still remain in work to go and do likewise'.[96] Perhaps not surprisingly, given this offer, the next day Swansea reported to the TUC that 'blacklegging is absolutely non-existent'.[97]

The end of the strike was signalled two days later to the considerable dismay and at times bitter anger of many workers in South Wales. The Bedlinog Council of Action passed a resolution protesting the abandonment of the strike and 'expressing our disgust at the way in which the settlement was made'. It was sent directly to the TUC.[98] Cardiff Trades and Labour Council informed the TUC that they deeply deplored the action they had taken and demanded the resumption of strike action. Cwmamman Trades and Labour Council did the same, calling on the TUC to 'get on or get out'. Workers in Tumble, Gorseinon, Bedwas, Gwaun-Cae-Gurwen, Ystradgynlais, Glyn-Neath, and Ammanford, all registered their outrage in strongly worded communications to the TUC offices in London. The following day, more protests were sent from South Wales than any other region in the country. Maerdy Lodge even went so far as to label the TUC traitors. A mass meeting in the Rhondda on 17 May declared the General Council's actions in calling off the strike to be the 'blackest betrayal in history and a blow to future trade unionism'. In many places the railwaymen remained out. In Pontypridd, a meeting of the railwaymen urged the strike to continue 'in view of [the] tendency of employers to victimise'[99] And in Ebbw Vale, they resolved to stay out until the miners had won a decent standard of living.

Confusion was particularly acute in the Rhondda. E. W. West, manager of the Central Cinema in Porth, observed in a letter to his bosses in Cardiff that things seem more confusing now than they were before, the tram cars are running in Porth today but below everything is on stop as before and I believe those are going to stop again tonight. The railways of course are still out, it's difficult to know what is really going to happen now.[100]

Eventually the railwaymen did go back to work, as did the tram drivers, but the transformation of the strike into the miners' lockout hardly eased the economic bleakness evident in the coalfield. Indeed, things went from bad to worse. West wrote again on 15 May:

Business has been very quiet this weekend and under the circumstances one cannot expect much, there being no money about.[101]

Two days later he said simply, 'one really feels the stoppage'.[102]

Lockout

The decision of the miners to carry on delayed final defeat for months, but inevitably exacerbated the destructive effects of the lockout on the SWMF and on mining communities. An enormous amount of organisational energy was expended during the lockout as the result of holding the community together. In reality, victory had already been made unobtainable five years earlier. Neither the general strike, nor the miners' lockout, altered that fact. And yet, precisely because the lockout became not about winning the strike but about the preservation of community, a new form of collective politics came into being which sustained the coalfield through the hardships of the 1930s and beyond. In essence, the lockout was about adjusting to life without the regularity of employment and a functioning economic system, and accepting Labour's radical pragmatism rather than the CPGB's rejectionist position. Communities and councils established soup kitchens and made the best of the situation in the short term, but it fell to local councillors and MPs to try to find longer-term solutions so that great vats of soup and stew and the temporary distraction of carnivals did not become the normal way of life for hundreds of thousands of people. What has sometimes been depicted as an 'alternative social and political culture' with people willing to engage in direct action and 'resourceful illegality', was more like a means of survival in the absence of a more meaningful alternative.[103]

As several testimonials from the lockout demonstrate, communal action relied on the embers of the old prosperity. In Ammanford, as James Griffiths recalled, lodges could not afford to pay out even one week's strike pay and so had to establish soup kitchens to ensure the communal money stretched out further.[104] In Porth, the remaining reserves were used in the same way; whilst at Maerdy, the lodge underwrote any shortfall in fundraising for the local soup kitchen. Its funds did not last long.[105] The co-operative societies, too, which had more substantial reserves, took almost every measure they could to underwrite mining communities, although they stopped short of deliberately imperilling themselves financially – although that did not prevent a severe impact on resources. The Ynysybwl Co-operative Society alone provided twenty thousand pounds in financial support.[106] To enable Aberdare Co-operative Society to provide a limited dividend of one shilling and sixpence in the pound to members in desperate need of credit (and to encourage them to spend Guardians' relief notes there), society employees took a fifteen percent cut in their wages.[107] Newport Co-operative Society, which had branches in mining villages such as Llanbradach, Machen, and Bedwas, registered a sharp drop in sales from around one hundred and fifteen thousand pounds in 1925 to under one hundred thousand in 1926. In Bedwas alone sales fell from nearly seven thousand pounds in January 1926 to little more than four thousand a year later.[108] Whilst debts accrued by members over the course of the lockout were so burdensome on Caerau Co-operative Society as to be 'crippling the society's progress'.[109]

Communal kitchens ensured that the threat of starvation was kept away. However severe lack of money had other effects on the fabric of the community. There was a visible decline in the quality of boots and clothing, particularly those worn by children. At Bedlinog, one headmaster recorded distressingly that half of his pupils had shoes that were in a poor state of repair and that for many their 'footwear [is] so bad as to allow contact with the floor and bare feet. Only ten percent keep out water'.[110] Things were not much different in Porth, either.[111] In July 1926, Mountain Ash Education Committee pressed the Board of Guardians to provide assistance to families who were keeping their children away from school because they no longer had clothes and shoes for them. When the Guardians refused to help, the committee turned to other sources including the Society of Friends, and the Save the Children Fund, and the Board of Education to whom they wrote hoping that officials in London would be able to convince those in Wales to act. When this also failed, the committee held a public meeting on 11 October and the following week, on the initiative of Ynysybwl councillor Richard Woosnam, established their own network of ward boot committees with a central committee led by William Hazell (also of Ynysybwl) to coordinate fundraising efforts to buy new boots and repair old ones. Fundraising efforts, including concerts, street collections, and whist drives, came from local jazz bands and labour party branches.[112] As the Schools Medical Officer for the district recorded, this intervention had a transformative effect and led to widespread improvement.[113]

The same active intervention took place in Pontypridd where, by September 1926, nearly half of local schools reported children attending barefoot and in clothing that was 'somewhat deteriorated'. The education authority implemented a scheme of voluntary boot repair centres, liaising with the strike committee, and issued headteachers with tickets to give to the neediest children to get their boots repaired. The scheme appears to have been successful: by the end of October, only three schools in the area reported children attending barefooted (although this does not discount the possibility that parents kept their children away from school, as was the case in Mountain Ash).[114] In the Rhondda, children who could not attend school through lack of boots and clothes were also unable to attend the canteens. Supplies of clothes and leather were granted to schools by the Quakers to help with repairs, but as one headmaster recorded 'the demand is more than the volunteers can cope with'. Eventually schools were issued with funds provided by Battersea Grammar School, the Save the Children Fund, and the Heads of Council Departments Fund, to enable them to buy boots. Most of this money was issued in the form of vouchers to spend at the local co-operative store.[115]

The impact of the lockout on the health of South Walians has long been debated. At the time, the general perception amongst medical officers was that health, particularly amongst children, improved, although this was vigorously contested by the labour movement. The Schools Medical Officer for Pontypridd, E. J. Griffiths, remarked, indicatively, that children 'were not undergoing what can be called suffering at the present time'.[116] In Mountain Ash, the view was that children had 'never looked so well'.[117] Likewise, historian Steven Thompson has suggested that the decline in death rates in 1926 – the year was the lowest for the entire interwar period – implies that the 'population was somewhat healthier in 1926 than previously'.[118] This is a problematic conclusion. Medical officers were not universal in their belief that health had improved, especially for women. In Abertillery, for example, the medical officer noted that the 'health and stamina of a great many mothers depreciated considerably' and elsewhere in Monmouthshire children were at a greater risk of rickets and other similar diseases associated with malnutrition.[119] They may not have died, but this did not mean that they were healthy; indeed, the Medical Officer recorded a sharp increase in the death rate and the rate of infant mortality in 1927.[120] He also reflected tellingly that 'one has been surprised by the maintenance of bodily weight and resistance to disease in children living in homes where the pinch of poverty must have been felt. But one cannot help thinking that the mothers' resistance to tuberculosis has broken down under the strain'.[121]

The conclusion to be drawn, readily available from medical officer of health reports, is that so long as families had access to food, they could survive. But members of those families did not eat equally: typically, priority was given to children, then to men, and finally to women. As Gwyn Thomas reflected:

> When the school holidays came we took to the mountain tops, joining the liberated pit ponies among the ferns on the broad plateaux. That was the picture for us who were young. For our fathers and mothers there was the inclosing fence of hinted fears, fear of hunger, fear of defeat.[122]

Fear, too, perhaps, of having to make a choice to survive by breaking the strike. It was a choice some made willingly, fed up of the direction the miners' federation leaders had taken, others because they felt they had reached the end, and were desperate.

One of those who broke with the SWMF was William Gregory who worked at the Raglan Colliery at Heol-y-Cyw, near

Bridgend.[123] Until June 1926, Gregory had been a member of the SWMF but resigned his membership, together with many others at the colliery, and went back to work. News of this action was seized on by the press as a sign of fractures in the SWMF resolve, but it was greeted by many in the SWMF with determination and several meetings were held to discuss a collective course of action. One such, held at Porth, resolved to form a demonstration to march to Heol-y-Cyw to convince Gregory and his compatriots to resume the strike. However, because of the distance from the Rhondda, a smaller group were mandated to travel to discuss the matter in a less confrontational manner. This they did, but it made little difference.[124]

Gregory and his compatriots were the most serious, but not the only, symptom of a slow breakdown in the solidarity of the strike-cum-lockout. In August 1926, there was a concerted effort by strikebreakers in New Tredegar to effect a return to work, only to face a fierce resistance from picketers in the village. At Llanharan, figures tallied by the police suggest a steady growth in the number of strikebreakers, although significantly it does not tally with those printed in the newspapers. The latter was always a higher figure. For instance: the *Glamorgan Gazette* recorded a return rate at Llanharan of over one hundred miners by 13 August, whereas the police record suggests this figure was not in fact reached until early September.[125] One community where strikebreakers are generally thought to have had a major impact is Ynysybwl. In his history of the Lady Windsor Lodge, John E. Morgan records that there were as many as forty blacklegs working at the Lady Windsor Colliery and seemingly more at the smaller Mynachdy Colliery, although he does not record the final tally. The first to break at the Lady Windsor was David Thomas, followed by a miner who travelled into the village from Pontypridd. By September, they had been joined by more than a dozen others.[126]

There is, however, other evidence that moderates what Michael Lieven has referred to as a 'fractured working-class consciousness'. The employment registers for the Ocean Coal Company suggest far stronger levels of solidarity in Ynysybwl than Morgan allowed for; indeed, the first occasion that any strikebreakers are reported as working at the Lady Windsor was at the end of September, when five colliers and two timbermen broke the strike and returned to work. The following day, three of the colliers struck again, and by 1 October only the timbermen remained at work. Their last shift was on 2 October and they did not return until 27 October. No colliers returned to work at the colliery until 17 November and then only to the same extent as in late September – that is, five colliers in total and a single timberman. Given a workforce of over one thousand at this stage, this was a minor wobble and hardly a fractured consciousness.[127]

Whatever the realities of fracture in Ynysybwl, the Lady Windsor Colliery was not the frontline of attempts to break up the South Wales Miners' Federation and replace it with a union more amenable to the coal owners. That was at the new Taff-Merthyr Colliery near Bedlinog, a joint venture by the Ocean Coal Company and the Powell Duffryn Combine. In a lapse of judgement, albeit one clearly aimed at providing employment after the lockout, the SWMF agreed to limited working at the pit to prepare it for full production. It was to prove a costly mistake, and one that the SWMF leadership would rue for many years, since non-unionised labour, running into the hundreds of men, was brought in by the companies to work underground. They soon formed their own union, initially called (in a deliberate echo of pre-Federation terminology) the Taff-Merthyr Works Committee. 'This is the first occasion in the coalfield for such drastic action to be taken', the *Western Mail* enthused, 'and this example will probably soon be followed by many other colliery workers elsewhere'.[128] Deliberately 'non-political' the Works Committee would provide provident insurance but would eschew any political fund. 'We are not going to subsidise the Minority Movement, the Labour Party, nor the daily newspaper of any Party', the members asserted.[129] Nevertheless many of the leading members of the Works Committee were active in the Conservative Party.[130]

Within a week, the Taff-Merthyr Works Committee had a new name: the South Wales Miners' Industrial Union (SWMIU). It grew rapidly, drawing on the disaffection caused by the breakup of the lockout. A few weeks earlier, the *Western Mail* had reported (almost certainly erroneously) that as many as twenty thousand miners had returned to work.[131] SWMIU officials sought to tap into this possible well of support with a simple question – 'Are you in favour of a trade union free from all party politics?'[132] The core of SWMIU support lay in the Rhymney valley (centred on the Taff-Merthyr Colliery) and by the new year as many as twenty-one branches had been formed with a membership of between five and ten thousand. Through the early months of 1927 this apparently accelerated to over one hundred branches and (wildly exaggerated) membership figures of up to thirty five thousand.[133] In fact, membership was much lower with fewer than three thousand in the union during 1928. The membership range after the initial surge in late 1926 and early 1927 was between two and six thousand depending on how many collieries the SWMIU controlled.[134] The SWMIU's presence emphasised the fragility of the South Wales Miners' Federation and compounded the effects of the defeat in the strike and the lockout. The employer-backed insurgents ensured also that the post-lockout rebuilding of the SWMF took place in the context of civil war. The 'loyalists' rallied to the Federation to help rebuild it. Pontypridd Women's Co-operative Guild, for example, established a special ha'penny-a-week fund to this aim.[135] The coal owners and their allies, with far greater resources, channelled funds into the SWMIU and used the media to continually build a red scare.

There was, in effect, a power struggle at all levels evident in South Wales after the lockout – the coal owners against the SWMF, Labour councillors against Conservative ministers in London and the police in South Wales, and the Labour Party versus its political antagonists on the left and right – all for the right to present the victor as the legitimate voice of South Walian society. It was a battle that, together, the Labour Party and the South Wales Miners' Federation won convincingly. There can be little doubt that Labour-controlled administrations throughout the coalfield felt the full antagonism of a hostile Conservative government, particularly through the Board of Education, the Ministry of Health, and the Home Office, all of which were openly antagonistic to elected representatives in South Wales. There were severe consequences. Forced to find thousands of pounds of additional revenue to meet the costs of the school feeding programme, which had kept children alive during the lockout, education committees appealed to the Ministry of Health and the Board of Education for assistance to ensure that debts did not threaten the viability of schools. This was not forthcoming. Pontypridd Education Committee wrote to the Board of Education to complain of the indifference to their plight shown by the Ministry of Health and its minister, Neville Chamberlain. In stark terms, they stated that they 'fully realise the attitude of the Ministry [...] towards education in this area' and went on to insist that

> while the authority realise that the financial condition of the council as a whole has to be borne in mind they naturally regard it as a very serious matter that the children of miners should be denied the inalienable right of a public education because of

the stoppage of the mines to which they are not parties and in respect of which they have suffered and are still suffering.[136]

The Board of Education ignored the plea.

A bigger struggle came locally between Labour councillors and the police in Monmouthshire and Glamorgan. In Monmouthshire, there was a tense standoff between Victor Bosanquet, the chief constable, and the Labour-controlled Standing Joint Committee which oversaw policing in the county. When the committee demanded his resignation on the basis that 'his actions in times of emergency are calculated to disturb the peace of the country', Bosanquet refused taking some delight in describing the councillors as 'my little lot of Communists'. Upon receiving the support of the Home Office, Bosanquet succeeded in forcing the Labour members to back down.[137] The *Western Mail* thundered against the 'attempt of the Labour majority [...] to exert undue influence over the action of the Chief Constable' and demanded a national police force administered 'directly by the State', removing any local influence.[138] It failed to see the irony of calling for the nationalisation of law and order! The antipathy between the two sides remained. During the lockout, Bosanquet had been labelled a 'dictator' and 'a man of overpowering ego' by Labour members; his defenders pointed conversely to his just 'war with the red peril'.[139] If Bosanquet was victorious in keeping his job, he failed to get his way on police spending during the lockout. In 1928, the Labour Party noted in a retrospective on their administration of Monmouthshire since 1925 that:

During the lockout of 1926, we took a firm stand in resisting expenditure upon special constables, specials' uniforms, and imported police. As Labour representatives, we believed in our people's desire and ability to keep the peace, if dealt with reasonably. Our belief proved to be well founded, for our people maintained order under great provocation and distress. They knew that Labour was in power in Monmouthshire and that we were doing our best in their interests.[140]

The *Western Mail*, thought this 'wicked', pointing to the thirty thousand pounds of additional police expenditure in Glamorgan.[141] In private, Bosanquet was highly antagonistic towards the Labour Party. Writing to Lionel Lindsay in 1928, he observed that he 'only requested help from Newport Borough for a short time, the only cost incurred was £321 12/4'. Nevertheless, he continued, 'we got no kudos or thanks, but the Labour Party purred loudly over their own imagined cleverness'.[142] It was hardly surprising that the Labour councillors in Monmouthshire took the Home Office's support for Bosanquet as further evidence of Westminster's open hostility towards them. 'The Home Office' explained one councillor, 'has set its face against us'.[143]

Had local government been of a different political hue in the early 1920s, it is difficult to imagine the industrial disputes lasting as long as they did, and certainly impossible to envisage the same degree of open hostility between local representation and central government. Appreciating the solidarity of Labour councillors and Guardians with their colleagues in the trade union movement and the co-operative societies, particularly the South Wales Miners' Federation, helps to explain why the miners' defeat in 1926 did not shatter the spirit of collectivism that had by then emerged, it also helps to explain why Labour, rather than an alternative voice, such as the CPGB, remained the dominant political force. Indeed, Labour became even more dominant. The 1921 lockout, the general strike and the 1926 lockout, consolidated rather than weakened the wholesale shift of the political culture of the coalfield from liberalism to social democracy, and together they ensured the extension of industrial polarisation to the different layers of the state. Glamorgan and Monmouthshire county councils, together with Labour-controlled Boards of Guardians, county borough, borough, urban and rural district councils, acted in congruity with the wider labour movement standing oftentimes against central government, the police, and the press. In less than a decade, the South Wales Coalfield had undergone a silent revolution. Labour had proven the viability of socialism with a South Walian accent, but it would now have to govern in a region where the economy and its central industrial force had been thoroughly broken.

Notes

[1] Davies, *Cook*, 49.

[2] *SWDN*, 11 April 1921.

[3] *Colliery Guardian*, 7 January 1921.

[4] As above, 14 January 1921.

[5] As above, 24 March 1921.

[6] As above, 22 April, 3 June 1921.

[7] *PO*, 30 April 1921.

[8] SWMF, *Minutes*, 10 October 1921.

[9] *Colliery Guardian*, 10 June 1921.

[10] TNA, CAB 24/123/36: 'Feeding of Necessitous School Children, 10 May 1921'.

[11] GA, DX816, Llanbradach Workmen's Hall and Institute, Minute Book, 1920-1925: entries for 5 March, 14 May 1921.

[12] Pontypridd UDC, Education Committee: 'Minutes of a Special Meeting, 13 April 1921'.

[13] As above, 'Minutes of Education Committee Meeting, 28 June 1921'.

[14] SWMF, *Minutes*, 16 July 1921.

[15] *Colliery Guardian*, 21 October 1921.

[16] As above, 28 October 1921.

[17] Rhondda No. 1 District, Minutes, 25 July 1921; Davies, *A. J. Cook*, 55.

[18] *Colliery Guardian*, 5 August 1921. Hartshorn noted that miners in Penrhiwceiber and Ynysybwl had both voted against affiliation to the Third International by large margins.

[19] SWMF, Minutes, Annual Conference 22-23 July 1921.

[20] Davies, *A. J. Cook*, 59.

[21] TNA, CAB 24/126/15: 'Report on Revolutionary Organisations in the United Kingdom, No. 113, 7 July 1921'; CAB 24/126/81: 'Report on Revolutionary Activities, No. 116, 28 July 1921'.

[22] SWCC, Lady Windsor Lodge, Minutes, 1 July 1921.

[23] *DH*, 7 March 1922.

[24] *Colliery Guardian*, 23 September 1921.

[25] ALS, PY7/1/21: *Aberdare Division Labour News*, 11 November 1922.

[26] ALS, PY7/1/26-27: Charles Stanton Election Addresses, 1922.

[27] Edmund Stonelake, *The Autobiography of Edmund Stonelake* (Bridgend, 1981), 167.

[28] ALS, PY7/1/24: George Hall Election Address, 1922. The political agent for Labour in Aberdare in 1922 was Rev. George Neighbour.

[29] The historic Zinoviev Letter, which formed part and parcel of the 1924 election campaign but which, in retrospect, had little real impact on Labour's fortunes was brought to Ramsay Macdonald's attention whilst he was on the campaign trail in Aberdare. Edmund Stonelake, the election agent in Aberdare in 1924, received a telegram addressed for Macdonald and handed it to him 'when we met his car near the level crossing just above Hirwaun'. Stonelake reflected later that 'although he [Macdonald] said nothing upon reading it; a very marked effect was obvious'. My thanks to Alun Williams for access to this note from Stonelake which is appended to a copy of Fenner Brockway's *Socialist Over Sixty Years* (London, 1946), once owned by Alun's father. On p. 221 of that volume Brockway records that 'On the day of the *Daily Mail* revelations, Macdonald was inaccessible; he was speaking in some remote Welsh village'. See also Stonelake's memoir, p. 168, although he does not indicate the location so precisely.

[30] *Mineworker*, 20 September 1924, cited in John Shepherd and Keith Laybourn, *Britain's First Labour Government* (London, 2006), 94.

[31] *The Times*, 29 July 1922.

[32] Schemes laid out this way included Garth Welfare Ground, near Maesteg, opened in 1924 and extended the following year. *Glamorgan Advertiser*, 30 May 1924, 24 April 1925.

[33] *GFP*, 15 May 1925.

[34] Francis and Smith, *The Fed*, 431.

[35] *Herald of Wales*, 19 June 1926; *South Wales News*, 23 July 1923.

[36] *CJ*, 15 December 1923.

[37] *AL*, 19 January 1924; *CJ*, 4 August, 8 December 1923, 9 February, 5 April, 12 April, 26 July, 1 November 1924; *Glamorgan Advertiser*, 3 April 1925, 14 May 1926.

[38] *Glamorgan Advertiser*, 3 September 1926.

[39] *GFP*, 2 May, 16 May, 8 August, 5 November 1924.

[40] *GFP*, 1 March 1912.

[41] *Merthyr Pioneer*, 15 January, 29 January, 5 February 1921; SWCC MNA/PP/124/2/2 – Neath ILP Choir; *Glamorgan Advertiser*, 18 June 1926; *MEx*, 26 July 1924; ILP, *Annual Report of the National Administrative Council, 1925* (London, 1925), 27.

[42] *MEx*, 22 March 1924. Cited in Demont, 'Tredegar', 353.

[43] *PO*, 23 November 1935.

[44] GA, DCON/UNL/144: 'Great Western Colliery Police Journal, 1924-1926', entries for 1 May-31 May 1926.

[45] *EEx*, 7 May 1926.

[46] *EEx*, 1 May 1926.

[47] Edwin Greening, 'A Collier Boy in the 1926 Coal Lockout', in *Old Aberdare* 8 (1997), 1.

[48] *EEx*, 1 May 1926.

[49] Thomas Jones (ed. Keith Middlemass), *Whitehall Diary* (Oxford, 1969), 23 April 1926.

[50] The Monmouthshire and South Wales Coal Owners' Association, *Statement on the Owners' Terms and Conditions of Work from the 1st May, 1926* (Cardiff, 1926).

[51] GA, DLOV/148: Letter dated 22 April 1926.

[52] As above, DLOV/149: List of Volunteers, 1926.

[53] E. W. Edwards, 'Pontypridd', in Margaret Morris (ed.), *The General Strike* (London, 1976), 420.

[54] Rachelle Hope Saltzman, *A Lark for the sake of their country: The 1926 General Strike volunteers in folklore and memory* (Manchester, 2012).

[55] Alun Burge, 'In Search of Harry Blount: Scabbing Between the Wars in one South Wales Community', *Llafur* 6, no. 3 (1994), 58-69.

[56] A. J. Cook, *The Nine Days* (London, 1926), 16.

[57] *SWA*, Coal Crisis Emergency Issue, 6 May 1926.

[58] *EEx*, 4 May 1926.

[59] Parliamentary Archives, Lloyd George Papers, LG/G/17/7/1: 'Letter from D. T. Salathiel to A. J. Sylvester, 6 May 1926'.

[60] *WM*, 11 May 1926.

[61] Parliamentary Archives, LG/G/17/7/2: 'Letter from D. T. Salathiel to A. J. Sylvester, 8 May 1926'.

[62] Alun Burge, 'The 1926 General Strike in Cardiff', *Llafur* 6, no. 1 (1992), 42-61. They would eventually result in the dissolution of the Cardiff Trades and Labour Council in 1940 and the separation of industrial organisation and the Labour Party in the city. MRC, TUC Papers, MSS.292/79C/9: 'Proposed Re-organisation [of Cardiff Trades Council], 1940-1'.

[63] *Workers' Weekly*, 23 April 1926; Burge, '1926', 44.

[64] *Aspects of the General Strike*.

[65] MRC, TUC Papers, MSS.292/252.62/1/24: 'Letter from Mrs F. Handy, Glyn-Neath and District Trades and Labour Council to Walter Citrine, 5 May 1926'.

[66] *EEx*, 7 May 1926.

[67] London Metropolitan University (LMU), General Strike 1926 Collection: 'Report from Chepstow Joint Strike Committee, 7 May 1926'.

[68] As above, General Strike 1926 Collection: 'Notice from Pontnewynydd Joint Industrial Council of Action, 10 May 1926'.

[69] GA, UDMA/E/1/24, Mountain Ash UDC, Education Committee, Minutes, 11 May 1926.

[70] *WM*, 6 May, 7 May 1926; Edwards, 'Pontypridd', 415.

[71] GA, DCON/293/3/16, Pontyclun Cottage Station Strike Journal 1926: entries for 4 May, 6 May, 9 May, 12 May 1926.

[72] *Clevedon Mercury*, 8 May 1926.

[73] MRC, TUC Papers, MSS.292/252.62/99/6: 'Report from Arthur Leveson, Newport Industrial Labour Council to Trades Union Congress, 5 May 1926'.

[74] E. Hughes (Chair), Walter Collier (Vice-Chair), and Arthur Pearson (Secretary).

[75] LMU, General Strike 1926 Collection: 'Letter from Merthyr Tydfil Central Strike Committee to TUC Publicity Department, 9 May 1926'; *Merthyr Tydfil County Borough: Souvenir of the General Strike, May 4th to May 12th 1926* (Merthyr, 1926), 10.

[76] Morgan, *VWC*, 27.

[77] This was also a feature of the Gwaun-Cae-Gurwen Council of Action. Emile Burns (ed.), *The General Strike, May 1926: Trades Councils in Action* (London, 1926), 129.

[78] SWCC, MNA/PP/24, Bedlinog Council of Action, Minute Book: entries for 4 May, 7 May, 8 May, 11 May 1926.

[79] As above, 13 August 1926.

[80] Francis, 'South Wales', 238-9.

[81] *British Worker*, 5 May 1926.

[82] *Sporting News*, 15 May 1926; *British Worker*, 8 May 1926.

[83] *British Worker*, 7 May 1926.

[84] Edwards, 'Pontypridd', 413.

[85] MRC, TUC Papers, MSS.292/252.62/21/13: 'Summary of BBC News Broadcast, 6 May 1926, 4th Bulletin, 7pm'.

[86] *Aspects of the General Strike*; *Merthyr Souvenir*, 11.

[87] *Colliery Workers' Magazine*, April 1926; the idea was raised initially at the East Glamorgan Labour Women's Advisory Council meeting in March. NLW, Labour Party of Wales Archive, East Glamorgan Labour Women's Advisory Council: 'Minutes for 1925-6, 6 March 1926'. I am grateful to Sue Bruley for this reference.

[88] GA, Stan Awbery Papers, DAW/V/1/1: 'Diary, 1926', entry for 10 May.

[89] *British Worker*, 10 May 1926; MRC, Warwick University, TUC Papers, MSS.292/252.62/20/12: 'TUC Official Bulletin, 10 May 1926'.

[90] *Swansea Labour News*, 12 June 1926.

[91] Women's liberal and nationalist politics is the major theme of Masson, *For Women, For Wales and for Liberalism*. For comparable analysis of women in British labour politics see: Pamela M. Graves, *Labour Women: Women in British Working Class Politics, 1918-1939* (Cambridge, 2008); Christine Collette, *For Labour and For Women: The Women's Labour League, 1906-1918* (Manchester, 1989); June Hannam and Karen Hunt, *Socialist Women: Britain, 1880s to 1920s* (London, 2001); and Karen Hunt, *Equivocal Feminists: The Social Democratic Federation and the Woman Question, 1884-1911* (Cambridge, 2002).

[92] Sue Bruley, *Leninism, Stalinism, and the Women's Movement in*

Britain, 1920-1939 (London, 1986), 152. For a more recent study of Scotland see, Neil Rafeek, *Communist Women in Scotland: Red Clydeside from the Russian Revolution to the End of the Soviet Union* (London, 2014).

[93] Burge, '1926', 49, 57.

[94] *WM* 5 November 1926; *SWDN*, 3 November 1926; Francis and Smith, *The Fed*, 65.

[95] DCON/293/3/16, Pontyclun Strike Journal, 14 May 1926.

[96] GA, National Union of Railwaymen Records, Llantrisant Branch, DNUR/3/1/3: 'Statement Issued by Swansea Joint Strike Committee, 9 May 1926'.

[97] MRC, TUC Collections, MSS.292/252.62/20/12: 'Official Bulletin No. 7, 10 May 1926'.

[98] SWCC, Bedlinog Council of Action, Minute Book, 14 May 1926.

[99] GA, Pontypridd No. 2 Branch National Union of Railwaymen, DNUR/1/iii: 'Minute Book, 1925-1928: entries for 13 May 1926, 14 May 1926'.

[100] GA, DAB/18/9/59: 'Letter from E. W. West to Head Office, 13 May 1926'.

[101] As above, DAB/18/9/60: 15 May 1926.

[102] As above, DAB/18/9/61: 17 May 1926.

[103] Francis, '1926', 248.

[104] Griffiths, *Pages from Memory*, 31.

[105] SWCC, Maerdy Lodge, Minutes of Committee, 1924-1926: 8 May 1926.

[106] Burge, *Gleaming Vision*, 67.

[107] ALS, CSS/2/5, Aberdare Co-operative Society, Half Year Report, 1 September 1926.

[108] Newport Library, Local Studies Department, Newport (Mon) Co-operative Industrial Society, Annual Reports: Half Yearly Report, 7 January 1927.

[109] SWML, Caerau (Maesteg) Industrial Co-operative Society, *Half Yearly Report October 1927*.

[110] GA, ECG/5/2/3: Bedlinog School, Log Book, 2 November 1926.

[111] GA, ER/32/4: Porth Boys' School, Log Book, 15 November 1926.

[112] Mountain Ash UDC, Education Committee Minutes, 20 July, 21 September, 5 October, 19 October, 2 November 1926.

[113] Mountain Ash UDC, School Medical Officer Annual Report 1926, 28.

[114] Pontypridd UDC, Education Committee Minutes: 28 September (Report of the Schools Medical Officer), 26 October 1926. See also Pontypridd UDC, *Annual Report of the School Medical Officer, 1926*, 47.

[115] GA, ER22/4, Llwynypia Mixed School Log Book, 1915-1958: 31 August, 14 September 1926.

[116] Pontypridd UDC, Education Committee Minutes: 26 October, 30 November 1926'.

[117] Mountain Ash UDC, Schools Medical Officer, Annual Report 1926, 28.

[118] Steven Thompson, '"That Beautiful Summer of Austerity": Health, Diet and Working-Class Domestic Economy in South Wales in 1926', *WHR* 21, no. 3 (2003), 555.

[119] As above, 567.

[120] Monmouthshire CC, Medical Officer of Health, *Annual Report for 1927*, 5-7.

[121] As above, 56.

[122] Gwyn Thomas, *Gazooka and other stories* (London, 1957), 64.

[123] Montagu Slater, *Stay-Down Miner* (London, 1936), 23. What follows draws on Francis and Smith, *The Fed*, as well as Smith, 'Rebuilding'.

[124] SWCC, Maerdy Lodge Minutes, 7 September 1926.

[125] *GG*, 13 August 1926; GA, DCON/52: 'Llanharan Strike Journal,1926.

[126] Morgan, *VWC*, 29.

[127] GA, DNCB/28/91, Ocean Coal Company, *Summary of Daily Reports, 1925-1927*.

[128] *WM*, 22 November 1926.

[129] *MEx*, 27 November 1926.

[130] *Workers' Life*, 4 March 1927; *South Wales News*, 22 November 1926.

[131] *WM*, 5 November 1926.

[132] *WM*, 30 December 1926.

[133] *WM*, 7 May, 21 May 1927.

[134] Francis and Smith, *The Fed*, 116.

[135] GA, D1006/2/2: 7 December 1926.

[136] GA, UDPP/E/3/5: Letter to Board of Education, 4 October 1926; Letter to Board of Education, 20 November 1926.

[137] TNA, HO 45/24707: 'Police, Action taken during the General Strike by Mr Victor Bosanquet, Chief Constable of Monmouthshire Force; call for his resignation'. I am grateful to Professor Keith Laybourn for sharing his notes on this file with me.

[138] *WM*, 26 June 1926.

[139] *Colliery Guardian*, 23 July 1926.

[140] *Where Labour Rules: A Record of Labour Administration, 1925-1928* (Cardiff, 1928), 14.

[141] *WM*, 1 December 1929.

[142] GA, D463/Box 15: 'Letter from Victor Bosanquet to Lionel Lindsay, 1 May 1928'.

[143] *WM*, 1 December 1929.

PART III

Defending South Wales

CHAPTER FIVE

Picking Up The Pieces

In a single year, between April 1926 and April 1927, over twenty thousand miners lost their jobs. During the last week of production prior to the General Strike, some two hundred and sixteen thousand miners were employed in the pits of South Wales, itself a dramatic decline from the more than two hundred and seventy thousand working in 1920. By 1927 that had fallen to under one hundred and ninety five thousand, declining still further over the course of the decade so that by 1936 there were just one hundred and forty thousand miners. The industry had halved in little more than fifteen years. Almost two hundred and fifty pits had shut. It was an industry that was dying. The Mining Association, the national employers' union, was resolute and insisted that despite such levels of unemployment there was 'no question of victimisation ... [and] if market improvements continued and the output increased, there was no reason why all the unemployed miners should not eventually be absorbed'. They never were; it was self-evidently a lie.[1] As Gwyn Thomas was to later remark, he was, like so many of his generation,

> Denied the sight of a society that was economically sure of itself, confident that we had got hold of a productive system that was on the make, on the way, glad to be making the things it was making, devoutly proud of its money.[2]

Everywhere the complaint was the same. 'The continued slump in trade has led to prolonged unemployment', reflected the medical officer for Barry, Dr Percy Kent. What work there was had become casual in nature.[3] In its absence, many left: Glamorgan's population fell by several thousand between 1926 and 1927, and continued to fall sharply in following years. In 1926, the county council recorded a population in its boundaries (which did not include Cardiff, Merthyr or Swansea) of around eight hundred and forty thousand; within a decade it had fallen to just over seven hundred and thirty thousand.[4] The rate of decline in Merthyr was no less dramatic, from a population of around eighty thousand in 1921, the population by the mid-1930s was around sixty five thousand and falling.[5]

The first port of call for many was Bristol. In 1926, the almoner of the Bristol Cambrian Society reported on the sums of money given in response to cases of need that year.[6] One hundred and nineteen men and ten women had been given a small sum of money to enable them to return to Wales having come to Bristol in a vain search for work. Most of those relieved were not miners, for whom the Society held a strong degree of suspicion, but those who previously worked in service industries directly impacted by the economic slump such as hotel porters, plumbers and chefs.[7] The following year, the rate of demand grew sharply: two hundred cases were heard by the almoner but fewer were given money and passage back to South Wales – there was little point. These were desperate individuals. One man, who was otherwise refused by the Society because he could apply for the dole, was given a few coppers when he sang *Hen Wlad Fy Nhadau* to convince the almoner of his case.[8] By 1928, the almoner could scarcely cope. So many people had arrived from the mining areas, the almoner wrote in his report, that 'he is frequently reminded that it is almost one's work to answer the door for them'. The support given was mostly in the form of vouchers for food and lodgings at the Salvation Army Hostel. There they stayed, to pick up the pieces of lives devastated by an economic system – and an industry – seemingly broken beyond repair.[9]

Some were determined to make a stand. In February 1927, a dispute over SWMF membership led to a strike in Gwaun-Cae-Gurwen. A few months later, a more serious dispute on the same issue in Maesteg saw the town crier march through the town declaring that there would be no more work at the pits surrounding the town. The same month saw almost every household lose their incomes in Nantgarw, near Pontypridd, when the colliery was closed by its owners – Baldwin's Limited, the family firm of the prime minister, Stanley Baldwin. In parts of Monmouthshire, where half the miners were out of work and one in seven of the general population was already unemployed, anger was at boiling point. And then, amid it all, Stanley Baldwin travelled to South Wales with his wife to attend a Cymmrodorion Society dinner in Cardiff. They stopped off at Cwm near Ebbw Vale to pay their respects to the families of the fifty two victims of an explosion at the Marine Colliery on St David's Day, twenty men were reportedly still trapped underground. The confrontation was inevitable. As the Baldwins arrived at the colliery offices in their chauffeur driven car, the site filled with angry miners and their families. They booed and shouted: 'why don't you go down the mine yourself'. The newspapers reported that Baldwin stood, silently, smoking his pipe in visible distress and that Mrs Baldwin had returned to the car on the verge of tears. She 'sank back in her seat with a look of pained amusement'.

The local MP, Evan Davies, shocked at the behaviour of the crowd, hurried to blame a 'band of irresponsibles', earning himself, in turn, a censure from the SWMF executive.[10] But the demonstration was welcomed by those on the Labour left. The former secretary of mines, Emanuel Shinwell, was supportive. In a speech to the ILP in Northallerton a few weeks after the event he remarked that 'Mr Baldwin went about with a Bible in one hand and a blunderbuss in the other, and ought to be ashamed to show his face in the coalfields of this country'.[11] Little could be done to change the government, but Evan Davies's position was far from secure. He had proven to be a mediocre member of parliament and, despite everything that was going on in his constituency in the 1920s, made little contribution to political debate, either in the Commons or at large. The wheels were set in motion by a group of conspirators that would eventually cause his deselection and his replacement. The man who stood to gain was Aneurin Bevan. It was Bevan's close friend, Archie Lush, secretary of the Ebbw Vale Divisional Labour Party, who masterminded the plot. He used Davies's actions in response to the colliery dispute as the excuse to effect what was, at the time, an unprecedented deselection process. As well as the censure, Lush successfully convinced the SWMF executive to sanction a selection ballot for Ebbw Vale ahead of the next general election (due in 1929). This was held in March 1929. Aneurin Bevan came top in each round and went on to be elected as MP for the constituency a few months later.

Bevan's victory was even more remarkable because it broke, for the first time, the traditional route into parliament in a mining constituency in South Wales. Although he was a councillor, and had been a checkweigher, Bevan was neither a miners' agent nor a senior SWMF official and so had not served the apprenticeship traditional to almost all mining MPs. S. O. Davies, who was to be selected as the Labour candidate in Merthyr Tydfil in 1934 typified the traditional route having served as checkweigher, miners' agent, SWMF vice president, and finally member of parliament. Bevan's selection, at the age of thirty one, was not for services rendered, but for the possibilities that were to come.[12] The difference in political tone was immediate. In his first speeches to parliament, sitting on the backbenches of a Labour government, Bevan attacked the legacies of the previous Conservative administration, particularly those of the former Minister of Health, Neville Chamberlain, who had been ruthless in his application of the poor law and failed to listen to medical officers from South Wales who pointed to the growing health problems in the region's poorest communities; and he clashed almost immediately with Winston Churchill. As had been the case during his period as a Monmouthshire county councillor, Bevan also willingly reproached Labour colleagues notably Margaret Bondfield, the Minister of Labour, and Philip Snowden, the Chancellor, when they did not go far enough in using the powers at their disposal to ameliorate poverty and unemployment 'to stiffen their people's resistance' to the ill-effects of capitalism.[13]

Bevan refused to be entirely bound by the rigid conventions of constitutionalism and the existing parliamentary rule book and sought practical mechanisms for putting into practice the principles he held. He developed, in Dai Smith's characterisation, an effective 'twinning of the ideally imaginative and the strictly realizable'.[14] This meant that he could, on the one hand, campaign in favour of CPGB affiliation to the Labour Party but on the other never seriously consider joining the communists.[15] He bridged the gap between the language of idealism and the politics of practicality. As he put it in 1929, 'the workers were at last awakening to a realisation of the power which lay in their grasp and were beginning to use it'.[16] It was a bridging that most in either party spurned. For the communists, who were ostensibly to the left of Bevan, this meant a failure to appreciate the potency of Bevan's social democratic politics, and for the moderates in the Labour Party it meant giving far more credence to principled action rather than cautious inaction. This was the essence of his observation to Arthur Horner after the Rhondda East by-election in 1933, that had Horner stood as a miners' candidate he 'would have spoken on his behalf'.[17] But then Horner was the most Bevanite of the British communists.

Most of the CPGB after 1926 came to see the Labour Party in much the same light as the Conservatives and Liberals, the old parties of capital. As one communist organisation from Monmouthshire put it, Labour were 'now the real bulwark of capitalist administration'. One of those whose voice was particularly loud was Wal Hannington, a founding member of the CPGB from London and one of the leaders of the national unemployed movement. In the autumn of 1928, Hannington visited South Wales to agitate amongst the unemployed. There, he wrote afterwards, he saw 'terrible poverty ... thousands of men, women, and children in the mining valleys ... sinking deeper and deeper into the morass of destitution and actual starvation'.[18] Others told of unemployed in Cardiff seeking refuge in the city's dust carts because unemployment relief was too meagre to afford proper accommodation.[19] This kind of rhetoric, which was undoubtedly reflective of actuality, if written up for effect, was used by the CPGB and associated organisations like the National Unemployed Workers' Movement to attack all those in positions of power, regardless of their political allegiances. It was indicative of the CPGB's rejectionism and stood in stark contrast with the realism of the Labour Party. These were the twin paths followed by the left after 1926.

The division was as bitter and personal as it was unhelpful. In a circular issued by the SWMF executive in 1928, Thomas Richards, the general secretary, complained of a

Perfidious frantic effort by the emissaries of the Communist Party to further disrupt the unity of the Federation in the hope of its ultimate suppression and the substitution of revolutionary destructive action.

He continued:

> For a long time we have been subjected to a campaign of abuse and vilification which has recently been prosecuted with added vigour in response to the command from headquarters to besmirch the reputation and destroy the confidence of the workmen in what they designate the 'reformist leaders'. They are now engaged in a veritable orgy of falsehoods and abuse in an attempt of portraying a maladministration of the funds of the Federation, with special emphasis upon the disbursement of the monies received for the relief of the miners arising from the 1926 lock-out.
>
> The full heinousness of this campaign can only be realised when it is known that Mr Arthur Horner, who initiated it, was a member of the council during the distribution of this fund and must be fully conscious that he is responsible for writing and stating a deliberate falsehood that his expense as an executive committee member, or the salaries of the officials, were paid from relief funds.[20]

The situation was potentially a perilous one. To the right of the SWMF was the employer's union, the South Wales Miners' Industrial Union, which was determined to take advantage of the SWMF's post-1926 weakness and exhaustion to break its influence over the coalfield. As A. J. Cook put it in a speech to miners at Llanharan in May 1927, the SWMIU was

> Born in the colliery office, supplied with Tory beer, and fed in the Tory clubs, and when the employers withdraw their support from it, it will die. The *Western Mail* is its mouthpiece. [...] We have in South Wales the dirtiest and most vile press in the country which has done all it could to utilise its columns, to try

317

to support the Non-Political Union and smash the Miners' Federation.[21]

To the left was the increasingly sharp rhetoric of some within the CPGB who had switched from supporting ginger groups within existing trade unions under the umbrella of the National Minority Movement, to establishing their own alternatives. One such alternative could have been the United Mineworkers of Great Britain, a left alternative to the SWMF modelled on the United Mineworkers of Scotland, a communist splinter union which formed in Fife in 1929, with Maerdy Lodge at its core. Most refused to go along with the idea. As one leading communist explained to leaders in Moscow:

> In a whole series of lodges in South Wales where formerly our party or left wingers were in control, we have been eliminated not by the manoeuvres of bureaucrats but the open vote of the workers at their annual meeting. ... our general influence ... has gone down.[22]

The red union was a blind alley, but the fact that it was discussed at all demonstrated the extent of the divisions across the left between ideological purity and practicality. In the face of such external pressure, and the push within the SWMF from left-leaning members such as S. O. Davies, it was no surprise that the SWMF executive gave no quarter to internal demands for wholesale change. Their focus was, instead, on overcoming the existential threat. The more the left pushed, the more the moderates dug in. The division was first exposed by the hunger march in the autumn of 1927.

On 18 September 1927 – Red Sunday in the Rhondda Valley, as the posters proclaimed it – ten thousand people gathered from across South Wales on Penrhys mountain in the Rhondda to listen to speeches by A. J. Cook, Wal Hannington, and the local miners' agents. At the rally, Cook called for 'a great march to London' to interview government ministers and press their case. Although the initial enthusiasm was broad-based, by the time the march set off in November this had all but collapsed with almost all the South Wales Miners' Federation districts refusing to support it financially: only the Rhondda district remained steadfast, as did the Dowlais Agent, S. O. Davies. Other local leaders who joined the march included Arthur Horner. The core of the march's support derived from the Communist Party and its rhetoric was determinedly radical; therefore, the Federation executive and the Labour Party withdrew their support. Two hundred and seventy marchers with haversacks, army kit bags, and home-made banners, set off on Wednesday 9 November from across South Wales in high spirits. Along the route they sang a wide variety of popular Welsh songs, such as *Cwm Rhondda* and *Sospan Fach*, as well as old war-time favourites such as *Pack Up Your Troubles*, and perhaps less well-known socialist songs that included *March Song of the Red Army* and James Connolly's *A Rebel Song*.

In Bristol, their first stopping point along the route, they were greeted enthusiastically by members of the city's trades and labour council and some university students and were joined by local unemployed.[23] From Bristol, they marched to Bath, arriving there on Thursday afternoon. That evening was spent at the Friends Meeting House on York Street.[24] The morning of Armistice Day was spent at the Bath Labour Party's headquarters. Before setting off for Chippenham and Swindon, several of them indulged at the mineral water fountain on Bath Street 'a proceeding that was watched with considerable interest by many citizens'.[25] By the time the marchers reached Swindon on Saturday evening, they appeared tired, but knew that Swindon would provide respite as they were not due to leave for Reading until Monday. Whilst in the town, there were reports that the marchers had burned copies of a London daily in protest at its anti-march propaganda.[26] In Reading, the march was hosted at the town's communal kitchen with meals provided by the local Labour Party and they stayed overnight at the Corn Exchange.

Their arrival at Reading came at dusk and the spectacle of nearly three hundred miners, lit by the safety lamps they were carrying, was remarkable, although the press preferred to comment on the badge that Wal Hannington was wearing – three red stars, a sickle, and a hammer. A 'Soviet Symbol' as the *Western Morning News* declared it.[27] But there was disquiet amongst members of the Reading Labour Party at the presence of the march, not least from the secretary, who gave an interview to the press in which he remarked:

> during the last five years in Reading we have had to find accommodation for five groups of hunger marches, for a score of miners choirs, jazz bands etc, and seventy miners' children for a period of several months [...] in the light of experience we are thoroughly convinced that these marches do little good. [...] they certainly are an embarrassment to the Labour Parties in the towns en route.[28]

Hostility of a different nature grew the closer the marchers came to London. In fact, such was the level of anticipated violence that organisers went to the trouble of organising a group of one hundred uniformed ex-service men drawn from the ranks of the Labour League of Ex-Service Men who marched alongside the Welsh miners from Chiswick to Trafalgar Square.[29] They were also joined by members of the Durham Miners' Association who had cycled down from the North-East to meet them.[30] There were intermittent scuffles with members of the British

Fascisti.[31] At a mass rally in Trafalgar Square, A. J. Cook declared the object of the march had been to bring before the public the poverty of the miners and the callousness of Baldwinism. 'Baldwin, you must go!' he declared, a slogan that was repeated by the crowd three times. 'Public sympathy with the unfortunate miners ... would have found fuller expression yesterday', remarked the *Gloucester Citizen*, in reaction, 'if they had not been so ostentatiously taken in hand by the Communists for propaganda purposes and if Mr Cook had not made a characteristically violent speech in Trafalgar Square'.[32]

By the time the marchers returned to South Wales, by train, on 28 November, two of their comrades had died of natural causes and the march organisers had broadly failed in their objective of convincing the government to listen to the voices of the suffering. For a moment, however, the march had a galvanising effect and helped to overcome some of the divisions apparent following the SWMF's withdrawal of official support, but not all. At a rally in Pontypridd, on the afternoon of their return, the platform included representatives from the Labour Party, the CPGB, local SWMF officials, and local councillors. Speeches were given by (amongst others) W. H. Mainwaring, Arthur Horner, and S. O. Davies. The procession itself was headed by D. L. Davies, miners' agent for the Pontypridd district (and the town's MP 1931-37); councillor Arthur Pearson (Pontypridd MP 1938-70); and Jesse Powderhill, chairman of the Pontypridd Trades and Labour Council.[33] The march had generated hope, perhaps even hopes of a truce within the labour movement, particularly given the external challenges faced, but it was not yet to be realised as such. Dai Lloyd Davies, one of the communist lodge officials in Maerdy, had suggested in Trafalgar Square that 'the march marked the beginning of a new era'. He was right, but not in the way he might have wished, or imagined.

The ten years that followed the 1926 miners' lockout were marked by Labour's steady consolidation of its strength in South Wales, together with indications of its future potential (in 1929, the party won all three Cardiff parliamentary seats and Llandaff and Barry, for example), despite the hostility of central government, the antagonistic attitude of the CPGB, and the calamity of the 1931 general election. It refused to go along with the 'alternative culture' instead making 'the existing culture its own [rather] than demolish it'.[34] But it also faced internal problems masked, to some extent, by that outward progress, but no less threatening. In the Rhondda, senior councillors and future MPs, were concerned about apathy and disengagement. 'I have been in the labour movement in the Rhondda for forty years', complained Treorchy councillor Rhys Evans in 1933, 'but have never experienced anything so depressing as the present lack of enthusiasm and interest'. The counterpoint of communist consciousness raising, through hunger marches, street rallies, pit papers, daily newspapers, and pamphlets, which together brought attention to the worst excesses of government policy, was apparent.

Although Labour refused to go down the route of political rejectionism, as advocated by the CPGB, the alternative of managing austerity was difficult and potentially damaging particularly if pragmatism became passivity in the face of encircling dangers. This was Bevan's charge and he argued in favour of a working class that was 'well organised, disciplined and courageously led'.[35] To senior figures in the Labour Party it sounded too much like the CPGB's message but Bevan's aim was to

> promote all forms of working class resistance to a lower standard of life and to vitalize all institutions which serve the workers, such as trade unions, co-operative societies, etc.[36]

As Dai Smith records, this was 'undertaken by the SWMF within a year and with dramatic results'.[37] Others organised grassroots resistance to unemployment regulations. In Aberdare, the trades and labour council secretary, Ted Stonelake, developed a training programme for miners called before the Court of Requests (the debtor's court). As he recalled in his memoir, 'I asked them all the stock questions, and when they fell down on them, as most of them did, I provided the correct answers, warning them not to forget'.[38] In this way Labour navigated a way through the administrative challenges of the interwar depression and found solutions, as best they could, to the central questions of the day: how to mitigate the cuts insisted upon by central government, how to prevent the future collapse of the local economy, and how to ensure that the social democracy that had been steadily built up since the end of the First World War did not fail.

Labour in the Downturn

It was the financial fragility of the interwar years, alongside Labour's social democratic politics, that brought large swathes of previously non-municipal institutions and resources under the auspices of the state. To protect parks, libraries, and hospitals, Labour expanded the reach of councils even as central government insisted on spending restraint and cuts to public expenditure. Here was the essence of the party's radical pragmatism. In healthcare, Labour councils began to move into provision in the 1920s, expanding the reach of the state beyond the regulatory capacities of medical officers of health and sanitary inspectors. This was notably true of maternity, infant welfare, and birth control, but was also the case for environmental protection, housing, food supplies, and recreation.[39] It meant that councils were willing to innovate, as with the birth control and social welfare clinic opened in

Abertillery in the summer of 1925.[40] The clinic had been encouraged by David Daggar, brother of the town's future MP George Daggar, in his capacity as miners' representative on the Abertillery and District Hospital Committee, and was supported by the birth control campaigner Marie Stopes. Such innovation was met with hostility by the chapels. They denounced 'the placarding of our streets with such posters as would bring the blush of shame to the cheeks of our mothers and would make our youth prurient'.[41] The impact of the miners' lockout forced the clinic's closure the following year.[42]

The next to open was in Pontypridd, initially as a voluntary initiative and then as a municipal clinic.[43] Once the clinic was municipalised the council met the cost of treatment for those who could not afford to pay and provided services to patients from Glyncorrwg on the same basis.[44] Similar municipally-run clinics opened across much of Glamorgan in the 1930s, particularly in the central districts of the coalfield, with the rate in Monmouthshire affected by the virulent opposition of the county medical officer to birth control. Kate Fisher, in her work on the provision of birth control clinics in South Wales, has questioned the extent to which the existence of a municipal clinic reflected the willingness of the Labour Party to act on the question. A similar stance has been taken by Pamela Michael. Certainly, there is evidence from the Rhondda – albeit from the middle of the 1926 lockout, which undoubtedly coloured the response – where calls made by the Co-operative Women's Guilds, amongst others, for information on birth control to be made available in council clinics were ignored.[45] And from Newport, where the Labour Party executive refused to allow the party to be associated with motions promoting birth control.[46] But this must be balanced by the greater reality that almost all of the local authorities in South Wales which did provide birth control and gynaecology were run by the Labour Party, and, in

Pontypridd at least, that very same Labour Party was quite willing to press the local authority and its committees on precisely this issue whether in power or not. In 1920, for example, Pontypridd Trades and Labour Council presented a lengthy motion calling for sex education in the town's schools:

> This Pontypridd Trades and Labour Council are emphatically of the opinion that, in the interests of the rising generation, boys and girls approaching the age of fourteen should be instructed in sex problems. That this instruction should be given by those best qualified to do so, e.g. in the case of boys, the school medical doctor; in the case of girls, the school nurses. That this instruction should be given at a centre, the opinion of the Trades and Labour Council being that the school clinic would be the most suitable place.[47]

The motion was ultimately rejected by the council's education committee on the basis that 'parents are the proper persons to instruct their children in matters of this kind', but it does nevertheless demonstrate a determination to provide state intervention in the field of sex and family planning.[48]

It was a similar story in other aspects of healthcare, too. A network of maternity and child welfare clinics was established in the 1920s in response to the Maternity and Child Welfare Act of 1918 obliging local authorities to do just that. By 1930, there were more than one hundred across Glamorgan, some in temporary locations such as chapel vestries, workmen's halls, and public libraries, and others in genuine clinics.[49] Some councils went even further. In Maesteg, councillors established their own maternity hospital in 1921 paid for out of local rates; the general hospital in the town was paid for primarily by the miners' lodges.[50] Mountain Ash UDC opened its maternity hospital in 1925.[51] And there was considerable effort expended across the coalfield providing antenatal advice and support services, despite the economic circumstances of the period. As the medical officer for Gelligaer UDC wrote, 'much trouble is taken to instruct and help mothers in matters of good health, food, clothes, etc., and if only times had been normal, the results would have been more marked than they are'.[52] For the youngest children, state intervention was considerable. In Ogmore and Garw, for example, the council provided dental and optical treatment for all under-fives through its school medical service.[53]

The intervention of Labour councils over birth control and on the earliest years of a child's life reflected a determination to ameliorate the effects of a poor economy on individual lives. The stress was not merely on health, either, with an equal desire to effect meaningful change in the field of early years education apparent. But it was housing that most exercised concerns about public health and the general fitness for life of mining communities in the modern world. Housing was also an area in which the local authority had little choice but to intervene since, as early as 1906, the private sector for housing had all but collapsed. Although the rates of decline were felt differently depending on location, by the mid-1920s it was apparent everywhere. In the Rhondda, for instance, the private sector could maintain a house building programme through to the outbreak of war in 1914, but it came to a sudden halt thereafter and was not revived after the war.[54] Indeed, in the absence of private sector investment after 1918, councillors began tentatively to engage in council housing schemes with houses let to tenants by the housing committee. Given the economy, the rate of construction was painfully slow and could not keep up with demand. In 1924, it was estimated that more than five thousand homes were needed in the Rhondda but fewer than two hundred – almost all of them council housing – had been built. The following year, with little sign of improvement, the district's medical officer declared the provision of housing 'the most obviously urgent of all the problems with which the Council is faced'.[55]

Across the coalfield, particularly following the passage of the 1919 Housing Act, medical officers, borough surveyors, and councillors, recognised the challenge and sought solutions. But they were not easily implemented. In Tredegar, for instance, the medical officer noted that in the decade since the outbreak of the First World War the private sector had managed to build a mere seven houses a year. 'The consequences', he reflected, 'are very deplorable'.[56] Across Monmouthshire, ambitious plans were put in place after 1919 for thousands of homes to be built including more than seven hundred at Abercarn, a thousand at Abersychan, eleven hundred at Bedwellty, and more than five hundred at Tredegar. But few were ever built and by the middle of the 1920s, even in areas where housing problems were less acute, such as Caerleon or Risca, councillors admitted defeat.[57] 'The original housing schemes', reflected Monmouthshire's medical officer in 1924, 'are not likely to be attained under the present economic conditions'. Most house building was, by then, confined to the 'residential class of property, the outlook for houses for the working class is depressing, and constitutes the biggest obstacle to an improved public health'.[58] The same sentiment was expressed year after year for the next two decades.

And so, by the second half of the 1920s and into the first half of the 1930s, most houses built in the coalfield were constructed because of local authority initiative. In 1927, Tredegar UDC constructed fifty homes compared with just fifteen built by private enterprise, in Bedwas and Machen the ratio was forty eight to six, and in Nantyglo and Blaina it was twenty to none.[59] The following year the disparity was even more stark – more than two hundred and sixty houses were constructed across the urban districts of Monmouthshire by local councils, compared with just ninety seven by private enterprise. But both figures were dwarfed by the more than seven hundred houses built by private contractors in the prosperous St Mellons in the green belt between Cardiff and Newport, and by the regularity of private sector housing being built in areas such as Porthcawl.[60] Although it was noted in the case of the latter that the new homes were unaffordable for working class families.[61] In addition to being priced out of the market, the ambition to build a better type of housing for working people vanished: lower density, better quality housing constructed at the beginning of the 1920s gave way to higher density housing thereafter reflecting the withdrawal of central government support. As Aneurin Bevan lamented, he was 'sick of hearing the phrase "working men's dwellings", as if a working man's house should be a rabbit warren. A rabbit warren house led to a rabbit warren life'.[62]

Bevan knew that overcrowding in those 'working men's dwellings' remained shockingly high and was determined to do something about it. In Nantyglo and Blaina, for example, some thirty percent of houses were deemed to be overcrowded and housing inspections in Tredegar revealed a rate of overcrowding of fifty percent.[63] The only reason that South Wales did not suffer an even greater housing crisis in the interwar years was because of depopulation – the result of out-migration because of a lack of employment – but that served only to delay the problem rather than resolve it.[64] The problem was multifaceted for those forced to exist in the housing conditions which prevailed into the interwar years. As the medical officer for Monmouthshire reflected in 1931,

> This state of affairs is not conducive to good health or decent morals. At many of the older houses where the accommodation is limited it is quite common to find two families living in the

same house. Parents and children, some of whom have reached puberty, are compelled to sleep in the same bedroom, whilst it is not uncommon for members of both sexes of advanced ages to use a common sleeping room. These houses have in addition none of the advantages that tend to promote a health life, as most of the household washing, cooking, etc, have to be carried out in the one living room which is often the only room on the ground floor. Many of these older type are in a condition only fit for demolition, but it is unfortunate that most of these houses are to be found in the areas where the industrial depression has been most keenly felt and the tenants, in most cases, are not in a position to avail themselves of better housing accommodation, even when provided.[65]

Those bedrooms were often internally divided with curtains or other makeshift screens to offer the semblance of privacy.[66]

Councils could not, of course, spend money that they did not have and despite a clear desire to act, they struggled either to develop housing to meet modern needs or to alleviate some of the pressures on existing housing stock. Writing in 1938, the medical officer for Nantyglo and Blaina lamented that 'I am constantly receiving letters imploring me to find some better accommodation for families ... but I am quite helpless, as we have nothing to offer'.[67] Financial constraint placed clear limits on what Labour could achieve at the local level without clear support from central government or the willingness of banks and building societies to lend money to private businesses even with local authority backing. In the Rhondda, builders told councillors bluntly that house building 'could not be regarded as adequately remunerative' because tenants could not pay a market rent, they made a better return on housing repairs and even funerals instead. Councillors then offered to act as an intermediary to secure the agreement of banks and building societies to provide loans to house builders to restart the market. It failed. The Principality Building Society told Rhondda UDC bluntly that they were 'not prepared to entertain the suggestion'. House building fell back on what resources the council itself could provide.

Given these experiences, it should be of little surprise that councillors became steadily more convinced of the need for the state to be the driving force of essential public services. Having entered office in the early 1920s on broad platforms of change including tackling pollution, improving public libraries, even building crematoriums, and with a desire to implement social democratic ideas of government, the challenge for Labour councillors by the end of the decade and in the 1930s was how to implement them in a period of high demand and severe budgetary constraint. This led to innovative solutions – one of which was the opening of the crematorium at Glyntaff, Pontypridd, in 1924. It was intended to tackle the steady increase in the cost of burials in public cemeteries and therefore to reduce the cost of one aspect of local government. As the district's medical officer remarked in 1925, 'it is estimated that if one half of the people now buried in Glyntaff Cemetery were cremated there would be no burial rate'.[68] Likewise, because councillors recognised that businesses were unlikely to act on issues of pollution, it fell to them to implement regulations to improve the public environment. Those caught polluting rivers were subject to hefty fines.[69] And all rubbish collected from homes and businesses was burned at Pontypridd UDC's incinerator, rather than buried at landfill, with the resulting energy used to produce cheap electricity for the town.[70]

Other innovations involved the careful encouragement of private enterprise, particularly in new sectors of the economy such as the rapidly developing entertainment industry. Entertainment, including professional sport, was one of the growth sectors of the interwar economy and a major modernising influence.[71] It brought jobs, new infrastructure, and vital investment, and was greatly aided by the popularising medium of the radio; and sports broadcasting began, if at first tentatively, to bring mass commercial sport into the reach of everyone including many women who otherwise might not have attended. Thus, in coalfield towns such as Pontypridd and Tredegar in which investment was otherwise leaving, crowds of thousands flocked to stadiums built or renovated to house speedway, greyhound racing, professional boxing, cycling, and, for a time, rugby league. And Labour began to see itself as an ally of this new industry that was providing, however temporarily, new jobs. Indeed, the party gave tacit sponsorship to commercial sport to encourage economic growth in the coalfield – they could not, after all, adequately claim to represent working-class people and turn away, as the churches, chapels, and communists demanded, the employment opportunities that came with commercial entertainment. The stakes were too high: conversion of Taff Vale Park in Pontypridd in 1927, for instance, involved private investment of twenty five thousand pounds.[72] Few other businesses were investing on that scale in the coalfield, most were still feeling the impact of the previous year's mining lockout.

For those who weren't employed at the tracks there were also financial appeals. The regular prize money of between one and five pounds offered to victorious racers was a clear temptation given that, according to contemporary estimates, some eighty percent of male breadwinners in the region were earning less than four pounds per week in the early 1930s. The opportunity of doubling (or greater) one's weekly income could not be turned down.[73] Commercial sport caught, if only for a moment, the imagination of those living in the coalfield in its most economically stark years: for a shilling or two at tracks from

Bedwellty to Caerphilly to Aberdare, Merthyr, and Pontypridd, spectators could enjoy one of the newest sporting imports. It should not be a surprise that the Labour Party actively encouraged the development of greyhound racing and speedway and refused to bow to pressure from opponents to prevent their arrival in the coalfield. This was in line with the party's aim to create a country in which opportunities were made universal. As Aneurin Bevan wrote later, the purpose of democratic socialism was to 'universalise the consumption of the best that society can afford'. When speedway arrived in Tredegar in 1929, Bevan, the newly elected MP for Ebbw Vale, was present at the opening ceremony and spoke in praise of the committee that had delivered the track and other improvements.[74] His direct support for greyhound racing was evident when he attended the annual meeting of the National Greyhound Racing Society in 1933.[75]

Bevan was, in this way, indicative of Labour's efforts to find solutions in the decade after the miners' lockout in 1926: his experience of the failure of private enterprise to provide housing in Tredegar led to his determination, as post-war housing minister, that local authorities should be the primary body responsible for house building, but this did not prevent him from engaging with and encouraging private enterprise in other areas of the economy.[76] He, like the Labour Party, was able to bridge the divide where it suited the greater aim. Indeed, radical pragmatism, which guided Labour's actions in South Wales in the 1920s and 1930s, neither rejected business or commercial interests outright, nor fully committed itself either to statist or voluntaryist models of socialism. Instead it embraced and engaged with all three, albeit with increasing recognition of the necessity of the state. This was the major reason for the party's success in South Wales in a period when it could quite easily have lost momentum, as it did elsewhere in the country. It enabled negotiation and negation of the often-competitive internal instincts of the labour movement: Labour as an effective political organisation capable of winning elections and governing, Labour as an activist movement campaigning and engaging on a wide range of issues but rarely holding power, and Labour as an industrial force fighting (in conjunction with the trade unions) industrial battles about industrial matters. It was a triumvirate that Labour's opponents on the left sometimes failed to understand.

Indeed, it might have been very different. Given the economic circumstances of the coalfield and the clear antagonism of the Conservative government, Labour could easily have become far more oppositional and rejectionist as the CPGB did in the late-1920s and early 1930s. That option was certainly available. But the Labour Party was largely defined by its ability to 'focus the attention of the electorate' and by its ability to navigate the problems of the day without ending up in a political cul-de-sac of radical words but little in the way of material result.[77] Labour adopted positions of radical pragmatism that set out to achieve the most given the tough economic circumstances. Thus, 'keeping their hands on the reins of power, if only to administer relatively harsh regulations as sympathetically as possible, was considered preferable to any abdication of control'.[78] That, rather than the rejectionist attitude of the CPGB, was the only way to improve the lot of the individual South Walian, and demonstrated Labour's real understanding of the possibilities of political action over grievance politics. Indeed, in the worst years of the Depression, Labour councils bent the rules as far as they could to ensure the lowest possible rates of destitution, in effect creating a policy of 'non-administration' of government regulations. It meant that, following the introduction of means testing of unemployment benefits in 1932, for instance, applications for transitional assistance were refused at a rate of more than one in every three in Birmingham, which was not controlled by Labour, but at a rate of less than one per cent in Merthyr Tydfil, which was.[79]

Counting Comrades

But why did the CPGB, which emerged out of the miners' lockout with more members than it had ever had, and persons sympathetic to its message in positions of influence, squander its only significant opportunity to seize the initiative from Labour? Certainly, the communists hardly helped their own cause by entering a period of absolutist dogma, the so-called Third Period of 'class against class', insisted upon by Moscow and readily implemented by the faithful in Britain. Although resisted, to an extent, by activists such as Arthur Horner, who recognised its folly and impracticality, they could not prevent its implementation and it undermined the case that activists were able to put to would-be voters and supporters. Indeed, speaking to senior communist figures in Moscow in 1932, Harry Pollitt, the head of the CPGB, who had himself encouraged some of the worst follies admitted that the party was using language such as 'social fascism' which workers did not understand and which was therefore of no use in political agitation or in the *Daily Worker*. By then the damage had already been done. Party membership in South Wales fell from nearly two and a half thousand in 1927 to fewer than three hundred by 1930.[80] Labour Party membership was officially more than eleven thousand, by contrast. In relative terms, there were as many communists in South Wales in 1930 as there were Labour members in Montgomeryshire, the only constituency in Wales never to have elected a Labour MP. Their influence had eroded in all but a few places.

These membership figures serve as an illustration of the fact – easily forgotten given some of the mythologies of the interwar years – that there were never very many card-carrying communists in South Wales, even at the height of the party's fortunes (which were, in any case, after the Second World War). Herein lies part of the reason for the CPGB's failure: it failed to create a broad appeal as a political movement and it squandered opportunities by turning away from practical politics just when they were needed most. This was particularly evident in the failure of the CPGB to appeal to working-class women: there were never more than a few hundred women communists in South Wales in the interwar years, mostly concentrated in the Rhondda. This compared with more than ten thousand in the Labour ranks by the end of the period with women's sections found in every part of the region; particularly large women's sections could be found in towns like Newport and Caerphilly.[81] The few communist women that there were forged their own model of left-feminist politics activism, to the bafflement of many communist men who thought they had no place in the party. Their focus on matters that had a direct impact on women's lives mirrored the initiatives put forward by the women's sections of the Labour Party and included malnutrition, family planning, housing, welfare, and employment. They held relatively well-attended demonstrations to mark international women's day, organised dedicated women's conferences, and they went on the hunger marches.

It was, of course, to men that the CPGB appealed most determinedly and through a variety of organisations such as the National Minority Movement and the unemployed movement that supplemented the work of CPGB itself. Despite their best efforts, recruitment activity produced uneven results and was more successful amongst the unemployed than any other group. In 1932, the communists recruited six unemployed members for every one member who was employed.[82] This meant that, even with a determination to improve recruitment amongst those who were working, by February 1937, of the seven hundred and seventy male members in South Wales, four hundred and twenty were unemployed (or fifty five percent) compared with three hundred and fifty who were employed.[83] In the Rhondda, of the nearly two hundred men who were members, one hundred and thirty were unemployed; in Pontypridd it was twenty nine out of thirty two; and in Dowlais four of the five members were out of work. This serves to qualify the sense given, chiefly in the CPGB's own publications, but which has had some resonance in historical writing about the interwar years, that the communists were able to wield mass influence and leadership on the coalfield through the South Wales Miners' Federation. To what extent was that really the case?

By the beginning of 1937, the CPGB claimed twenty one trade union branch chairmen and twenty seven secretaries, in addition to Arthur Horner's role as president of the South Wales Miners' Federation. Most of these men were, like Horner, in the SWMF, and in that sense the CPGB was justified in claiming a certain degree of local leadership in the coalfield, with a small number to be found in the National Union of Railwaymen and the Transport and General Workers Union in port communities and towns. Yet even the communists were uncertain about the overall effects of this level of 'leadership', certainly in comparison to the strength of the Labour Party. As Idris Cox, the district secretary, lamented in 1937 'if it were judged from the standpoint of the number of communist recruits that have been gained, then our work in the trades unions is a complete failure'.[84] The problem, as they saw it, was that 'leadership of the trade unions is regarded in many places as a substitute for the work of the Communist Party'.[85] Indeed, precisely because of the emphasis on trade union activity, rather than the political work of the party, it was possible for some in the coalfield to vote for Arthur Horner as SWMF president and vote other in parliamentary elections; many more voted for Horner and maintained their allegiance to the Labour Party.[86]

Emphasis on trade union activity was entirely deliberate, for this was the focus of Horner, the leading communist in the South Wales Coalfield. In 1929, Horner had taken a political position, standing as the CPGB candidate in Rhondda East at the general election and winning more than five thousand votes. He had received the support of Maerdy, Ferndale, and Tylorstown lodges in contradiction of SWMF rules which insisted on exclusive support for the Labour Party. The SWMF executive moved to expel Maerdy and on 24 January 1930 it agreed that 'Mardy Lodge shall no longer be recognised and that the officials of that Lodge shall not be entitled to receive contributions on behalf of the SWMF'.[87] Ferndale and Tylorstown backed down and agreed to support the Labour Party in future elections, avoiding Maerdy's fate as a result. Others who had been supportive of Horner were not so fortunate: Will Paynter, checkweigher at Cymmer Colliery and an increasingly prominent communist, was also expelled from the SWMF. He denounced the executive as 'social fascists', but it was empty rhetoric; he left to study in Moscow in 1932.[88] The episode was a blow to the far left's credibility.[89] Horner himself faced hostility within the CPGB executive from younger political radicals who refused to accept his antagonism to class against class and tried to have him expelled from the party. Although eventually rehabilitated, Horner was never fully reconciled to the CPGB as a political force – his own campaigns in Rhondda East in 1931 and 1933 were very much conducted as personal ones. Indeed, in 1931 Horner won more than ten thousand votes and in 1933 over eleven thousand, but in 1932 the party lost every seat it held on Rhondda UDC whilst Labour's cohort of councillors grew to twenty seven.

What Horner understood, and many in the CPGB did not, was that they were in danger of becoming a 'leadership without an army to lead'.[90] As one activist from Maerdy put it, 'in the mining villages, once you were a militant you were known by everyone in the village and the district'.[91] In other words, you had to demonstrate leadership, or else such militancy had little tangible effect other than to prompt personal ostracism. Instead the CPGB pushed for the creation of separate trade unions and lashed out at the Labour Party, even more virulently than it did the Conservatives and Liberals, going so far as to blame Labour councillors for the actions of the police despite the clear disdain of the police for the very same councillors and denouncing Rhondda UDC for 'evicting tenants from their houses'.[92] And Cwmtillery communists declared that 'the treacherous betrayal of the miners by the Labour Party and the SWMF officials is an accomplished fact ... the Labour Party and the SWMF executive committee is one force and the workers in the coalfield is another'.[93] The interests of the former, they stated, was the defence of capitalism. Particular disgust was reserved for Margaret Bondfield, the minister of labour, whom the communist press frequently denounced as the 'great Maggie' using language that would not be out of place in the left's depictions of Margaret Thatcher fifty years later.[94]

To prove the validity of its own propaganda, the CPGB set about establishing an 'alternative culture'. Instead of getting news from the 'mainstream media', there were pit papers such as the *Cambrian X-Ray* published by Lewis Jones in Blaenclydach or the *New Dawn* published by communists in Ferndale or the *Red Challenger* published in Merthyr Tydfil, together with the *Daily Worker* which first appeared on 1 January 1930. There was communist sport, communist eisteddfods, communist holidays, communist funerals, and even communist Christmas.[95] But it didn't really work as a means of growing the movement, and was always subject to stresses and strains, particularly in areas where branches were thinly populated in the first place. Tensions over whether social activity or political activity should be the primary purpose always threatened to tear branches apart and often did.[96] As a report to the CPGB politburo noted in April 1936, there had been half a dozen attempts at forging a communist youth movement in South Wales but it had failed each time. This led to 'complete confusion'.[97] The pit papers, which fell in number from sixteen at the beginning of 1926 to just one by the summer of 1933, had very low circulation in the early 1930s of between three and seven hundred. The *Daily Worker* fared better, increasing its national circulation from eight thousand seven hundred in 1930 to more than twelve thousand by 1931, although distribution outside London had to be made by passenger train because wholesalers refused to carry it.[98] Most copies were delivered by hand by the party faithful.

1933 was when CPGB fortunes began to improve. D. Watts Morgan, the Labour MP for Rhondda East died in February, prompting a by-election. Arthur Horner, who had won more than ten thousand votes at the 1931 general election stood again as the communist candidate; his opponent was W. H. Mainwaring, agent for the Rhondda No. 1 district, and a determined anti-communist. Horner conducted a populist campaign focused on the poverty of the constituency, linking, as one internal report later noted, 'its general fighting slogans against capitalism, the state and reformist policy, with concrete local demands'.[99] Much was made of Horner's own charisma and standing within the miners' lodges. For his part, Mainwaring received the support of leading Labour and SWMF figures, notably the Labour leader George Lansbury and the SWMF president, Enoch Morrell. More than fifty campaign meetings were held involving local and national figures. In the event, the by-election was a close-run contest with Mainwaring winning by a margin of less than three thousand; two years earlier the Labour majority had been nearly twelve thousand. But most of the lost Labour votes went to the Liberal candidate, William Thomas, not to Horner.[100] The CPGB had not advanced.

The value of Horner's campaign lay not in the extent to which it was able to whittle away at Labour's majority, but in convincing the CPGB leadership of the validity of populist electoral campaigning. A few weeks after the Rhondda East by-election, the party won four district council seats, restoring representation on Rhondda UDC and winning in Pontypridd for the first time. One of those elected in 1933 was Llew Jenkins of Cilfynydd, whose work was illustrative of this new turn. Jenkins had worked at the Albion Colliery prior to its closure in 1928 when the Albion Steam Coal Company went into liquidation. As vice chair, and from 1932 chair, of the Albion lodge, it was his responsibility to respond to the changing circumstances in the village. The Albion was eventually bought by the Powell Duffryn combine and reopened in 1933, but a significant proportion of the workforce remained unemployed – many of them Powell Duffryn refused to re-employ because they were regarded as politically problematic.[101] Jenkins was caught up in this victimisation having first come to the notice of the police as a radical during the 1926 lockout. By the early 1930s he was a member of the CPGB, secretary of the party's Pontypridd branch, a correspondent for the *Daily Worker*, a member of the Miners' Minority Movement, and the local organiser in Pontypridd for the NUWM.[102] In 1931, he was even nominated by lodges in Pontypridd as a left candidate to replace Thomas Richards as secretary of the SWMF.[103]

Then, in 1932, in an act that ran the risk of the Albion lodge being expelled from the SWMF on a similar basis to Maerdy two years earlier, Jenkins was nominated by the lodge to run against long-standing Labour councillor Artemus Seymour. There was palpable anger that Seymour had taken a job at the colliery as a company checkweigher and his own election campaign was supported by the increasingly notorious colliery management. Jenkins's run was the first time a CPGB candidate had stood in Pontypridd and was taken as a sign of the discontent in Cilfynydd with the new Powell Duffryn regime and Labour's apparent collusion with it. Seymour triumphed but it was a close run thing: Jenkins secured five hundred and thirty nine votes to Seymour's six hundred and seventy. A few months after the election, nearly half the workforce at the Albion were issued with termination notices. Writing in the *Daily Worker*, Jenkins noted that 'the management are clearly trying to break the resistance of the men by issuing notices and subsequently taking back whom they will'.[104] In the autumn, managers at the Albion issued orders that effectively aimed at breaking up existing 'butties' and other underground support systems which enabled SWMF organisation. In protest, the lodge issued a Sunday stoppage, but it did not prevent the orders from being implemented.[105]

The following year, not surprisingly, Llew Jenkins was again nominated by the Albion lodge to stand in the municipal elections. On this occasion he triumphed, albeit by the slimmest of margins, beating the sitting Labour councillor, Ben Meredith, by seven votes.[106] Jenkins's victory over Labour raised their ire and led to several attempts to minimise communist influence in the village and on council committees. In 1935, Labour gerrymandered committee positions in such a way as to ensure that the only positions Llew Jenkins held were on the libraries and town planning committees. As the *Pontypridd Observer* reported, 'on a number of occasions he moved himself, but failed each time to obtain a seconder'.[107] A few weeks earlier, the Labour chairman of the council (and fellow Cilfynydd councillor) George Paget had remarked at a chamber of trade dinner that 'some of my colleagues cow tow to the communists but I am not taking their orders. I am trying to administer this town in the interests of all'.[108] But Jenkins was not easily side-lined and in 1936, because of the prominent role he took in the unemployed movement and the campaign against the means test, he was re-elected with a majority of nearly five hundred.[109] He stepped down at the 1939 elections to take a job at the Bargoed Educational Settlement and soon after joined the Labour Party.

It is doubtful that Llew Jenkins could have been elected, or re-elected, without having taken prominent roles in the Albion lodge or within the unemployed movement. These enabled him to demonstrate the efficacy of his communist politics at the local level and to build the personal relationships necessary to dislodge the incumbent Labour Party. This was also true of other individuals elected as communists elsewhere in the coalfield, such as John Roberts (known as Jack Russia) in Abertridwr, Trevor Williams in the Blaengwawr ward in Aberdare, Alistair Wilson in Aberaman, Mavis Llewellyn in Nantymoel, or Edgar Evans in Bedlinog. This was quite different from the large concentration of communist councillors in the upper Rhondda Fach, since they could sit together not as single members but as the largest opposition bloc on Rhondda UDC. Outside of the Rhondda, the CPGB relied on strength of personality to get members elected in places that were slightly out of the way and which were on the front lines of the political and economic turmoil that engulfed the coalfield in the 1930s. Wherever there was a confrontation with the forces of capital or with the police, as Hywel Francis and Dai Smith reflected, communists were 'invariably to be found'.[110] By having a visible presence and always being – or appearing to be – at the forefront of campaigns around unemployment and living standards, the communists drew attention to those places most affected by the turmoil of the decade and they were – eventually – able to articulate what was happening in readily appreciable terms.

But there were limits. Because of the trajectory that the CPGB had taken between 1926 and 1933, it had lost practical momentum just as a series of opportunities presented themselves. In 1931, Thomas Richards, the SWMF general secretary, died and was replaced by the moderate Oliver Harris, who easily defeated the left candidate S. O. Davies. Davies, vice president of the SWMF since 1924, resigned from that post in 1933 for family reasons and was succeeded by Arthur Jenkins. And in 1934, Enoch Morrell, the SWMF president died. James Griffiths, widely seen as the protégé of Thomas Richards won the contest easily. Although it was unlikely that the CPGB could have prevented this moderate swing entirely had it been more willing to participate in practical politics, since this was about the consolidation of the SWMF as an effective administrative body rather than as an ideological megaphone, it was possible that the left could have won at least one of the three positions. It was a sharp lesson that some of the alternative courses available were more fruitful than others, and that to achieve anything substantive the communists would have to find an accommodation with the radical pragmatism of the Labour Party as the central political force in South Wales and with the reconstructed South Wales Miners' Federation within which power was firmly in the hands of anti-communist moderates. They chose unemployment, the central issue of the 1930s, on which to seek it.[111]

Valleys in Revolt

The anti-means test protests of 1934 and 1935 were significant both because of their size – as many as a quarter of a million people took part – and because they enabled the Labour Party and the CPGB to set aside, temporarily, bitter antagonism for the greater good. 'As one watched the huge streams of protesters pouring up and down the two gulches on their way to Tonypandy', Gwyn Thomas wrote many years later, 'one could have sworn the very blood of the place was on the boil'.[112] But it was an uneasy truce, and one that soon unravelled – it was not a popular front of the kind which was formed in France and Spain in the middle of the 1930s, as Gwyn Thomas's observations, contained in the difficult and deeply pessimistic climax of his novel *Sorrow For Thy Sons*, illustrated. His fictional characters were all drawn into the anti-means test protests and went along to the meetings and rallies, as did he.[113] One of the meetings they attended took place at Cymmer Library in mid-January 1935. On the dais, ready to address the four hundred and fifty-strong audience, were leading Labour figures including Mark Harcombe and W. H. Mainwaring. As in the novel, the meeting was partly disrupted from the floor by a group of communists.[114] It was a similar experience to one in Aberdare.[115]

But by the summer of 1935, ahead of a possible general election, Labour's enthusiasm for joint working had cooled substantially and it organised its own mass demonstrations from which the communists were, organisationally at least, excluded. One such 'victory for socialism' rally, held in Pontypridd in June 1935, brought together George Lansbury, the Labour leader, as well as the MPs for Pontypridd, Aberdare, Merthyr, and the two Rhondda constituencies. It sought to demonstrate Labour's independent capacity to organise on a vast scale. It was a rally held as if to say to the CPGB, you are not needed. The Labour Party's National Executive Committee similarly reiterated its ban on a range of left-wing organisations including the CPGB, the NUWM, and the ILP, members of which could not be members of the Labour Party.[116] In Pontypridd there was even an attempt to force communists out of the co-operative guilds, although this was strongly resisted by the guilds themselves mindful of their own independence rather than because of any commitment to the communist cause.[117] Labour's closed ranks had the desired effect: communist membership, which had risen during the agitation at the beginning of 1934, sharply declined once more. And in the general election the CPGB failed to make a breakthrough, including in Rhondda East where Harry Pollitt increased the number of communist voters but could not dislodge W. H. Mainwaring. The latter's majority rose to more than eight thousand.

Speaking in Moscow in December 1935, Pollitt sought to explain the CPGB's performance in, and the political consequences of, the general election and the overwhelming return of, the National Government. He held little back.[118] 'The Welsh people' he began, 'are very narrow and nationalist in outlook, and this is the only place in the whole country where they question the right of an outsider, who is not a miner or a Welshman, to go in and fight'. He could report that the party had sold forty pounds worth of literature and had been able to attract three hundred new members to the cause, half of them in the Rhondda, but it had little real impact on the result.[119] He blamed Arthur Horner. Pollitt suggested that Labour had promoted the idea that Horner was no longer a member of the CPGB and pointed to his absence from the contest in the Rhondda and his support for Labour whilst campaigning in Oxford. 'For three days', Pollitt complained, bitterly, 'I had seventy five meetings in the streets, with a microphone, and was only answering one question: that Horner was a member of our party'. It was Horner's face that was plastered everywhere on communist posters in Rhondda East, although the central message of the election literature 'Horner says vote for Pollitt' had nothing to do with him. As Pollitt admitted, he had written it himself. Horner had refused to get involved. 'He could not go out in the streets in the same way I went to answer the lie of the Labour Party'. In a scored-out line in the transcript, Pollitt reflected angrily, 'I personally never felt so humiliated in my life'. He knew, however, that nothing could be done about Horner – 'we are not strong enough to take disciplinary action against him'.[120]

Four months later, Pollitt was back on the campaign trail in South Wales during the by-election in Llanelli in March 1936. There was no communist candidate this time, just James Griffiths, the SWMF president and his National Liberal opponent. For the communists, the 1936 by-election was a chance to prove to Labour the value of a united front, and so a number of communists moved to Llanelli for the duration of the campaign, including Alistair and Olive Wilson of Aberdare. The Wilsons took charge of the party bookshop, and there they sold books such as the *Ragged Trousered Philanthropists* and contemporary pieces such as Montagu Slater's *Stay Down, Miner* eschewing traditional communist literature. Alistair Wilson later recalled, 'my impression was that Pollitt was concerned to remove sectarian practice from the Party as rapidly as possible'.[121] Of course, Pollitt and others knew that Griffiths's probable victory in Llanelli would lead to the possibility of the most significant prize of all: the presidency of the South Wales Miners' Federation. As the *Western Mail* pointedly observed, 'the heir presumptive to the President of the SWMF [is] none other than the chief Communist agitator of the South Wales coalfield'.[122] James Griffiths duly won his seat in parliament, with a majority of more than sixteen thousand. Two months later, Arthur Horner was elected president of the South Wales Miners' Federation.

Horner's election was a moment of personal triumph and a vindication of the strategy he had pursued since the early 1930s. He was convinced that the SWMF, not the CPGB, provided the platform for left-wing politics and he was now the most powerful communist in Britain. Horner understood that the Labour Party would never allow a united front through political parties, but he recognised that miners' lodges provided a mechanism by which members of both parties could work together to improve the lot of South Wales. He also knew that the SWMF, as the sponsor of miners' MPs, could wield considerable influence over the Labour Party. This did not mean that Labour would commit to joint working, however, but it made for more probable circumstances than had Horner not been elected president. In the event, however, the sense of elation was short lived. Less than two months after the ballot, on 18 July, the rebel generals launched their coup against the Republican government in Madrid. As Arthur Horner settled into his office in St Andrew's Crescent in Cardiff, and the hunger marchers prepared, once more, to walk to London, the world's eyes were drawn to Spain.

Notes

[1] Francis and Smith, *The Fed*, 505-7.

[2] Gwyn Thomas, *The Subsidence Factor* (Cardiff, 1979), 15.

[3] Barry UDC, Report of the Medical Officer of Health for 1927, 4.

[4] Glamorgan CC, Report of the Medical Officer of Health for 1937, 24.

[5] Merthyr Tydfil CBC, Report of the Medical Officer of Health for 1937, 16.

[6] The Bristol Cambrian Society had been founded in 1869 ostensibly to organise an annual St David's Day dinner for Welsh residents in the city. It quickly became a more general philanthropic organisation akin to the Caledonian Society and Hibernian Society which served resident Scots and Irish. *Bristol Daily Times & Mirror*, 29 January, 8 February 1869; *Western Daily Press*, 2 March 1869.

[7] Bristol Archives, Bristol Cambrian Society Records, 40499/1: *Almoner's Report for 1926*.

[8] As above: *Almoner's Report for 1927*.

[9] As above: *Almoner's Report for 1928*.

[10] Smith, *Aneurin Bevan*, 226-7.

[11] *Western Morning News*, 3 March 1927; Yorkshire *Post*, 18 March 1927.

[12] Smith, *Aneurin Bevan*, 225.

[13] As above, 221; Laybourn and Shepherd, *First Labour*, 83; Howell, *Macdonald's Labour*, 8-9.

[14] Smith, *Aneurin Bevan*, 222.

[15] *DH*, 5 August 1936.

[16] *MEx*, 8 June 1929.

[17] Francis and Smith, *The Fed*, 194.

[18] *Unemployed News*, 17 December 1928.

[19] *Out of Work* 1, no. 19 (October 1921.).

[20] SWCC, Digital Circulars, File F10: Circular dated 10 November 1928.

[21] *WM*, 7 May 1927.

[22] RGASPI, 495.72.75: Meeting of the Anglo-American Secretariat of the Communist International, 15 May 1930.

[23] *Western Daily Press*, 9 November 1927.

[24] *Bath Chronicle*, 19 November 1927.

[25] *Bath Chronicle*, 12 November 1927.

[26] *Western Daily Press*, 14 November 1927.

[27] *Western Morning News*, 17 November 1927.

[28] *Lichfield Mercury*, 25 November 1927.

[29] *Sunday Worker*, 20 November 1927; *Hull Daily Mail*, 19 November 1927.

[30] *Nottingham Evening Post*, 17 November 1927.

[31] *Nottingham Evening Post*, 28 November 1927.

[32] *Gloucester Citizen*, 21 November 1927.

[33] *GFP*, 3 December 1927. In later years Powderhill was a keen advocate for the abolition of corporal punishment in schools. See, Jesse Powderhill, *The Children's Charter and the Plimsoll Line* (Pontypridd, 1945).

[34] Williams, *Democratic Rhondda*, 114.

[35] Smith, *Aneurin Bevan*, 239. The quote from Rhys Evans can be found here also.

[36] As above, 240.

[37] As above, 240.

[38] Stonelake, *Autobiography*, 172.

[39] Rhondda UDC, Report of the Medical Officer of Health for 1925, 15-23.

[40] Kate Fisher, '"Teach the Miners Birth Control": The Delivery of Contraceptive Advice in South Wales, 1918-1950', in Pamela Michael and Charles Webster (eds.), *Health and Society in Twentieth-Century Wales* (Cardiff, 2006), 143; Margaret Douglas, 'Women, God and Birth Control: The First Hospital Birth Control Clinic, Abertillery, 1925', *Llafur* 6, no. 4 (1995).

[41] Cited in Douglas, 'Abertillery', 117.

[42] Caroline Walker, 'Making Birth Control Respectable: The Society for Constructive Birth Control and Racial Progress, and the American Birth Control League, in comparative perspective, 1921-1938 (Unpublished PhD Thesis: University of Bristol, 2007), 238-9.

[43] The Committee for Constructive Birth Control's mobile caravan clinic was present in the town in January 1930, for example. *Birth Control News*, 8, no. 9 (December 1929), 139.

[44] Pontypridd UDC, Medical Officer of Health, Annual Report for 1937, 14-15.

[45] Rhondda UDC, *Minutes*, 1 June 1926.

[46] Tanner, 'Gender, Civic Culture and Politics', 178.

[47] Pontypridd UDC, Education Committee, Minute Book, entry for 27 July 1920.

[48] Pontypridd UDC, Education Committee, Minutes, entry for 15 September 1920.

[49] Glamorgan CC, Medical Officer of Health, Annual Report for 1920, 20-23; Monmouthshire CC, *Report upon Maternity and Child Welfare for the year 1921*, 11; Glamorgan CC, Medical Officer of Health, Annual Report for 1930, 29; Mountain Ash UDC, Medical Officer of Health, Annual Report for 1927, 59; Pontypridd UDC, Medical Officer of Health, Annual Report for 1929, 7.

[50] GA, Maesteg General Hospital Records, DHMA/4: 'Maesteg Urban District Council Maternity Home', *Register of Births, 1921-1947*.

[51] Mountain Ash UDC, Medical Officer of Health, Annual Report for 1925, 18.

[52] Gelligaer UDC, Medical Officer of Health, Annual Report for 1925, 20.

[53] Ogmore and Garw UDC, Report of the Medical Officer of Health for 1925, 8.

[54] Malcolm J. Fisk, *Housing in the Rhondda, 1800-1940* (Cardiff, 1996), 83-4.

[55] Rhondda UDC, Medical Officer of Health, Annual Report for 1925, 15.

[56] Tredegar UDC, Medical Officer of Health, Annual Report for 1925, 11.

[57] Caerleon UDC, Report of the Medical Officer of Health for 1925, 6-7; Risca UDC, Report of the Medical Officer of Health for 1925, 7.

[58] Monmouthshire CC, Medical Officer of Health, Annual Report for 1924, 59.

[59] As above, Medical Officer of Health, Annual Report for 1927, 23.

[60] As above, Medical Officer of Health, Annual Report for 1928, 23; Porthcawl UDC, Report of the Medical Officer of Health for 1937, 27.

[61] Porthcawl UDC, Report of the Medical Officer for 1938, 27.

[62] Nicklaus Thomas-Symonds, *Nye: The Political Life of Aneurin Bevan* (London, 2014), 42-3.

[63] Monmouthshire CC, Medical Officer of Health, Annual Report for 1925, 18-19.

[64] See the comments in Ogmore and Garw UDC, Medical Officer of Health, Annual Report for 1937, 22.

[65] Monmouthshire CC, Medical Officer of Health, Annual Report for, 1931, 44.

[66] He first made the complaint in 1929. See Monmouthshire CC, Medical Officer of Health, Annual Report for 1929, 29.

[67] Nantyglo and Blaina, Medical Officer of Health, Annual Report for 1938, 9.

[68] Pontypridd UDC, Medical Officer of Health, Annual Report for 1925, 49.

[69] As above, Medical Officer of Health, Annual Report for 1925, 24; Aberdare UDC, Medical Officer of Health, Annual Report for, 1925 64; Mountain Ash UDC, Medical Officer of Health, Annual Report for 1925, 32. The Clydach, which ran through Ynysybwl, was regarded as unpolluted.

[70] Pontypridd UDC, Medical Officer of Health, Annual Report for 1937, 37.

[71] Stephen G Jones, 'The Leisure Industry in Britain. 1918-39', *The Service Industries Journal* 5, no. 1 (1985), 90-106.

[72] *PO*, 13 August 1927.

[73] Gareth Williams, 'The Road to Wigan Pier Revisited: The Migration of Welsh Rugby Talent since 1918', 29; *PO*, 9 April 1932.

[74] *WM*, 7 August 1929.

[75] *The Times*, 14 February 1933.

[76] Thomas-Symonds, *Nye*, 42, 153.

[77] Chris Williams, 'Labour and the Challenge of Local Government, 1919-1939' in Tanner et al (eds.), *The Labour Party in Wales*, 149.

[78] As above, 155.

[79] As above, 156-7.

[80] Andrew Thorpe, 'The Membership of the Communist Party of

Great Britain, 1920-1945', *Historical Journal*, 43, no. 3 (2000),
777-800; see also his *The British Communist Party and Moscow,
1920-43* (Manchester, 2000). Where possible I have returned to the
original sources in providing membership figures below.

[81] In 1924, as an indication of its strength, Newport Labour Party's
women's section organised a trip to London for two thousand
members. *DH*, 17 June 1924.

[82] RGASPI, 495.14.190, 'Proposals to improve the recruitment of
members for the CP of Great Britain, 9 April 1934'.

[83] RGASPI, 495.14.156, 'Registration of the Party Membership in
South Wales, February 1937'.

[84] Idris Cox, 'A United Labour Movement Depends on the Number of
Recruits to the Communist Party', February 1937. RGASPI,
495.14.156.

[85] CPGB, *It Can Be Done, It Must Be Done, It Will Be Done* (Cardiff,
1937).

[86] My thanks to Dai Smith for relating the story of his maternal
grandfather who voted for Horner in 1936 and thought that Winston
Churchill should be Prime Minister in 1945.

[87] SWMF EC 'Minutes, 24 January 1930'.

[88] SWMF, EC 'Minutes, 29 April, 10 September 1929'; Maerdy
Lodge: 'Minutes, 24 September, 26 September 1929, 5 October
1930'.

[89] Nina Fishman, *Arthur Horner: A Political Biography, Volume I,
1894-1944* (London, 2010), 197.

[90] *Workers' Life*, 6 December 1929.

[91] As above, 20 December 1929.

[92] As above, 1 November, 8 November 1929; *Cambrian X-Ray*, 17
July 1929.

[93] *Cwmtillery Searchlight*, 12 December 1930

[94] *Workers' Life*, 4 October 1929.

[95] As above, 21 December, 28 December 1928, 18 January, 25
January, 1 February 1929. Thomas Linehan, *Communism in Britain,
1920-39* (Manchester, 2007).

[96] Of course, young members could never escape party work entirely.
For all that they enjoyed a kickabout, reading literature, watching

films, acting in plays, or singing revolutionary songs, they were part of a political movement and were, of necessity, encouraged to stand for election to further the cause, particularly on youth issues, and to deliver leaflets and sell copies of the party newspapers. *Young Worker*, April 1933; Alun Hughes, 'Pontypridd Communist Party Notes', PLS. I am also grateful to Ceinwen Statter and Ann Wilson who reflect a similar form of party work.

[97] CPGB Politburo Minutes, 16 April 1936. The YCL had around two hundred members by the end of 1931. RGASPI 495.72.145.

[98] Matthew Worley, *Class Against Class: The Communist Party in Britain Between the Wars* (London, 2002), 259; RGASPI, 495.72.97: statement on the places to which papers are despatched and quantities, 17 January 1930; 495.20.73: Report on the London 'Daily Worker', 16 November 1936.

[99] RGASPI, 495.20.37: Improvement of the Agitational Activity of the Communist Party of Great Britain, 13 August 1933.

[100] Williams, *Democratic Rhondda*, 159-60.

[101] *PO*, 18 March 1933.

[102] Weekly Intelligence Summary, 3 July 1926.

[103] *DW*, 21 December 1931.

[104] *DW*, 15 June 1932. The correspondent was Llew's younger brother Ben, also a miner at the Albion Colliery.

[105] *DW*, 21 November 1932, 23 November 1932.

[106] *GFP*, 8 April 1933.

[107] *PO*, 20 April 1935.

[108] *PO*, 16 February 1935.

[109] *GFP*, 11 April 1936.

[110] Francis and Smith, *The Fed*, 269.

[111] As a joint resolution from Ward 9 Branch of the Rhondda Labour Party and the Rhondda No. 1 District of the South Wales Miners' Federation put it pointedly in December 1933, the party should 'agitate or risk losing the sympathy of the rank and file and it should actively take up the unemployed case instead of leaving it to others'. NLW, A1995/62, Rhondda Borough Labour Party, General Committee Minutes, 9 December 1933.

[112] Gwyn Thomas, *A Welsh Eye* (London, [1964] 1984 edn.), 24.

[113] Gwyn Thomas, *Sorrow For Thy Sons* (London, 1986), 213. The novel was written in 1936-7.

[114] *GFP*, 26 January 1935. Harcombe's centrality to Rhondda Labour in the interwar years is described in Williams, *Democratic Rhondda*, 207.

[115] Greening, *From Aberdare*, 47-52.

[116] LHASC, LP/GS/ILP/34-5: National Executive Committee's List of Proscribed Organisations.

[117] Pontypridd TLC, Minutes, 30 April 1934.

[118] What follows draws primarily on a transcript of Pollitt's remarks to the Communist International on 9 December 1935. RGASPI, 495.18.1036. Quotes are from this document, except where otherwise indicated.

[119] The three hundred figure derives from Morgan, *Harry Pollitt*, 120.

[120] This may usefully be compared with Nina Fishman's account which paints a rather friendlier relationship and takes the involvement of Horner in the campaign rather more for granted. Fishman, *Arthur Horner*, 300-1. A file of Pollitt's election materials is held at LHASC, CP/IND/10/4.

[121] LHASC, CP/IND/MISC/22/14: Alistair and Olive Wilson, Recollections of CP Activity in Llanelli, 1936.

[122] *WM*, 25 March 1936.

CHAPTER SIX
A Sad But Beautiful Joke

In September 1936, two months after the outbreak of the Spanish Civil War, twenty-three-year-old Gwyn Thomas delivered a lecture to a crowded room at Porth Unemployed Club. Drawing on his own experiences of having travelled and studied in Spain, he held the audience's interest for over an hour 'presenting a full, clear and intelligent picture of the truth about Spain', as the *Rhondda Leader* glowingly reported. Conditions in the country for working people were 'tragic and revolting', Thomas stated, 'an unpleasant mass of starvation, illiteracy, prayers, suicides, and blind revolts'. For the rebels – including General Franco – he had little enthusiasm. In his words:

> Their political philosophy, on the one occasion it rises above the dirty, indecent and sub-human pornography of an officers' mess, consists of detesting democracy, which as the ordered will of the common people, would like to put salt on their be-medalled tails and see them do something useful for a living.

The Catholic Church, too, was 'more intent on collecting rents than spreading light'. The Spanish Republic had endeavoured to break down the ignorance and caprice of dictatorship and self-indulgent monarchy, and now faced the wrath of those who stood to lose out.[1]

The Spanish Republic was formed in 1931 and Gwyn Thomas first went there in 1933 as a student of Spanish at Oxford University.[2] He later insisted that he did not go there by choice.

It was, he recorded in his autobiography, *A Few Selected Exits*, a requirement of the degree. 'Had it not been', Thomas wrote, 'I would not have stirred'.[3] And yet Spain, particularly the glimmering Guadarrama mountains and the mining region of Asturias, made up for the 'eroding humanity' that he found at Oxford by bringing him into direct contact with a people and a landscape he considered to be much like his own.[4] The streets of Madrid, of course, were not free from the snobbery and looks-down-the-nose that he had encountered in plentiful supply in Oxford, nor were they anywhere near as safe. Throughout the early 1930s, after shaking off 'the nightmare of the Middle Ages', as Arthur Koestler put it, and the formation of the Republic, violence in Spain was endemic and the government seemingly unable to stop it.[5] Brutal suppression of strikes in Asturias in 1934, the declaration of martial law in Barcelona, and, during the municipal elections of April 1933, the murder of four men and one woman on the streets of the southern town of Hornachos by the Civil Guard, all marked the country as dangerous and hostile.[6] Writing from Madrid to the bursar of St Edmund Hall in May 1933, Gwyn Thomas set the scene:

> Everyone sits about, looking sweaty and political, praising or cursing the Republic according to the position of the sun ... I am not at all pleased with the enthusiasm with which the Spanish nation takes to the delights of bomb throwing. They almost make it a winter sport ... they have set up civil slaughter as a rival attraction to the public dispatch of bulls.[7]

By then, the Republic was in the throes of a deep crisis from which it would never really recover. The contours of the civil war were becoming increasingly evident and right-wing opinion was open in expressing its belief in the necessity of the Republic's destruction. Only that would restore Spain to its true

Catholic purpose. Sitting at a table in a café in central Madrid, Gwyn Thomas experienced the full force of this rhetoric and incitement to violence for himself from a senior army officer:

> Of course, it will have to be destroyed, this peasant government, this system of ideas ... cataclysmically destroyed. ... The guns that won South America, will again regain Spain for the faith and traditional values.

It was, and remains, a remarkable statement of intent. And for Gwyn Thomas it was a startling expression of values alien to his own. As he recalled many years alter:

> I had never heard this kind of language in my life. It was astounding. But this was it you see. This was it in a capsule. This marvellous idea that if you have a hundred thousand people in a state, organised in one small system of ideas, and ideas based on a technology, which is the technology of death, you were on to a winner. And so it proved. That despite all these marvellous donations of love and valour from all four corners of Europe and the world, it was that man, sitting next to me on that table in Madrid who decided the issue. He knew precisely what he wanted, he knew precisely what he hated. And he won.[8]

What Gwyn Thomas saw and heard on the streets of the Spanish capital in 1933, he could just as easily have heard in Germany a few months earlier. One of those who did bear witness to what was going on in Germany was Morien Morgan, son of John E. Morgan of Ynysybwl, who was a languages student at Cardiff in the mid-1930s.[9] His political education and development came through discussions with his family, through debates with fellow students, particularly in the wake of the Abyssinian crisis of 1935, and through experiences during a holiday-exchange spent at the University of Strasbourg. Travelling along the Rhine, Morgan observed many soldiers, new fortifications, and training camps, the material reality of rearmament. 'It hit me like a bomb', he explained later, 'because until then I'd lived in this village, we were never aware of military might whatsoever'. He wrote up his experiences, and views, in an essay for the university magazine, *Cap and Gown*, and began his own newspaper, *Why Not?*, to encourage other students to think critically about the global situation.

Morgan's agitation in the university corridors of Cardiff was a small part of a growing movement in the summer of 1936 which expressed anxiety at what was going on in Germany and outrage at the actions of the rebels in seeking the overthrow of the Spanish Republic. However, much of this reaction was mediated through a belief in the viability of the League of Nations, which seemed to have been bolstered (on paper at least) by the entry of the Soviet Union in September 1934, and frustration at the inaction of the National Government in Britain. In early August 1936, for instance, some three thousand liberals, labourites, and communists, held a rally in Pontypridd to demonstrate their support for the League of Nations and the cause of international peace. On the platform were D. L. Davies, the town's Labour MP, Lewis Jones, communist County Councillor from the Rhondda, and local dignitaries including E. R. Thomas, the headmaster of Pontypridd boys' grammar school and secretary of the local branch of the League of Nations Union. The march through the town began with a round of community singing ranging from *Cwm Rhondda*, which everyone sang, to the *Red Flag* and *Tipperary* which were sung by communist and non-communists (respectively) in competition with each other. In his speech, D. L. Davies declared that 'we congratulate the Workers' Popular Front Government of Spain on its magnificent determination and stand against the Fascist rebels'. Cheers followed but little was achieved beyond a reaffirmation of belief in democracy.[10]

A few weeks later, Pontypridd played host to a party of German students on an exchange visit. The students went to the boys' club, the historic old bridge, and the lido and Ynysangharad War Memorial Park. Insofar as the trip was enjoyed by the students themselves, it passed without incident, but then it emerged that the students were members of the Hitler Youth, and this drew strident protests from the local branch of the Communist Party and a degree of contrition from the town's Labour Party who had been caught unawares. The town's communist councillor, Llew Jenkins, remarked that it was 'wrong for representatives of the labour movement to associate themselves with it [the Hitler Youth]'.[11] But it was not the last time that a local authority in South Wales would find themselves in this kind of situation. In September 1938, the signing of the Munich Agreement was marked by the Lord Mayor of Cardiff, Oliver Cuthbert Purnell, a staunch Conservative, ordering the flying of the national flags of the four nations involved over city hall. The flags of the United Kingdom, France, Italy, and Germany, were duly run up the flag poles on the roof: the red and white swastika had become the German national flag three years earlier. Two Labour councillors hauled it down almost immediately and Arthur Horner, the president of the South Wales Miners' Federation, remarked in an interview with the *Western Mail* that 'to see the Nazi flag flying … is, I feel, a disgrace to the people of Wales'. Purnell responded by ordering a replacement flag to be flown. It remained up for several days.[12]

Nor did the city learn the lessons of Purnell's political naivety. The following year, in July 1939, a visit to Cardiff by the Soviet ambassador, Ivan Maisky, resulted in the red hammer and sickle being flown over city hall for more than twenty four hours, this time on the orders of William Gough Howell, Purnell's successor as Lord Mayor. The itinerary of Maisky's tour was relatively typical, he went to the National Museum, to the Temple of Peace, was taken down a mine, in this instance, Nine Mile Point, and he had tea in the colliery canteen. But the ambassador was most astonished by the sight of the red flag flying over Cardiff, one of the first occasions it had ever been raised above a city hall anywhere in Britain, and recorded in his diary that 'nothing like that had ever occurred in the history of Anglo-Soviet relations'.[13] The last time a major city in Britain had raised the red flag over its council chambers was in Glasgow in 1919, and that was during a strike which the Scottish Secretary, Robert Munro, thought tantamount to a Bolshevik uprising.[14] Cardiff, on the other hand, much like the National Government, struggled to know which way the international winds were blowing.

There were those who viewed the 1930s with far greater clarity than the lord mayors of Cardiff. Brinley Thomas, economics lecturer at Cardiff, for example, wrote in the *Welsh Outlook* in March 1933 that 'the situation is pregnant with ominous possibilities and, whatever the outcome, one cannot help feeling that Germany, and probably Europe, will have reason to regret President Hindenburg's grave decision of January 30th'.[15] That decision had been to name Adolf Hitler Chancellor of Germany. Writing six months later, one observer reflected that 'one's first impression of the Third Reich is an impression of colour and of movement. Every bookshop is a blaze of colour – the Bismarckian black, white and red'. He continued:

First colour with the mystic symbol everywhere of the hooked cross, the Swastika, then movement. Awakened Germany is on the march! I had not been in a German town for five minutes before I saw marching along an officer and a company of men. As they marched, they sang one of the popular patriotic airs.

Although undoubtedly impressed by the visual spectacle of early Nazi Germany, he nevertheless warned that 'nobody who really cares for freedom can come away from a German frontier station without a feeling of relief at being back again in an atmosphere of liberty, no one who cares for peace can leave ... without profound misgiving about the trend of things'.[16] And there was Gwyn Thomas, who wrote in his diary that 'a victorious democratic outcome in Spain in 1939 would have brought unassessable benefit to Europe, so a victorious Fascist regime contributes powerfully to the forces of oppression and backwardness throughout the continent'.[17]

The growth of fascism on the continent, whether in Germany in 1933 or Spain in 1936, prompted a desire for left-wing unity after many years of internecine conflict. Aneurin Bevan, the one South Wales MP who seemed able to bridge the gap between the lofty idealism of the Communist Party and the pragmatic social democratic politics of the Labour Party, was the one to make the overture. Albeit he did so only in the aftermath of the 1933 Rhondda East by-election in which Arthur Horner pushed within three thousand votes of Labour's W. H. Mainwaring. The by-election was held at the end of March, Bevan wrote to Horner at the end of April to arrange a meeting to discuss a way forward.[18] Tentatively, and not always happily for MPs such as Mainwaring, Labour, the CPGB, and the ILP, began to work together on major issues such as the Means Test and the Spanish Civil War.[19] It helped that, across much of South Wales, and not just in the coalfield, Labour eventually refused to be bound by what they regarded as the overly-moderate and cautious policies pursued by the national Labour leadership and were willing to lead the more fluid extra-parliamentary activity that Bevan sought to foster.[20] But there remained limitations.

The attendant danger of infiltration of the Labour Party by communists was apparent and encouraged the national executive's caution, but was easily exaggerated from both sides, at least at first, as local Labour activists seem to have understood.[21] The CPGB's figures for February 1937 show that just ten communists had found their way into women's sections, just under seventy held membership of Labour Party branches, and just twenty four had been selected as delegates from those branches to constituency committees. Moreover, the CPGB fretted constantly that those sympathetic to the cause in South Wales were too willing to put aside the party in favour of working for the SWMF, and that Labour could act turncoat at any moment. One internal memorandum recorded bluntly in the autumn of 1936 that

> The membership of the Communist Party in South Wales is smaller than in any other district of the country. While the mass movement has been growing, the Communist Party has been losing members. While united action has given new life to the Labour Movement in South Wales the Communist Party, which has led the fight for unity, has fallen back in membership. ... Unless we can increase our membership and strengthen the Party as a whole, the leadership of this united movement will be in the hands of reactionary elements who will take the first opportunity to stake a drive against the Communist Party.[22]

By 1938, communist presence within the Labour Party in South Wales had grown, but remained small: one hundred communists held membership of Labour branches, twenty one of which were members of branches in Cardiff, and there were twenty communists within women's sections of the Labour Party.[23] The fear in the upper-echelons of the Labour Party nationally, and the TUC, was always greater than the reality but that did not mean its determination to stamp out communist influence was easily ignored. The true source of strength for the CPGB even in this period of the popular front were the hundreds of card-carrying communists to be found within the SWMF, a group that included key figures such as Arthur Horner, Will Paynter, Dai Dan Evans, and Harold Finch (then working as the SWMF's compensation secretary but later Labour MP for Bedwellty). Their presence was felt and was strong enough that neither Labour nor the CPGB could ignore it.[24]

These, then, were the fluid political boundaries of the second half of the 1930s in South Wales. Thus, there was indeed a popular front in South Wales, for a time, but it was guided by the SWMF, the Labour Party, and the CPGB, in that order, and was often subject to the enthusiasms of Labour activists regardless of whether 'it was the CP that captured the limelight'.[25] It existed because of a desire to act in response to the Spanish Civil War, fascism, and continued unemployment. But it also satisfied certain priorities. For Labour, there was a determination to balance militancy with practical action (the constant theme of the interwar years), and to show leadership rather than to abdicate responsibilities. The popular front demonstrated that the party could do both, maintaining the principle of radical pragmatism rather than being forced to decide between 'practicalism' and radicalism.[26] For the communists, there was a clear need for rehabilitation after the disaster of class against class – somewhat successful given the steady growth in membership, reaching one thousand members by 1939. And for the SWMF, this was an opportunity to move on from the long, but ultimately successful, battle against the employers' union and to reinvigorate its own position as community leader.

Towards a Popular Front?

The experience and existence of the popular front was invariably different in each district of South Wales (even down to the ward level) and waxed and waned according to local circumstances. In the Rhondda, where the communist influence and electoral presence was at its strongest, the popular front failed, culminating in the decision of Rhondda Borough Labour Party to approve the national executive's expulsion of Stafford Cripps and Aneurin Bevan in 1939 for having campaigned for one.[27] Yet that same month, Labour figures in Pontypridd attended a popular front meeting at the town hall at which Aneurin Bevan spoke on colonialism and war.[28] Likewise both of Pontypridd's MPs in the 1930s, D. L. Davies and Arthur Pearson, were willing to share platforms with communists and work with them to pass motions in the council chamber, and parts of the town clearly supported CPGB affiliation to the Labour Party.[29] Bevan's own constituency party in Tredegar was warned that if it was 'unable or unwilling to take such steps as may be necessary to ensure party discipline [it] cannot be permitted to remain affiliated'.[30] The issue at hand in the popular front – as Bevan conceived it – was how vigorously Britain should oppose fascism on the continent, and how strong the Labour Party should be in pursuit of action.[31] In the words of Arthur Pearson,

> The government had cold shouldered Russia but the rank and file of the labour movement had concluded that unless France, Poland and Russia and other nations held together, there was a danger of their freedom being lost and all that they loved would be laid at the feet of dictators.[32]

Just as occurred in Spain.

From the perspective of Labour's national executive, the popular front was a dangerous initiative and they endeavoured accordingly to stamp it out. In 1937, the South Wales Regional Council of Labour was established to coordinate party activity, to develop uniformity of action and programme across the region, and to implement the national executive's position on communist collaboration. As a body, it was closed to delegates with any potential links to the CPGB and enforced the strict London line.[33] In Newport this resulted in a rapid succession of twists and turns from a seemingly pragmatic decision not to support affiliation to the Labour Party but to accept communist support locally, to an insistence that constituency officers not attend popular front meetings, to eventually resolving 'to have nothing to do with such futility'.[34] In reality, the communists themselves were too few in number in Newport to really have much influence. As an internal CPGB report observed in December 1937, 'the Newport branch has a membership of thirty on its books and of these only a very small proportion (about half a dozen) are active' and it 'plays very little part in the political life of the town'. The extent of its infiltration of the Labour Party was a mere one member in a constituency party of several thousand, and two of the three communists on the town's trades council were from the unemployed movement.[35]

A similar trend was evident in Swansea, another town in which (the miniscule) communist presence was perceived chiefly because of the actions of the Labour Party membership. In 1939, for instance, the constituency party asserted that the national leadership were 'apparently unaware of the feeling in South Wales regarding the Means Test, Munitions and Rearmament, Distressed Areas and Spain'.[36] But it was in the Rhondda, where Labour's determination to foil communist activity was at its sharpest, that the popular front most obviously failed. Given the CPGB's electoral strength of seven urban district councillors and one county councillor – the equivalent of half the communists' interwar peak of seventeen councillors across South Wales – together with rising communist electoral performance in the Rhondda East parliamentary constituency, this determination (and anxiety) was understandable. Labour steadily withdrew from united action in the aftermath of the means test protests of 1935, with the United Front deliberately dissolved in June of that year. Thereafter collaboration was on a temporary, issue-by-issue basis – chiefly in response to fascism, unemployment, and the Spanish Civil War, and was in any case undertaken primarily through the SWMF.[37] An internal Labour report explained the process:

> It has become necessary, for a number of reasons, for us as a Party to review our position and to reconsider the question of associating with certain other organisations in the furtherance of Party aims and policies. This, particularly, is the case with regard to the so-called United Front activities in which for some months past we have been to some extent associated with Communists on and off public platforms. ... It is impossible here in the Rhondda to continue to associate with the Communist Party in any shape or form and that is the case not merely in the Rhondda but throughout South Wales, where they have boasted of having won a dominating position. The United Front has become, at once, a device for preventing Labour Party propaganda and the means of advancing in every way Communist influence and policy.

When the Central Committee was set up for the Rhondda, the Communist Party was allowed representation thereon, and it was hoped that all energies would be concentrated without reflecting one upon the other, to the end of securing the withdrawal of the regulations passed under the Employment act 1934. The experience gained since has shown how vain was the hope of those elements agreeing to common aims. It speedily became clear that for them the United Front was an excuse through which the workers might be brought under their influence, and not merely in relation to Unemployment Regulations but any other question they cared to raise. In common therefore with the National Committee it is idle for us to ignore fundamental differences of policy and method that distinguish the Labour Party from the Communist Party – these differences arise in relation to industrial and political problems and the approach to them.

> This has been clearly shown in relation to local agitations during the past months. Communists participate for no reason but to advance their own views and to denounce other actions. To continue the associations therefore is to betray every principle that the Labour Party stands for separately and to abandon for good or ill the policy and method laid down by National Conference from time to time. There is but one sure basis upon which to pursue our political agitations and upon which we can hope to secure certain triumph and victory and that is the tried basis of real working class unity, namely, the trade unions, co-operative, and political organisations of labour in which are to be found mutual trust, co-operation and confidence.[38]

The chief antagonist of the CPGB in the Rhondda was the Rhondda East MP W. H. Mainwaring, whom the communists hated and were determined to unseat. He 'loses no single opportunity to attack and slander the Communist Party' noted one internal report compiled in 1937.[39] Mainwaring's actions proved successful. Communists completely failed to infiltrate the Rhondda Borough Labour Party, although when asked by the CPGB's national leadership why, they claimed they were too well-known to get in anyway, and membership declined rapidly after 1935. Some two hundred members had drifted away by the end of 1937, leaving just one hundred and fifty. This led to a 'good amount of personal bickering' and ineffective group meetings, and eventually the loss of councillors on Rhondda UDC. The primary successes were the election of Lewis Jones as county councillor in 1937 and the publication of the *Rhondda Vanguard*, the communist halfpenny newspaper which first appeared in the summer of 1935.[40] Sales ran into the thousands. But it prompted an almost immediate response from Labour (on Mainwaring's initiative): the *Rhondda Clarion*.[41] This first appeared in September 1935. Through the pages of the two, readers could appreciate the deliberately sharp boundaries between Rhondda's Labour and Communist parties as the possibility of a popular front evaporated. Although ostensibly written from the position of strength, the *Clarion* in fact left the impression of reacting to and trying to contain the communists rather than presenting a more forthright summary of Labour's own point of view.

It was the failure of the CPGB to infiltrate the Labour Party and to establish ginger groups within it able to pull the party to the left that prompted the more enthusiastic embrace of cultural initiatives such as workers' theatre, cinema, and the Left Book Club, at the end of the 1930s. Established in May 1936, the Left Book Club was the brainchild of left-wing MPs Stafford Cripps and John Strachey, the Marxist philosopher Harold Laski, and the publisher Victor Gollancz, and aimed at introducing a new form of political education and furthering a popular front. Discussion groups and local branches (or study circles) were established to debate the ideas presented by the monthly choice, together with a monthly newsletter, annual rallies locally and nationally, and summer schools. Although close to the CPGB, the Left Book Club was never exclusively communist and featured writers from the Labour Party, the ILP, and the CPGB, including Clement Attlee, GDH Cole, George Orwell and Ellen Wilkinson, some of whom diverged from the broader aims of the club. Attlee's contribution, *The Labour Party in Perspective*, published in August 1937, for instance, rejected a popular front and instead insisted on the democratic aims of the Labour Party that he was leading.[42] Ironically the previous month's title, Cole's *The People's Front* had questioned whether 'some of our official leaders to-day are any more Socialists than Mr Ramsay MacDonald and Mr J. H. Thomas'.[43]

Following its establishment, the Left Book Club proved popular in South Wales with study circles formed across the region, thirty eight in total.[44] In the view of Hywel Francis, they 'not only filled the vacuum left by the collapse of the United Front, but continued and extended the United Front in a different form'.[45] We should perhaps exercise more caution: whilst there seems to have been broad engagement in parts of South Wales, particularly in the coalfield, in other areas there were clearly limits to the willingness of the Labour Party to accept communist front organisations, which is what the study circles were for the most part. Thus, in Aberdare, the study circle drew in speakers such as John Strachey, T. E. Nicholas, and George Hall, the local MP.[46] In Pontypridd, members included communists, labourites, and even elderly former members of the Social Democratic Federation.[47] But in Newport, the Left Book Club was deemed 'inconsistent' with Labour's aims and objectives.[48] Likewise, although the Swansea study circle met at the Labour Club in the High Street, its meetings were organised in conjunction with the local branch of the Friends of the Soviet Union, another front organisation, rather than the Labour Party.[49] And in Cardiff, the study circle moved from the May Street Labour Institute in Cathays to Collet's Bookshop in the Castle Arcade following communist infiltration.[50]

A truer measure of the success of the Left Book Club in South Wales was its impress on the miners' institute libraries – the prominence of the club in the lists of books acquired by institute libraries in the 1930s (and which have subsequently survived through deposit at the South Wales Miners' Library) was indicative of the relative success of the Left Book Club in shaping political views of users. Works dealing with Spain, such as Arthur Koestler's *Spanish Testament*, published in 1937 and Harry Gannes and Theodore Repard's *Spain in Revolt*, published in 1936, together with studies of fascism on the continent, such as Jan Petersen's *Our Street*, published in 1938, were particularly popular amongst South Walian readers.[51] Jonathan Rose, in his *The Intellectual Life of the British Working Classes* has, however, issued a note of caution about the reading habits of most library users in South Wales in 1930s based on a study of library issues. 'Though Tredegar eventually acquired the complete works of Lenin, he remained unread', Rose noted indicatively.[52] He has stressed similar trends in other parts of the coalfield as well, notably Tylorstown.[53] In Merthyr, literature and fiction dominated loans from public libraries but the tallies also indicated that history and politics were the most popular non-fiction titles borrowed across the borough.[54]

In addition to the books on the shelves, there were newspapers, journals, magazines, and pamphlets made readily available both in public libraries and in the reading rooms of the miners' institutes but not available for loan (and so absent from Rose's analysis). One young activist later recalled the range of material available to him in Pontypridd Free Library, and which was formative to his political education, included publications such as the *Daily Worker*, Aneurin Bevan's left-wing *Tribune* magazine, and the journal of the Labour League of Youth, *Challenge*. There was, he said, also 'excellent coverage of Marxism and the Soviet Union'.[55] Surviving photographs of reading rooms in miners' institutes in the Rhondda, such as Ton Pentre, show that the *Daily Worker* and the *Daily Herald* sat alongside the local and regional press. This was also true of Tredegar.[56] There was, then, clearly a demand in the coalfield for knowledge about politics, philosophy, economics, and industrial history, in contradistinction to the observations made by Rose. Activists undoubtedly read more in the way of pamphlets and books to support their political education than did most others – and in some cases sought them out in places such as Collet's in Cardiff or from the Collet's van that travelled the coalfield – but this had (and has) always been the case.

The Left Book Club appeared, fortuitously, albeit coincidentally, a matter of weeks before the outbreak of the Spanish Civil War, and provided intellectual ballast and a degree of organisational rigour to the popular response to that conflict. Many of the volunteers who fought in Spain acknowledged their debt to the Left Book Club and 'a recurring feature was the pride and diligence with which they [the volunteers] built up their own small but revealing libraries'.[57] Harry Stratton, a taxi driver from Swansea, drew on volumes such as *Spain in Revolt* to fill in his own knowledge about the immediate causes of the war before he left to fight. In the absence of the Left Book Club, that could have been much more difficult. 'The existing literature on modern Spain is extremely limited and inadequate', wrote that volume's authors in 1936, 'there is no coherent, systematic account of the history of Spain since 1933 in any language'.[58] There were novels, though, such as Ralph Bates's *Lean Men* (1934) and *The Olive Field* (1936), and journalistic reportage such as Claud Cockburn's *Reporter in Spain* (1936) which added to contemporary knowledge and understanding.[59]

The Spanish conflict encouraged a renewed attempt at forging a popular front in South Wales placing considerable strain on the Labour Party as it endeavoured to maintain increasingly impossible foreign policy positions.[60] At the party's conference in Edinburgh in the autumn of 1936, Dai Grenfell, the long-standing MP for Gower and close ally of Clement Attlee, had stressed the national executive's view that neutrality should be maintained, a position supported amongst others by Morgan Jones, the pacifist MP for Caerphilly, and by a large proportion of the conference delegates. This stance was strongly criticised by those on the left who were in favour of a more robust defence of the Spanish government, most notably Aneurin Bevan and Stafford Cripps.[61] Bevan and Cripps urged engagement with the Soviet Union, the development of a popular front at home, and the delivery of arms to the Spanish government. 'The alternative to a front populaire government', Bevan had explained at a meeting of Labour's national council in July 1936, 'was a government of the Right'.[62] Attlee's view, shared by Labour's moderate wing, was that the alliance needed to be transatlantic, with Britain and France the lead partners in Europe.[63]

In private, Grenfell was more robust, recognising that 'pacifism was not enough' but that 'it was difficult to eliminate from men's minds the beliefs of a lifetime'. There was, he thought, a dilemma facing the country, 'but there was a set of people in this situation who have no dilemmas, and they were the fascists and Nazis'. Nevertheless, he refused to adopt Bevan's position except insofar as it was apparent that there had been a breach of the non-intervention treaty by foreign powers. 'I think we could very well have left the Spanish nation alone', he said, 'if there had been no intervention from outside. But there is intervention on the side of the rebels'. And so, he concluded, 'this party must make up its mind ... and he would commit himself in public and private to their taking an anti-Fascist side of the struggle. .... There is no other hope'.[64] In November, after having visited Spain as part of a cross-party delegation of MPs, Grenfell went even further: 'the war is on now ... and the Fascists are winning all along the line. ... With arms in their hands they are fighting a campaign, even in this country – I am sure we are losing ground in this country every day. The idea is gaining ground'.[65]

The twists and turns in Labour's national executive were to prove frustrating to the robust response provided by the party's grassroots in South Wales, with the support and leadership of the South Wales Miners' Federation. Between the end of July and the end of September 1936, Labour's 'Help for the Workers of Spain Fund', had raised thousands of pounds for the cause. The Miners' Federation of Great Britain contribution was around three hundred and sixty pounds, of which two hundred and eighty five pounds, or eighty percent, came from the fundraising efforts of the South Wales Miners' Federation. It was the ninth largest trade union donation in the period.[66] Much of this was raised after mid-August, since the focus of the coalfield remained primarily on the battle against the Means Test and on the hunger march to London.[67] Thereafter, the South Walian response was robust and widespread. There were rallies and meetings held in Port Talbot on 5 September, in Abertillery and Merthyr on 17 September, each organised by the constituency labour party or trades and labour council.[68] And the CPGB claimed a network of more than eighty councils of action across the region, established to coordinate a response across the Labour Party, the CPGB, the ILP, and other religious and secular organisations.[69]

The extent to which the councils of action and the Aid for Spain movement were, in fact, a mechanism for the development of the popular front depended primarily on the receptiveness of the local Labour Party. As Idris Cox explained in February 1937, from his point of view, lamentably, but from the historian's, indicatively, there was a 'tendency to wait for the Labour Party to act and then [for communists to] react'. The strongest unity work, he went on to record, was in Cardiff, most especially on the Spanish question, with localised agreements in Ogmore Vale, Neath, and Rhigos.[70] The Cardiff Spanish Aid Committee was, therefore, based at Collet's Bookshop, rather than at either the Labour or CPGB headquarters in Charles Street.[71] In the Rhondda, the CPGB and the Labour Party worked largely independently of each other, as befitted the latter's antagonism towards joint effort.[72] Where there was joint effort, it was through the auspices of the SWMF, which satisfied those in the Labour Party who refused to work with the CPGB, and antagonised those within the CPGB who wanted more overt 'party' action.[73]

The window for collaborative action was, in retrospect a narrow one. Following sustained grassroots pressure, Labour's annual conference in Bournemouth in 1937 overturned previous resolutions supporting non-intervention and committed the party to campaigning to press for its abandonment.[74] To do so, Labour established its own Spain Campaign Committee that autumn, with members that included James Griffiths, Dai Grenfell, Stafford Cripps, and Ellen Wilkinson. Major demonstrations were held in Swansea and Newport on 28 November 1937, and the Milk for Spain Fund was launched in collaboration with co-operative societies across the country. Aneurin Bevan, although not co-opted onto the committee (nor was he invited to be) was engaged as a speaker at the Committee's Birmingham rally.[75] Bevan and Grenfell, together with Megan Lloyd George, then Liberal MP for Anglesey, were similarly members of the cross-party Parliamentary Committee for Spain. Grenfell was one of three honorary secretaries for the Duchess of Atholl's National Joint Committee for Spanish Relief, and subsequently served as one of three honorary secretaries the national Basque Children's Committee. The South Wales Regional Council of Labour, too, launched its own appeal. In addition to food, milk, and clothing, party branches collectively fundraised hundreds of pounds. Between them constituency parties in Llanelli, Swansea, Rhondda, and Neath, raised two hundred pounds.[76]

Labour's own efforts were matched by those of the SWMF. By October 1938, the SWMF had raised, in common with the Durham and Yorkshire coalfields, more than sixteen thousand pounds in support of the Miners' Federation of Great Britain's Spanish Aid Fund (although a portion was returned to each district as over-payment).[77] It was probably the case, although we should not discount the support provided by the NUR and the TGWU, that 'the SWMF contributed more financially to the Spanish Republican cause than any other British trade union, certainly more than any other regional union'.[78] Lodges also contributed to the South Wales Regional Council of Labour's own fundraising initiatives. It is therefore equally probable that the contribution of the SWMF (including the individual contributions made directly by lodges) was closer to twenty thousand pounds over the period of the conflict, a vast sum considering the financial constraints of the interwar Depression.

Of course, money and moral support alone could not win a war, especially when those on the opposite side were more than willing both to supply and to take up arms in support of their own cause. On this, Labour were far more anxious than were the CPGB, who clearly advocated the supply of volunteers from Britain to fight fascism in the International Brigades, or the South Wales Miners' Federation, which financially supported the International Brigades Dependents' and Wounded Aid Committee. The SWMF secretary, Oliver Harris, served as a patron. Several lodges, chiefly those led by communist officials, also called for the formation of volunteer battalions, although this was sensibly turned down by Oliver Harris because of its illegality.[79] Had it occurred, the ramifications for the SWMF could have been very serious indeed. Even the provision of financial support for dependents of volunteers was problematic, since the normal rules and regulations of trade unions did not necessarily permit it. In fact, in the TUC's view, there was nothing in the rules of the Miners' Federation of Great Britain that allowed for dependents' support when the member had volunteered for the International Brigade.[80] What the SWMF were doing was, in the strictest sense, illegal, but they regarded it as the right and moral thing to do.

There's a Valley in Spain

Although the significance of the Spanish Civil War is not easily conveyed by statistics, there is one statistic from South Wales that stands out above all others, and serves to illustrate why the contribution of the coalfield was not only financial. By January 1939, there were around one thousand members of the CPGB in South Wales: this figure included two hundred or so women, and around eight hundred men. Almost all the two hundred and six volunteers for the International Brigades from Wales were communists (only a handful were not). These two figures put together mean that somewhere between one quarter and one fifth of the entire male membership of the CPGB in South Wales served in Spain between 1936 and 1938. In the Rhondda, a district that sent thirty two volunteers to the International Brigades, the figure was closer to one in every three. And in Merthyr and Dowlais, where the CPGB membership was small, it was at least one member in every two. This was unparalleled in Britain. For all the organisational problems that beset the South Wales District, for all the apparently unfulfilled promises of radicalism and militancy, there was a remarkable efficacy – and ruthlessness, given internal conscription took place – in its response to Spain.[81]

That you were more likely to fight in Spain if you were a member of the CPGB, than if you were not, cannot, then, be doubted. There were also those, such as the novelist Gwyn Thomas or the poet Alun Lewis, who imagined service in the International Brigades, but who never went. Lewis was active in Left Book Club meetings in Aberdare at the end of the 1930s and, like Gwyn Thomas, taught for the WEA. His own views on the conflict were revealed in a short story, 'Private Jones' that included a character who had 'fought two years in Spain', and in letters to the *Aberdare Leader* warning that 'democracy is more likely to perish than thrive on a European war'.[82] Gwyn Thomas was too ill to go to Spain and instead devoted his energies initially to the fundraising effort and then through work with the Basque refugee children at Cambria House near Caerleon.[83] And there was the people's remembrancer Gwyn Alf Williams, barely a teenager, who imagined himself as part of the wider communist movement. His chapel gang, he imagined, was an 'extra-mural branch of the Third International'. Williams was present at the funeral of J. S. Williams who had returned from service in Spain – the ceremony comprised Dowlais-Spanish communists in red ties and brown boots singing the *Internationale*. Encouraged by the scene, the young boy

rushed down to the International Brigade office near the remains of the old [Dowlais] works, my head full of a "give me a gun and send me to Spain" zeal. But as I shot in through the door, I froze. I stood there speechless. There was a high counter and, after a while, a face appeared over it. 'Oh!' it said. 'Young Williams, is it?' Our family were known in Dowlais as the Bloody Williamses. After another pause, he said ... 'Son, come back when we're desperate'.[84]

One who, at least initially, would have gladly gone to fight was the Rhondda novelist Lewis Jones. Aside from Arthur Horner, Jones easily had the highest profile of any communist in South Wales. As a hunger march leader, writer, county councillor, and charismatic agitator, Jones was the kind of communist who drew public attention to the cause and gained a loyal following of fellow travellers. He also shared Horner's determination to work under the auspices of the SWMF. Jones's life had 'the taste of legend' and when Gwyn Thomas was asked by the BBC in the 1970s to choose the greatest Welshmen, he did not hesitate to select his hero. 'Never has anyone orchestrated the rage and bitterness of bewildered communities as he', Thomas told listeners.[85] But Lewis Jones did not go to Spain. He was not allowed to do so. The party hierarchy were wary of removing from South Wales one of its finest assets and, in any case, after several years of unemployment he was not fit enough to go (although this did not prevent men such as J. S. Williams from doing so). When the CPGB revised its position in February 1938, and offered Lewis Jones a second chance, this time he refused pointedly to go.[86] Within a year, he was dead, and his partner, Mavis Llewellyn, finished his second novel, *We Live*, in line with the party's expectations. Rather than dying exhausted in South Wales, Len Roberts travelled to Spain and gained his martyrdom.[87]

As *We Live* showed, travelling to Spain involved considerable personal cost, from the danger of the journey to the impact of loved ones who were confronted with sudden disappearances. When Will Paynter left to become Political Commissar of the British Battalion at Albacete in 1937, he faced the 'private personal drama' of being separated from his new wife Irene. This time apart became even more poignant when Mrs Paynter died in childbirth in 1939.[88] Most International Brigaders followed instructions and said nothing and left in the middle of the night, but one of those who did tell his family what he was doing was Leo Price of Abertridwr. Only at the final goodbye did it seem real. 'I took my daughter to bed', he reflected later, 'and that was the hardest thing that ever I did was to leave her there and go'.[89] And despite his own decision not to go, Lewis Jones agonised over the fate of his friend Jack Jones (Blaenclydach) who volunteered in March 1938 and was captured by Franco's forces a few months later. Jack was released from prison in Burgos in January 1939 but did not return home until after Lewis had died. In a letter to his parents written on 13 March 1938, Jack reflected on his decision: 'you will be concerned to know as to how I am getting on. Let me say I have never felt better in my life'.[90] But Jack had left his parents in the middle of fighting a compensation case and remained as much concerned for their well-being as his own.[91]

The case of Morien Morgan of Ynysybwl provides a useful example of how personal desire to support the Spanish Republican war effort fused with political activity, and a degree of CPGB encouragement, to create a volunteer for the International Brigades. At the time the war broke out, Morgan was studying modern languages at Cardiff and had been active in the Labour Party.[92] He had grown up in a political family – his father, John E. Morgan was the secretary of the Lady Windsor Lodge in Ynysybwl, one of his uncles, Abel, was a district councillor and prominent in the Ynysybwl Co-operative Society, and another, Bethuel, had been imprisoned as a conscientious objector during the First World War. Frustrated by the 'bits and pieces' approach of the humanitarian aid given to the Spanish Republic, and the failure to overturn the non-intervention treaty, he was steadily drawn into communist activity in Cardiff, resolving in the autumn of 1936 that he would go to Spain. He did not, however, leave until the end of 1937. According to the schedule provided by the South Wales District Committee, he travelled to London and then on to Paris before eventually arriving at a safe house in Carcassonne in the south of France. After a few days, a bus arrived in the middle of the night to take a group of volunteers, including Morgan, to the Pyrenees from where they walked over the mountains into Spain. He did not see Wales again for more than a year.

The communist world that Morien Morgan entered in Cardiff in 1936-37 was amongst the most sophisticated in South Wales. There was the Left Book Club study circle, initially formed by Harry Greenwall, the pro-Republican foreign correspondent of the *South Wales Echo*, but which soon fell under the control of the local CPGB committee.[93] It attracted eminent speakers, including Arthur Horner and discussed books such as Allen Hutt's *The Post-War History of the British Working Class* (1937) and Archie Lush's *The Young Adult in Wales*, although the latter was not published by Victor Gollancz. There was the League of Nations Union branch, both of which mimicked the Left Book Club study circle model. They debated foreign policy, the International Labour Organisation, communism, and even 'the position of an individual in the event of war'.[94] And there was the university socialist society which, despite 'a certain amount of apathy in the political life of the college', engaged its members on matters such as Spain, Indian nationalism, and the fortunes of the League of Nations; they showed Soviet films, denounced the Munich agreement, and above all worked hard to convince fellow students of the necessity of international intervention on behalf of the Spanish Republic.[95]

The films were almost certainly loaned to the university socialist society by the local branch of Kino, the workers' film society, which was based at Collet's.[96] Formed in January 1936, the branch initially attempted to organise the local premiere of *Battleship Potemkin*, although intervention by the city police prevented it from taking place.[97] Members instead turned their attention to the provision of mainly Soviet audio-visual material to leftist meetings across South Wales (notably in miners' institutes in the coalfield[98]) using a network of contacts developed by radical bookshops, the *Daily Worker*, and the CPGB. In January 1938, for instance, they arranged for a showing of Nikolai Ekk's 1931 drama *The Road to Life* at the

Elysium Hall in Swansea, the proceeds of which went to the Spanish Medical Aid Committee. The Republican newsreel, *News From Spain*, was also shown.[99] Maerdy Institute cinema had showings of *The Defence of Madrid* in 1937 and Tredegar Institute cinema showed *They Shall Not Pass* and *Spanish Earth*, together with Walter Wagner's *Blockade*. Stephen Ridgwell has argued that films from socialist and pro-Soviet workers' film societies were rarely that successful and could not compete with the mainstream offerings of British and American film companies such as MGM, Disney, and Warner Brothers.[100] But that was not the mindset that the exhibitors had, for them workers' film had an intrinsic value and served its purpose during the period of the Spanish Civil War.[101]

Together with the newspapers, pamphlets and Left Book Club editions, leftist films encouraged political talk. Certainly, in Cardiff, political discussion was a dimension that the CPGB carefully cultivated, at first providing speakers to existing organisations – the university socialist society or the League of Nations Union branch – and then steadily drawing the curious into its own organisations. Amongst those who spoke to the socialist society was Alec Cummings, the Rhondda-born former army sergeant turned WEA lecturer and communist agitprop organiser.[102] Before he left for service in the International Brigades, Cummings worked closely with Cardiff's Young Communist League organiser Elin Davies, an Oxford graduate then undertaking teacher training in the city. Davies had been tasked by Will Paynter to get a 'bunch of BIs [Bloody Intellectuals] together to hold political discussion', and many of the sessions were held in Cummings's flat.[103] Morien Morgan went along and there he met Gilbert Taylor, the manager of Collet's Bookshop, and Sid Hamm, a student at Cardiff Technical College and a close friend of Leo Abse, as well as other members of the Cardiff Communist Party. Both Taylor and Hamm served, and died, in Spain.[104]

The Young Communist League was mirrored in parts of Cardiff by branches of the Labour League of Youth, itself long considered (nationally as well as in Cardiff) to be overly close to the CPGB. In Splott, the Labour League of Youth was led by Bill Coles, a tall 'little bolshie' radicalised by long stints of unemployment and engagement with political literature. He got the pamphlets and books from a radical bookshop on the corner of Park Lane and Queen Street, which was run by Gwen Jones, another of Paynter's BIs. Coles was one of the few communists in Cardiff who had successfully entered the Labour Party.[105] There was also the Cardiff United Youth Movement formed in 1936 by Leo Abse and Sid Hamm as a means of bringing unity amongst the politically active young people in the city. Members initially met in the backroom of Collet's bookshop but moved subsequently to 53 Charles Street, home of the CPGB. The group held meetings in the open and in their meeting room, with denouncing the government's policy on Spain high on the agenda. Aspects of their activities were semi-fictionalised in Dannie Abse's 1954 memoir, *Ash on a Young Man's Sleeve*.[106] The CUYM organised memorials for fallen comrades such as Sid Hamm and enjoyed the support of leading communists such as Lewis Jones – it was, in effect, a popular front organisation for young people.[107]

Whatever may be thought of the methods by which men and women travelled to Spain, and their political reasons for doing so, it would be churlish (and certainly disrespectful) to suggest that their actions and the way they have subsequently been presented were part of a 'need to manufacture a history of popular struggle and armed resistance', as Robert Stradling has.[108] Rather, we should recognise the late-1930s for what they were: a period in which communist determination to organise armed resistance to fascism in Spain (and to spread Soviet ideas to that country, undoubtedly) was broadly successful in the South Walian context; and in which the Labour

Party, far from being inactive, as was once argued by guardians of the communist narrative, sought to shape its radical pragmatism to the Spanish cause, to navigate its ingrained anti-communism, and to overcome the pacifistic instincts of an entire generation of local leaders. The dearest cause, in the end, was not only Spain, which was but a cipher of the larger issue, but the defeat of fascism across the European continent. After all, it was not only Nazi Germany that had its work camps for those whom the government deemed 'undesirable'.

The international conflict had its own home front.

'Nie Mair': Breaking the Unemployed

In 1938, Gwyn Thomas was pulled away from his work with the Basque children in Caerleon, indeed from Wales entirely, when he took a paid position as a tutor at one of the government instructional centres at Cranwich Heath near Thetford in Norfolk. The 'instructional centre' was part of a network of labour camps set up for the long-term unemployed in 1929 and were intended to 'harden' young men for work through a period of heavy manual labour, to make them more masculine – the idea being that through unemployment men became weak (and by implication more feminine). At that time they were hardly controversial, but the arrival of the Nazis to power in January 1933, and the establishment of the first concentration camps – as opposed to the extermination camps of the holocaust – soon afterwards, quickly changed that.[109] 'They were just like concentration camps', recalled William Heard, who attended a centre near Hereford after two years on the dole in Ebbw Vale. He continued: 'the first thing they did was supply you with a pair of heavy nailed boots, a pair of corduroy trousers, and some kind of shirt. So, wherever you did go people know who you were – you were a convict in a sense, because you were all dressed the same'.[110]

Gwyn Thomas wrote to his sister, Nan, in similar terms:

> There is scarcely a man in these camps who is not saddled with
> the Nazarene error of some hire purchase swindle ... Apparently
> the wives get the idea that the fact of their husbands being in a
> training centre gives them immunity from the debt. ... If any of
> these trainees is found to be in debt and trying to escape the
> responsibility, the centre management co-operate with the
> police to put him in the jug. ... Between jail and training centres
> there is little difference.

Having only just about escaped the blunt impact of
unemployment himself, the three months spent as a tutor at the
camp in Norfolk gave Gwyn chance to reflect on his own
situation and the 'there but for the grace' position he found
himself in. He was an angry young man and angry at the world
around him: 'There is nothing here, nothing, from the work of
the place to the state of my soul, that does not make me snarl'.
As he moved around England from one instructional centre to
another, one short-term teaching contract to another, he
encountered men who had been utterly broken by the years of
distress that they had endured. Towards the end of his life, he
reflected on his experiences in Norfolk, Bury, Rochdale and
Derbyshire, and on the men that he met there. 'About the only
thing on the curriculum was knotting – making knots – and I
had never made a knot in my life; I had no idea what to do but
they gave me a board full of all kinds of knots'. He continued:

> The poor chaps in the camps, they were desperate men, they
> were very sad men and I gave these lessons in knotting; you
> know, how to attach a yacht to a mooring point [...] but it's a
> very funny thing, because so many of these lads would come
> up to me and they'd say "what is the execution knot?" Well, I

didn't have much of an idea, but I sort of probably gave them some instruction in knotting for something totally different but one of them at least acted on the shape and killed himself.

The men at the camp in Cranwich Heath were principally from the North-East, from the mining communities of Durham and Northumberland, or from industrial towns such as Jarrow. Tough, physical men, like the miners of the Rhondda, these were 'men of dignity'.[111] They had had their backs broken, Gwyn Thomas reflected angrily, 'by an act of social idiocy':

> And these men were bitter, but impotent, of course, impotent – there was very little they could do about this. And there they would sit in these awful bunks – there were nine great huts – and there'd be silence, terrible silence for half an hour in the evening. Maybe the odd crooning of a Northumbrian song, something of that sort, you know, and then a voice would cry: "Nie Mair!" – No More. "Nie Mair!" And it would be taken up until it became a great prairie fire of wrath and anguish and despair.[112]

The camps provoked bitter outcry from amongst the organised unemployed, not least because they removed individuals from their homes and placed them in camps in isolated areas for several weeks at a time.[113]

The more that information became available about circumstances in Germany, the more this sort of government sanction evoked the sinister idea of 'concentration camp'. There were warnings from the left that the National Government was creeping, bit by bit, even as it appeared to do nothing at all, towards establishing a fascist regime like those on the continent. The communist-led NUWM encouraged active boycott of the camps and direct agitation inside and outside.[114] At Brechfa in

Carmarthenshire this meant strikes and eventually a mass walkout of the men with complaints about damp bedding, bad food, the semi-militarised disciplinary system, and an eight pence stoppage a day if they fell ill.[115] Conditions at Brechfa had already prompted the South Wales NUWM to commission a report, written by William Picton, Arthur Evan Short, and Richard J. Perry, and to distribute it to employment exchange managers in the vain hope that they would not send men there.[116] In 1935, the local NUWM branches had convinced fifty men to get off the bus taking them to Brechfa and the Cambrian Combine lodges agreed to support them financially.[117] Locally, the Llanelli United Front Committee undertook a campaign for the closure of Brechfa camp, in one protest they took a group – dressed in the uniform of the camps – to the site and held a protest march.[118]

Brechfa had originally opened in May 1934 and had accommodation for two hundred people at any given time. By the end of that year, nine hundred and forty men had passed through and just thirty five had found work of any kind.[119] The following year, nine hundred and thirty four men attended and just sixty one gained employed thereafter.[120] In fact, by the end of 1938, a further three thousand, three hundred and one people had passed through Brechfa Instructional Centre, and only two hundred and eleven were working. It was a dismal failure: the equivalent of just six percent of those interned.[121] The government claimed the 'success' rate was nearer sixteen percent.[122] 'We therefore see', remarked Wal Hannington, the national organiser of the NUWM, 'that the majority of the men who went to these Camps on the grounds that they were to be made fit again for work, simply returned to their normal dreary conditions of unemployment to become unfit again'.[123] The non-residential camp at Rheola near Resolven, which also opened in 1934, was more successful, with around ten percent finding work after spending time there, but this also fell short of the national average. Complaints continued to be made, but nothing was done to resolve them.[124] In fact, by 1939, the system had expanded to four camps across Wales.[125]

For almost two decades, by that point, unemployment had stalked the South Wales Coalfield. Personal distress and consistent policy failures by successive governments had, on the face of it, transformed a region that was once vibrant and economically powerful into a problem, a special area, a distressed area, a national headache. During a debate on unemployment measures in July 1936, James Griffiths, MP for Llanelli and formerly the SWMF president, summed up the changes that had taken place in Carmarthenshire, Glamorgan, and Monmouthshire over the previous generation:

Compare the South Wales of to-day with the South Wales of 20 years ago, a South Wales full of virile people, people full of the joy of life, people contributing in no small measure to the songs and the poetry of our nation. Compare Tonypandy 15 years ago with the Tonypandy of to-day. We did not need to discuss unemployment benefit then. What we were discussing was the money spent on sending police there to keep those people quiet. Now we have valleys condemned to perpetual unemployment under the policy for which Ministers are responsible. Ever since 1920 the South Wales coalfield has been condemned to ever greater misery every year because of the policy of successive Governments.[126]

Griffiths, together with fellow South Wales MPs including S. O. Davies, Morgan Jones, and Aneurin Bevan, endeavoured to give voice to that former vitality and the current lamentable economic situation. They faced jibes from Conservative MPs. Nancy Astor, for instance, begged the Labour benches – and the

South Wales MPs, particularly – to 'not give us any more sob stuff'. But it was difficult not to. National unemployment had fallen to (the still very high) thirteen and a half percent by the summer of 1936 but in parts of South Wales it was many times that: sixty percent in Merthyr and Dowlais.[127] Even those who were employed faced poor living standards.[128] And populations were falling dramatically: Rhondda's medical officer observed in 1938 that 'since 1924 over 56,000 persons have emigrated from the district'. The emigration rate that year for Rhondda was two thousand, two hundred and sixty.[129]

Those who left found work in London and the South East, notably at Slough, or in the car plants at Oxford and Birmingham. But for those left behind, there was a continued degradation in health and a reliance on a raft of initiatives designed to mitigate the boredom of unemployment: allotment societies, physical training classes, public parks, and unemployed clubs.[130] One such initiative was the educational settlement, of which there were nine across South Wales by 1939.[131] By the late-1930s, Merthyr was home to two of them: one run by the Quaker John Dennithorne, at Dowlais, which opened as a club in 1928 and became a settlement in 1935, and the other opened in Merthyr itself in 1930. At its peak, the Merthyr settlement had a membership of over three thousand and organised nearly sixty clubs across the county borough. The programme of activities ranged from public lectures to drama productions, musical groups including a string quartet, a glee club, and a thrift club for women that made clothes from recycled material. The settlement at Merthyr was indicative rather than unique: in nearby Aberdare, the town's settlement opened in 1936, claimed a membership of around one thousand, and offered a full range of clubs and talks.[132]

The settlement at Pontypridd, opened in 1937, and with a membership of more than five thousand was similarly impressive. It had a film society, choral society, orchestral society, brass band, drama society, and a modern language society. It supported the town's network of boy's and girl's clubs, which collectively had hundreds of members. And it ran a full programme of lectures and classes in subjects ranging from sociology to international affairs, German language training, and practical drama.[133] Many of the education classes provided at the settlements were run in conjunction with the WEA and the extra mural department of University College Cardiff and added once more to the intellectual and social fuel of the period.[134] Merthyr's classes varied from Welsh literature and social history, to philosophy, economics, political theory, and logic.[135] In the second half of the 1930s, there was a very strong focus on international affairs with lectures on Hitler and Mussolini and a day school on the 'League [of Nations], the Empires and the Hungry Powers', which was accordingly popular with members – it was attended by one hundred and fifty people. The following year, lectures focused on the 'need for a thinking democracy', 'is there a danger of war', issues of youth disaffection, and a presentation on life in the Soviet Union by Pat Sloan, a prominent writer on Soviet affairs who had lived there for much of the 1930s.[136]

The settlements were an effective riposte to the government's attempt to break the unemployed through the instructional centres, even if that had not been their original intention. They took the principles and forms of independent working class education and blended them with popular recreation and leisure, in effect creating significant centres of activity and of resistance to government policy. It has been shown, categorically, in recent years that continuing education improves mental and physical health and provides increased self-confidence and determination, and a sense of belonging, particularly amongst those without work.[137] This is not a recent phenomenon and evidently it applied to the settlements, in vivid contrast to the instructional centres. The central theme was history: members of the settlements, particularly those attending classes, had a determination to make sense of the various reasons why the world had ended up in the manner that it had, and to learn lessons. Infused with politics, philosophy, and economics, this was labour history or, as Gwyn Thomas termed it, for his class in Ton Pentre, the 'political history of South Wales'.[138] It was the sort of history that others sought to capture and present, too. For them, it was one last attempt to build a popular front on the coalfield: before it was too late.

In the March of History

On 21 March 1937, communists marched through Mid Rhondda with banners and portraits of events and figures drawn from working class history. It was their first attempt at a pageant of mining history and was called 'South Wales in the March of History'.[139] The souvenir programme, decorated with some of the portraits featured on the march, ranging from Simon de Montfort and Lord Byron to Keir Hardie and Oliver Cromwell, set out the timeline of radical history and declared South Wales to be 'symbolic of progress and struggle. A name beloved by the heroes of progress throughout the civilised world'.[140] The purpose of the pageant and march, as Idris Cox reflected, was to make communist activity 'attractive not only to the politically conscious workers, but the mass of unthinking workers as well'. It was Cox who wrote the programme (evident in the tinges of nationalism that run through it) and he was determined to ensure its success. 'We are confident', he said, 'that this pageant will become the talk of the whole of South Wales, we need more colour and style and music in the whole of our activity, and this should be the keynote of our public meetings so that communist meetings become the centre of attraction with all progressively thinking people'.[141] The Rhondda event was followed by a May Day Pageant in Pontypool the following year.[142] They were followed by the even more ambitious Pageant of South Wales in 1939.

The Pageant of South Wales was initially conceived of by a small group on the SWMF Executive, namely W. J. Saddler, the vice president, and W. H. Crews, neither of whom were in the Communist Party, and Dai Dan Evans and Will Paynter, who were. It was indicative of the co-operation between Labour and the CPGB under the auspices of the SWMF. The group met for the first time on 1 December 1938 to sketch out their ideas. Having determined that they wanted to tell the story of labour struggle since the Chartists, they then approached the communist-led Labour Research Department for advice and assistance. Oliver Harris, the Federation general secretary, wrote 'if you could help us in suggesting some twenty outstanding phases of incidents in the working class movement during the last one hundred years who would be suitable for representation in a pageant'. They received a reply from Bill Williams, the Monmouthshire-born secretary of the LRD, who suggested that:

> It might be worthwhile ... to include broad movements of social struggle, such as, for example, the very important struggles of the Welsh working class against the English landlords and capitalists, which took the form of a strong nationalist movement with a working-class content. Then, also, the election of Keir Hardie for Merthyr was an event of considerable importance.[143]

Over the next few months, the pageant was developed by Montagu Slater, André van Gyseghem, the composer Benjamin Britten, and the sub-committee, with input from Ness Edwards, as a historian and theorist of workers' theatre, David Williams, history lecturer at Cardiff who had been commissioned by the Newport Chartist Centenary Committee to write a history of the Newport Rising, and Robin Page Arnot. Slater and van Gyseghem were both active in the Left Theatre movement in London as well as the Communist Party, as was Britten. Van Gyseghem was also president of the Unity Theatre, the lead organisation for communist theatre in Britain which had been founded in 1936.[144] Slater had been chosen as the writer in part because of his earlier work on the stay down strikes at Nine Mile Point in Cwmfelinfach. His book, *Stay Down, Miner*, and the subsequent play, *New Way Wins*, were intended to force audiences to confront their own class awareness with the goal of consciousness raising.[145] Audiences in London, it was hoped, would stand up in solidarity with the miners. Eventually the Pageant took on its final form: Slater had retained much of the original idea but extended the chronology to include the Spanish Civil War. This made the links between the past and the present deliberately overt, as Oliver Harris, reflected in the Pageant programme:

> The story of the miners of Wales, during the last century and a-half, is one of hardship, suffering and struggle, but it records steady progress, in face of many difficulties, and of the callous opposition of employers, the privileged classes, and the governments of the day. It is fitting that on the hundredth anniversary of the Chartist movement some of the incidents of the miners' struggle should be recalled in pageant form, to remind the present generation of the dark periods through which our forefathers passed on the road to the present better and brighter days.[146]

On May Day, 1939, the SWMF together with the Labour Research Department hosted the Pageant of South Wales in Abertillery, Pontypool, and Ystradgynlais. A further silicosis pageant was held on the same day at Cwmamman. With a cast made up of members of those communities and a script divided into two 'episodes', the second of which was entitled 'Yesterday, To-Day, and To-Morrow', the Pageant of South Wales held up a mirror to a society that had indeed travelled on a considerable journey over the previous century. That journey, unlike the by-ways and meandering paths taken on the actual historical route, was here presented as a seamless one despite its arduous nature. A mapped-out history was to take the denizens of the present in 1939 out of the past from 1839 into the future. Out of the ideals of the Chartist movement sprang the fight for better conditions and a happier life for everyone in South Wales, so the programme declared, and on then to the South Wales Miners' Federation and its struggle for democratic principles which were carried through to that auspicious centennial year of 1939. Onto the stage steps the narrator:

It was in 1839 when John Frost marched to Newport, and a hundred years is a long time. It has been said that in the first weeks of its pre-natal life the human embryo lives through aeons of the history of the race. In the first years of their lives the South Wales children live in a sense through the intervening years of our history.

In our villages they learn of the miners' lodges and of organisation for bargaining. They learn what a hard bargain is driven. They learn of accidents in the mine. They see friends or relatives dying of silicosis. And if they are over 13 they will remember something about 1926, and all that the great strike and lock-out means in working-class history. What is more important than all this they learn in every day's life in the valleys that against the inertia of all that is mean and miserable the men of their class and nation have found a force.

On then came the procession of men, women, and children, one of whom is stopped by the narrator. His name is Tom Jenkins, who tells the crowd that he works from six in the morning to six in the evening and sometimes from three in the morning. At nine years of age he is already at work; so is the little girl who comes along next, she is just five. Says the narrator:

> To fight this universe of evil, men unite to form the first embryo of our Federation ... they meet illegally, at night, swearing a secret oath. Listen.

The meeting is secret, yes, with oaths sworn on the bible, but it has the appearance of a chapel meeting too and to emphasise that impression choirs take up the classic hymn, *Cwm Rhondda*. And, as *Cwm Rhondda* gives way to *England Arise*, a new procession takes to the stage carrying banners for each trade union and society and organisation associated with the collier: ostlers, hauliers, engine drivers, firemen, and ambulance men. Suddenly as the music moves to the *Red Flag* a man runs onto the stage and tells the assembled that they're on strike at a nearby pit. It's time to form up together. But soon there are police and militia – an echo of Tonypandy – and finally a coffin. 'In South Wales we know another kind of procession', the narrator explains, 'when a man is killed in the pit, his workmates down tools and form a procession to the widow's house'. The stage is given over to four dead miners, all to tell their tales.

Then, behind them, emerges a single figure, together with a painted portrait of A. J. Cook. For that is who the figure is, and he is there to tell the story of 1926. At the end of his speech, the choirs take up the American labour hymn, *Solidarity Forever*, with lyrics speaking to the purpose of the labour movement and the hardships that everyone in the audience had endured in the years since 1926:

Oh we who suffered in the fight with hunger and with cold,
Have known from day to weary day the tale that here is told;
Read in the faces of the dead the hope that we shall hold,
Till democracy has won.

Solidarity for ever,
Solidarity for ever,
Solidarity for ever,
And democracy has won.[147]

But the struggles were not yet over and onto the stage step four
new people, a miner's wife, a miner's daughter, a miner's son,
and an unemployed miner. Each tells their own story. 'I am a
miner's daughter. There are no jobs here. I had to leave home
and go to London in service. There are a lot of Welsh girls here.
But if you keep together all of you we'll win through – then we
can come back'. And at the very end of the episode, and of the
Pageant, comes the last hero of the South Walian century: the
international brigader. 'I am', he says:

One of the little band that went out from South Wales to fight
in the international brigades in Spain. I am going to ask you to
rise, all of you, and swear with me this oath of victory.

In the name of Wales and its people, in the name of our high-
wrought past, in the name of our traditions, in the name of all
our battles in the fight for freedom, on this day 1 May 1939,
we solemnly swear not to relax until freedom, and the
prosperity that can only be brought by the power of the people
bring back the sunshine to our land.

The actors, the choirs, and the crowd, then sang the
Internationale. And understood and believed its words. At least,

that was the intention. However, rain, high winds, and even snow, this being South Wales in the summer, after all, dampened the effect.[148]

If the curtain were to be drawn down at this point, on that soggy May afternoon just before the Second World War, there would be a rather downbeat ending. The history popularised in the pageants, despite the attempt at a heroic conclusion and the singing of the *Internationale*, was mired in defeat and a sense of loss. As the last of the International Brigaders returned home, some of them after nearly a year of incarceration, there was an opportunity to reflect on what they had seen and experienced. Morien Morgan explained to reporters on his arrival that many prisoners had been beaten and tortured and that, when they were fed, meals consisted of dry sardines or soup. The prison at San Pedro de Cardeña was a 'huge stone building lying at the bottom of a shallow vale – a vale poplared with beauty in summer; in winter, ugly as death'.[149] The economic turmoil had still to be resolved despite the new factories at Treforest or the instructional centres, and there was a sense that, for all the effort put in to build a public consciousness, 'our children are not so well informed on the history of these valleys as we would wish'.[150]

With a spirit of high idealism, leading communists on the SWMF executive sought to develop and sustain a popular history of the South Wales Coalfield and to present to the public the idea of struggle as a collective experience.[151] It was the theme of the popular front as they saw it. Having failed to convince the Labour Party, these activists turned to artists and filmmakers to support their efforts, a process that began at the end of the 1930s and continued into the 1940s. In the aftermath of the war, this same group of communists instituted fully-fledged social and cultural initiatives including the South Wales Miners' Eisteddfod, the South Wales Miners' Gala, the youth committee, a series of education classes, international activism, pageantry, and a strong legacy of sponsored documentary film-making. It was this group which successfully courted Paul Robeson and Humphrey Jennings, and encouraged the making of a succession of films in the coalfield including *Spare Time* in 1939, *This Proud Valley* in 1940, the *Silent Village* about the Nazi destruction of Lidice in Poland in 1943, and *A Diary For Timothy* in 1945. These initiatives were the fulfilment of ideas that emerged in the 1930s as a way of making the labour movement, particularly its communist wing, seem less austere and more popularly accessible, but they were about the failure of the popular front rather than its success.

Significantly, this group contributed to a popular inculcation of what the coalfield and its society was (for them) all about. As the initial script for a pageant to be held in the Dulais Valley put it, 'you are about to witness the portrayal of the struggle of the mining population of Wales against the most tyrannical and fierce opposition'. History with the definite article. And yet, because of the continued economic situation, mitigated only by war, there was a deep pessimism about South Walian society that could not be masked by heroic theatre and history-making. Nor, indeed, could it be masked by the utter triumph of the Labour Party in many parts of the South Wales Coalfield. As one correspondent of the *Daily Herald* remarked in 1937:

When I was speaking in Ynysybwl in the Aberdare Division, George Hall [the MP] actually appealed for Labour workers because, owing to the predominance of the Socialist vote, there was no organisation apart from the Miners' Federation! All the local councillors were Labour men, except one veteran of 83, who invariably voted with them! So "propaganda" is unknown. The old Socialist gospel is so much taken for granted that the young have never heard it preached![152]

One of those who felt that pessimism completely was Gwyn Thomas who, in his private notebooks, laid out the tortured passions of his twenties and the ferment of a society he could never really detach himself from, not that he ever really wished to do so. Sitting in Barry, many years later, he reflected on the certainties of the past. 'The Wales of my childhood' he wrote, despairingly, 'the libertarian noon, was intelligent, altruistic, aglow, a place of strong-voice dreamers and comedians. All gone'.[153] Such feelings echoed those he had in the 1940s. Then they may have seemed misplaced: the high-water mark of the British labour movement was seemingly not behind him, but in front of him – the Labour governments of 1945-1951. But even in later life, when possessed of the knowledge of those administrations, he returned to this idea of the passing away of South Walian brilliance and the descent of the region and its people into apathetic decay. Into, in other words, a world where people laughed but did not really understand the joke. As he put it in 1969:

> In Wales an industry was dying, a massive popular religion was dying. And most important of all, the most dynamic and passionate political belief in Britain was dying.[154]

The South Wales Valleys would never be lit up in quite the same way again.

Notes

[1] *RL*, 5 September 1936. This is discussed more broadly in my 'The World Cannot Hear You: Gwyn Thomas (1913-1981), Communism and the Cold War', *WHR* 28, no. 2 (2016), 335-362.

[2] 'Application Form for Admission to St Edmund Hall, Gwyn Thomas, 19 September 1931'. St Edmund Hall Archives, Oxford, Gwyn Thomas Student File.

[3] Gwyn Thomas, *A Few Selected Exits* (Bridgend, 1993 edn.), 63.

[4] 'Gwyn Thomas', in Meic Stephens (ed.), *Artists in Wales* (Llandysul, 1971), 71.

[5] Arthur Koestler, *Spanish Testament* (London, 1937), 50.

[6] For a broader sense of this wave of violence see: Paul Preston, *The Spanish Holocaust: Inquisition and Extermination in Twentieth-Century Spain* (London, 2012), 3-33; Chris Ealham, *Anarchism and the City: Revolution and Counter-Revolution in Barcelona, 1898-1937* (Edinburgh, 2010), 130-148.

[7] 'Letter to Bursar, St Edmund Hall, from Gwyn Thomas, 10 May 1933'. St Edmund Hall Archives, Oxford, Gwyn Thomas Student File.

[8] 'The Colliers Crusade: Interview with Gwyn Thomas', Gwyn Thomas Papers, NLW, G169, 16-17.

[9] What follows here draws on an interview conducted with Morien Morgan for the Imperial War Museum in September 1987. Imperial War Museum, London, Recording IWMSA/9856.

[10] *GFP*, 8 August 1936.

[11] *GFP*, 22 August, 12 September 1936.

[12] *WM*, 3 October, 4 October 1938. The incident introduces Richard Wyn Jones's, *The Fascist Party in Wales? Plaid Cymru, Welsh Nationalism and the Accusation of Fascism* (Cardiff, 2014).

[13] Gabriel Gorodetsky (ed.), *The Maisky Diaries: Red Ambassador to the Court of St James's, 1932-1943* (New Haven, 2015), 208-210.

[14] W. W. Knox, *James Maxton* (Manchester, 1987), 29.

[15] Brinley Thomas, 'The Critical Struggle for Power in Germany', *The Welsh Outlook* 20, no. 3 (1933), 80-2.

[16] Gwilym Davies, 'In the Third Reich', *The Welsh Outlook* 20, no. 10 (1933), 263-5.

[17] 'Cardigan County School Notebook, 1942', 11-12, NLW, Gwyn Thomas Papers, N2.

[18] SWCC, MNA/PP/46/13: Letter from Aneurin Bevan to Arthur Horner, 30 April 1933.

[19] The CPGB regarded Spain to be the 'main lever in the struggle to develop united action and has developed a movement in South Wales of some consequence'. RGASPI, 495.14.261: 'Communist Party of Great Britain, South Wales District Report, 1938'.

[20] Smith, *Aneurin Bevan*, 238-9.

[21] When the CPGB applied for affiliation to the Labour Party in November 1935, for example, the proposal was supported by the SWMF but by relatively few Labour branches (twelve in total) and just one trades and labour council. In Scotland, by contrast, the figures were thirty one Labour branches and ten trades and labour councils. RGASPI, 495.14.178: 'Information on Britain, 1. Affiliation, 20 July 1936'.

[22] RGASPI, 495.14.156: 'The Crucial Test for Our Party in South Wales, 12 November 1936'.

[23] RGASPI, 495.14.261: 'Registration of Party Membership in South Wales, 1938'.

[24] RGASPI, 495.14.215: 'Information Material Concerning Party Organisation and Cadres, 17 December 1936'; 495.14.261: 'Communist Party of Great Britain, South Wales District Report, 1938'.

[25] Williams, *Democratic Rhondda*, 190.

[26] NLW, South Wales Regional Council of Labour, Minutes: 23 February 1937.

[27] *DH*, 22 May 1939.

[28] *PO*, 20 May 1939.

[29] *PO*, 9 February, 16 February 1935, 1 August 1936; Pontypridd TLC, Minutes: 30 April 1934, 24 May 1937.

[30] MRC, TUC Papers, 292/79T/20.

[31] Smith, *Aneurin Bevan*, 229-31.

[32] *PO*, 13 May 1939.

[33] Matthew Worley, *Inside the Gate: A History of the Labour Party in Britain Between the Wars* (London, 2005), 212. LHASC,

LP/GS/WRCLP/1, Annual Report, South Wales Regional Council of Labour, 1938; LP/GS/WRCLP/2, Standing Orders of the South Wales Regional Council of Labour, 1938; GA, DNUR/2/5: Annual Report, South Wales Regional Council of Labour, 1939.

[34] Newport Labour Party, Minutes: 28 February, 4 May, 11 September 1936, 8 February, 12 July 1937, 23 January 1939. Cited in Worley, *Inside the Gate*, 212.

[35] RGASPI, 495.14.239, Position of Communist Party Organisation in Newport, December 1937.

[36] Swansea Labour Party, Annual Report, 1939.

[37] Williams, *Democratic Rhondda*, 201-2.

[38] RGASPI, 495.14.178: 'Report by the Executive Committee of Rhondda Borough Labour Party, c. 1935'.

[39] RGASPI, 495.14.239: Report of Visit to Rhondda Area, December 1937.

[40] There was an equivalent published by the Cardiff Communist Party, the *Searchlight*, although copies are rare. For an example see, RBA, 2013/23, *Jubilee Searchlight* (May 1935). Likewise, the Cwmtillery *Searchlight* which was the least professionally produced of the three.

[41] Williams, *Democratic Rhondda*, 197.

[42] C. R. Attlee, *The Labour Party in Perspective* (London, 1937); John Bew, *Citizen Clem* (London, 2016), 214-5.

[43] GDH Cole, *The People's Front* (London, 1937).

[44] Branch locations draw on information in the *Left Book News* and its successor the *Left News*.

[45] Francis, *Miners Against Fascism*, 115.

[46] *The Left News* 10 (February 1937); *The Left News*, 16 (August 1937).

[47] *Left Book News* 9 (January 1937), 197; Notes from telephone interview with Dr Alun Hughes conducted in February 2013; LHASC, CP/IND/MISC/22/4, Memoirs of Pontypridd Communists in the 1930s.

[48] Worley, *Labour Inside the Gate*, 212.

[49] *The Left News* 10 (February 1937), 225

[50] As above, 224; *Left Book News* October 1936.

[51] Hywel Francis, 'The Origins of the South Wales Miners' Library', *History Workshop Journal*, 2 (1976), 201; Chris Baggs, 'How Well Read Was My Valley? Reading, Popular Fiction and the Miners of South Wales, 1875-1939', *Book History* 4 (2001), 288.

[52] Rose, *Intellectual Life*, 248. See also Robert James, *Popular Taste*, which follows Rose's line of argument. As an indicative example of Rose's argument, the surviving copy of Gwynne Meara, *Juvenile Unemployment in South Wales* (Cardiff, 1936) once held by Llwynypia Workmen's Institute was not borrowed. (Copy in author's possession.)

[53] Although ironically, the centerpiece of the two thousand volume Tylorstown Institute Library rescued for the South Wales Miners' Library was a nearly complete set of Left Book Club volumes. Hywel Francis, 'Survey of Miners' Institute and Welfare Libraries', *Llafur* 1, no. 2 (1973), 60. The Labour Book Service (which published around forty books), a rival of the Left Book Club launched in 1939, has survived less well at the SWML, primarily from the library of George Daggar, Labour MP for Abertillery. The Labour Book Service also had its own *Bulletin* as a rival to the *Left News*. Even fewer books from the Right Book Club, which launched in 1937, have survived (if they were widely available in South Wales at all). Of the Liberal Book Club, which was supported by John Maynard Keynes and AA Milne, amongst others, there is nothing.

[54] Merthyr Local Studies Library, Merthyr Tydfil County Borough Council, Public Libraries Committee Minutes, 7 February, 10 October 1938.

[55] Alun Hughes, 'Notes on Communism in interwar Pontypridd', held at Pontypridd Local Studies Library; Pontypridd Free Library, *Catalogue of Books in the Central Library* (Pontypridd, 1927).

[56] D. J. Williams, *The Tredegar Workmen's Hall, 1861-1951* (Tredegar, 1952)

[57] Francis, *Miners Against Fascism*, 197.

[58] Harry Gaines and Theodore Rapard, *Spain in Revolt* (London, 1936). Copy previously owned by Harry Stratton. In author's possession.

[59] Rose, *Intellectual Life*, 252, notes the increase in popularity for Bates's work. The copy of Claud Cockburn, *Reporter in Spain*

(London, 1936), held in the SWML was part of the library of S. O. Davies. Bates and Cockburn were both members of the Communist Party.

[60] The wider story of Labour's response to the Spanish Civil War can be found in Tom Buchanan, *The Spanish Civil War and the British Labour Movement* (Cambridge, 1991), and his 'Britain's Popular Front? Aid Spain and the British Labour Movement', *History Workshop Journal* 31, no. 1 (1991), 60-72.

[61] This was also the official view of the South Wales Miners' Federation. MRC, TUC Papers, 292/946/10/117: Letter from Oliver Harris to Walter Citrine, 2 September 1936.

[62] MRC, TUC Records, 292/946/14/42: 'Discussion at National Council of Labour, July 1936'.

[63] Bew, *Citizen Clem*, 211-2.

[64] MRC, TUC Papers, 292/946/14/20: 'Draft Report of Meeting of National Council of Labour, 25 August 1936'.

[65] MRC, TUC Papers, 292/946/15a/1: 'Draft Report of Meeting of National Council of Labour, 28 October 1936'.

[66] MRC, TUC Papers, 292/946/28/23: 'Help for the Workers of Spain Fund, Statement of Donations Received by the National Council of Labour, 30 September 1936'.

[67] Francis, *Miners Against Fascism*, 107. Indeed, the total raised by the SWMF before 15 August was only four pounds. MRC, TUC Papers, 292/946/28/5: 'Help for the Workers of Spain Fund, Statement of Donations Received by the National Council of Labour, 15 August 1936'.

[68] MRC, TUC Papers, 292/946/14/3(ii): 'List of Labour meetings held on behalf of Spain'.

[69] Francis, *Miners Against Fascism*, 108.

[70] RGASPI, 495.14.239: Speech by Idris Cox to the South Wales Communist Party Congress, February 1937.

[71] MRC, TUC Papers, 292/946/21/83: Letter from JC Harries, Cardiff Spanish Aid Committee, 1 March 1937.

[72] Williams, *Democratic Rhondda*, 190.

[73] RGASPI, 495.14.239: Report of the South Wales District, October 1937.

[74] For instance, the letter from Evan Williams, Secretary of Cwmavon Ward Labour Party, 16 May 1937, MRC, TUC Papers, 292/946/37/179.

[75] MRC, TUC Papers, 292C/946/3/8(iii): Minutes of the Spain Campaign Committee, 4 November 1937.

[76] MRC, TUC Papers, 292/946/32/97: South Wales Regional Council of Labour, Welsh Spain Effort, 17 February 1939.

[77] MRC, TUC Papers, 292/946/30/28(i): Statement Showing State of Spanish Aid Fund, 3 October 1938.

[78] Francis and Smith, *The Fed*, 360.

[79] Francis, *Miners Against Fascism*, 142-3.

[80] MRC, TUC Papers, 292/946/34/188L Trade Union Financial Aid to Dependents of Spanish Volunteers, 23 March 1937. See also the letter from George Morris, Secretary of the SWRCL, 23 August 1938, 292/946/34/156.

[81] Francis, *Miners Against Fascism*, 159.

[82] Alun Lewis's life is charted in John Pikoulis, *Alun Lewis: A Life* (Bridgend, 1995). An updated version, *Alun, Gweno & Freda*, which places greater stress on Alun Lewis's relationship with Freda Aykroyd, was published by Seren in 2015.

[83] Gwyn Thomas, 'Transcript of an interview with Hywel Francis, 21 September 1970'. NLW, Gwyn Thomas Papers, B17. Cambria House had been established on the initiative of Christopher Hill, then a history lecturer in Cardiff, and J. F. Rees, the principal of University College Cardiff.

[84] Gwyn A. Williams, *Fishers of Men: Stories Towards An Autobiography* (Llandysul, 1996), 21.

[85] Dai Smith, *Lewis Jones* (Cardiff, 1982), 2; Gwyn Thomas, 'Script for The Greatest Welshman: Lewis Jones, 4 February 1977', NLW, Gwyn Thomas Papers, G231.

[86] South Wales Miners' Library, AUD/14: 'Interview with Billy Griffiths conducted by Hywel Francis, November 1969'; AUD/212: 'Interview with Edgar Evans conducted by Hywel Francis, 1975'; Francis, *Miners Against Fascism*, 168-174.

[87] Lewis Jones, *We Live* (London, 1978 edn), 303-334; *WM*, 1 February 1939.

[88] Hywel Francis, 'Say Nothing and Leave in the Middle of the Night: The Spanish Civil War Revisited', *History Workshop Journal* 32, no. 1 (October 1991), 72.

[89] SWML, AUD/384: 'Interview with Leo Price conducted with Hywel Francis, 24 July 1969'; AUD/385: 'Interview with Lillian May Price conducted by Hywel Francis'.

[90] 'Letter from Jack Jones (Blaenclydach) to his parents, 13 March 1938', held at RBA, SWCC, MNB/PP/41. The letter is appended to Francis, *Miners Against Fascism*, 285-6.

[91] 'Letter from Jack Jones to his parents, 7 August 1938'.

[92] Morgan interview, IWMSA/9856; I am also grateful to Hywel Francis for discussions about Morien Morgan, and to the late Elaine Morgan for conversations about the Morgan family.

[93] *Left Book News*, August 1936, October 1936. Although Greenwall did not sever his connection and was active with the branch in organising conferences, rallies and film shows, in support of the anti-fascist movement. *Left News*, August 1937.

[94] *Cap and Gown* 31, no. 1 (December 1933), 44.

[95] *Cap and Gown* 33, no. 2 (May 1936), 35; *Cap and Gown* 36, no. 1 (December 1938), 28; *Cap and Gown* 36, no. 2 (March 1939), 22.

[96] A workers' film society had previously existed in Cardiff in the early 1930s. Worley, *Class Against Class*, 225, fn. 135; *Left Film Front* 1 (July 1937), 3. Aneurin Bevan served on the General Council of Kino.

[97] *Left News*, October 1937. Bert Hogenkamp, *Deadly Parallels: Film and the Left in Britain, 1929-1939* (London, 1986), 140-1. Kino itself was the subject of sustained surveillance by MI5. James Smith, 'Soviet Films and Britain Intelligence in the 1930s: The Case of Kino Films and MI5', in Rebecca Beasley and Philip Ross Bullock (eds.), *Russia in Britain 1800-1940: From Melodrama to Modernism* (Oxford, 2013), 241-257.

[98] This is based on a reading of *Kino News*, the organisation's newsletter.

[99] *Left News*, January 1938; Hugo Garcia, *The Truth About Spain! Mobilizing British Public Opinion, 1936-1939* (Eastbourne, 2010).

[100] Stephen Ridgwell, 'Pictures and Proletarians: South Wales Miners'

Cinemas in the 1930s', *Llafur* 7, no. 2 (1997), 77-8; Robert James follows Ridgwell in this analysis. James, *Popular Culture*. Although as Peter Stead usefully notes, American cinema of the 1930s was full of New Deal motifs that were clearly political in nature. Peter Stead, 'Kameradschaft and After: The Miners and Film', *Llafur* 5, no. 1 (1988), 37-44.

[101] As noted by Bert Hogenkamp, 'Miners' Cinemas in South Wales in the 1920s and 1930s', *Llafur* 4, no. 2 (1985), 64-76.

[102] *Cap and Gown*, 33, no. 1 (January 1936), 29-30; *Cap and Gown* 33, no. 2 (May 1936), 33. A wealth of biographical detail, drawing on his international brigade service file held in Moscow, can be found in Robert Stradling, *Wales and the Spanish Civil War: The Dragon's Dearest Cause* (Cardiff, 2004), 145-150.

[103] John D. Mehta, 'Forgotten Names, Remembered Faces – The Bookshop Manager' in Anindya Raychaudhuri (ed.), *The Spanish Civil War: Exhuming a Buried Past* (Cardiff, 2013), 46. These details are also relayed in Stradling, *Dragon's Dearest*, 68. Stradling gives Elin Davies's activities under the pseudonym Helen Smith. She later married John Williams, a close friend of Sid Hamm whilst at Cardiff. See Frank Thomas (edited by Robert Stradling), *Brother Against Brother: Experiences of a British Volunteer in the Spanish Civil War* (Stroud, 1998), vi-vii.

[104] Mehta, 'Forgotten Names', 46.

[105] Stradling, *Cardiff and the Spanish Civil War*, 88; MRC, TUC Papers, 292/946/31/192: 'List of Trade Unionists & Labour Party Members in the International Brigade, 22 February 1937'.

[106] Dannie Abse, *Ash on a Young Man's Sleeve* (Cardigan, 2006 edn).

[107] SWCC, Lewis Jones Diaries: entries for 6 September, 23-24 November 1937. Cited in Smith, *Lewis Jones*.

[108] Stradling, *Dragon's Dearest Cause*, 177.

[109] John Field, *Working Men's Bodies: Work Camps in Britain, 1880-1940* (Manchester, 2013).

[110] Dave Colledge and John Field, '"To Recondition Human Material...": an Account of a British Labour Camp in the 1930s', *History Workshop Journal* 15 (1983), 163; the 'uniform' is also described by Gwyn Thomas. *A Few Selected Exits*, 103.

[111] On relative militancy see: Len Edmondson, 'Labour and the Labour Camps', in Keith Armstrong and Huw Beynon (eds.), *Hello, Are You Working? Memories of the Thirties in the North East of England* (Whitley Bay, 1977), 65-68; George Beresford, 'When You're Starving It's Pretty Tough', in ibid, 79.

[112] Gwyn Thomas, 'Interview with Denis Mitchell for Private Lives, Granada Television 1975'. NLW, Gwyn Thomas Papers, G166.

[113] Croucher, *We Refuse*, 163.

[114] *Unemployed Leader*, May 1934.

[115] Croucher, *We Refuse*, 165; John Field, *Learning through Labour: Training, Unemployment and the State, 1890-1939* (Leeds, 1992), 127.

[116] SWCC, MNA/PP/91/1: 'Letter to William Picton from the Manager of Ferndale Employment Exchange, 8 September 1936'; MNA/PP/91/2: 'Report on a visit to Treglog and Cynarth Instructional Centres, 1936'.

[117] *DW*, 28 March, 8 April 1935; Unemployed Assistance Board, *Annual Report for 1935*, 269.

[118] *DW*, 13 March, 21 March, 9 April, 23 April. 30 May 1935.

[119] Ministry of Labour, *Annual Report for the year 1934*, 114.

[120] Ministry of Labour, *Annual Report for the year 1935*, 112.

[121] Ministry of Labour, *Annual Report for the year 1936*, 111; *Annual Report for the year 1937*, 106; *Annual Report for the year 1938*, 106.

[122] HC Deb, 4 February 1937, vol. 319, c. 1744.

[123] Wal Hannington, *Ten Lean Years* (London, 1940), 184.

[124] SWCC, MNA/PP/91/7: 'Letter from William Picton, Tom Brooks, and Arthur Evan Short to Divisional Controller, Ministry of Labour, Cardiff, 25 May 1938'; MNA/PP/91/8: 'Letter from William Picton, Tom Brooks, Arthur Evan Short to Divisional Controller, Ministry of Labour, Cardiff, 1 June 1938'.

[125] Brechfa, Coed-y-Brenin near Dolgellau, Dovey near Machynlleth, and Capel Curig. HC Deb, 16 March 1939, vol. 345, c. 638.

[126] HC Deb, 22 July 1936, vol. 315, cc. 541, 761.

[127] Merthyr Tydfil CBC, Medical Officer of Health, Annual Report for 1937, 10.

[128] Mountain Ash UDC, Medical Officer of Health, Annual Report for 1937, 6; Abercarn UDC, Medical Officer of Health, Annual Report for 1937, 4.

[129] Rhondda UDC, Medical Officer of Health, Annual Report for 1938, 14.

[130] Tredegar UDC, Medical Officer of Health, Annual Report for 1937, 4-5.

[131] Percy E. Watkins, *Educational Settlements in South Wales and Monmouthshire* (Cardiff, 1940).

[132] Aberdare Valley Educational Settlement, *Bulletin* (October 1938), SCOLAR, Settlement MSS, File 16.

[133] Pontypridd Educational Settlement, 'Minutes of Governing Body, 2 May 1939'; 'Minutes of Governing Body, 19 October 1938', SCOLAR, Settlement MSS, File 17.

[134] Aberdare Valley Educational Settlement, *Warden's First Annual Report, 1936-1937* (Aberdare, 1937), 12-13.

[135] Merthyr Tydfil Settlement, Draft Annual Report for 1932.

[136] Notably his *Soviet Democracy* (London, 1937).

[137] Eiluned Pearce, Jacques Launay, Anna Machin, and Robin Dunbar, 'Is Group Singing Special? Health, Well-Being and Social Bonds in Community-Based Adult Education Classes', *Journal of Community and Applied Social Psychology* 26, no. 6 (2016), 518-533. Anecdotally, this is much in evidence in my own WEA classes delivered in Merthyr Tydfil, Neath, Port Talbot, and Swansea.

[138] The South Wales District of the Workers' Educational Association, *Annual Report for 1937-1938* (Cardiff, 1938), 40.

[139] *DW*, 23 March 1937. There had been a 'Peace Pageant' in Blaina the year before arranged by wealthy philanthropists from Kent. *DH*, 14 July 1936.

[140] Rhondda Communist Party, *South Wales in the March of History* (Tonypandy, 1937).

[141] RGASPI, 495.14.239: *A United Labour Movement*.

[142] SWCC, MNA/NUM/3/4/45.

[143] London Metropolitan University, Labour Research Department Records, LRD/1/E/08/4: Letter from Bill Williams to Oliver Harris, 6 January 1939.

[144] Unity Theatre, *Handbook* (London, 1939), MRC, MSS.148/UCW/6/13/42/9.

[145] Montagu Slater, *Stay Down Miner* (London, 1936); Montagu Slater, *New Way Wins: The Play from Stay Down Miner* (London, 1937).

[146] South Wales Miners' Federation, *The Pageant of South Wales* (Cardiff, 1939), 5.

[147] The original song was written in 1915 by Ralph Chaplin for the International Workers of the World. The tune, *The Battle Hymn of the Republic* emerged during the American Civil War. See: Ralph Chaplin, *Wobbly* (Chicago: University of Chicago Press, 1948); Ralph Chaplin, 'Why I Wrote *Solidarity Forever*', *American West* (1968). Available online: https://www.iww.org/sv/history/icons/solidarity_forever/1 [Accessed: 15 March 2018].

[148] *WM*, 2 May 1939; *DH*, 2 May 1939.

[149] *Daily Mirror*, 8 February 1939; *WM*, 8 February 1939. The experiences of several British and Irish prisoners at San Pedro de Cardeña is discussed in David Convery, 'At Their Most Vulnerable: The Memory of British and Irish Prisoners of War in San Pedro de Cardeña' in Raychaudhuri (ed.), *The Spanish Civil War*.

[150] LRD/1/E/08/18: Letter from Councillor Evan T. Lewis to Bill Williams, 5 May 1939.

[151] Notably, Arthur Horner, Will Paynter, Dai Dan Evans, and (after the war) Dai Francis.

[152] *DH*, 18 January 1937.

[153] NLW, Gwyn Thomas Papers, N2: Notebook 27, 2.

[154] Gwyn Thomas, *One Pair of Eyes* (BBC TV, 1969).

PART IV

A New South Wales?

CHAPTER SEVEN
Labour's Citadel

After nine years in the wilderness, Labour re-entered government on 15 May 1940 amid Britain's worst wartime crisis. The ineffectual National Government, led by Neville Chamberlain, had fallen five days earlier and Winston Churchill appointed prime minister of an all-party coalition. As the government expanded during the war, Labour's position within grew steadily, particularly after 1942 when Clement Attlee was appointed Britain's first deputy prime minister. He was, in effect, prime minister for the home front. Labour's participation in Churchill's war ministry was a vital testing ground for the party and did far more to rehabilitate it in the eyes of voters than if they had remained in parliamentary opposition.[1] Two Labour MPs from South Wales entered the government alongside Attlee (part of a Labour cohort of sixteen): Dai Grenfell, the most senior, served as secretary for mines from 1940 until 1942; and George Hall who served, in the same period, in a variety of junior posts in the Colonial Office, Admiralty, and Foreign Office. In 1942, Will John, the veteran Rhondda West MP, joined them as a government whip. He too served until 1945. And in March 1945, the Pontypool MP, Arthur Jenkins, was appointed to the town and country planning ministry. Of the four, only George Hall had any ministerial experience, having served as a junior minister at the Admiralty in the short-lived Labour government of 1929-31. Despite the relatively long parliamentary careers of most of the Labour MPs from South Wales by 1940 – an average of ten years – none attained the cabinet rank achieved by Vernon Hartshorn in 1924 and 1929.

The role played by the South Wales Labour MPs during the war was nevertheless crucial to the maintenance of democracy: they served on the opposition benches and pressed the government for domestic legislative reform, ensuring that it accorded with Labour's own pre-war position. If Labour were truly serious about change, they argued, then this was a golden opportunity to put it into practice. In 1941, a gang of six including Aneurin Bevan, S. O. Davies, W. H. Mainwaring, and Ness Edwards, led a rebellion on the government's flagship Determination of Needs Bill because of its failure to abolish the means test.[2] The concern was that continued means testing of income would unnecessarily impact on productivity, since if 'their earnings rise above the prescribed amount, all the supplementary pension goes – all of it – and five shillings "dignity money" remains for the unemployed'. And if a person did not 'dig in for victory' because of the likelihood of losing financial support for their family, they might be sacked; or, as Aneurin Bevan interrupted to say, 'be called saboteurs'. Ness Edwards, who moved the opposition amendment, agreed. In his own speech Bevan reminded colleagues that abolishing the means test involved the honour of the Labour Party since there was 'no single issue upon which we have pledged ourselves so deeply'. But it was not without its consequences. Edwards was accordingly told by Attlee that he would never be a member of a future Labour government.[3]

The following year, they rebelled again, this time on the government's pension measures, which the group regarded as inadequate and unfair.[4] In the words of Arthur Pearson, the Pontypridd MP, 'these people have had a bad bargain in their lives, with long terms of unemployment and very little in the way of social services. Now that they have reached a pensionable age we are trying to squeeze little advantages which I maintain should be theirs'. The group also took up the demand to implement the terms of the Beveridge Report. Nor were rebellions limited to economic matters and the pursuit of socialist reforms to hated welfare legislation. In December 1943, in response to the government's decision to release Oswald Mosley from prison, the group supported a motion decrying the action as injurious to the war effort. Dai Grenfell, by then released from his ministerial role, took up the charge: 'he is a bad man; he is a worthless man. Why was it necessary to convey to the world outside an impression that we cannot avoid conveying that we are becoming tender to the Fascists, that while men are sent abroad to fight and die against Fascism the prophets of Fascism at home are being pampered'. There was, one critic suggested, one rule for the rich and another for the poor.[5]

The most consistent rebel, the leader of the opposition, in practice if not in title, was Aneurin Bevan. His actions during the Second World War have often been regarded as controversial, perhaps even at odds with wartime sentiment.[6] But his purpose was to have Labour set the agenda, not be led into 'docile acceptance' of the conservative status quo. His finest hour, in wartime at least, came in July 1942 when he led a no confidence motion on the 'central direction of the war'. 'It is the duty', he said, 'of Members of Parliament to try and reproduce in the House of Commons the psychology which exists in the country, and there can be no doubt that the country is deeply disturbed by the movement of events'. He continued by pressing for soldiers in the field to be given the right arms to win the war, to be backed by modern technology. Britain's politicians had failed to understand the situation they found themselves in, and they had failed to overcome the very thing – the class prejudices of the country – that held back success:

The Prime Minister must realise that in this country there is a taunt, on everyone's lips, that if Rommel had been in the British

Army, he would still have been a sergeant. There is a man in the British Army – and this shows how we are using our trained men – who flung one hundred and fifty thousand men across the Ebro in Spain, Michael Dunbar [sic – it should read Malcolm Dunbar]. He was chief of staff in Spain; he won the battle of the Ebro and he is a sergeant in the British Army.

The motion of no confidence was supported by Bevan and twenty four others; four hundred and seventy five MPs opposed it. Thirty abstained.[7] The following morning, almost alone in refusing to denounce Bevan's actions, the *Daily Herald* declared the speech the most considerable backbench delivery in many years.[8] It was a clear expression, perhaps the clearest expression of all between 1939 and 1945, of Bevan's determination to change Britain's political direction and of his belief in Labour's own responsibilities.

He began to set out his case in written form, too. In a contribution to the 1943 Fabian Society collection, *Plan For Britain*, he argued in favour of nationalisation as part of his 'plan for work'.[9] And in late 1944, he produced an impassioned plea for an end to coalition government once the war had been won.[10] Published by Victor Gollancz, *Why Not Trust The Tories?* was a stark warning and a reminder to Labour colleagues that, when faced with the same offer in 1918, they had chosen to stand on their own. 'You may have laughed at the 1914-18 generation, and the way it was deceived', he wrote, 'watch you are not caught the same way'. If you are, he concluded, this will not be the last war.[11] The book was widely read, both by civilians and members of the armed forces, although the right-wing press (inevitably) declared it 'easily the weakest' in Gollancz's latest series of political texts.[12] It was hardly that, for it showed Bevan's deep understanding that there would, in all likelihood, be a Labour government at the end of the war

416

and the need for it to be a radical government, not one that settled for modest alterations of policies which had prevailed for over twenty years.

One of those who joined Bevan in the intellectual remaking of Labour's policy platform was James Griffiths. In 1939, he published a determined summary of the impact of poverty on health; three years later he followed that up with a study of industrial strife in the coalfields and re-asserted the demand for coal nationalisation; and he spent much of the war heavily involved in the Welsh Reconstruction Advisory Council, a body tasked with generating proposals to revitalise the Welsh economy after the war so that it could avoid a return to the dark days of the 1930s.[13] This collectively informed his 1945 essay 'Industry – the Servant of the Public' published as part of a Fabian Society book, *What Labour Could Do* published shortly before the general election.[14] What Griffiths received through his work on reconstruction committees was data, and rather a lot of it. His was an intellectual remodelling based on deliberate empiricism. In 1940, for instance, a series of manpower surveys of South Wales produced a set of clear needs ranging from housing to jobs, health, and the economic fragility of women.[15] These were then followed by a series of reports conducted by the Nuffield College Social Reconstruction Survey, that considered electricity, transportation, industry, and town planning. In one indicative report, they even proposed that a new town should be built at Church Village (between Cardiff and Pontypridd) to provide modern accommodation for the Treforest Industrial Estate.[16]

Labour's victory in 1945, then, was hardly accidental. Rather, it was the product of the careful demonstrative work of government, as Attlee believed, and of the radical investments made intellectually and organisationally by Aneurin Bevan, James Griffiths, and the other South Wales

MPs who stood up for what they believed in (and what they felt Labour believed in). In South Wales, that victory was total. From Llanelli in the west to Pontypool in the east, and from Barry in the south to Radnorshire in the north, Labour won every seat – twenty three MPs out of a possible twenty four. Fourteen of the seats (or sixty percent) were held by former miners, two by teachers, two by former officers in the armed forces (one a solicitor, the other, James Callaghan, a former tax officer), and one each by a railwayman, steelworker, academic, and businessman. That was a clear shift in the complexion of the parliamentary cohort. In 1935, Labour held sixteen seats, of which twelve (or three quarters) were held by former miners.[17] The remaining seats were held by two teachers, a doctor, and a boilermaker. In effect, Labour as elected in 1945 represented the entire spectrum of Welsh society and could claim, with no meaningful opposition, to be the national party of Wales – a point underlined in May 1947 when the Welsh Regional Council of Labour was created. At the local level, Labour's triumph was equally total. South Wales truly was Labour's citadel.

Given this level of electoral success, there was undoubtedly a burden of expectation placed on the post-war Labour government. As had been recognised during the war, the most fundamental need was to avoid going backwards and to avoid a return of the hardships of the interwar years. There was a need, too, to overcome the antagonism between government and people that had resulted in the hunger marches, mass protest against the means test, and disgust at the labour camps for the unemployed. As James Griffiths was later to reflect, 'in the nineteen-forties we fought and won a battle for the cause of social security. We rejoice that the present generation knows not the poverty and distress of the thirties'.[18] There can be no nobler aim of any government than that. Labour councils, which had held the line of radical pragmatism in the previous decade, hoped, too, to benefit from the extension of that governing philosophy to central government. For its part, the non-Labour left pressed the government to go further, to hold more concretely to a socialism that was peaceful, more dedicated to the common weal, and more responsive to grassroots needs, but its message was incoherent. As the *Pontypridd Observer* commented in 1945, it was 'baffling to vote for [Arthur] Pearson in Pontypridd but not for [W. H.] Mainwaring in Rhondda East', as the CPGB advised voters to do.[19]

The list of achievements of the first majority Labour government were enormous and transformed Britain in some, though not all, of the ways that Aneurin Bevan and James Griffiths had hoped for. The pinnacle of that achievement was the National Health Service, but no less important was the establishment of the welfare state and the nationalisation of coal and the railways. Despite post-war austerity, there was a clear, determined commitment to improve housing, to full employment, and to remodel towns and cities for the modern age. At the centre of these changes, pushing and pressing as far as he could, and always with the understanding that the only real way to do anything was to hold power, was Bevan. Clement Attlee no doubt appointed Bevan – whom he originally had in mind as minister of education – to the ministry of health to keep him from being a rallying point for backbench discontent. This was a lesson learned from wartime experience: Attlee had no desire to sit and listen to a speech about himself akin to the one Bevan had made about Churchill in 1942. Certainly, he was concerned, as he had been ahead of the 1945 general election, that 'a silly speech by Aneurin Bevan might easily be used to stampede the electors away from Labour'.[20] But Bevan, too, was ready to serve and to put into practice the principles and policies for which he had so long fought.

But how might we truly measure the prowess of Labour's South Walian citadel in its postwar heyday? Perhaps by the standards established by the party and its members itself, and by the expectations of ordinary voters. There were three broad aims, as there had been throughout the interwar years: to provide a decent home, to provide a job, and to ensure a decent standard of living. But this had to be achieved whilst considering a changing economic environment, with some of the older certainties based on the overwhelming dominance of staple industries starting to disappear. To take Merthyr Tydfil as a clear, indicative example: by the mid-1950s, just twenty percent of the county borough's workforce were employed in the coal mining industry, the equivalent of around four thousand, two hundred workers, with others involved in textile manufacture and engineering. Twenty years earlier, coal mining accounted for nearly twelve thousand workers in Merthyr or forty percent of the workforce. Coal was undoubtedly still an iconic feature of the town's sense of itself in the 1950s, but many workers were by now employed making washing machines, toys, chemicals, and ladies underwear.[21] It was to this that Labour had to respond.

Labour in Power

Writing in 1945, the medical officer for Tredegar, Dr Edwin Davies, reflected on the challenges that faced the council after the war – there were familiar themes. With the coal mining industry still in gradual decline, the best hope for employment came from the new industries which the council sought to attract to the area. This could bring 'a measure of prosperity', he wrote, but also 'stem the tide against a falling population, brought about by the exodus of so many of its young people, forced by the local unfavourable industrial position to seek employment elsewhere'.[22] He was not the only medical officer that year writing with concern about and aspiration for the future. In Glyncorrwg, Dr Taylor noted the trend of young men to abandon the mines altogether seeking better pay and an easier working life in factories. It was a general trend. There was another: the continued failure of the private sector to build the modern homes that the coalfield desperately needed, and the struggle of councils to meet the challenge on their own. As the medical officer for Rhymney, Dr Evans, remarked in 1946, there had been no housing scheme in the district since 1920 and even at that time the number of houses built was insufficient. 'The long list of applicants for houses becomes larger each week', he wrote, 'and it appears that it will take a few years to improve the position to any appreciable extent'.[23]

As housing minister, in addition to his duties as minister of health, Aneurin Bevan was responsible for remedying a major deficit of the interwar years and for overcoming, particularly in working-class areas of the country, the private sector inadequacy. As he put it in *Why Not Trust The Tories*: 'between the wars private enterprise produced a shocking state of affairs. The population was distributed in a most lop-sided fashion ... some parts of the country were converted into distressed areas, denuded of their industries, and others became congested'.[24] As Nicklaus Thomas-Symonds has noted in his biography of Bevan, the latter's record as housing minister has tended to be the focus of more resolute criticism than as health minister. But are the criticisms, notably that he failed to build enough houses, and that he had too much faith in the capacity of local councils, fair? Certainly not in the South Wales context which was what Bevan knew best. Given his experiences as a councillor in Tredegar, he understood the possibilities – and the limitations – of councils taking on the bulk of the building work: these included labour shortages, shortages of building materials, and lack of finance. But he also knew that there was no other alternative. By the mid-1950s, with the Conservatives in office and house building proceeding apace, private sector house building far outstripped that of the public sector across Britain: the ratio was three private sector houses for every one public sector house built. But in Merthyr, the ratio was more than nine to one the other way; in Ebbw Vale, it was ten to one; and in Abertillery, it was sixteen to one.[25]

In more concrete terms, the rate of house building between 1945 and 1950 vastly outpaced that of the period 1918 to 1945, in large part because of central government support, and because of the initiative and determination of the minister of housing. Across Glamorgan, except for Cardiff, Merthyr, and Swansea, which were administered separately, the interwar period saw the construction of around twelve thousand houses by local authorities – an average of about four hundred and fifty a year.[26] In the five years between 1945 and 1950, with Bevan as housing minister, the total number of homes built by local authorities was more than ten thousand, or a rate of about two thousand a year.[27] By any measure, it was a dramatic rate of increase, despite the range of shortages that impacted upon development. And it continued to grow, particularly as materials became more readily available in the early 1950s: by 1960, a further twenty three thousand houses had been constructed by local councils (around two thousand three hundred a year) bringing the total since 1945 to around thirty three and a half thousand.[28] This was a major intervention by the public sector and transformed councils from inspectors of housing to landlords. In 1946, for instance, Rhymney UDC owned just ninety houses but within a decade it owned nearly five hundred.[29] And in Merthyr, ten percent of the borough's entire housing stock was owned by the council by 1951.[30] These were the new homes 'built by a Labour council, under a Labour government' that Neil Kinnock, who benefitted from one of them in Tredegar, was to reference in his famous conference speech in Bournemouth in 1985.

Little wonder, then, that officials thought of this period as a new era. In the words of Dr Jones, the medical officer for Ogmore and Garw UDC,

> The valleys are now, in 1950, embarking upon a new era, when there will be, I trust, a period of lasting prosperity which depends not upon the exigencies of a world war but upon the requirements of a planned economy. This prosperity does not mean overcrowded dwellings, denuded mountain sides, stark and grim coal tips rising higher each day, rivers choked with filthy scum, but houses built on open sites containing the most labour saving devices, mountains with freshly planted trees, playing fields where tips formerly raised their ugly heads, rivers where fish may live and mines the entrance to which are disguised by flower gardens and trees.[31]

To make good on such promises and aspirations, some councils, notably Tredegar UDC, began to offer non-repayable home improvement grants to modernise houses, ensuring more widespread provision of indoor toilets, hot running water, and modern electric lighting even in those homes that were many decades old.[32] They also established a scheme whereby would-be home owners could purchase a home by means of a council mortgage. As the medical officer for the town observed in 1960, 'today, owning one's own house is no doubt the best investment possible'.[33] Everyone, councillors might have said in Tredegar, had the right to buy from the private market if they wished to. Labour did not entirely solve the housing problems of the postwar period, given the challenge they faced that was almost too much to ask of them, but it would be a misrepresentation of the extraordinary efforts undertaken to suggest, as some have, that housing was a 'gaping hole in the government's clothing'.[34] It was hardly that.

Jobs were a major area of concern inherited from the interwar years. Labour were especially anxious about the undulating fortunes of coal and the possible impact of new factories on the complexion of the workforce – many employed a largely female workforce and so were not well suited to taking up slack from pit closures when those occurred. Nevertheless, jobs appeared in factories making (amongst other things) furniture and upholstery, clothes, boxes, watch straps, and spectacles, and did offer a way out of the mines, or of domestic labour, for those who wanted to take that opportunity. Nationalisation inevitably altered the nature of employment for many: two and a half million workers moved from private employers to the state as employer, more than one hundred thousand miners in South Wales among them.[35] There was clear optimism, with appeals for more men to work in the mines, and the industry was calm even as the least productive and least modernisable pits were closed down (thirty four between 1947 and 1951). 'At the moment', wrote one official in Ogmore and Garw in 1947, coal mining 'appears to be in a flourishing condition'.[36] A few years later, they went further and declared coal to be the 'great white hope of the British economy'.[37] A corner had been turned.

Coal nationalisation was a key transformation, and had an 'underlying symbolic value for miners' providing both fulfilment of political purpose and a degree of certainty and security.[38] It was meant to demonstrate the central role played by the miner in the British economy and to prevent a return to the pre-war situation of opposition between employers and employees, low wages, and idle pits. As Dai Francis put it in 1945, nationalisation was 'an imperative for the future economic prosperity of the nation'.[39] Most miners' leaders, of course, understood that nationalisation was not a perfect solution (nor was it entirely in keeping with the ideology of socialisation of industry) and worked to resolve some of its limitations. That involved settling disputes through discussion and compromise rather than through strike action, and accepting pit closures when they occurred, since they went together with investment in modernisation, for the sake of coal's longevity. Retrospectively this gave the impression that the miners' leaders of the 1940s and 1950s were unduly supine in their relations with the National Coal Board, and, in any case, were part of an industry that was owned by the government not by the people; but that was hindsight.[40]

The Labour governments were, for the most part, enthusiasts of nationalised coal and, because it had come about as a reaction to the state of the industry before the war, expected the National Coal Board to be a model employer. The NCB was to have modern training initiatives providing scholarships, apprenticeships, and career-improving educational opportunities.[41] As Clement Attlee wrote in his memoir, 'it was obvious, for instance, that the coal industry was more urgently in need of reconstruction than iron and steel ... First things had to come first'.[42] Reconstruction was intended to be wide-ranging. But the coal industry was struggling to move on from the twin exhaustions of the interwar depression and the Second World War. The workforce was ageing, many of the pits were old and difficult to modernise, and it unsurprisingly disappointed the planners in Whitehall by failing to meet productivity targets. The South Wales Coalfield was one of the worst performing precisely because it exemplified the major problems facing the industry at the time of nationalisation. The more miners' leaders became disillusioned with the experience of working for the government, the warier the Labour leadership became at replicating the process elsewhere. Steel nationalisation, which Bevan had pushed for inside and outside cabinet, was passed in 1949 but delayed until 1951. It was re-privatised by the Conservatives when they returned to office.

Indeed, it was the Conservative Party, which avoided re-privatising coal in the 1950s, which began the slow process of disintegrating the industry. In December 1958, Lord Mills, the minister of power, submitted a memorandum on fuel policy to cabinet reflecting on the challenges that lay ahead of the industry. One was the need to keep unemployment in mining areas to a minimum and another was to avoid too great a dependence on deep-mined coal since it was expensive to produce and demand was, in any case, falling. He continued, 'the high cost pits are situated chiefly in Scotland and Wales and special unemployment problems are created by the closure of pits owing to the fact that mining is carried on in close-knit communities'.[43] As news of the considerations broke into the newspapers, having been leaked to *The Times*, there was a feeling that rather than a fuel policy, the government were determined to create (in the words of one journalist) 'unemployment in our South Wales valleys'.[44] Will Paynter, the president of the South Wales Area, responded in similar terms:

> We are not prepared to face a resurrection of unemployment in our mining communities ... Never again will we allow any government to create the distress and misery that we suffered in the inter-war years.[45]

But speeches and marches had little real impact on the decisions made by the National Coal Board and government ministers (of either party), particularly regarding poor performing pits. Cwmllynfell Colliery had the worst output record of any colliery in Britain in the late-1950s, prompting its closure in early 1959; although the economics of closure provided little material solace to the miners who lost their jobs or to the communities that again spoke of death.[46] When a journalist from the Bevanite newspaper *Tribune* interviewed one shopkeeper in Gwaun-Cae-Gurwen in 1958 about life in the area, he was met with a stark response: 'You should write a bloody obituary!'[47] It was little different in Gilfach Goch when the Britannic Colliery closed in 1960. 'It is no longer a bustling industrial village with the sounds of men's working boots on the pavement' lamented one council official, 'the hooters and ventilating fans are silent and the inhabitants complain that it seems the village of the dead – quiet and sad'.[48]

To remain in the industry, miners faced longer journeys to work by car. Many of those from the Britannic were transferred to the Cwm Colliery at Llantwit Fardre, a ten-mile journey by car that could only be done in that way with any ease. As a result, colliery closures coincided with, and to some extent accelerated, the trend away from public transport and passenger rail services in many mining valleys were withdrawn in the 1950s and early 1960s – ahead of the more famous Beeching Axe. The lengthened working day was mitigated by recreation at home, with television replacing the cinema, and community life, some felt, suffered directly as a result. 'Family unity and loyalty is to be commended', suggested the Ogmore and Garw UDC medical officer in 1958, 'but not when such a way of life excludes partisanship in the world around. Much can be learnt from television and from travelling through the countryside, but never can such knowledge take the place of education gained by rubbing shoulders with the rest of the world and by active participation in community life'.[49] Talk of apathy was widespread in the 1950s, but what was meant by 'apathy' was that the old radical spirit seemed to have disappeared, people had become more individualistic and less interested in the day-to-day functions of politics.

Labour in opposition

Labour's response to these trends as a political force, rather than as a party of government or local administration, was complex and drew on a desire to present itself as being at the forefront of modernisation whilst also safeguarding traditional interests and achievement in office. It was successful in doing so, with South Wales becoming even more of a bastion for the Labour Party in the course of the 1950s. In 1952, for instance, it took control of Barry.[50] Then, in 1958, it took control of Bridgend UDC for the first time defeating the Conservative chairman, H. F. Toms, in the process; elsewhere Labour consolidated its hold on Newport council (thirty three seats compared with the Tories' thirteen), and had the largest number of city councillors in Cardiff.[51] In mining constituencies, Tory voters allegedly felt 'intimidated' and uncomfortable, with few openly admitting their political allegiance to their Labour-voting neighbours.[52] But even those who did openly declare they were Tories could find little to complain about. The vice-chair of Pontypridd Conservative Association wrote in 1956 that 'whilst my Association is opposed to the politics of the majority of the members of the Council at the present time, it is nevertheless satisfied that the Urban District Council of Pontypridd has a record in the field of local government administration of which the District can be proud'.[53]

The real tussles of Labour's years in opposition came from within the party itself, between 'modernisers' and 'traditionalists', Bevanites and Gaitskellites, young and old, men and women. The question that obsessed them all after 1951 was how to win back power and to continue the work of implementing socialism (although they differed as to the form it would take). A start was made in October 1951 with the launch of the *South Wales Democrat*, a monthly newspaper published in Swansea and dedicated to Labour's intellectual renewal. Its second issue, which appeared after Labour's narrow electoral defeat, featured a lengthy article by James Griffiths on 'the challenge facing the labour movement'. He insisted on the revolutionary changes that had taken place in the economy, with the growth of factory-based industrial production as a complement to the old staples of coal and steel. As he put it, this was the age of the overalls. For Labour to grow and to return to power, Griffiths insisted, it had to adapt to the new circumstances, particularly to the sharp rise in the number of women working in factories and to the steady rise in the number of university students. We must, he said, 'pay attention to this new potential source of leadership for our movement: the graduates from working class homes'.[54]

One such graduate was his parliamentary colleague, Roy Jenkins. The son of Arthur Jenkins, former Vice President of the South Wales Miners' Federation and MP for Pontypool, Roy Jenkins had been elected to parliament in 1948 for the London constituency of Southwark. A graduate of Cardiff University and Oxford University, he was part of the wave to which Griffiths was referring and was active in presenting the intellectual case for egalitarian reform in the moderate, Gaitskellite mode. In 1951, he published a *Tribune* pamphlet calling for redistributive taxation; the following year, an essay on equality appeared in Richard Crossman's *New Fabian Essays*; and in 1953 a critical examination of Labour's present fortunes, *Pursuit of Progress* in which he asserted that the left would not always win on its own terms.[55] James Griffiths, too, took up the message of equality, calling for the abolition of the colour bar in Newport in 1953.[56] Bevan, on the other hand, who had (in any case) called for the end of imperialist exploitation in Pontypridd in 1939, focused his attention on a different kind of egalitarianism.[57] An egalitarianism which, he believed, derived not from growing wealth across the board (redistributed where necessary) but from public ownership and the balancing effects that resulted from a planned economy. The purpose, as he saw it, of the Labour Party in parliament, indeed in government at any level, was to take control of the economy and to set it towards a collective interest to alleviate poverty and individual suffering, rather than accept, meekly, that some are poor and others are rich and the most that could be done was to move money around. That was the essence of his testament, *In Place of Fear*, published in 1952, and was the hallmark of parliamentary Bevanism.[58]

After a second electoral defeat for Labour in 1955, Clement Attlee retired. Aneurin Bevan entered the contest to succeed him as the left-wing candidate. From the centre-right of the party came Hugh Gaitskell and Herbert Morrison. In the first ballot Bevan placed second, winning around a quarter of the vote, but it was Gaitskell who ultimately triumphed. Bevan lost again a few months later in the deputy leadership contest with James Griffiths drawing the support of the moderate wing of the party. Grassroots support for Bevan was considerable, however, and had either ballot been open beyond the Parliamentary Labour Party it was entirely likely that Bevan would have won. Indeed, in parts of South Wales, branches protested the method of voting claiming it unrepresentative of the 'true voice of the rank and file' and demanded one member, one vote.[59] Similarly, whereas Gaitskell's authority at the upper echelons of the party was secure, amongst the rank and file there was clear unease at the way Labour was being led and the policy decisions being made. Speaking in January 1956, Brynmor John, who was later to serve as MP for Pontypridd, complained that the leadership lacked policy, had failed to give a vigorous lead to the rank and file, and was in danger of 'parliamentary paralysis'.[60] In Hirwaun, too, there was a call for a 'truly strong socialist policy in reply to the present Tory government'.[61] Both branches strongly backed Bevan's alternative course.

In May 1959, James Griffiths retired as deputy leader, and Aneurin Bevan was elected, unopposed, to replace him. It marked Bevan's accommodation with Gaitskell's leadership and his determination to help Labour win power by effecting unity rather than division.[62] Five months later, in October, Bevan fought his last election campaign; he remained innovative to the last. Perhaps in recognition of the role played by television in the election, particularly Tony Benn's well-received and effective 'Britain Belongs To You' party political broadcasts, Bevan proposed that parliamentary proceedings be televised on their own special channel.[63] (That did not happen until 1992.) In December 1959, Bevan underwent exploratory surgery for a stomach ulcer, but what doctors found was advanced cancer. He died seven months later on 6 July 1960, aged just sixty three. His entire political career had been to advance the cause of social democracy. 'I am not a communist', he said in his last speech to Labour's annual conference in 1959, 'I am a social democrat'. His comparatively early death robbed the Labour left of its most charismatic and important figure and in South Wales, particularly, there was no obvious figure to replace him. He became an icon of a lost left alternative to Labour's centrist revisionism.

That was how Gwyn Thomas saw him. Two years after Bevan's death, Gwyn Thomas, by then much in demand as a television personality and commentator about Welsh life, let it be known that he was working on a play to dramatise the former's life and politics.[64] Richard Burton, whose socialism was equally Bevanite in character, wrote offering his services in the lead role. It was, potentially, the perfect match. As Gwyn Thomas explained:

I would say the strange essence of Nye finds its only perfect response in the core of your own immense talent. I wish the piece in no way to be a chronicle of things that pushed a dead man towards his end. I want to go right into the hinterland beyond Nye, all the voices in the valleys that were faintly heard but never truly sounded … I would like to express the valour, wisdom, laughter of all the men and women in our part of Wales who thrust Aneurin like a lance at the spiteful boobs at Westminster who regarded us in their inmost thoughts as a kind of intolerable dirt. A thundering vindication of us and our kind.

The play, titled *Return and End*, was destined never to be performed in either's lifetime, but its themes were the summation of Gwyn Thomas's outlook on the world. As he saw it, this was about more than the singularity of Bevan; it was, too, about the toughness of hard, industrial work, the relative tranquillity of the mountainsides, the angular geography of the valley communities that exacted its own toll on the population, and the wide availability of learning and communitarian politics that made him so potent a symbol of hope. Gwyn Thomas explained during an HTV broadcast in 1960 that Bevan

took the image of this place [Ebbw Vale] out of the valleys in which he was born, and presented it, its imperfections, its struggles, its humour, as a challenge to those parts of Britain that have never been scarred by poverty or the monstrous toll that heavy industry exacts from beauty.

That was Bevan's legacy and the true meaning of the opposition that he had provided in the 1940s and 1950s.

Labour did not hold office again until 1964 when Harold Wilson won a narrow victory over the Conservatives. The student socialist society in Swansea responded to the new government by launching a new journal, *Swansea Left*, in October. They were particularly enthused by the victory of Alan

Williams over Hugh Rees, the Conservative who had unexpectedly won the marginal (but Labour-leaning) Swansea West constituency in 1959, and felt that the time for the left-right splits in the party had come to an end. 'Let us hope now that both Left and Right are a little chastened and recognise the part they have played in keeping Labour in the wilderness for thirteen years', remarked one contributor to the journal.[65] But such pragmatism did not last very long. 'What progress has been made towards a socialist government', *Swansea Left* asked six months later. 'A start has been made: old age and widows' pensions have been raised ... a bill has been drafted to bring in fair redundancy payments, as well as another dealing with racial discrimination, and the recent budget made a start on the march towards social justice'. A strong record, the journal remarked, 'at first sight'. But all was not well: 'the racial discrimination bill is being applied only to PUBLIC places, this savours of the sacrifice of principle to political expediency ... we must not let the government lead us, willy-nilly, down the road to neo-conservatism'. It was hyperbole but indicative of the growing radicalism of the student left in the 1960s.

Alan Williams, however, was more cautious and reminded students of the need for pragmatism as well as radicalism. 'Be critical', he counselled, 'but not indiscriminate and deliberately destructive'. It was a message only partly heeded by the university socialist society. The issues discussed in the pages of *Swansea Left* pointed to wide concerns: immigration, education, housing, employment, Vietnam, women's liberation, and the way in which the media manipulated the news for effect, particularly on the role of immigrants in British society. 'We feel that the press's role in fomenting racial discontent should be investigated ... slanted headlines have been numerous and the word "coloured" has been used in circumstances which did not merit its mention'.[66] In this way, *Swansea Left* was an admirable attempt at exploring the issues of the 1964-66 Labour government through a student left perspective, and it was sufficiently aware of the wider ramifications of the legislation discussed and proposed in the mid-1960s by that Labour administration to be of continuing interest even today. One such issue was whether Britain should join the European Common Market. For younger MPs, such as Donald Anderson, who won the Monmouth constituency for Labour in 1966, this was a key indication of the party's reform agenda. In an interview with the university newspaper, *Crefft*, he remarked that 'I would like to see Harold Wilson lead us into Europe'.[67]

Anderson was a member of the pro-European Labour Committee for Europe alongside Leo Abse (elected as the MP for Pontypool in 1958 and previously a city councillor in Cardiff), who was as committed a European as he was bitterly opposed to Welsh nationalism. Ifor Davies, the Gower MP, was similarly active in the campaign for British entry into the European project. The issue was widely debated across the labour movement in the 1960s, particularly at trade union education classes and in Young Socialist meetings, but alongside the enthusiasm of some there was considerable opposition (notably amongst MPs and the NUM) as well as widespread agnosticism. George Thomas, for example, was active in Labour and the Common Market, a campaign group formed by the former Llandaff and Barry MP, Lynn Ungoed-Thomas, and which opposed British entry.[68] Another was Neil McBride, the Scottish-born MP for Swansea East, who remarked, indicatively, in the Commons in 1972 that 'Welsh prospects will be severely injured if Britain becomes a member state of the European Economic Community and aligns herself with the Community's economic and social policies'. It was a debate that lingered through the 1960s and into the 1970s, in part because when Britain applied for membership in 1963 and again in 1967 the application was vetoed by the French government, but also because the Common Market posed significant questions about the sort of country Britain wanted to be as it approached the last quarter of the twentieth century.

Cracks in the Wall?

The European question, which posed a dilemma for British relations with its continental neighbours and its former empire in the form of the Commonwealth, was mirrored by consideration of constitutional reform at home. Devolution was one area of policy, much discussed in the 1950s and 1960s, sometimes bitterly, for which Aneurin Bevan and many others on the left, justifiably, had little real enthusiasm. Bevan, in fact, regarded devolution not as 'socialism' so much as 'escapism'.[69] However, given the advent of devolution in 1999, it is a topic that has garnered considerable academic attention in recent years, often to the detriment of other aspects of Labour's history. Indeed, although devolution was much discussed, it is possible to overstate the significance of Labour's internal conversation about the subject in the 1940s and 1950s. Much of the real interest in constitutional reform came from outside the Labour Party – the CPGB were notable for their engagement with national identity once they realised they could not dislodge Labour as a political force. In 1946, the Labour government rejected a secretary of state for Wales on the basis that it would interfere with national planning and, in any case, 'Wales could not carry a cadre of officials of the highest calibre'.[70] Attlee was similarly equivocal: 'I do not accept the view that the appointment of a Secretary of State would solve the economic problem'.[71]

It was S. O. Davies who pursued devolution with the most vigour in the 1950s, prompting a degree of annoyance from his colleagues, even from those who were otherwise sympathetic to the cause of Welsh self-government. Writing in the *South Wales Democrat*, James Griffiths explained that he had refused to sign Davies's petition calling for a parliament for Wales because

> A Welsh Government relying on its own financial resources cannot possibly finance an insurance scheme on the scale that is now being made possible by the British Treasury.

He continued:

> I want to see the largest amount of devolution in all essentially Welsh affairs within the framework of our British economy. I would like to see our Labour Movement undertaking a thorough examination of this problem of devolution. Let us go fully into the question of what services we believe can be best administered in Wales.[72]

Griffiths's reasoned opposition to the course of action taken by S. O. Davies was the most moderate reaction to be found in the pages of the *South Wales Democrat*. A response soon followed from George Thomas. He wrote:

> I am not one who believes in a Secretary of State for Wales because I have studied carefully the way in which the Scottish Secretary of State acts merely as a buffer between the MPs and Ministers with real authority over departments.

He concluded, forcibly, that 'what Wales wants is economic security ... our culture itself rests upon this basis'.[73]

For George Thomas, as with many Labour MPs from South Wales in this period, the reawakening of nationalism was regarded as both dangerous and a potential gateway to fascism. It was a regular accusation levelled at Plaid Cymru by Labour members chiefly because of the nationalists' refusal to take part in the war effort. The Rhondda West MP, Iorrie Thomas, a vigorous opponent of devolution, went so far as to denounce the 'mental neurosis associated with the virus of nationalism'.[74] Likewise, the Labour Party secretary in Rhondda West, D. J. Davies, insisted that 'it was industrialisation far more than cultural oppression which had upset the old Welsh way of life'.[75] Nevertheless, with some grassroots support for home rule, as one correspondent to the *South Wales Democrat* put it 'if Wales is to live, her people must act',[76] the Welsh Regional Council of Labour had to find a pragmatic way forward and so, despite its opposition to the parliament for Wales campaign, proposed in January 1952 that

> Labour will leave to others the creating of meaningless titles such as "Minister of Wales" or frothy tirades against English Despotism. The problem of devolution is a practical solution which can only be solved by practical proposals.[77]

This was echoed nine months later in a contribution from one writer under the pen-name 'mab y werin' (son of the people), who suggested that

> In tackling the needs of the Welsh people and helping to preserve the language and culture, Labour should not be swept into a romantic but unreal worship of a bogus nationalism. Instead, it should seek a solution whereby national differences in the cultural and linguistic field are enhanced but where political boundaries in the shape of new state boundaries are avoided.[78]

The debate was picked up again in February 1953, suggesting that self-government would 'divide not unite', and that 'national consciousness belongs mainly to those areas where the language and culture is strong'. It was inevitable, they said, that 'a sharp nationalist trend would divide the allegiance of the majority of Welsh people who are not mainly Welsh in culture and speech from the minority'. Another correspondent agreed, stating that 'nationalism becomes unhealthy when it is political'. Both determined that devolution, inspired as it was by political nationalism, was incompatible with Labour's desire for social justice and economic democracy.[79]

In the event, Labour came around to the idea of a Secretary of State for Wales, largely because of the influence of James Griffiths during Hugh Gaitskell's leadership. Griffiths was to serve as the first Welsh Secretary in 1964. But the debate on devolution had prompted the question not only of Wales's constitutional future, but also of the persistence of the South Wales to which Aneurin Bevan had been committed. From inside and outside the Labour Party, those who saw Wales as a unity, not as a region of regions clearly divided between north and south, English-speaking and Welsh-speaking, went on the attack. 'We Welsh' Gwyn Thomas observed knowingly on St David's Day 1963, 'are not a united people. But I won't say that we haven't enjoyed our divisions. ... We have two languages and plenty to argue about in both. English poured in in the wake of industry and many of us in our childhood heard the language of our fathers die on our tongues'. The following year, his most enduring and popular book, *A Welsh Eye*, appeared. Although for the most part it was pitched in the darkly humorous tone with which Thomas was then associated, bubbling under the surface was a fierce critique of the authoritarian elements that he perceived as being present in Welsh-language culture and its political dynamic.

This is nowhere more in evidence than in his discussion of the poet Huw Menai (1886-1961). Although a fluent Welsh speaker, born in Caernarfon, Huw Menai lived his adult life in the central

438

Glamorgan valleys and wrote his poems in English.[80] He was an ardent member of leftist political organisations such as the Social Democratic Federation and the Independent Labour Party, his political outlook was internationalist, and he held no truck with the nationalist movement of his time. 'When some fanatical separatist told him that the Welsh language was the "tongue of paradise"', Thomas wrote, 'Huw's look suggested that he had always expected the worst of paradise'. The language hardly needs explanation. Nor was Gwyn Thomas finished. In the next chapter of *A Welsh Eye* (which draws on an article he wrote for *Punch*), he was even more forthright. Here he argued that Welsh nationalism signalled the total retreat from the internationalist high noon of the interwar years: 'the national brain now bulges with such projects as the need to deny Welsh rainwater to the Liverpool water-board and a demand that the present limited education we now give our children in English should be replaced by an even more limited education in Welsh'.[81] This was not, he thought, the point of socialism.

In a moment of frank openness on the subject during a television interview in the 1960s, Gwyn Thomas reflected that 'I never wanted to be emotionally involved in the Welsh language'. This followed from his experiences of his own childhood when, despite the busy bilingual bomb of a kitchen, he grew up, as he said, with the top half of his family speaking Welsh and the bottom half (of which he was the last) speaking English only. He explained:

> I simply had to make the best of this. And I don't think that people in this dilemma in Wales have quite had the amount of understanding from their Welsh-speaking brethren as they should have done. Because after all when you lose a language for say ten years, if you are at all proud you are not going to try to learn it again.

Nowhere in Wales was the decline in the Welsh language more apparent than in the central valleys of the coalfield, the very communities that Gwyn Thomas was identified with and took as the focus of his work. His own family eventually all stopped speaking the language.[82] It became a sharp dividing line within the Labour Party, especially, with those uncomfortable with language revival and self-government demanding 'a firm assurance from pro-Self Government supporters that it is NOT their intention should they gain their demand to make the Welsh language in any way compulsory'. It would 'ensure a more friendly attitude from the vast majority of the Welsh nation who do not use Welsh as their native tongue'.[83] When, in 1965, the David Hughes-Parry report argued that all heads of government departments should be Welsh speaking, ostensibly to make administration easier, there was an outcry. Amongst the most vocal opponents was Leo Abse, who addressed the matter in the House of Commons. 'I am sure', he said, 'that Monmouthshire will welcome ... [the] statement which made it abundantly clear that the government have no intention of allowing any preference to be given in any job or post in Wales as a consequence of a man or woman having the ability to speak Welsh in addition to English, and that all applications for post will be dealt with on merit, and on merit alone'.

Abse was by no means a lone voice in the Parliamentary Labour Party on this issue and it was a clear dividing line between members representing seats outside of the coalfield and those in Glamorgan and Monmouthshire. Most South Wales MPs expressed anti-nationalist and anti-devolution views.[84] In George Thomas's case, virulently so. In 1956, Ness Edwards launched a volley at the growing nationalist movement with his pamphlet *Is This The Road?* Recognising the need for democratic renewal to avoid lapsing into managerialism, he nevertheless disregarded what he saw as 'narrow nationalism'. He wrote:

'nationalism, devolution, federalism are all forms of a protest against the political vacua of their lives'. He continued:

> This must be said for them all. They have a vision. And it is this visionary quality that stimulates the virile, thinking section of any community. Whatever criticism one may indulge of the form it takes, this reaching out for a form of social organisation which will give significance to the life of a community, is a good thing. Far better activity of this sort than dull apathy. But the creation of new boundaries and new separations is no solution ... A time when the nations of Europe find that they are too small singly to develop their own atomic energy programme, upon which the industrial future depends, is not the time to cut the United Kingdom into small parts.[85]

Arthur Pearson the MP for Pontypridd, similarly, warned that Welsh nationalism 'draws young people onto extremes' and that the nationalists were 'narrow and without vision'.[86] He undoubtedly took some pleasure in announcements from Plaid Cymru branches in the town that praised Labour's social radicalism in office and their insistence that 'only socialism can solve our problems'.[87]

But then, in the 1960s, Labour got caught in the headlights. After several false starts, and a few victories at local government level in parts of Merthyr and the Cynon Valley, Plaid Cymru shook the Labour Party in a series of by-elections. Although Gwynfor Evans's victory in Carmarthen in 1966 is often highlighted as the major earthquake, since he was the only Plaid Cymru MP elected, this is easily exaggerated. Carmarthen was really a Liberal constituency and Evans positioned himself as the heir-apparent of Megan Lloyd George. In that he proved victorious. Nor was the Carmarthen CLP very strong: in Carmarthen itself the party had little more than one hundred members. Concern about membership had been a regular feature of the secretary's reports to annual meetings and in internal correspondence in the decade leading up to 1966, and there was a clear belief that Megan Lloyd George had carried the seat because of her own force of personality rather than through Labour's own electoral machine.[88] As the CLP secretary reported, tellingly, in April 1971, Labour's recapture of the seat at the 1970 general election came about because the party 'worked along the line, not top to bottom'.[89]

More obviously damaging to the Labour Party's fortunes were the by-election results in Rhondda West and Caerphilly in 1967 and 1968, since these were genuine Labour heartlands. Iorrie Thomas, whose death in December 1966 resulted in the by-election in Rhondda West, had been an opponent of the parliament for Wales campaign in the 1950s, and the devolution question was used by Plaid Cymru and the Communist Party in their campaigns to suggest that Labour was not representing the Welsh people. Arthur True, the communist candidate, published a list of things 'I want to see' in his election literature, which was topped by a demand for a 'parliament for Wales with real powers to plan our industry and bring new life into our country'. He went on to explain his position:

> We need a parliament for Wales to develop our economic and social resources to the full. It could plan the all-round growth of Wales as a nation, while maintaining our voice in the affairs of Britain as a whole. All-Wales economic development and full employment for our people in their own country is a vital basis for preserving our culture and language.[90]

It was a perspective shared by communists and nationalists in the Rhondda.[91]

In the aftermath of the by-election, which was won narrowly by Labour, the communists reflected on Plaid Cymru's near-miss and noted that the nationalists had seized on the economic misfortunes of the Rhondda, notably the pit closure programme, and offered 'loosely socialist policies' alongside a clear demand for independent representation outside of what they perceived to be the Labour machine. The nationalists had also brought in 'coach-loads of young supporters from all over Wales' who canvassed in the streets, packed public meetings and had 'Welsh flags flying all over the constituency'. This contrasted with the traditional campaign fought by Labour and the Communist Party, both of whom, to some extent, relied on the 'older committed generations and traditions of the labour movement'. There was 'no special women's activity' and most of the youth work conducted by the communists in the Rhondda was carried out by students and young communists brought in from Cardiff and branches in Monmouthshire.[92] The result was a firmer commitment to devolution and a left-wing nationalism by the Communist Party. Ironically, Alec Jones, the new Rhondda West MP, was himself a keen advocate of devolution, helping to steer proposals through parliament as Welsh Office minister between 1975 and 1979.

Dr Alistair Wilson, writing in the Communist Party's new journal, *Cyffro*, in 1970, concluded that 'the Labour Movement will not unite Wales and lead it forward without drastic changes in its policy'. This meant:

The adoption of a radical socialist programme and the revival of the spirit of popular, democratic agitation for change. Secondly in placing itself at the head, instead of at the tail, of the movement to force genuine democratic rights for Wales, and essentially the establishment of a Welsh Parliament. The uniting of the militant left movement which was already beginning to show itself in the final year of the Labour Government, with the broad national movement in Wales, is the key to the revival of the Labour Movement as a pioneering and revolutionary force in Welsh life.[93]

Labour had lost votes to the nationalists, Wilson argued, because they had 'in general neglected to recognise the widespread demand for a Welsh Parliament'.[94] Until the Labour Party, and the wider labour movement, settled in favour of such an institution, so the communist analysis went, the revolt against their singular dominance of Welsh affairs would continue. Having lost the general election, Labour had the opportunity to reconsider its position on devolution, which it did do, but not without considerable internal consternation. But was there really such widespread demand for devolution? Voters in Caerphilly in 1968 had in fact elected an anti-devolutionist, Fred Evans, who regarded the idea of an Assembly as an 'expensive anachronism', rather than a pro-devolutionist in the form of Plaid Cymru's Phil Williams. The same was true of Pontypool, where Leo Abse was vehement in his opposition to devolution, going as far as to denounce the proposals put forward by the Labour government in the 1970s as unbecoming of the Labour Party. He had, he said, 'no time for narrow nationalism ... it had nothing to do with socialism'. Even the choice of St David's Day, 1 March 1979, for the referendum, Abse thought had been undertaken for 'the most miserable, chauvinistic reasons'.

In retrospect, the by-elections of 1966, 1967, and 1968, were flashes in the pan. At the 1970 general election, Fred Evans won nearly twenty five thousand votes in Caerphilly compared to the nearly twelve thousand won by Phil Williams for Plaid Cymru; Alec Jones captured nearly nineteen thousand votes in Rhondda West compared with the paltry three and a half thousand won by Plaid Cymru; and in Carmarthen, Gwynoro Jones won back the seat for Labour with a majority of nearly four thousand over Gwynfor Evans. Only in the Aberdare constituency did Plaid Cymru register a more long-lasting advance, winning more than eleven thousand votes at the 1970 general election and again in February 1974. But Labour's vote there was more than twenty thousand. Plaid Cymru had little real hope of winning outside of a sudden by-election. Yet, the nationalist tide at the end of the 1960s, and the near losses in Caerphilly and Rhondda West, pushed Labour down a path that, in normal circumstances, it would have and probably should have avoided.[95] There was evidently an air of panic. In the autumn of 1966, a debate organised at University College Swansea and attended by James Griffiths and Gwynfor Evans saw the proposition that 'this house believes that Labour government is good for Wales' defeated by two hundred and thirty five votes to ninety. The loudest cheers, if the college newspaper, *Crefft*, was accurate in its reporting, were for Gwynfor Evans who insisted that 'Labour [are] just not serious about Wales'.[96] It was mere rhetoric. As the secretary of Carmarthen CLP reflected ruefully, 'our movement has much experience of splinter organisations cashing in on our hard work'.[97]

A few weeks after the Swansea debate, *Crefft* published an angry interview with George Thomas, then Minister of State at the Welsh Office, in which he repudiated the claims made by Gwynfor Evans in the debate (it had been broadcast on BBC Radio), and by colleagues on the Labour benches, not least James Griffiths, in favour of devolution. He pointed out that

the amount of economic help we get today is STAGGERING, and I don't think the nationalists realise it. And our standard of living would go down like a stone in a pond if we followed that will-of-the-whisp, a parish-pump parliament.

445

He then went on to remind readers that more than twenty ministers, including the Chancellor of the Exchequer (James Callaghan), were either Welsh or held Welsh seats. And he pointed to the diversification of the economy of South Wales which meant that miners were leaving mining not because they were 'going up the mountain to play [or...] going down the Exchange to sign on the dole'. This point was borne out in the reports of careers officers in mining districts who noted the trend themselves. Thomas's loyalty to the Prime Minister and his persistence on the matter was soon rewarded by his promotion to become Secretary of State for Wales in 1968, replacing the pro-devolution Anglesey MP, Cledwyn Hughes.[98] Hughes had succeeded Jim Griffiths in 1966. Had Labour been truly concerned about a rising tide of nationalism in its coalfield heartland at the end of the 1960s, it is hard to conceive of George Thomas becoming Secretary of State in 1968 – his views on devolution were too alien. That he was appointed, suggested, instead, that Wilson, who had little personal enthusiasm for or interest in devolution, believed he had weathered the storm. The party approached the 1970 general election from a position of strength and with the belief that Harold Wilson would do what Clement Attlee could not – win for a third time.

Notes

[1] Clement Attlee regarded it as his 'proudest act'. Bew, *Citizen Clem*, 252. See, also, K. O. Morgan, *Labour in Power, 1945-1951* (Oxford, 1984), *passim*.

[2] The others were W. G. Cove (Aberavon) and George Daggar (Abertillery). *WM*, 14 February, 19 February 1941.

[3] David, *Remaining True*, 45. It was not the only rebuke Edwards received because of his stand – members of the Glamorgan Public Assistance Committee were similarly unimpressed and he was called to give an account of his actions to members of Caerphilly Divisional Labour Party a few days after the vote. *WM*, 3 March, 20 March 1941.

[4] *WM*, 31 July 1942.

[5] *WM*, 3 December 1943. Mosley had been imprisoned in May 1940. Stephen Dorril, *Blackshirt: Sir Oswald Mosley and British Fascism* (London, 2006).

[6] Thomas-Symonds, *Nye*, 95.

[7] *WM, 3 July 1942.*

[8] *DH*, 3 July 1942.

[9] Aneurin Bevan, 'Plan for Work', in GDH Cole (ed.), *Plan For Britain: A Collection of Essays Prepared for the Fabian Society* (London, 1943). The book also included a chapter by Jim Griffiths: 'Plan for the Key Industries'.

[10] The Labour leadership announced their determination to do so in March 1944, some months prior to the book's publication, but Bevan was determined to hold them to their decision. Bew, *Citizen Clem*, 311.

[11] Aneurin Bevan, *Why Not Trust The Tories?* (London, 1944), 89. A similar warning was given by Emmanuel Shinwell in his *When The Men Come Home* (London, 1944), 5.

[12] My own copy was once owned by someone serving in 1944 at RAF Nassau in the Bahamas, for example; *Birmingham Daily Gazette*, 11 January 1945.

[13] James Griffiths, *The Price Wales Pays for Poverty: Wales and Health* (Llanelli, 1939); idem, *Between Two Wars: Coal* (London, 1942); Welsh Reconstruction Advisory Council, *First Interim Report* (London, 1944).

[14] James Griffiths, 'Industry – the servant of the public', in Fabian Society, *What Labour Could Do* (London, 1945)

[15] Nuffield College Archives, Oxford, G. D. H. Cole Papers, GDHC/F2/61/1-8: Reports of Local Surveys, Cardiff and District, 1940.

[16] Nuffield College Archives, Nuffield College Social Reconstruction Survey Papers, NCSRS/Box 89: C1/321-353. The Treforest material is contained in C1/336: South Wales Survey, The Industrial Future of the Region (October 1941), 6. The idea was subsequently rejected in order to exploit the coke reserves found underground.

[17] W. G. Cove, the Aberavon MP, was himself a former miner but had been a teacher prior to entering parliament. It is under that profession that he is categorised here.

[18] Griffiths, *Pages*, 89.

[19] *PO*, 23 June 1945.

[20] Bew, *Citizen Clem*, 335.

[21] Merthyr Tydfil CBC, Report of the Medical Officer of Health for 1954, 35.

[22] Tredegar UDC, Report of the Medical Officer of Health for 1945, 2.

[23] Rhymney UDC, Medical Officer of Health Report for 1946, 8.

[24] Bevan, *Why Not*, 66.

[25] Thomas-Symonds, *Nye*, 161; Merthyr Tydfil CBC, Report of the Medical Officer of Health for 1954, 84-5; Ebbw Vale UDC, Report of the Medical Officer of Health for 1950, 45; Abertillery UDC, Report of the Medical Officer of Health for 1950, 31.

[26] Glamorgan CC, Report of the Medical Officer of Health for 1945, 16.

[27] Glamorgan CC, Report of the Medical Officer of Health for 1950, 58.

[28] Glamorgan CC, Report of the Medical Officer of Health for 1960, 88.

[29] Rhymney UDC, Report of the Medical Officer of Health for 1956, 10.

[30] Merthyr Tydfil CBC, Report of the Medical Officer of Health for 1951, 8.

[31] Ogmore and Garw UDC, Report of the Medical Officer of Health for 1950, 14.

[32] Tredegar UDC, Report of the Medical Officer of Health for 1956, 24.

[33] Tredegar UDC, Report of the Medical Officer of Health for 1954, 28; Report of the Medical Officer of Health for 1960, 24. More

than two hundred thousand pounds in mortgage loans had been provided by 1960 (the equivalent of more than four and quarter million pounds today).

[34] Martin Johnes, *Wales Since 1939* (Manchester, 2012), 39.

[35] Leon Gooberman, *From Depression to Devolution: Economy and Government in Wales, 1934-2006* (Cardiff, 2017), 33.

[36] Ogmore and Garw UDC, Report of the Medical Officer of Health for 1947, 5.

[37] Ogmore and Garw UDC, Report of the Medical Officer of Health for 1951, 4.

[38] Bill Jones, Brian Roberts, and Chris Williams, 'Going from the darkness to the light: South Wales Miners' Attitudes towards nationalisation', *Llafur* 7, no. 1 (1996), 101.

[39] SWCC, Dai Francis Papers, File B16: 'notes for a speech "Nationalisation of the Mines", 1945' cited in Jones et al, 'Darkness', 103.

[40] Francis and Smith, *The Fed*, 487, fn. 27; Hywel Francis, *The Tower Story: Lessons in Vigilance and Freedom* (Hirwaun, 1997), 14.

[41] National Coal Board, *Annual Report for 1948*.

[42] Clement Attlee, *As It Happened* (London, 1954), 164.

[43] TNA, CAB 129/95/58: Memorandum on Fuel Policy and Problems, Lord Mills, 19 December 1958.

[44] *South Wales Evening Post*, 30 December 1958.

[45] *South Wales Evening Post*, 24 January 1959.

[46] Lyn Evans, 'Death of a Village', *The Miner* 7, no. 5 (1959), 8-9; cited in Francis and Smith, *The Fed*, 491, fn. 74.

[47] *Tribune*, 12 December 1958.

[48] Ogmore and Garw UDC, Report of the Medical Officer of Health for 1960, 8.

[49] Ogmore and Garw UDC, Report of the Medical Officer of Health for 1958, 7.

[50] *South Wales Democrat* 1, no. 9 (June 1952).

[51] *WM*, 9 May 1958.

[52] Sam Blaxland, 'The Conservative Party in Wales, 1945-1997' (Unpublished PhD Thesis, 2017), 106.

[53] Pontypridd UDC, *Petition for Incorporation* (Pontypridd, 1956).

[54] *South Wales Democrat* 1, no. 2 (November 1951).

[55] Roy Jenkins, *Fair Shares for the Rich* (London, 1951); idem, 'Equality' in Richard Crossman (ed.), *New Fabian Essays* (London, 1952); idem, *Pursuit of Progress: A Critical Analysis of the Achievement and Prospect of the Labour Party* (London, 1953).

[56] *South Wales Democrat* 1, no. 14 (January 1953).

[57] *PO*, 20 May 1939.

[58] Aneurin Bevan, *In Place of Fear* (London, 1952). It was echoed in Barbara Castle, *How Can We Avoid the Tragedy of Back to the Dole* (London, 1951); Aneurin Bevan, Harold Wilson and John Freeman, *One Way Only: A Socialist Analysis of the Present World Crisis* (London, 1951).

[59] GA, D1433/1, Hirwaun Joint Ward Labour Party, Minutes 1952-1958: entry for 10 February 1956.

[60] Pontypridd TLC, Minutes: Entry for 2 January 1956.

[61] Hirwaun Joint Ward Labour Party, Minutes: entry for 9 March 1956.

[62] A point made by Megan Lloyd George when speaking to a meeting of Carmarthen Constituency Labour Party in December 1960. Carmarthen CLP, Minutes, 12 December 1960.

[63] *South Wales Echo*, 3 November 1959.

[64] NLW GTP/K52: 'Nye Bevan inspires a play'. This is discussed in Smith, *Aneurin Bevan*, 13 and more broadly in Dai Smith, *Wales! Wales?* (London, 1984), 132-133.

[65] *Swansea Left* 1 (October 1964).

[66] *Swansea Left* 2 (April 1965).

[67] *Crefft*, 5 May 1966.

[68] *The Times*, 31 July 1962. George Thomas, *Mr Speaker: The Memoirs of the Viscount Tonypandy* (London, 1985), 83.

[69] Cited in Vernon Bogdanor, *Devolution in the United Kingdom* (Oxford, 1999), 152.

[70] TNA, CAB 129/6: The Administration of Wales and Monmouthshire, January 1946; Cited in K. O. Morgan, 'Power and Glory: War and Reconstruction, 1939-1951' in Tanner et al (eds.), *The Labour Party in Wales*, 179.

[71] LHASC, Labour Party Archive, LP/GS/9/2: Letter from Clement Attlee to D. R. Grenfell, 5 September 1946 (as above).

[72] *South Wales Democrat* 1, no. 2 (November 1951).

[73] *South Wales Democrat* 1, no. 3 (December 1951).

[74] Mari Wiliam, 'Labour, the Union and the Rebirth of Welsh Devolution', in Chris Williams and Andrew Edwards (eds.), *The Art of the Possible: Politics and Governance in Modern British History, 1885-1997: Essays in Memory of Duncan Tanner* (Manchester, 2015), 150

[75] *South Wales Democrat* 1, no. 9 (June 1952).

[76] *South Wales Democrat* 1, no. 14 (January 1953).

[77] *South Wales Democrat* 1, no. 4 (January 1952).

[78] *South Wales Democrat* 1, no. 12 (September 1952).

[79] *South Wales Democrat* 1, no. 15 (February 1953).

[80] Huw Menai, *Through the Upcast Shaft* (London: Hodder and Stoughton, 1920); *The Passing of Guto* (London: L. & V. Woolf, 1929); *Back in Return* (London: William Heinemann, 1933); *The Simple Vision* (London: Chapman & Hall, 1945).

[81] Gwyn Thomas, *A Welsh Eye*, 103.

[82] Gwyn Thomas, 'The Welsh Dreamer' in Michael Parnell (ed.), *Meadow Prospect Revisited* (Bridgend, 1992), 119. The article was originally published in the *Liverpool Post* in 1977.

[83] *South Wales Democrat* 1, no. 5 (February 1952).

[84] Notably George Thomas (Cardiff West), W. H. Mainwaring (Rhondda East), D. J. Williams (Neath), Iorrie Thomas (Rhondda West), Ioan Evans (Aberdare), Donald Anderson (Swansea East), Arthur Pearson (Pontypridd), and Ness Edwards (Caerphilly).

[85] Ness Edwards, *Is This The Road?* (Wrexham, 1956), 6-7.

[86] *PO*, 6 October 1967.

[87] *PO*, 15 December 1967.

[88] This is based on a reading of the Carmarthen CLP records for this period. These are held CA, 8048/1-18. The archive is uncatalogued. My thanks to the staff of the Glamorgan Archives, where the records were housed on consultation, for facilitating access and providing guidance in their use.

[89] Carmarthen CLP, Secretary's Report for 1971, Presented at the Annual General Meeting, 24 April 1971. Contained in CA, 8048/4 (but consulted at GA). The secretary also reported the 'self-isolation'

of several wards in the constituency, hampering the party's efficacy at election time.

[90] Arthur True, 'Election Material, 1967', contained in LHASC, CP/CENT/PC/09/15, 'Report on Rhondda West By-Election, March 1967'. Nevertheless, as the report suggests, the CP felt they had to 'overcome the basic and still deep problem of getting a large mass acceptance [sic] of Communism and the Party, dispelling the prejudice and effects of past history'.

[91] See, for instance, the report by Syd Morgan and Roy Roberts in *Crefft*, 2 March 1967, which was typical of the steady merger of the two parties on the question of national representation. This was a silver age for the CP (electorally) in Rhondda West with the election of Annie Powell in Penygraig, George Baker in Ystrad, and Arthur True in Treherbert. Annie Powell's career was capped in 1979 when she served as mayor of the Rhondda, the first woman communist ever to hold such an office in Britain. LHASC, CP/CENT/EC/11/02, Report on Rhondda West Constituency, February 1966. But this masked wider problems elsewhere – every branch of the CP in Rhondda East was smaller than those of the Dulais Valley and fewer copies of the *Daily Worker* were sold in Maerdy than in Onllwyn. LHASC, CP/CENT/PC/06/17-18, Reports on Rhondda East and Neath constituencies, 1962.

[92] LHASC, CP/CENT/PC/09/15.

[93] Alistair Wilson, 'Editorial Notes', *Cyffro* 1, no. 3 (Summer 1970), 5-6. I am grateful to Brian Davies for talking through the development of *Cyffro* with me.

[94] A point echoed by Arthur True in 1975. See, *Morning Star*, 21 November 1975.

[95] Richard Crossman, *Diaries of a Cabinet Minister* (London, 1977), 29 April, 6 May, 9 May, 27 May 1968.

[96] *Crefft*, 3 November 1966.

[97] Carmarthen CLP, Secretary's Report for 1967-8, Presented at the Annual General Meeting 16 March 1968.

[98] Hughes became Minister of Agriculture.

CHAPTER EIGHT

The Fall

Little was expected to change at the 1970 general election, at least in South Wales. Only two seats exercised much in the way of public attention: Carmarthen, where Gwynfor Evans, Plaid Cymru's first MP, looked to hold onto the seat he had won in a by-election four years earlier; and Merthyr Tydfil where the left-winger S. O. Davies hoped to defy the party machine and hold the seat he won in 1934. Davies was, by this time, in his late eighties and party members in Merthyr felt it was time for him to retire in favour of a younger candidate, Tal Lloyd.[1] It was the first time that the Labour Party had deliberately 'retired' someone on the grounds of old age but most of S. O. Davies's cohort had already died or otherwise left the House of Commons.[2] Davies refused to stand aside and insisted on standing as an independent, 'they're behaving like a bunch of ambitious school kids', he told the *Sunday Express* describing the actions of his constituency party executive.[3] Lloyd was a Labour stalwart: he had been mayor of Merthyr and was the local organiser for the engineering union, AUEW, then the largest union in the town. He was also more in line with national policies, for instance, on entry into the Common Market, which S. O. Davies opposed. One by one the major unions, including the NUM, fell in behind Lloyd, leaving S. O. Davies with only the tacit support of local members of the NUR and the NUM. 'Whoever holds the Labour titles', the *Merthyr Express* declared confidently, 'will be Merthyr's next MP'.[4]

In typical circumstances that would have happened, but loyalty to S. O. Davies, together with political opportunism by

Plaid Cymru activists, was strong enough to ensure his victory. It was the lowest number of votes he had ever won at a parliamentary election, but it was enough to give the Labour Party a bloody nose.[5] The Merthyr result was broadcast shortly after Harold Wilson's speech from his constituency at Huyton and it prompted the commentator David Butler to remark that it was 'really quite extraordinary' because 'it has been said that this could no longer be done'. In the aftermath of the election, S. O. Davies and several supporters were expelled from the Labour Party.[6] Some of the supporters eventually joined Plaid Cymru, whereas Davies sat in the House of Commons until his death in February 1972 as an 'independent Labour' MP. For the first time since the early 1930s, Merthyr was no longer held by the Labour Party. It remained the case until the by-election following Davies's death, when it was won back by Ted Rowlands. His majorities soon resembled those of S. O. Davies at the height of the latter's popularity. Normal service had been restored, or so it seemed.

In 1972, Merfyn Jones published his bleak study of contemporary unemployment in Merthyr, *Life On The Dole*. It pointed to the return of the dark days. Although the rate of unemployment in the town was under ten percent, which was a fraction of what it had been in the 1930s, it was still about twice the national average and left more than eighteen hundred people without a job.[7] The Labour-controlled council sought solutions. John Reddy, the chair of Merthyr's housing committee, pressed for the establishment of apprenticeships so that trainees could be set to work building council houses. Without government intervention, for which Reddy appealed to the Welsh Office, but was turned down, that was impossible, and the modest council scheme Reddy introduced using the council's own resources provided only for housing repairs.[8] Yet it was an attempt at developing a practical response to prevailing conditions; to continue to deliver socialism in a form that working people understood and valued.

This was notably true in 1971 when Labour councillors took a stand against the removal of subsidies for milk for school children aged seven to eleven years. The Education (Milk) Act was passed by the Heath government in 1971 and introduced into the House of Commons by Margaret Thatcher as Education Secretary ostensibly as part of a range of measures designed to reduce public spending. The backlash in Merthyr was significant and prompted a widespread campaign organised by the Welsh Regional Council of Labour to support Merthyr members.[9] Gerry Donovan, the Mayor of Merthyr, famously declared that he was prepared to go to prison in defiance of the new legislation, and councillors resisted all attempts at coercing them into compliance. 'The history of Merthyr Tydfil itself', Donovan remarked in an interview with the BBC, 'proves the necessity of milk to children between the ages of seven and eleven, and we feel that what we are doing is preventative medicine rather than defying a government'.[10] The town's trades and labour council, too, commended the action of councillors in resisting 'this reactionary approach'. As Fred Evans, the Caerphilly MP, observed in the House of Commons, 'they have also said that we should adhere to our tradition, set in 1932, when school fees were introduced into grammar schools and we said that we would not do that in Merthyr Tydfil – and won'.

But there were also grievances, which eroded confidence in local authorities and which, in Merthyr, resulted in defeat for the first time in more than half a century. Having won a mere three seats in the 1973 council elections, compared with Labour's twenty eight, Plaid Cymru won a notable victory in 1976 taking twenty one of the thirty three seats on the council. It was the first time that the nationalists had ever won outright control of a local authority.[11] The *Merthyr Express* searched for answers and focused on a small number of issues: perceived arrogance, poor judgement in selling off council-owned properties, and a failure to tackle the poor quality housing in the borough. Rising unemployment played its part, too. Plaid Cymru established Merthyr Housing Association, which was tasked with building new homes and renovating existing ones, and they established Merthyr Heritage Trust which was designed to promote the town's industrial heritage and safeguard it from destruction.[12] Labour had been evicted from the town hall because of a grievance but they were soon back in office: three years after their victory, Plaid were again reduced to a mere three seats.[13] Like the by-election scares of the late-1960s, and S. O. Davies's victory in 1970, it was but a flash in the pan.

Historians of the 1970s have suggested that it was during this decade that the 'traditional Labour synthesis fell apart', leading to reinvigorated and increasingly credible rivals on the left and right.[14] Certainly, in constituencies such as Carmarthen and the Rhondda, Labour Party organisers were concerned about the activity of Plaid Cymru in particular wards and the spread of hostility towards the party because of what was going on in the coal mining industry.[15] Indeed, there was a clear challenge for Labour in renewing its blend of radical pragmatism in a period of economic and industrial turbulence. There is clear evidence that they did undertake considerable investment and did attempt to renew communities across South Wales. In areas such as Taff Ely, the Cynon Valley, and the Rhondda, this effort resulted in a raft of new leisure centres and indoor swimming pools, for instance, which became symbols of a new era of public investment.[16] But was it enough? A series of studies produced by the Board of Celtic Studies and sponsored by the Welsh Office pointed at the underlying difficulties. In the words of John Sewel,

The major general question that clearly concerned all those who were actively interested in the future of the South Wales mining valleys was how the way of life was being affected by a series of colliery closures that were reducing employment opportunities throughout the South Wales coalfield.[17]

Mining communities began to decline in population: the upper Dulais Valley, for instance lost over one thousand residents in the decade between 1961 and 1971, or some fifteen percent.[18] There were similar rates of decline in Ammanford and other parts of the anthracite coalfield. Rhondda's population, too, fell by more than eleven thousand between 1951 and 1961, a rate of decline that continued into the 1970s.

The decline in the coal industry was mirrored by the dwindling influence of the South Wales NUM over the Labour Party: S. O. Davies was the last member of parliament from Wales to be sponsored by the NUM – sponsorship lost in 1970. This was to have an important effect on the nature of Labour politics after that point, particularly as the traditional economic base of male manual labour fell away. In Tonypandy almost half of all workers by the end of the 1970s were women, the figure in Treorchy was nearly sixty percent. Across Wales the largest group in the workforce were women in education and medicine.[19] It was a process of change that Labour struggled, at least initially, to deal with, although it slowly began to think and act differently. After the death of Megan Lloyd George in 1966, and the retirement of Eirene White in 1970, there were no women in parliament from Wales until the election of Ann Clwyd for Cynon Valley in 1984.[20] This prompted the women's organiser, Anita Holmes (later Baroness Anita Gale), to begin a concerted campaign in 1976 to force Labour to run women candidates in Welsh constituencies. She warned that unless action were taken 'this situation could remain the same for about fifteen years'.[21] It was little better at local government level, in 1976, just thirty five women stood as candidates for Labour in the local elections, although twenty seven of these were in the former counties of Glamorgan and Monmouthshire.[22]

What follows in this chapter explores this process of change and sets it alongside the growing militancy within the National Union of Mineworkers. That militancy was, however, never going to prevent the steady erosion of the mining industry, although it did temper the pace of decline during the 1970s. As Duncan Tanner suggests, Labour's central problem was not rising national identity or increased opposition, both of which gave rise to temporary expressions of grievance, nor was it identity politics, but rather the steady disappearance of the industrial basis on which the party's historic strength had been constructed. Failure to replace this foundation with something equally meaningful left Labour unable to reassert its once overwhelming dominance: its eventual embrace of a form of nationalism (pronounced in recent years) was a symptom of this inability to revitalise industrial activity. It was the easy answer. The miners' strike of 1984-5 was indeed a break point, but not one that, as is now widely assumed, gave way to the modern Wales of devolution. Rather, it accelerated the demise of the coal mining industry, sacrificed the remnants of that way of life, and left South Wales over-exposed to the bitter effects of Thatcherism. It need not have been that way.

The October Revolution

The march to the 1984-5 miners' strike began over a decade earlier following the revival of mass industrial action in response to political and economic change at the end of the 1960s. In 1966, responding to pit closures and the speed with which the mining industry was being shrunk by Labour's own energy policies, Dai Francis, the South Wales Area general secretary and leading communist, remarked that 'we do not want a perpetuation of Tory policy ... it is my personal opinion that this government is intent on creating a pool of unemployment'. But it was also the case that young South Walians were unwilling to enter the industry despite consistently positive propaganda published in the press that promoted mining as a modern and hi-tech job. The Youth Employment Service in Glamorgan warned about this deeper cultural reality throughout the 1960s, noting in its annual careers reports that mining was simply not attractive as a career for young men any longer, just as factory work was becoming unpopular amongst young women, and young unemployed people would rather do anything else – even nothing – than work underground. Consequently, by 1970, nearly forty percent of those working in the industry were over fifty years old, with only around ten percent aged under twenty five.

Yet, in the early 1970s, with unemployment rates amongst young people rising sharply, attitudes began to change, and rapidly. In February 1971, the divisional careers officer for Bridgend and Maesteg reported the changed mood:

> One encouraging feature about the employment situation is the increasing intake into the mining industry, whilst at present there is an insatiable demand for employees in the industry, there appears to be a marked difference of attitude by the public towards employment in the industry ... The ready co-operation of the officials concerned with the intake of employees has done much to dispel the image of the past.[23]

This growing cohort of younger workers, attached to their jobs and their long-term future in the mining industry, were willing to take more risks, were more politically attuned to the politics of their own time, and had fewer attachments to the principles and historic meaning of post-war nationalisation. They certainly had less time for the perceived 'aloofness' of the NUM concerning coal board policy making and the pragmatic, even 'right-wing' approach of the NUM to the state as employer.

The tipping point came in October 1969 with the surfacemen's strike, a moment later referred to by miners active in the 1972 and 1974 strikes as the 'October Revolution'. Two years earlier, in the summer of 1967, the National Coal Board announced the closure of Cefn Coed Colliery in the Dulais Valley, causing public protests led by the colliery lodge. These successfully prompted the Labour government to call a halt to the planned closures in October 1967, ostensibly to avoid winter hardship, but it was only a temporary delay. On 14 February 1968, the *Western Mail* carried the news that Cefn Coed would be shut down at the end of March. But the Prime Minister, Harold Wilson, was due in South Wales the following day and part of his tour was scheduled to pass through Crynant, and indeed by the colliery. Outside the colliery gates a crowd of protestors had gathered. Wilson decided to avoid the protest altogether and not to stop in the village, doing little to defuse the situation on the ground. Instead he issued a statement insisting that the procedures to close Cefn Coed had not been completed – all that remained was a report on the likely economic and social impact of closure – and that no formal decision had therefore been made. The report was duly written and submitted to Richard Marsh, the Minister of Power, who signed off the closure. It had been delayed by one month. Memories of the Cefn Coed closure led Dai Francis to reflect, years later, that:

> The Labour government which was returned in 1964, either Wilson forgot what he told the miners or they conveniently betrayed what they had said. But the fact of the matter is that

more pits were closed [...] during the period of the Labour government than there was under the Tories. It was a complete betrayal of the miners by the Wilson government. I wouldn't go so far as to call it a Labour government, I call it a Wilson government.[24]

Behind the scenes, the Wilson government had been debating how to implement their policy of providing low cost energy whilst mitigating the effects of 'readjustment' (that is, closure of expensive collieries) on regional economies and local communities. In a memorandum to the cabinet, Tony Benn argued that 'we must continue to give social help to the coal industry [...] if we do not, we must look forward to the worsening of our regional problems and we may damage morale or even risk industrial unrest'. Although there was broad agreement on the need to pare down levels of employment, to close unprofitable sites, and to look towards tapering off support by 1974.[25] In light of what had occurred in South Wales in the summer of 1967, cabinet agreed in November that year that 'much depended on the timing of closures'. Perhaps most interesting of all, in retrospect, was the belief amongst ministers that the most ardent opposition to the government's closure programme was not from the miners themselves but from the parliamentary miners' group and that the NUM were therefore in the awkward position of trying to convince their members of the need for pit closures in certain places to preserve the long-term economic viability of the industry whilst miners' MPs were agitating in opposition to any scheme.[26]

Whatever the broad merits of that perspective, it was soon overtaken by events in Yorkshire. In October 1969, nearly seventy thousand miners struck across the Yorkshire coalfield in support of wage claims by surface workers.[27] These men were the lowest paid in the mining industry and were typically those who had been invalided out of work underground either through accidents or diseases such as silicosis. Efforts to improve their wages had been ongoing for several years and in 1968 the NUM national executive agreed to help surface workers in their wage campaign. But the pace of change was slow and in the context of colliery closures and the apparent ambivalence of the NUM leadership to them, the issue became the focal point of wider frustrations and emerging militancy. The Yorkshire strikers were soon joined by workers at four pits in Scotland and another near Coventry in the West Midlands.[28] As the strike grew, with seventy five thousand out in Yorkshire and over three thousand in Scotland, pits in South Wales began to join in: by the 16 October nearly six thousand miners in the region were out and six pits in the centre of the coalfield shut down entirely – Cwm, Tower, Fernhill, Deep Navigation, Taff-Merthyr, and Coedely. The Tredegar workshops were also affected.[29] By the end of the strike's first week this had risen to sixteen thousand miners from twenty four pits, the core group had increased to nine including the Lady Windsor in Ynysybwl, Maerdy, and Wern Tarw.[30]

In interviews with the press, Dai Francis expressed regret at the outbreak of unofficial action, although thought it was 'understandable in the view of the stand made by the Yorkshire miners'.[31] The South Wales Area president, Glyn Williams, went further demanding that those lodges that had gone out fall back into line.[32] It was to no avail. The strike's leaders in South Wales, men such as Ron Saint (Coedely) and Cliff True (Fernhill, Rhondda), many of them communists, pointed to a change of attitude amongst the workforce. 'Men are realising that the pits will be closed whether they strike or not', they argued, 'and we might as well get the best out of it while we can'.[33] Saint had already warned that 'some of the best lodges in the coalfield' would strike anyway, in contravention of the line taken by the

Area executive.[34] The dilemma that faced the Area was whether it was to fragment or act in a unified manner. In the event, although South Wales did not act uniformly in the two-week strike, it was nevertheless one of the two major storm centres, alongside Yorkshire and gave considerable encouragement to the militants in the face of what they regarded as supine Area and national leadership (notably the NUM president Sidney Ford).

At the South Wales Area conference on 22 October 1969, members of the executive committee were mobbed by striking miners, and the left-wing NUM general secretary Lawrence Daly was jostled and booed outside the TUC headquarters in London at around the same time.[35] Seeking to build on the initiative of the strike, to harness increasing militancy within the NUM, and to effect a leadership change within the union, the strike leaders in the various coalfields formed a national unofficial strike committee to coordinate their activities into the 1970s. Ron Saint explained its purpose at the South Wales Area Conference held on 18 November 1969, making deliberate reference to the unofficial reform committee of an earlier age. He said:

> This Unofficial Committee is no frivolity. [...] The Cambrian strike of 1910-11 was an unofficial action, but this achieved the minimum wage. The unofficial movement was never at any time a dual leadership but a ginger group. The struggle will continue providing this is what the rank and file want. We will decide when to disband and this Union will never quite be the same as it was prior to the strike.[36]

Industrial history had begun to seep back into union activity, informing and guiding trade union action.[37] It was to the South Walian radical tradition that this new 'unofficial reform movement' looked for intellectual inspiration. In 1973, a new edition of the *Miners' Next Step* was published by Pluto Press with a foreword by Merfyn Jones, bringing into contemporary circulation the ideas of industrial democracy, antagonism towards leadership that had grown respectable by its accommodation with the state and institutions of power, and emphasis on rank-and-file movements that stood up for themselves.[38] The relative concentration of the unofficial movement in a small number of pits in the central coalfield – in an echo of its original formation – serves as a reminder that the process of radicalisation in South Wales after 1969 was precisely that – a process. There was a need to win over lodges that had been reluctant to take part in 1969 and to convince the Area leadership, with its attendant concerns about fragmentation of coalfield unity, that strike action was essential to winning the fight against the complete rundown of the industry.

It was not a straightforward process. Dai Francis, the leading communist in the Area, fell out of favour with the militants because of his reluctance to endorse unofficial action. And there was relatively little engagement with the left-wing initiatives evident in Yorkshire, notably the Miners' Forum, a rank-and-file organisation centred on Arthur Scargill that took responsibility for organising the 1972 miners' strike in that coalfield and provided a platform for Scargill's successful bid to become Yorkshire Area President the following year.[39] The closest contact the South Wales militants had with the Miners' Forum was through Emlyn Williams, a Labour Party member, who attended meetings and was tasked with spreading its influence in the South Wales Coalfield.[40] But Williams was a pragmatist and determined to preserve the unity of the South Wales Area and the resultant lack of pace in growing the influence of the Miners' Forum in South Wales earned him criticism from more militant – and communist – activists.[41]

But unity was essential to the conduct of official strike action, such as occurred in 1972 and 1974. The former, as Dai Francis later reflected, was the culmination of rising frustration across the whole of the NUM; it was 'when the miners told the coal board if this is the kind of wages that you're paying us, well you can run the industry yourselves. And it was the most successful strike in the history of the British miners'.[42] The 1972 miners' strike, the first national strike since 1926, lasted seven weeks and was the first successful national miners dispute since the minimum wage strike of 1912. It succeeded in part because it drew on widespread support outside of the industry, including from dockers, colliery office workers, petro-chemical workers, local authorities, transport workers, the unemployed and pensioners' organisations.[43] Women too were active in picketing and campaigning, foreshadowing the effective and significant intervention of women onto the front lines of the 1984-5 miners' strike.[44] A second victory for the miners in 1974 cemented the resurgence of the left within the NUM, much to the frustration of Joe Gormley, the NUM president, and the wealthier coalfields in the Midlands which were antagonistic to the militancy of Yorkshire, South Wales, and Scotland.

These antagonisms weakened any potential for unity across the NUM. The divergence was especially apparent in 1977 when Joe Gormley negotiated with the Callaghan government and the National Coal Board the introduction of a new incentive bonus scheme that, in effect, broke the principle of collective bargaining on wage increases that had been central to the NUM's industrial strategy for decades. Indeed, it had been one of the central reasons for creating a single mineworker's union in the first place. Championing the incentive bonus scheme was the Nottinghamshire Area, which stood to benefit, whereas the South Wales Area was deeply hostile for many of the same reasons of geology that had prompted South Wales miners to insist on national wage bargaining. In their connivance,

Gormley and the wealthier coalfields had split the NUM setting those Areas most supportive of incentivisation against those most hostile to it. It was a fracture that was clearly apparent in the 1984-5 miners' strike. As Hywel Francis observed in the aftermath of that dispute, 'all the disunity which manifested itself directly or indirectly ... stemmed from ... the introduction of the incentive bonus scheme in 1977-78'.[45] It was but a prelude, however, of the disaster that was to come.

The Year of the Plague

On 12 January 1978, Barry Constituency Labour Party met for its monthly management meeting. During that meeting, the constituency's prospective parliamentary candidate, Peter Stead, then a lecturer in history at University College Swansea, told members that '1978 will almost certainly be an election year' and that 'if the Labour government is to be returned with a working majority Barry is just the type of marginal which has to be won'.[46] For many months, the constituency party were convinced that the election was coming and worked on that basis, but this was also a constituency which was concerned at the direction in which party policy was heading.[47] Resolutions appeared opposing the extension of Welsh medium education, with the Penarth branch going as far as to declare that 'other aspects of education in Wales which deserved greater priority might well suffer'.[48] Then in October 1978, a motion to support devolution was defeated – a blow to Stead, who was pro-devolution.[49] In January 1979, Stead again spoke to constituency colleagues. Warning that a victory for the Conservatives would be a disaster, he reflected on the industrial situation which was in his view equally 'disastrous'. He continued: 'the unions have alienated public sympathy. The government has made mistakes, particularly in its handling of the low pay problem. There should be agitation for a low wage policy'.[50] The following month, the day before the devolution referendum, the constituency secretary warned that there was a low level of activity in Barry and that the vote would prove to be an anti-climax.[51]

The next day, 1 March 1979, after a decade of thought and consideration about the form and function of 'home rule', Wales voted on Labour's devolution proposals. Officially, the Labour Party campaigned for a yes vote, but six South Wales MPs broke rank and opposed, articulately but no less vociferously, what they regarded as a sop to the nationalists. Others had expressed misgivings in private. This 'gang of six' comprised Ifor Davies (Gower), Donald Anderson (Swansea East), Ioan Evans (Aberdare), Fred Evans (Caerphilly), Leo Abse (Pontypool), and, most high profile of all, Neil Kinnock (Bedwellty). Even the prime minister, James Callaghan, was fearful of the impact devolution would have on the integrity of the government.[52] In favour were most of Labour's MPs from outside the South Wales Coalfield, the Communist Party, and the South Wales Area of the NUM. Plaid Cymru, naturally, was active in support of devolution although the Communist Party regarded that support as 'only an opportunity to be seized to attempt to destroy the Labour Party'.[53] The referendum failed spectacularly (but unsurprisingly) with nearly one million votes against compared with around a quarter of a million in favour. Nearly ten thousand more had voted yes in Mid Glamorgan than in Gwynedd, the council area with the highest proportion of yes voters. Devolution ceased to be a viable means of renewal. For a generation anyway.

Two months later, on 3 May 1979, Britain went to the polls. Labour lost the General Election and the Conservative Party, led by Margaret Thatcher, entered office determined to solve the economic problems the country appeared to face. Considered as an electoral map, the 1979 general election did not really alter the political landscape of South Wales all that much: Labour regained Carmarthen having lost it in October 1974, but lost Brecon and Radnor for the first time since the 1939 by-election. In coalfield seats such as Rhondda, Labour's majority was still over thirty thousand and its percentage of the vote more than seventy five percent. Neil Kinnock even increased his share of the vote in Bedwellty, whereas the Plaid Cymru candidate lost his deposit. The bigger electoral earthquake came in 1983 after four years of internal wrangling, the formation of the Social Democratic Party (SDP), and the issue of a left-wing manifesto to the electorate that was clearly not universally welcomed. Labour's majority in the Rhondda, indicatively, fell by almost ten thousand. But 1979 did mark the beginning of a new kind of politics. Almost immediately, Labour activists found themselves challenging public expenditure cuts and there were calls within the party for more democratisation and a change of party leader.[54]

Within a year of the election, the Barry constituency found itself in the doldrums. There were fewer than five hundred members on the register, relatively few new members to speak of, and many of those who had previously been active had let their membership lapse.[55] The more active members pulled the constituency party to the left, virulently opposing those disposed to the Council for Social Democracy (the forerunner of the Social Democratic Party) and insisting on the 'implementation of Clause IV and the present policies of the Labour Party'.[56] Its motion to the 1981 Labour conference called for the next Labour government to withdraw from the EEC, to commit to unilateral nuclear disarmament, to implement full employment, to bring financial institutions into public ownership, to control foreign investment, and to restore Aneurin Bevan's model of the NHS.[57] The situation in Barry contrasted with constituency parties in the coalfield, for instance Cynon Valley. There an almost even split developed between those who supported Denis Healey for deputy leader and those who sided with Tony Benn. When the constituency vote was held in September 1981, nine voted for Benn, eight for Healey, with one abstention.[58] Nor was this divide properly healed: in August 1983, there was again an even split in favour of Michael Meacher (the left candidate) and Roy Hattersley (the centrist candidate).[59]

Alongside these debates, there was the rise of the Militant tendency, stoking the idea that, in the words of one activist from Cardiff, 'the previous Labour administration had pursued Tory policies at a lower level [which] the present Tory administration would take up in earnest'. Although never that powerful in South Wales, Militant did have a strong presence in Cardiff and Swansea, both cities where it had full-time offices and where it fought vitriolic campaigns against the Swansea West MP, Alan Williams, and James Callaghan in Cardiff South East.[60] And in the Cynon Valley there was concern that young people were being pestered to join Militant and that they were at risk because the far left were 'extremely persuasive'.[61] In the end, Militant faded, and Labour were saved by a turn towards a renewed form of radical pragmatism – a recognition of the need to develop a practical alternative to Thatcherism that was both popular and meaningful, rather than adopt a rejectionist mode of grievance politics that was far easier to pursue. Yet, the Labour Party which was emerging in the early 1980s was not entirely like the one which had existed twenty years earlier when its power rested on the strength of the NUM: it was under pressure to engage more fully with different minorities and many women who had been part of the women's liberation movement in the 1970s entered Labour in this period convinced that it, not a nationalist alternative such as Plaid Cymru, was the vehicle to bring about meaningful change.[62]

This offers us, then, a different perspective to what has become the generally accepted view of South Wales (and Wales more generally) in the aftermath of the 1979 referendum and general election. The standard view draws on the contemporary despair of certain intellectuals who regarded that moment as 'the year of the plague' whereby out of the crisis came the urgent need to reassert a singular Welshness. Much of the debate rested on ideas of Welsh identity and Welsh culture and what it was all about. 'The production of history in Wales', wrote Dai Smith in 1983, 'is now a battleground on which rival armies contend to dispel the confusion. It is not just an academic matter, even though the scholars enter the fray'.[63] One of the first to do so was Gwyn Alf Williams. Asked to deliver the annual BBC Wales radio lecture in the autumn of 1979, he posed the question 'When Was Wales?', concluding that

> There is no historical necessity for Wales; there is no historical necessity for a Welsh people or a Welsh nation. Wales will not exist unless the Welsh want it. It is not compulsory to want it. Plenty of people who are biologically Welsh choose not to be Welsh. That act of choice is beyond reason. One thing, however, is clear from our history. If we want Wales, we will have to make Wales.[64]

But what was Wales? It was, as Dai Smith noted in the opening words of the television series *Wales! Wales?* in 1984, not a singular thing but a plurality.[65] There was not a single 'Welsh' history, but many. And the recognition of that was necessary to understand why what happened in Tonypandy or Merthyr did not happen in Tregaron or Machynlleth. Why Tryweryn could safely be ignored but Taff Vale could not be. As he concluded, 'the meaning of Wales is "a cherished myth" since only that can support the fantasy of historical integrity' because 'the quintessential nature of Welshness this century is that of divided sensibility'.[66]

That division was entirely apparent in the television series *The Dragon Has Two Tongues* which broadcast between 1984 and 1985. It was not merely the debate between the Liberal Romantic Wynford Vaughan Thomas and the Marxist-Nationalist Gwyn Alf Williams that exposed the fractured Welsh past, but also the topics they chose to emphasise. Nor was the series originally intended to be a debate, but a singular vehicle for Vaughan Thomas. With the inclusion of Colin Thomas as director, the series changed into the dialectic form soon familiar to audiences, although the original choice of counterpoint, Angela John, was vetoed by Vaughan Thomas. The series had two major points of division: nation and class. Of the former, both presenters were convinced of the existence of a Welsh nation that could be measured and considered, but they differed sharply only on whether it was a timeless thing or something more temporally specific. On class, there was sharper debate. And yet this was a series that set out to trace Welsh history from the prehistoric to the contemporary in a broadly linear narrative for all the attempt in the first episode to suggest otherwise; this was also evident in the accompanying publications. The Romans came and went, Edward I built his castles, then came industrialisation, Tryweryn, and the miners' strike.

In his summary of the early 1980s, Wynford Vaughan Thomas stressed the industrial integration of Wales with the rest of Britain, noting that an industrial strike in South Wales was little different from one in the north of England or the west of Scotland. Nor was there any profound contradiction in that statement since the old certainties of identity seemed to be on the way out. As to the miners' strike: 'was there anything specifically Welsh in this', he pondered. The response from Gwyn Alf Williams was a straightforward, yes. But on what measure? There were those who, during the strike, declared it to be a 'regional crusade' but no real answer was given in the television series itself, except insofar as the strike was depicted as a 'last ditch stand against the death of Wales'.[67] The Wales at stake in 1984-5, of course, was not the Wales of Aberystwyth or Gwynedd or the farmland surrounding Lampeter, but industrial South Wales – Labour Country – which Wynford Vaughan Thomas correctly asserted was linked to the rest of Britain by the power of economics. He might also have pointed to the unionism of the labour movement. There can be little doubt, in retrospect, that the miners' strike posed questions for a Labour Party unclear about its own direction of travel, but opposed vehemently still to either nationalism or the sectarian left. It was to prove a difficult balance, exacerbated by the miners' strike itself.

The Great Strike

By now it is almost a cliché to say that the 1984-5 miners' strike marked the major turning point in the history of the British labour movement. Rhetoric aside, between March 1984 and March 1985, thousands endured bitter hardship and poverty to keep, so they believed, their jobs, to maintain the industry that had been the principal employer in mining communities for generations, and to sustain some element of life in those places. But it was in vain. The defeat of the NUM, the most iconic of postwar trade unions, albeit then no longer the largest and most powerful, shattered both the militant strategy that had been responsible for the fall of the Conservative government a decade earlier and the industry that it aimed at saving, leaving the communities to pick up the pieces and the Labour Party in South Wales, at least, with the need to rethink its mode of organisation. Miners, together with their communities and supporters, were readily characterised in private by the government as the 'enemy within', as the direct antagonist of British democracy and the British way of life.[68] It had been, in fact, the intention of the government to apply the same phrase to the entire labour movement, to discredit the Labour Party and its leader Neil Kinnock, but the Brighton bombing in the autumn of 1984 prevented that course of action.[69] Given how virulently Kinnock was being attacked from the left, perhaps that did not matter.

As in 1969, the 1984-5 strike began in the Yorkshire coalfield; and like that earlier dispute there was considerable disquiet in South Wales as to whether an all-out strike was warranted. There was undoubtedly lingering hostility towards the Yorkshire miners for their failure to support a strike over the closure of the Lewis Merthyr Colliery in the Rhondda the previous year, and there was certainly disquiet about the validity of a strike that lacked a national ballot to provide legitimacy. An Area ballot took place on 11 March 1984 with eleven of the twenty eight collieries in South Wales (or forty percent) voting against joining in. The press was excited and claimed a 'Welsh revolt'. Emlyn Williams, the Area president, conceded that he had 'never before encountered a rejection like this'. Some miners expressed sentiments such as 'Yorkshire owes us a fortnight, make them sweat', but many others had to be picketed out. For all that South Wales remained solid throughout the course of the strike, it was never entirely certain that the Area would join the dispute in the first place. Nevertheless, by 14 March, after concerted picketing of the reluctant pits, every colliery in South Wales had been shut down and every miner pulled out on strike.

With the South Wales Area solid, miners joined in the picketing of other pits around the country, including in Yorkshire and North Wales. One group, from St John's Colliery in Maesteg, ended up at the notoriously conservative Woolley Colliery near Barnsley where they were confronted by a contingent of police from Surrey. In the early days of the strike, relations were good natured and the Maesteg men could even share a joke with the police about a man racing past on a motorcycle. 'There's enough police here', the miners shouted, 'you could book him for speeding'. The local press recorded that the 'policemen raised a smile'.[70] Humour was vital for pickets who were stationed far from home. In a diary kept during the first weeks of the strike, Alun Jones, the vice chair of Maerdy Lodge, noted the hardships the men faced: sleeping in the back of transit vans in cold weather and the attitude of strikebreakers who laughed at them. By the end of March, however, the jokes shared between the police and the striking miners stopped and relations soured. The police, remarked Jones, 'are more brutal than ever'. A few days later, he wrote that things had got worse. 'Our anger is beginning to boil over. There is no justice any longer. They mean to destroy us as a union, then attack the trade union movement and labour movement. The people will have to choose what they want'.[71]

Looking back at the 1984-5 miners' strike with our gaze fixed on the support groups, the Wales Congress in Support of Mining Communities, the sacrifices made by miners and their families, and the diverse range of organisations that stood in solidarity with mining communities, it is hard not to feel a certain sense of regret that this has subsequently disappeared. Speaking at the women in struggle workshop held during the London-Wales Congress in Support of Mining Communities rally in March 1985, Angela John remarked that 'where communities are threatened, it rekindles the community spirit'. That is the lasting impression of the strike, and the result held onto by historian-activists and, in recent years, film-makers. But does it really help to think of the 1984-5 strike in those terms? For although there was a degree of unity, there was also diversity of opinion and action, and the coalfield was already an attenuated one. In the Rhondda, for example, there was just one colliery left open by 1984 (Maerdy) and across South Wales miners were a minority of the workforce. 1984-5 was not 1926. What the strike did do was throw into sharp relief the economic fragility of a region that had yet to develop a response either to the final withdrawal of coal or to the questions posed by Thatcherism.

In late November 1984, the industrial committee of Rhondda Borough Council received a 'dismal report' into unemployment in the borough. Of the twelve hundred young people eligible to leave school that summer, just sixty one had found a job. Unemployment in the Rhondda was twenty five percent. In neighbouring Cynon Valley, the equivalent committee heard that the unemployment rate there was over twenty percent, with young people out of work at a rate of more than one in every three. Barbara Williams, one of the leading women's activists in Maerdy, told an ITN news journalist what these figures meant for the young people of her community:

> If you were to go along the road and say to those young boys, what would you rather do, would you rather go and sign the dole or would you rather go to work at the colliery? They'll answer you: I'd rather go to work at the colliery. I know of boys that have walked up to that colliery to put their names down, begging to be taken on.

But coal mining could not provide the definitive answer anymore. It was seized on now only in the absence of any real long-term replacement for the industry. As one young miner explained in an interview with the BBC, the industry had become one in which short term work was the norm. We've worked, he said, 'then get laid off, get a job and work a month then get laid off ... it's ridiculous ... I'm twenty-six years old and this is my third pit I've worked'. Nor was he alone in that experience. The plea from many in the coalfield was a simple one: 'give us employment for our youngsters to have a life'.[72] Likewise Kath Evans, who served as secretary of the South Wales Women's Support Group during the strike, explained in a speech to the London-Wales Congress that 'the women knew that if the pits closed their children would either have to leave the valleys or be condemned to the dole queues'.

Those same children began to switch off from formal education. As one group of women from Maerdy reflected in interviews with the BBC, children as young as twelve refused to study for exams in school because they saw no purpose to and few opportunities arising from education. To pick up from an interview with Barbara Williams:

> If you've got children and they're willing to stay in school, get an education, you keep them in school and you know damn well at the end there's nothing for them. That's hellish hard to take.[73]

The long-term effects of this turn away from education are apparent: in 2004, a Welsh Government survey noted that a quarter of adults had entry level (or lower) literacy skills and more than half had entry level or lower numeracy skills.[74] Given the likely economic and social impact of the drawdown of mining on the family unit, as well as the future prospects of children, women were activated in the strike in ways that neither the women's liberation movement nor the organised women's sections of the Labour Party had previously been able to achieve. Women formed support groups which often provided the administrative and logistical organisation of food and clothing; they took part in direct action such as picketing and occupation of collieries, and provided the communal labour that enabled men to take part in pickets elsewhere in the country.[75]

Many of those involved in the women's organisations have

reflected on the positive benefits. Margaret Donovan, from the Dulais Valley, noted that before the strike 'I didn't really get to know anybody but since the strike, I know a terrific amount, and we are all good friends now. That's one good thing about it really: got me out of the house'.[76] Politicisation was rapid and transformative. Siân James, future MP for Swansea East, who was active with Margaret Donovan in the Neath, Dulais and Swansea Valleys' group, recalled:

> Through my involvement with other women who were active in the strike, I started going to the Miners' Welfare Hall in Onllwyn – or the Palace of Culture, as it was called. Here's where I had the chance to take part in creating action plans as well as discussions about the politics of the strike. Before long, those discussions turned into broader political debates.[77]

Freed from aspects of domestic labour – notably childcare, which was undertaken by her husband, Martin, who was on strike – she, and the other women on the committee, felt themselves part of the 'wider political *scene*'.[78] That meant debating issues common to the women's liberation movement, and eventually adopting much the same language and subject matter. In effect creating a new women's movement located within the wider labour movement; after all, the economic effects of the strike were not only felt by men. At the first official meeting of the South Wales Women's Support Groups' Committee, held at the Cwm Institute in Beddau in August 1984, one of the agenda points was 'to arrange adoptions by outside groups to provide toiletries that the women need'.[79] The language of liberation was powerfully expressed a few months later when, speaking at the *Pits and Perverts* benefit concert at the Camden Electric Ballroom in December 1984, Hefina Headon, secretary of the Neath, Dulais and Swansea Valleys' Miners' Support Group, declared 'the women of South Wales have been liberated. We had no idea of the power we had. That will not be suppressed. We will never go back to sitting at home'.[80]

Margaret Donovan took up the theme in her address to the 'women in struggle' workshop at the London-Wales Congress, and explained how this new current of women's liberation had come about:

> At first women in the mining communities were just raising money and packing food parcels, but then these became secondary to taking part in meetings, and speaking at political rallies and meetings then became more important. It was the first time for many women that they had been out of the house not looking after the children. The struggle during the strike had become the focal point, the family secondary.[81]

She insisted that the energy of the strike should be turned into providing opportunities for women to be involved in public life in normal times. 'Crèche facilities were needed', she said, 'these and nursery facilities must be fought for'. These were direct echoes of the women's liberation movement of the previous decade. As Jenny Lynn, a leading women's liberation activist in Swansea in the 1970s, has observed, the discussion in that earlier period focused on 'childhood, parental care, consciousness raising', the group also produced its own handbook on pregnancy and looking after children in their early years.[82] In the aftermath of the strike, women's groups established organisations such as the DOVE Workshop in Banwen that provided educational opportunities, training, and advice on small business start-up, mirroring initiatives such as the South Glamorgan Women's Workshop founded just before the strike broke out.[83] The latter provided courses to women in computing and microelectronics.[84]

Those debates mattered because it was women, not men, who bore the brunt of the economic transformations of the 1980s, particularly during the recession in the early part of the decade, and they did so regardless of the miners' strike. By the late-1980s, women made up between a third and half the Welsh workforce but many of them were in part-time or casualised work – not entirely out of choice – in catering, supermarkets, and other areas of the service sector. Only half were unionised.[85] Writing in the aftermath of the strike, Victoria Winckler described the 'new and deeply entrenched differences ... between men and women'.[86] And in 1988, Teresa Rees observed the

> strategies used by employers to ensure a flexible workforce, the recalcitrance of trades unions to involve their female members at decision making levels, and the persistence of the traditional patterns of domestic divisions of labour combine to ensure that women, rather than being the vanguard of the labour movement, are likely to remain a numerically substantial, but distinctly disadvantaged section of the workforce.[87]

It may well be, as Hywel Francis has recently written, that the 'most benign and lasting legacies from the strike ... involve women' but this tells only part of the story of what was going on in this period. The challenges women faced, particularly as workers, were not overcome by their role in support groups during the strike.

Indeed, it is important that we consider the strike carefully and avoid ascribing too much of an historical legacy to themes and agents that were significant in their own localised context but relatively marginal to the broader picture. In other words, what took place in the Dulais, Neath, and upper Swansea valleys, was not what took place, for example, in the Rhondda or Cynon Valley which were much larger, more populous areas, and more difficult contexts overall in which to build either a 'broad democratic alliance' between various liberation interests or a pan-Wales alliance. If we trace the lines of support from Welsh-speaking communities in North Wales or Ceredigion, these end up chiefly in Welsh-speaking mining communities in the anthracite coalfield in the Gwendraeth or Dulais valleys, not in the Gwent Food Fund, for instance, or in Penrhiwceiber in the Cynon Valley.[88] Likewise, the London-based Lesbians and Gays Support the Miners, which had its origins in the Communist Party and the Labour left, focused its attention on the Dulais Valley, and although a similar lesbian and gay group from Southampton had links to Abercynon Colliery, and lesbians and gays did raise money in Cardiff and Swansea, these had none of the presence in larger mining communities that LGSM had in a small one.

Support for Maerdy, in the Rhondda, came initially from the Labour Party in Bristol and subsequently from Oxford and Cambridge, whose support groups also provided assistance to miners from Merthyr Vale and Abertillery (respectively); Maerdy also enjoyed the support of activists from the Netherlands including young members of the Dutch Labour Party and trade unionists who organised holidays for miners' children, solidarity evenings and collection weeks, and held a range of benefit concerts in Amsterdam, Maastricht, Rotterdam, and Leiden. Support flowed into the Rhymney Valley from France and West Germany, notably the steel town Ludwigsburg which had twinned with Caerphilly in 1960. The Cynon Valley Miners' Support Group was twinned with the Islington Miners' Support Group and enjoyed the support of the Turkish community in London. And money also flowed into Maerdy and Maesteg from both the miners' support group and the women's support group established by Birmingham Trades Council.[89] There was little directly 'Welsh' about this kind of fundraising activity or where it came from and it should serve as a reminder that, as with LGSM, the lines of support for mining communities in South Wales were, international links aside, largely British.

Moreover, and despite the hostility levelled then (and still) at the national leadership, the Labour Party was key to all of these lines of support. The Cardiff Miners' Support Group, for example, was established in early April 1984 on the initiative of the Cardiff Central and Cardiff West CLPs, drawing support from branches in Barry and Penarth as well.[90] Torfaen CLP organised collections for the Cwmbran miners' support group to go alongside the money and food raised from collections outside supermarkets and through jumble sales, raffles, and concerts. Even in the Dulais Valley, the question of how to support pickets away from home led to connections being built with host communities through the national structures of the Labour Party. 'I hit on the idea of ringing up Walworth Road [Labour Party Headquarters]', remarked Dai Donovan in an interview with Hywel Francis in 1986, 'and asking them for the secretary of the nearest Labour Party ward to where the boys were going'.[91] During his conversations he explained that the pickets were coming up and asked whether they could offer a bed for the night or something as simple as a cup of tea. In areas where the Labour Party ran the council, such as Rhondda, Cynon Valley, or Rhymney, this level of support went further still.[92]

In the Rhondda, the chief executive of the Borough Council met with the NUM and assured them that the council would go as far as legally possible in supporting the miners and placed a council van and buildings at the union's disposal. Following sequestration in the summer of 1984, a special trust fund was established, known as the Mayor and MP for Rhondda Distress Fund for Miners and their Families. Those on strike, together with their relatives, were given access to council leisure facilities and the cinema at the Park and Dare Hall at a fifty per cent reduction and the council issued food vouchers to the value of ten pounds. Similar efforts took place in neighbouring Cynon Valley, where food storage facilities at council-run day centres were made available, free use of leisure facilities granted, and substantial sums of money donated to the miners' support fund. An initial grant of five thousand pounds was made in July 1984, with a follow up of ten thousand pounds in late September 1984. As in the Rhondda, a mayor's fund was established. In the Rhymney Valley, the council authorised the use of council vans to deliver food, issued cards to striking families to enable them to use leisure facilities for free, and issued a substantial number of food vouchers.

Taff Ely council were a little more cautious in the action that they took, in part because more prosperous areas were less enthusiastic and advice from officers was mixed. Although the council made a permanent loan of a meals-on-wheels van to distribute food around the district, granted use of leisure facilities at the same rate as the unemployed (ten pence a session), and set up a mayor's fund, they initially stopped short of donating money directly to the local support fund on the advice of the district auditor. This decision was eventually reversed in November 1984 when the council authorised a donation of ten thousand pounds to enable the purchase of food for those on strike. One of the ways that the Taff Ely Mayor's Fund was intended to be financed was through collections at rugby matches. Although most clubs were amenable, some actively refused to permit collections to take place – hinting at some of the tensions in the district that the strike manifested. Similar tensions were evident amongst the student body at University College Cardiff, which in May 1984 elected a Conservative-dominated sabbatical team. Reticence on campus, as well as the logistics of student holidays, meant that the student miners' support group was not established until October 1984. The group had to raise funds from the steps of the student union building because Cardiff City Council banned street collections in support of the strike.

Such efforts by the Labour Party and community groups maintained miners and their families for a year, but that was all that they could do. They could neither defeat the government nor extend the strike beyond its immediate industrial-political purpose. The NUM national leadership, not least the union president, Arthur Scargill, was focused on the struggle for jobs and preventing pit closures, as well as delivering a bloody nose to the Thatcher government. Scargill's sense of the strike, which stressed the exclusive validity of industrial action, was not the same as the struggle imagined by those who had an investment in different ideas altogether. This became very apparent in the winter of 1984-5, as the strike neared its end. Writing in *Marxism Today*, Hywel Francis pressed the case for viewing the strike in South Wales as having provided the conditions for a 'broad democratic alliance'. He wrote:

What emerges is a network of the unexpected alliances which go far beyond the traditional labour movement. It is a broad democratic alliance of a new kind – an anti-Thatcher alliance – in which the organized working class has a central role but a role which henceforth it will have to earn and not to assume.

In this potentially permanent anti-Thatcher alliance, the women's movement and the peace movement will have prominence because, unlike the bulk of the trade union and labour movement during the run-up to the miners' strike, they have played a crucial role in raising the political consciousness of the British people. It is even conceivable that the churches will have a part in such an alliance because they have raised very pertinent political, social and moral questions during the strike concerning the nature and role of the state and of the dehumanizing character of capitalism.[93]

A similar logic was employed by Kim Howells, then research officer for the South Wales Area, who criticised mass picketing in the last weeks of the strike and in its aftermath posited the idea that a 'new kind of politics' had potentially emerged.[94] As he wrote later:

> At one moment, during a street battle outside a cokeworks in the Aberdare valley, there were visitors from six different countries watching or participating in the event. A film crew from Japan worked alongside crews from Paris, London and Cardiff. A week later, a benefit concert at Onllwyn was partly paid for by several gay and lesbian groups from London and the food provided by a London Turkish Society.[95]

The idea of a 'broad democratic alliance' was championed at precisely the time that behind the scenes, and in meetings in isolated places such as Llanwynno, a hamlet nestled between the Rhondda and Cynon valleys, there were moves to bring the strike to an orderly conclusion without a settlement – paradoxically, precisely the aim of the Thatcher government.[96] The 'broad democratic alliance' was based on experiences, chiefly, of the strike in the Neath, Dulais and Swansea valleys, and sustained by the intellectual debates evident within the Communist Party at that time.[97] It was not indicative of circumstances elsewhere in South Wales where such alliances were much harder to forge and had not really developed. Nevertheless, the irony of South Wales, traditionally seen as the most militant district, but which had been initially reluctant to strike and was now leading the return to work, was able to be explained by reference to this new alliance and to the need to preserve the NUM's integrity and unity.[98] If the anti-Thatcher alliance was 'potentially permanent' and was not to be led either by the trade union movement or by the Labour Party, it no longer needed the incubating context of the strike. The strike, therefore, could come to an orderly conclusion without threatening the 'new politics'.[99] Although soon reflections turned to 'coming to terms with defeat'.[100]

The most substantial outcome of the broad democratic alliance was the Wales Congress in Support of Mining Communities, which launched in October 1984, and its offshoots such as the London-Wales Congress, which was launched in London on 9 March 1985.[101] The Wales Congress saw itself as part of the politics of anti-Thatcherism, perhaps the leading Welsh edge, and so campaigned for gay rights, women's liberation, was active in anti-racism activity, the fight to save the Greater London Council and its equalities agenda, and members supported later campaigns against Section 28 and health cuts at the end of the 1980s. Peter Keelan, a Plaid Cymru activist who attended the early Wales Congress rallies, recalled the atmosphere being akin to the 'rainbow coalition' of anti-apartheid activism.[102] The most tangible outcome from the Wales Congress was the pressure placed on the NUM and then by the NUM on the wider labour movement to vote in favour of the gay rights motion tabled at the 1985 Labour Party Conference, which it did, but even this did not become party policy until the policy review conducted in the aftermath of the 1987 general election. Dai Donovan's now famous, and admirable, declaration at the Pits and Perverts benefit gig at the Camden Electric Ballroom in early December 1984 stated that

You have worn our badge 'coal not dole', and you know what harassment means, as we do. Now we will pin your badge on

485

us, we will support you. It won't change overnight, but now one
hundred and forty thousand miners know that there are other
causes and other problems. We know about blacks, and gays,
and nuclear disarmament. And we will never be the same.

It may have been true, but relatively little really changed. The
Wales Congress was, in retrospect, a chimera; although its aims
of building politics based on a renewed sense of community
were undoubtedly laudable in principle. Even in the Dulais
Valley, it was women rather than the striking miners who were
the most important figures in forging and sustaining the alliance
with Lesbians and Gays Support the Miners and with other
support groups. The miners themselves, as Hywel Francis has
subsequently noted, were 'for the most part passive
participants'.[103] Their attention was, ultimately, on the
industrial struggle not the creation of a 'broad democratic
alliance'. In any case, the Wales Congress, as a front
organisation, which the Labour Party could not lead without
compromising itself as a political force, rested largely on the
very narrow (and rapidly shrinking) shoulders of the Communist
Party in Wales.[104] By October 1985, there were fewer than eight
hundred members compared with more than one thousand
during the strike, and by the end of 1986 that number had
shrunk to little more than six hundred.[105] The Congress was the
last major initiative the Communist Party were able to embark
on in Wales but it did not last. It was disbanded in 1986. The
Communist Party itself became a tiny segment in South Wales
after the strike and continued to decline before the formal
dissolution of the CPGB in November 1991. Both Kim Howells
and Hywel Francis became Labour MPs: for Pontypridd (in
1989) and Aberavon (in 2001) respectively.

The miners' strike itself ended in March 1985. Nearly ninety
five per cent of miners in South Wales remained out on strike

until the very end. They returned to work marching behind brightly coloured lodge banners proclaiming well-entrenched socialist slogans such as 'workers of the world unite', but they knew that they had been defeated. Seeking to lift the mood, lodge chairmen such as Tony Ciano of Cynheidre Colliery spoke out into the darkness on the first morning back:

> I am delighted that over eight hundred of you marched in – united – behind the lodge banner this morning. I am proud you did this because although many of you went back to work in the last few weeks you were driven back through despair and suffering and not through any lack of loyalty to the union or its struggles. You are *not* scabs.[106]

Cynheidre Colliery closed in 1989 with the loss of over one thousand jobs. The schedule of pit closures in the second half of the 1980s reads as lachrymal poetry. 1985: Aberpergwm, Abertillery, Bedwas, Garw, Penrhiwceiber, Margam, St John's and Treforgan. 1986: Cwm and Nantgarw. 1988: Abernant and Lady Windsor-Abercynon. 1989: Six Bells, Merthyr Vale, Oakdale. 1991: Deep Navigation, Penallta. 1993: Taff Merthyr. 1994: Tower. Tower Colliery was officially closed by British Coal on 22 April 1994, ending the deep mining of coal in South Wales. That was not, of course, quite the end of the story because Tower was bought out by its workforce and run successfully as a co-operative from 1995 until 2008. In the eyes of its supporters, Tower's last decade proved the viability of the South Wales mining industry and that pit closures had been unnecessary.

And yet the pits were closed and mining did disappear. Tower was the exception, not the rule. In the immediate aftermath of the strike, journalists, historians, and activists, conducted numerous interviews with those involved to understand what had happened and what the likely long-term effects were going to be. Miners, overall, were reflective, as the *Guardian* found when it visited Ynysybwl in 1986 and again in 1988, with older members of the community concerned about the future and younger people content to take their redundancy and escape the merry-go-round of pit closures, job losses, and short-termism.[107] The anger, on the other hand, little dissipated. It steadily turned, over time, into deep-rooted apathy and strong cynicism about political action and the political class. Turnout at general elections fell rapidly. In Rhondda in 1974 it was eighty percent, in 1997 still just over seventy percent, but by 2001 it was little more than sixty percent, or about fifteen thousand voters added to the rate of abstention. These figures were repeated in every seat in the former South Wales Coalfield. Industrially, politically, and culturally, the miners' strike was a failure. It hastened decline and its effects were far reaching. In addition to apathy, there was the emergence of a little considered precariat whose economic fragility, evident in the experiences of working women in the 1980s, was amplified in the steady removal of social security, of social housing, and of stable employment. Above all, there was deep-rooted poverty that seemed unable to be shaken off.

That remains the South Wales of today.

Notes

[1] *The Guardian*, 11 May 1970.

[2] *The Guardian*, 26 March 1970.

[3] *Sunday Express*, 12 April 1970.

[4] *MEx*, 10 May 1970.

[5] *MEx*, 25 June 1970.

[6] *The Times*, 2 July 1970; Alun Morgan, 'The 1970 Parliamentary Election at Merthyr Tydfil', *Morgannwg* 22 (1978), 74.

[7] Merfyn Jones, *Life on the Dole* (London, 1972), 74.

[8] As above, 79.

[9] See the correspondence regarding the 'defiance of the School Milk Act, 1971', in the Islwyn CLP papers held at the Gwent Archives (D3784.18/2) and in the Carmarthen CLP papers held at the Carmarthen Archives. George Thomas even went so far as to declare in the House of Commons that 'I am prepared to go to gaol myself'.

[10] BBC News, 3 December 1971 – the clip was tweeted by the BBC Archive feed; *The Guardian*, 4 December 1971.

[11] *MEx*, 13 May 1976.

[12] Dafydd Wigley, *O Ddifri* (Caernarfon, 1992), ch. 6.

[13] *MEx*, 10 May 1979.

[14] Duncan Tanner, 'Facing the New Challenge: Labour and Politics, 1970-2000', in Tanner et al (eds.), *The Labour Party in Wales*, 265.

[15] Although in the Dulais Valley, Plaid Cymru were regarded with suspicion as a party that had little real connection with the mining industry and as opportunist. John Sewel, *Colliery Closure and Social Change: A Study of a South Wales Mining Valley* (Cardiff, 1975), 13.

[16] Taff Ely Borough Council, *Annual Report, 1991-1992*, which notes the construction phases of leisure centres and indoor swimming pools in the district. The flagship Michael Sobell Leisure Centre was opened in Aberdare on 10 November 1970.

[17] Sewel, *Colliery*, 1.

[18] Sewel, *Colliery*, 5.

[19] Gwyn A. Williams, 'Women Workers in Wales, 1968-82', *WHR*, 11 (1983), 530.

[20] Direct elections to the European Parliament in 1979 did, however,

produce two women MEPs: Ann Clwyd (Labour) and Beata Brookes (Conservative), although neither represented South Wales.

[21] GA, Women's Advisory Council Minutes, 16 October 1976.

[22] *Report of the Fifty-Second Annual Conference of Labour Women*, 1976, p. 21.

[23] GA, D801/1/2, Glamorgan Education Committee, Youth Employment Service, Minutes and Reports of the Youth Employment Service, 1962-1974: 'Report of the Division Careers Officer for 1 October 1970-31 January 1971'.

[24] SWML, VID/30: 'Dai Francis Interview'.

[25] TNA, CAB/129/145: 'Fuel Policy and Assistance for the Coal Industry, 14 October 1969', 3.

[26] TNA, CAB 128/42/67: 'Cabinet Conclusions, 21 November 1967'.

[27] *The Guardian*, 13 October 1969.

[28] *The Guardian*, 15 October 1969.

[29] *The Guardian*, 16 October 1969; *Morning Star*, 17 October 1969.

[30] V. L. Allen, *The Militancy of British Miners* (Shipley, 1981), 156; Francis and Smith, *The Fed*, 493, fn. 109.

[31] *The Guardian*, 17 October 1969.

[32] *The Observer*, 19 October 1969.

[33] *WM*, 22 October 1969.

[34] SWML, South Wales Area (NUM), 'Special Conference, 14 October 1969'.

[35] *WM*, 23 October 1969; *The Guardian*, 31 October 1969.

[36] SWML, South Wales Area (NUM), Area Conference 18 November 1969.

[37] Alun Burge and Keith Davies, 'Enlightenment of the Highest Order: The Education Programme of the South Wales Miners, 1956-1971', *Llafur* 7, no. 1 (1996), 120.

[38] Unofficial Reform Committee, *The Miners' Next Step* (London, 1973 edn). The volume was published on behalf of the Trotskyist International Socialists History Group. A reprint had been undertaken a decade earlier by the Cymric Federation Press, the publishing arm of the South Wales Area, National Union of

Mineworkers. Unofficial Reform Committee, *The Miners' Next Step* (Cardiff, 1964).

[39] Jonathan and Ruth Winterton, *Coal, Crisis, and Conflict: The 1984-85 Miners' Strike in Yorkshire* (Manchester, 1989), 18.

[40] Allen, *Militancy*, 139; SWML, AUD/33: 'Interview with Emlyn Williams, 22 October 1980'.

[41] SWML, South Wales Area (NUM), Special Conference, 25 August 1970.

[42] SWML, AUD/131: 'Interview with Dai Francis, c.1980'.

[43] Francis and Smith, *The Fed*, 470-476; *Red Mole* 35 (24 January 1972).

[44] SWML, AUD/345: 'Interview with Dulais Valley Strike Committee, 1973'; *Socialist Woman* (March-April 1972); https://www.jacobinmag.com/2015/01/pride-film-lgbt-miners-strike/ [accessed 4 June 2016].

[45] Hywel Francis, 'NUM United: A Team in Disarray', *Marxism Today* (April, 1985), 29.

[46] GA, D1212/1: Barry CLP, Management and Executive Committee Minutes, 1977-1983, 12 January 1978.

[47] They had first considered the prospect of a 1978 general election in December 1977. As above, 6 December 1977. Stead reflected on 25 October that 'we would have had a very strong chance of winning the seat' in a 1978 election.

[48] As above, 14 February 1978.

[49] As above, 25 October 1978. My thanks also to Peter Stead for discussing his position on devolution with me.

[50] As above, 31 January 1979.

[51] As above, 28 February 1979.

[52] Ewen A. Cameron, *Impaled Upon a Thistle: Scotland since 1880* (Edinburgh, 2010), 298.

[53] *Democracy, Devolution and Socialism* (Cardiff, 1977), 1.

[54] Barry CLP, Minutes, entries for 18 July 1979, 25 July 1979, 12 September 1979, 31 October 1979.

[55] As above, entry for 27 February 1980.

[56] As above, entry for 24 September 1980, 28 January 1981.

[57] As above, entry for 24 June 1981.

58 GA, D817/2/1: Cynon Valley CLP, General Management Committee Minutes, 1981-1985, 24 September 1981.

59 As above, entry for August 1983 (entry is otherwise undated).

60 Michael Crick, *Militant*; Ralph Griffiths (ed.), *The City of Swansea: Challenges and Changes* (Gloucester, 1991), 63; Morgan, *Callaghan*, 712.

61 Cynon Valley CLP, Minutes, 26 October 1985.

62 BLSA, C1420/41: Interview with Jane Hutt, 1 June 2012; this trajectory was also noted by Jenny Lynn in her talk given at the Llafur Day School on Women's and Gay Liberation in March 2017. Notes in possession of the author.

63 Smith, *Wales! Wales?*, 165.

64 Gwyn A. Williams, *When Was Wales? BBC Wales Annual Radio Lecture* (Cardiff, 1979). This was republished in his *The Welsh and their History* (1982).

65 Dai Smith, *Wales! Wales? Episode One: Who Do They Think They Are?* (BBC, 1984). This was first broadcast on BBC 1 Wales, 4 March 1984. Subsequent episodes were (in order): *The Longest Journey*; *Oh! What a Lovely Riot*; *Bitter, Broken Bread*; *The Crowd at the Ball Game*; *We're Still Here*.

66 Smith, *Wales! Wales?*, 168.

67 Raphael Samuel, 'Friends and Outsiders', *New Statesman* (11 January 1985).

68 The phrase was originally used in a speech to the backbench 1922 committee in the House of Commons in July 1984. Thatcher Foundation, 'Speech to 1922 Committee', 19 July 1984.

69 Thatcher Foundation, 'Draft Margaret Thatcher Speech, 8 October 1984'.

70 *Sheffield Star*, 19 March 1984.

71 Birmingham Archives, Paul Mackney Papers, MS1591/D/1/2: Maerdy Diary Kept by Alun Jones, entries for 16 March – 5 April 1984. See also my 'The Secret Life of Us: 1984, the Miners' Strike, and the Place of Biography in the Writing of History "From Below"', *European Review of History* 19, no. 5 (2012), 825-846.

72 'Pam', *Mardy: Last Pit in the Rhondda* (BBC Wales, 1984). This was first broadcast on BBC 2 Wales on 8 July 1984.

73 'Barbara', *Mardy: Last Pit in the Rhondda*.
74 Welsh Government, *National Survey of Adult Skills* (Cardiff, 2011).
75 The clearest indication of the role of women is the film *Smiling and Splendid Women* produced by the Swansea Women's History Group in 1986.
76 SWML, AUD/503: Interview with Margaret Donovan conducted by Ursula Masson, 5 November 1986.
77 Siân James, *O'r Llinell Biced i San Steffan* (Talybont, 2015), 41. My translation from the Welsh. Thanks are also due to Siân for discussing the strike and her experiences with me.
78 As above, 42.
79 GA, DWSG/2/1, Minute Book 1984-1986, 'Minutes of meeting held at Cwm Llantwit Welfare Institute, Beddau, 9 August 1984'.
80 *Capital Gay, 14 December 1984*.
81 GA, DWSG/7/3: Report on the Women in Struggle Workshop, 9 March 1985.
82 Notes from Jenny Lynn Talk, Llafur Day School, March 2017; see also the collection of papers on pregnancy at the West Glamorgan Archives deposited by Jenny Lynn. West Glamorgan Archives, WAW/3/4.
83 Mair Francis, *Up the Dove: The History of the DOVE Workshop in Banwen* (Ferryside, 2008).
84 *New Scientist*, 15 September 1983, 825; S. Essex, C. Collender, C. Rees, T. Winckler and V. Winckler, *New Styles of Training for Women: An Evaluation of the South Glamorgan Women's Workshop* (Manchester, 1986).
85 Victoria Winckler, 'Women and Work in Contemporary Wales', *Contemporary Wales* 1 (1987).
86 Victoria Winckler, 'Class and Gender in Regional Change: A Study of Office Relocation in Industrial South Wales' (Unpublished PhD Thesis, 1986), 217.
87 Teresa L. Rees, 'Changing Patterns of Women's Work in Wales: Some Myths Explored', *Contemporary Wales* 2 (1988), 127.
88 *Y Ddraig Goch*, August 1984; *Tafod y Ddraig* 173 (May 1984), 3.
89 Paul Mackney, *Birmingham and the Miners' Strike: The Story of a Solidarity Movement* (Birmingham, 1987), 21, 77.

[90] SCOLAR, Cardiff Trades Council Records, File 16/45: Cardiff Miners' Support Group. In particular, the letter from Steve Kinzett, Chairman of Cardiff Central CLP to Charlie Swain, Secretary of Cardiff Trades Council, 3 May 1984 and the surviving copies of the strike bulletin produced by the Cardiff group contained within, notably Cardiff Miners' Support Committee, *Bulletin No. 9* (September 1984). The Barry Miners' Support Group was based at the town's Transport and General Workers' Union offices in Coronation Street.

[91] SWML, AUD/547, 'Interview with David Donovan conducted by Hywel Francis, 10 April 1986'. My thanks to Dai Donovan for further discussions on the strike and the support groups he was involved in.

[92] The following paragraphs are based on a close reading of the relevant minutes for Rhondda, Taff Ely, Cynon Valley, and Rhymney district councils. These are held at the Glamorgan Archives.

[93] Hywel Francis, 'Mining the Popular Front', *Marxism Today*, February 1985; Hywel Francis, 'Confronting Reality: Coal and Trade Unionism After 1945', Unpublished Paper, October 1985, LHASC, CP/CENT/IND/07/02.

[94] *Daily Mail*, 21 January 1985; Kim Howells, 'Stopping Out: The Birth of a New Kind of Politics' in Huw Beynon (ed.), *Digging Deeper: Issues in the Miners' Strike* (London, 1985).

[95] Howells, 'Stopping Out', 146.

[96] Margaret Thatcher Foundation, Archive, THCR 1/13/8 f3: David Hart note for Margaret Thatcher, 7 January 1985. Available online: https://www.margaretthatcher.org/document/142233 [Accessed 26 October 2017]; the meeting in the Brynffynnon Arms, Llanwynno, is noted by Ben Curtis in *The South Wales Miners, 1864-1985* (Cardiff, 2013); see also Richard-Michael Diedrich, 'You Can't Beat Us! Class, Work and Masculinity in a Council Estate in the South Wales Coalfield' (Unpublished PhD Thesis, 1999), 61. Both rely on oral testimony.

[97] See, for instance, the comments in *Focus*, 9 May, 23 May 1985.

[98] Hywel Francis, 'Unfinished Business: The Breaking of the NUM?', *Marxism Today*, August 1985.

[99] Hywel Francis, 'NUM United: A Team in Disarray', *Marxism Today*, April 1985. This continued into the late-1980s. In 1987, Arthur Scargill gave the S. O. Davies Memorial Lecture, entitled 'New Realism: The Politics of Fear'. Hywel Francis responded with 'The Fear of Real Politics: Some Comments on an Infantile Disorder', which referenced Arthur Horner's positions in the 1930s and 1940s and carried a deliberately Leninist subtitle. The original being V. I. Lenin, *'Left Wing' Communism: An Infantile Disorder* originally published in 1920.

[100] Hywel Francis, 'Coming to Terms with Defeat: Recent Responses to Change in the British Coalfields with Particular Reference to South Wales', Unpublished Lecture Delivered to the University of Paris, 1986. Copy consulted, SWML.

[101] Papers relating to the Wales Congress in Support of Mining Communities are held at the SWML. The Cardiff Congress branch papers are held at SCOLAR, Cardiff Trades Council Records, 321/16.45-16.49.

[102] Interview with Peter Keelan, 13 February 2015. Keelan, now retired as head of SCOLAR at Cardiff University also explained to me that the strike's presence within Plaid Cymru circles was 'not that big', certainly not as large as often portrayed. There was, Keelan remarked, 'lots of coverage but [it was] one dimensional'.

[103] Francis, *History On Our Side*. This relationship is made more apparent in Tim Tate, *Pride: The Unlikely Story of the Unsung Heroes of the Miners' Strike* (London, 2017).

[104] Key figures included Hywel Francis who was Chair; Arfon Evans, the chair of the Rhondda branch of the Wales Congress, a member of the steering committee of the Wales Congress, and Maerdy Lodge Chair; and David Richards who was international secretary of the Wales Congress and secretary of the Welsh District of the Communist Party. Gareth Rees, then lecturer in sociology at University College Cardiff, a member of the Communist Party's Advisory Group on Fuel, and author of several articles on the miners' strike in South Wales, was also active in the Congress. Support was also forthcoming from Ann Clwyd, Dafydd Elis Thomas, and Ken Livingstone.

[105] LHASC, CP/CENT/EC/22/06: EC Materials, 1985, Memorandum, November 1985; CP/CENT/EC/22/11: EC

Materials, 1986, Executive Committee Meeting Materials, 13-14 September 1986.

[106] Cited in Francis, *History on Our Side*, 71.

[107] *The Guardian*, 21 February 1986, 26 March 1988.

CHAPTER NINE
Exit Labour Country

A trajectory leads from the end of the miners' strike both to the advent of devolution and the circumstances that led to the Brexit vote. It was mirrored in the parallel economic trends typically summarised as post-industrialisation. In 2016 the two paths collided. The consequences have already been dramatic. Without exception, the former South Wales Coalfield voted for Brexit. But should that result really be a surprise? Forty years earlier, in the 1975 referendum on membership of the Common Market, the lowest votes in favour in England and Wales were in the South Wales Coalfield: Mid Glamorgan, where support was below sixty per cent (the only region in England and Wales where that was the case), and in West Glamorgan and Gwent where it was around sixty two per cent.

Both results reflected a weakness in South Walian social democratic politics but of different kinds. In the 1960s and 1970s, the NUM was profoundly Eurosceptic, regarding Europe as 'an alliance of the upholders of anti-trade union capitalism'.[1] In 1967, the South Wales Area voted to oppose British entry into the Common Market and in 1971 pushed the NUM's national conference to use its block vote at Labour's annual conference that year to oppose entry – the resolution was co-sponsored by Dai Francis.[2] The Area even pushed the national executive of the NUM to withdraw financial support from NUM-sponsored Labour MPs who voted in favour of entry.[3] It was no surprise that the NUM's influence contributed to the referendum results in 1975. Nor did the Area's Euroscepticism cease with the referendum. Speaking in 1980, Emlyn Williams, the Area President, blamed European policy for the looming crisis in the mining industry.[4] The NUM was not alone in taking this stance. Wales Get Britain Out, formed in 1975, had as its chair the secretary of Cardiff South East CLP and parliamentary candidate for Barry in 1974, Jack Brooks, and as its secretary George Wright, the secretary of both the Welsh region of the Transport and General Workers' Union and the Wales TUC. The Wales TUC itself, headed by Dai Francis and George Wright, was Eurosceptic.[5]

Those in favour of entry into the Common Market in this period tended to come from the moderate wings of the Labour Party and from trade unions such as the clerical and administrative workers' union APEX, the municipal workers' union NUPE, the National Union of Railwaymen, and the steelworkers' union ISTC. The Wales Labour and Trade Union Committee for Europe was chaired by Cledwyn Hughes, member of parliament for Anglesey and former Welsh Secretary, with Tal Lloyd, the defeated Labour candidate for Merthyr Tydfil in 1970, as vice chair. Lloyd had defied his union, the AUEW, which was opposed to entry, in serving on the committee. He regarded British membership as an opportunity to galvanise social democracy across Europe.[6] In contrast to the NUM, the ISTC had long favoured entry, lobbying for Britain to join the European Coal and Steel Community in the 1950s. In 1962, the union's executive council passed a resolution stating that various industries 'would be encouraged by the expansion of economic frontiers which would follow Britain's entry into the Common Market'.[7] In 1975, the ISTC general secretary, Bill Sirs, went even further and declared that 'Britain's membership... [is] the only way in which to build a Socialist Europe.'[8]

Defeat on the European question in 1975 forced the left to reconsider its approach. Eurosceptic Labour MEPs, such as

Barbara Castle and Ann Clwyd (MP for Cynon Valley from 1984), who had both voted no in the referendum, rethought their position and began to embrace the European project more fully.[9] In a memorandum written for colleagues in the European Parliament in the autumn of 1982, ahead of a likely general election in the spring of 1983, Castle lamented the Labour Party's apparent about turn on the European question. 'After years of haggling about the right conditions for our membership', she complained, 'we have suddenly announced that we *know* membership would be incompatible with what a Labour government would want to do and that we are going to wash our hands with the whole show'. She continued:

We shall apparently have to spend the first months of office arguing about how we extract ourselves from our Treaty commitments instead of how we get the economy moving. The danger is that we shall lose sight of the economic battle in the complexities of the institutional one ... Anyone who believes that withdrawal policy is an automatic vote-catcher is living in cloud-cuckoo-land. Of course our membership of the Common Market is unpopular, but that is not necessarily a guide to the mood which will predominate when the election comes. It is one thing to register a complaint with an opinion pollster, quite another to cast a vote for going into the unknown.[10]

Perhaps most significant of all was Castle's reflection that by campaigning to leave, rather than to remain, the Labour Party left itself exposed to a 'split personality'. She noted: 'instead of crusading as a party which could mobilise fellow Socialists in the fight against unemployment and inequality, we shall be fighting for the right to wash our hands of them'. That, in the end, became the basis on which previously anti-market Labourites became steadily more pro-European. That sense of

European solidarity, and a mission associated with it, resonated during the miners' strike when aid entered the coalfields of Britain from across the European continent.

At the same time, a new generation was emerging that looked again at the possibilities of devolution seeing it as a panacea to the dilemmas posed by the demise of heavy industry on the one hand and on the other by Thatcherism triumphant. Just as there was a struggle within the Labour Party to overcome its swing back and forth between Euroscepticism and Europhilia, so too was there a struggle to win the party back around to the idea of constitutional reform and a further offer of devolved power to Wales. To overcome the circumstances that led to the 1979 vote against the idea required a revision of political terms, not in any sense straightforward given Neil Kinnock's previous opposition to devolution. The revisions required the steady delegitimisation of central government together with that form of unionist politics that rested on the shoulders of industrial labour and the trade unions. In the absence of heavy industrial unions such as the NUM and the ISTC, that was far easier to achieve. Nevertheless, appetite for devolution waxed and waned. Organisations and alliances formed in the miners' strike, such as the Wales Congress in Support of Mining Communities, came and went, and Conservative representation declined from the historic highs of 1979 and 1983, giving many within the Labour Party pause for thought.

There was no offer of devolution to Wales in Labour's 1987 general election manifesto, although this changed by the time of the 1992 general election with the party campaigning on a platform that offered an elected Assembly, albeit tentatively 'in the lifetime of a full parliament'. In other words, as far distant as 1997. In retrospect, historians and campaigners have afforded the miners' strike the badge of 'turning point' in the devolution story.[11] As Hywel Francis has written, 'the Congress was an important factor in the forging of a national consciousness of a new kind, which led to the successful Yes Devolution vote in 1997'.[12] But this merits reconsideration. The Wales Congress in Support of Mining Communities was formed in October 1984 and remained in existence only until 1986. Its base of support lay in the coming together primarily of the Communist Party (and its influences in the NUM) and left-wing elements in nationalist circles, a momentum that had been slowly developing in intellectual and rhetorical terms for a number of years, together with those parts of the Labour Party that had traditionally been inclined to a cultural nationalism.[13] This 'broad democratic alliance' (the terminology is that of the post-war Communist Party) may have seemed to bridge the gap between 'their respective, "historic" Waleses' but had little power to prevent central government from dismantling the 'mainstream structures of democratic Welsh politics'.[14]

So what changed? A new wave of pro-devolution members of parliament, such as Rhodri Morgan, the future First Minister of Wales, had been elected in 1987, thus bolstering that wing of the Labour Party. The continued significance of the Scottish Question and the attachment of key members of the shadow cabinet, not least John Smith, the Shadow Chancellor, to the establishment of a Scottish Parliament, certainly provided for ongoing debate about devolution. But Wales had not 'ridden on the coat-tails' of Scotland in 1979, so there was little likelihood that it would do so in any future referendum. More significant were the proposals for local government reform presented by the Conservative government in 1991.[15] This meant the end of two-tier local government and the creation of unitary authorities across Wales for the first time. Devolution no longer presented a probable third tier of local administration, but an intermediary step between local authorities and central government. For pro-devolutionists, the establishment of a Welsh Assembly was now able to be presented as administrative and constitutional 'logic' rather than as something based on Romantic fervour. Finally, defeat at the 1992 general election meant the end of Neil Kinnock's tenure as Labour leader. His successor, John Smith, the architect of Scottish devolution in the 1970s, regarded the Scottish Question as 'unfinished business' and committed Labour more fully to constitutional reform.

Together, these changes made for the steady encouragement of the devolution principle in the Welsh section of the Labour Party. Crucially, they were able to keep the issue on the party's agenda following the death of John Smith in 1994 and the election of Tony Blair as party leader. Blair's own interest in constitutional reform was relatively modest. In the event, despite some disquiet amongst MPs, devolution was offered to the public in Labour's election manifesto in 1997. After initially hesitating on a referendum in the run up to the election, this was eventually held in September 1997 and resulted in a very narrow vote in favour. Enthusiasm for the idea was still clearly limited. More people voted against devolution in Glamorgan in 1979, for example, than voted either yes or no in 1997. Moreover, an actually-existing National Assembly has hardly improved on the situation. Turnout figures for the 2011 referendum on the extension of powers were embarrassing for any exercise in democratic engagement, and none of the five elections to the Assembly held between 1999 and 2016 have had a turnout above fifty per cent. Of the three devolved institutions, the Northern Ireland Assembly, the Scottish Parliament, and the National Assembly for Wales, the body in Cardiff Bay has had, by a considerable margin, the weakest democratic performance. Rather than heralding a new era of representation and accountability, and a reconstruction of the social democratic model destroyed in the 1980s, devolution rested on a series of mirages. Gone was the fuel that was South

Wales, in its place the quasi-nostalgia of 'clear red water' and the soft nationalism exemplified by Welsh Labour.

It need not have been this way.

Social Democracy Revived?

In 1928, the Labour Party published its most significant policy statement of the interwar years, *Labour and the Nation*. It set out, in the words of Ramsay Macdonald, to 'rescue socialism entirely from the turning of phrases and impossible policies and make it a living and constructive thing'.[16] The message, developed and refined since the middle of the First World War, was wide ranging and proposed a charter for the trade unions; the implementation of a living wage; to provide 'humane and adequate' support for the unemployed; to bring about public ownership of the 'foundational industries' including the land, the railways, coal, electricity, and social security; to introduce rent controls; to provide effective maternity and infant welfare; and to provide an education highway from nursery school to university. Thus ensuring that 'the children of the workers shall have precisely the same opportunities of entering [universities] as the children of the rich'. This was practical democratic socialism and a manifesto for the transformation of Britain from a liberal democracy into a genuine social democracy. Its legacy is still apparent in aspects of the Labour Party's thinking in the twenty-first century.

The ideas encapsulated in *Labour and the Nation* found expression in those parts of Britain where Labour were in effective control. When Labour came into power municipally across much of South Wales after 1918, it set about transforming areas using the democratic levers at its disposal. In this way, South Wales was set on the road towards social democracy, with power assigned to working-class political parties and major trade unions, most especially the South Wales

Miners' Federation, playing a significant role in shaping public policy.[17] Nowhere was this more apparent than Merthyr Tydfil. In 1939, at a stormy meeting about rates and expenditure cuts, councillors reflected that 'the only way to bring about a reduction in the [council tax] rate, was to refuse to spend'. But:

> What item or items could they refuse to spend? Were they going to curtail facilities provided for people living on the verge of starvation? Did anybody suggest they should spend less on combating the scourge of tuberculosis? Were they to stop building houses for people who lived in hovels?[18]

With annual expenditure of nearly four hundred and fifty thousand pounds, the largest items were 'quasi-national services': social security, education, and health. Together these accounted for more than two hundred and seventy thousand pounds, or approximately half the council's budget. Spending on education was amongst the highest anywhere in Britain because 'Merthyr was the first town in Great Britain to provide secondary education with the objective of providing higher education free of all charges to children of poor parents'.[19] This was the education highway set out in Labour's interwar policy statements being put into action despite the implications it had for the council's budgets and fears that similar actions would mean Merthyr becoming a 'financial wreck' devoid of private enterprise by 1945.[20]

This kind of political activity and administration complicates the story we are usually told about interwar Britain. For Britain in those years was not a social democracy but one of the few remaining liberal democracies.[21] Its politics were characterised by a centre-right consensus and the weakness and isolation, particularly pronounced in the 1930s, of the Parliamentary Labour Party. Typically, the years between the foundation of the

Labour Representation Committee in 1900 and the coming to power of the Attlee government in 1945 are split in two, the age of Liberal dominance and the power struggle between Herbert Asquith and David Lloyd George which came to an abrupt end in 1922, incidentally the same year that Labour first took a majority of Welsh parliamentary seats, and the age of Conservative dominance interrupted by two brief Labour minority governments in 1924 and 1929-31, and the Churchill coalition during the Second World War. Historians of politics in England have often remarked on the potential for, but ultimate failure of, social democracy across large swathes of the country, even in 1945. Whilst some areas such as Poplar in London, and in the industrial north and north-east of England, certainly did enjoy strong and vigorous social democratic politics, these were exceptions rather than rules and the apparent strength of Labour in these areas could not prevent the party's parliamentary collapse in 1931.

In Durham, for instance, Labour lost fourteen of its sixteen seats. In Leeds, where more than one hundred thousand people had voted Labour in 1929 and Labour held four of the city's six seats going into the 1931 general election, the party fell back to around seventy five thousand votes and just one parliamentary seat. The story was little different in Scotland. With thirty six seats in 1929, Labour were by a considerable margin the largest party, particularly across the populous central belt, but in 1931 all but seven seats (most located in Glasgow) had been lost. The party was weakened even further by the disaffiliation of the ILP, the central force in Scottish Labour politics, in 1932. Yet in South Wales, despite the loss of seats in Cardiff and in rural areas such as Brecon and Radnor, Labour's vote share went up (from forty three per cent in 1929 to forty four per cent, then its highest ever). Of the fifty two seats Labour won across Britain in 1931, sixteen were in South Wales – the equivalent of approximately one in every three – and no fewer than four constituencies went uncontested: Aberdare, Abertillery, Bedwellty, and Ebbw Vale. This consistent strength proved that South Wales was the social democratic exception.

There are many ways to examine and seek to understand the emergence and development of such a social democracy: through ideas, through the implementation of those ideas, through the organisations that sustained the ideas, and through the built environment that gave a physical manifestation of those ideas. Each of these has had some bearing on *Labour Country*. But in the final analysis, the emphasis must be on the practical expression of social democratic ideas. There can be no doubt that social democracy, as with liberalism before it, and neoliberalism after it, was written into the urban landscape. Amidst the terraced houses and the institutions of capital and liberal nonconformity – the colliery and the chapel – there was, and in some places remains, a range of institutions that were instinctively of the labour movement: workmen's halls, miners' institutes and miners' hospitals, welfare grounds, paddling pools, and open-air swimming pools. All of them served as markers of a working-class urban environment that sat alongside, and was eventually to replace, the earlier landscape put there by rulers of a different kind. Much of this has now been lost, through demolition or decay. Recreation grounds, alongside a handful of miners' hospitals and workmen's halls, and a lido, remain as one of the tangible links with the built legacy of labour and the form of social democracy that developed in South Wales.

This book has examined the rise of fall of that social democracy, from the period in which ideas about socialism and democratic values first began to emerge in Merthyr in the early nineteenth century through to the last great set piece of this phase of South Walian history in the miners' strike of 1984-5. Gwyn Alf Williams was fond of remarking that Welsh history moved forward as a result of brutal ruptures. We may conclude of the miners' strike that it was the latest brutal rupture in our history. It killed off, in many ways, the way of life, the form of politics, and the organising ethos that had sustained South Wales since before the First World War. Yes, the coal industry limped on afterwards, but, in whichever cliché is used, the strike brought down the curtain. It precipitated the final collapse of Labour Country. What has followed since has been a departure. Little wonder that bitterness reigned for many years afterwards and the moment is now properly understood as a major strategic defeat. Indeed, a disaster. Writing in 1998, on the SWMF's centenary, Hywel Francis and Dai Smith reflected on the aftermath of the strike and what had happened since the publication of *The Fed* in 1980:

> There was nothing that occurred, in general, in South Wales in the 1980s that had not been anticipated, but expecting an outcome one day is not quite like meeting your fate today. The Welsh coal industry had been in long term, if sporadic, decline since the 1920s, and, at least since then, the easy assumption that the 'management' of economic change could be wantonly separated from the attendant social and cultural structures which had evolved had met with fierce opposition in word and deed, from the people most affected.[22]

Those words were written just as devolution, the attempt by politicians to press reset on the South Walian story, gained institutional form. It has not worked. We require a different answer to the question posed after 1985: what now?

So, what might the answer be? Firstly, we should be honest in our appraisal of the present: there was a social democratic politics in South Wales. But it was, by 1997, a feature of the past. South Wales today is certainly not a social democracy as it once was. That does not mean it cannot be one again. If it chooses to be. After all, history may not predict the future but it can, and does, offer clear examples of how things were once achieved. It is in that spirit that *Labour Country* has been written. The idea that South Wales is not a social democracy is, of course, contrary to the self-assessment offered by many in Welsh Labour who would point to the principles of 'clear red water' as evidence enough of the divide between neoliberal governance in Westminster and social-democratic governance in the National Assembly.[23] To say nothing of the widespread, but now difficult to justify, assumption that Labour in Wales is to the left of Labour elsewhere. In 2002, Rhodri Morgan could point to free museum entry, free prescriptions, and free bus travel for pensioners, all of which, at the time, were available in Wales but not England, as indicators of the policy divide. Welsh social democratic politics desired public services that were 'free at the point of use, universal, and unconditional'.[24] The divide is much less stark today – free bus travel for pensioners, a signature endeavour of early devolution, was introduced in England in 2008.

Secondly, we should seek to understand how historians and writers and thinkers came to 'invent' South Wales after 1945 and so helped to fashion a wider intellectual curiosity about the coalfield, its communities, and its past. This history had previously been the preserve of activist-historians such as Ness Edwards and Mark Starr and, in a different vein, writers such as Lewis Jones and Jack Jones. In 1917, Starr published *A Worker Looks At History* which was based on classes in industrial history that he taught in the Cynon Valley for the Central Labour College and the South Wales Miners' Federation. Although it was widely read and discussed, Starr's work had relatively little to say about South Wales, and was pitched as 'English industrial history'.[25] Nevertheless, it did identify turning points such as 1898 and 1910 which had specific meanings for his South Walian students. More obvious 'South Walian industrial history' was published by Ness Edwards in the 1920s. Starting with pamphlets on *The Early Trade Unions of South Wales* and *John Frost and the Chartist Movement in Wales*, and *The Industrial Revolution in South Wales*, Edwards then moved on to the organisational history of the South Wales miners, culminating in his *History of the South Wales Miners' Federation* published in 1938, shortly before he was elected to parliament.[26] The second volume remains unpublished.[27]

A further wave of at least fifty 'new era' histories appeared after the Second World War as miners' lodges, trades and labour councils, and co-operative societies looked back on half a century, and more, of 'action, struggle, achievement'.[28] Most were written by participants. John E. Morgan's classic *A Village Workers' Council* was typical. Writing to Thomas Jones CH in the summer of 1952, Morgan explained that the book was intended to describe the activities of a 'typical mining village' from the formation of the South Wales Miners' Federation 'until it became merged with the N.U.M., and the taking over of the industry by the state', but it did far more than that.[29] As one review, published in *Reynold's News*, put it:

The Lodge has not concerned itself only with fighting industrial disputes. It has been an example of democracy in its bolder, deeper meaning, concerning itself with the entire life of the community. The people themselves organising soup kitchens, a fish market and boot repairing centre in times of strikes, working out schemes for a garden suburb to replace the miners' rows, building an institute for cultural and recreational use; running a hospital and ambulance service; making a people's park and welfare ground; and fighting for the right of way over the mountains. This is true democracy at work, something infinitely more fundamental than dropping a vote into a ballot box but once in five years![30]

Put together, the interwar activist histories and the postwar 'new era' histories told a story of achievement. The message, particularly after 1945, was a simple one. Look at what could be done to bring about socialism without the powers held by central government, imagine the future now that we hold power. It was idealism anchored by practical success – the Bevanite creed. That Morgan – and his reviewer – identified recreational space as important serves as a reminder that these successes were about everyday existence as well as symbolism. Alongside a rigorous defence of local people during the Depression, Labour's ability to rally communities into effective self-help schemes backed up with the powers of the municipality showed that it was very much 'out of the people'.[31] Labour councillors sitting on recreation associations and welfare associations were at the forefront of organising grant applications and negotiating with landowners or colliery companies, and thereby made strong the ties between community action and political representation. That was how social democracy succeeded.

The Labour Party, quite as much as the South Wales Miners' Federation, was 'an artifice, the outward emblem of the organisation of the miners' collective existence, made by the men themselves'. Both were products of 'a self-conscious industrial society that developed in places a sophisticated class consciousness'.[32] This was the essence of the labour history written between the 1960s and the 1990s, exemplified by Hywel Francis and Dai Smith's *The Fed* and Chris Williams's *Democratic Rhondda*. Key to the sense of South Wales presented by that generation of labour historians were the central valleys of the South Wales Coalfield – Rhondda, Cynon, Taff – and their towns and townships, Merthyr Tydfil, Tonypandy, Dowlais, Maerdy, Pontypridd, and Porth, for example. As Williams concluded, 'Rhondda acted ... as a beacon to the rest of the coalfield, signalling its history'.[33] It provided leadership for the entire region. Attempts by recent revisionist scholarship to demolish this understanding of the past – or to cloak it with questions of identity, constitutionalism, and nationhood – offer little meaningful alteration to those fundamental terms. South Wales may now find itself reduced in rank to a lower-case geographical expression but its upper-case vitality remains apparent in the historical record. It was as South Wales, not south Wales, that this social democracy was envisaged and thought and written about. There is much to be gained from a revival of the capital.

For what lies ahead of South Walians in the twenty-first century has much in common with the challenge met by earlier generations of voters in the terraces. How to build a better society, to endow institutions with intellectual drive and imagination, to instil a commitment to radicalism and democratic values, without losing the essence of individual experience and idiosyncrasy. To avoid uniformity and top-down determinacy. To blend idealism with practical action. In his classic novel, *Border Country*, Raymond Williams examined the dilemmas of the interplay between individual essence and a wider social and cultural collective.[34] It was based on Williams's own father's experiences as a railway signalman and Labour Party activist in the border village of Pandy. This was a community at a remove from the party's heartland in the coalfield, but in touch with it because of the railway and shared events and circumstances such as the 1926 General Strike and Labour's dominance on Monmouthshire County Council. Harry Williams was himself a parish councillor for the Labour Party and he ran the local party branch (which he had helped to set up). His Labour politics, as Dai Smith showed in his biography of Raymond Williams, *A Warrior's Tale*, diverged little from those in evidence elsewhere in South Wales. Having worked to build community organisations and to develop socialist forms of self-help, Harry Williams also recognised the value of the state-as-guarantor and the validity of the municipal solution. There was no contradiction.

As in the coalfield, Pandy had its own form of social democratic associational welfare: a bowling green laid out at the end of the 1920s and opened in August 1929. Harry Williams was its groundsman. He helped to lay out tennis courts, too, and to run adult education classes. But the municipal also had a role to play. When, in 1957, Pandy was connected to the mains water supply for the first time, 'communal self-help was lessened but a community's worked-for well-being increased'. Harry, observes Dai Smith, 'had always seen the connections'.[35] In earlier versions of *Border Country*, so too did Raymond Williams. He utilised the bowling green as a symbol of 'how the "common good" can be attained by working together'. Or in Williams's words: 'Down here, in the centre of the valley, the village had come together, and a new organisation had begun'. It was the same instinct in the coalfield. But by the time *Border Country* came to be finalised, this episode in grassroots social activism had been excised from the novel and instead the bowling green and the groundsman's job appears as a form of supplementary labour rather than as an exercise in grassroots communitarianism.

This revealed something of Raymond Williams's own political enthusiasms and the conclusions that he drew from asking similar questions to his father but in 'a different idiom'. As he reflected many years later, his approach in the 1930s had been, in contrast to his father, international rather than local. It was a telling distinction. The 'traditional politics of locality and parliament in the Labour movement was seen as part of a boring, narrow world with which we were right out of sympathy', he confessed.[36] Williams refused his father's overtures to join the Labour Party in 1936, although often campaigned for the party at election time, and eventually joined the Communist Party in Cambridge in 1939. Although he was sympathetic to the Bevanites in the 1950s, Williams was nevertheless pessimistic about the potential of the Labour Party to bring about the change that he wished to see. He regretted the model of nationalisation created after the Second World War, which his father had seen as positive, and tried instead to encourage socialisation and grassroots democracy – the essence of working-class culture as he saw it – which was distinguished from the 'welfare capitalism' that he associated with post-war Labour's embourgeoisement. Aneurin Bevan came to symbolise Williams's pessimism:

> it was very difficult to know what Bevan ... believed ... if you look at his book ... you can take it as a set of strongly held emotional convictions which come out of a peculiarly Welsh experience – that of a people who have been united for so long in wanting change, yet in relative isolation, that they think that they have really only to sound the trumpet and the walls will fall down.

And then came his conclusion:

> After all, if it could have been done by talking, Wales could have been a socialist republic in the twenties.[37]

Ironically, the South Wales of the interwar years came closer to Williams's own socialist ideal than at any other point in his lifetime. It was a strong and vibrant social democracy anchored in working-class political activity and democratic culture. Williams's attraction to utopianism and, of course, the contemporary experience of the late-1970s, meant that he failed to see it. *That* South Wales was achieved both by talking and by practical action of precisely the kind that Aneurin Bevan – and Harry Williams – campaigned and worked for. In the end it was Gwyn Thomas rather than Raymond Williams who better understood the urgency of South Wales and its radical politics, and, bursting with indignation, set them down in his writing, pointing to the absurdity of reality and the need to understand the joke.[38] How far have we come from that South Wales? The South Wales of A. J. Cook or Noah Ablett? Of Arthur Horner or Aneurin Bevan? Of Minnie Pallister or Elaine Morgan? Of Gwyn Thomas? Well. 'The distance is measured, and that is what matters', reflected Matthew Price in *Border Country*. He concluded: 'By measuring the distance, we come home'.[39] Home, in fact, to *Labour Country*.

Notes

[1] National Union of Mineworkers, *Report of Annual Conference, 1961*, 338. The National Coal Board supported entry into the Common Market.

[2] L. J. Robins, *The Reluctant Party: Labour and the EEC, 1961-1975* (Ormskirk, 1979), 109.

[3] Andrew Mullen, *The British Left's 'Great Debate' on Europe* (London, 2007), 95.

[4] SWML, AUD/33: Interview with Emlyn Williams, 1980; this Euroscepticism is reflected in the final chapter of *The Fed* written by Hywel Francis. Francis and Smith, *The Fed*, 480. My thanks to Hywel for discussing the composition of this chapter with me, although the conclusions I draw are my own.

[5] Dai Francis, of course, was chair of the Wales TUC. Denis Balsom and P. J. Madgwick, 'Wales, European integration and devolution', in Martin Kolinsky (ed.), *Divided Loyalties: British Regional Assertion and European Integration* (Manchester, 1978), 75. The Wales TUC was pro-devolution.

[6] David Butler and Uwe Kitzinger, *The 1975 Referendum* (London, 1976), 154.

[7] Jeremy Moon, *European Integration in Britain Politics, 1950-1963: A Study of Issue Change* (London, 1985), 186-7.

[8] *Man and Metal*, May 1975.

[9] Ann Clwyd, *Rebel With A Cause* (London, 2017). Clwyd was elected MEP for Mid and West Wales in 1979.

[10] Barbara Castle, 'Memorandum on The Labour Party and the E.E.C., September 1982'. Historical Archives of the European Union, European University Institute, Florence, GSPE-072.

[11] Wiliam, 'rebirth of Welsh devolution'; Lee Waters, 'From Little Acorns'. Available online: sites.cardiff.ac.uk/wgc/files/2014/04/From-little-acorns-lee-waters.pdf [Accessed: 1 July 2017]

[12] Hywel Francis, *History On Our Side: Wales and the 1984-85 Miners' Strike* (London, 2015 edn.), 73-4.

[13] See my, 'A Miner Cause? The Persistence of Left-Nationalism in Post-War Wales' in Evan Smith and Matthew Worley (eds.), *Waiting*

515

for the Revolution: The British Far Left from 1956 (Manchester, 2017). An alternative view is offered by Douglas Jones, *The Communist Party of Great Britain and the National Question in Wales, 1920-1991* (Cardiff, 2017)

[14] Dai Smith, *Wales: A Question for History* (Bridgend, 1999), 27.

[15] Labour, too, had favoured the implantation of a single-tier of local government to replace the situation left by reforms in the early 1970s. See NLW, Wales TUC Archives, Box 92 H6/8/1; Box 222 H6/8/2; Box 223 H6/8/3; NLW, Labour Party Wales Archive, S/12: The Future of Local Government in Wales, 1986-89.

[16] Cited in Duncan Tanner, 'Labour and its Membership', in Duncan Tanner, Pat Thane and Nick Tiratsoo (eds.), *Labour's First Century* (Cambridge, 2000), 267.

[17] For a wider consideration of this theme See: Rebecca Gill and Daryl Leeworthy, 'Moral Minefields: Save the Children Fund and the Moral Economies of the Nursery School in the South Wales Coalfield in the 1930s', *Journal of Global Ethics* 11, no. 2 (2015), 218-232; Duncan Tanner, 'Gender, Civic Culture and Politics in South Wales: Explaining Labour Municipal Policy, 1918-39', in Matthew Worley (ed.), *Labour's Grassroots*; Pat Thane, 'Women in the British Labour Party and the Construction of State Welfare, 1906-1939', in Seth Koven and Sonya Michael (eds.), *Mothers of a New World: Materialist Politics and the Origins of Welfare States* (London, 1993), 343-377.

[18] *WM*, 25 April 1939.

[19] *Western Morning News* (Plymouth), 11 October 1933.

[20] *WM*, 19 July 1939.

[21] For a comparison between Britain and Norway, see: David Redvaldsen, *The Labour Party in Britain and Norway: Elections and the Pursuit of Power Between the Wars* (London, 2011). For Sweden see: Mary Hilson, *Political Change and the Rise of Labour in Comparative Perspective: Britain and Sweden, 1890-1920* (Lund, 2006).

[22] Hywel Francis and Dai Smith, *The Fed* (Cardiff, 1998 edn).

[23] Nick Davies and Darren Williams, *Clear Red Water: Welsh Devolution and Socialist Politics* (London, 2009). The context of the idea and the speech given at Swansea University in 2002 which set

out its principles is outlined in Rhodri Morgan, *Rhodri: A Political Life in Wales and Westminster* (Cardiff, 2017).

24 Rhodri Morgan, 'Clear Red Water: speech to the National Centre for Public Policy, Swansea, 11 December 2002'. Available online: https://www.sochealth.co.uk/the-socialist-health-association/sha-country-and-branch-organisation/sha-wales/clear-red-water/ [Accessed: 14 October 2017].

25 Mark Starr, *A Worker Looks At History* (London, 1917). It carried a foreword by George Barker. It may be compared usefully with W. W. Craik, *Outlines of the History of the Modern British Working Class Movement* (London, 1917).

26 Ness Edwards, *The Early Trade Unions of South Wales* (Abertillery, 1923); *John Frost and the Chartist Movement in Wales* (Abertillery, 1924); *The Industrial Revolution in South Wales* (London, 1924); *The History of the South Wales Miners* (London, 1926); *The Workers' Theatre* (Cardiff, 1930); *History of the South Wales Miners' Federation, Volume I* (London, 1938).

27 The proofs survive and are held at the library of Nuffield College, Oxford.

28 Alun Burge, 'New Era Histories: Local Labour Movement Histories in the 1940s and 1950s'. Unpublished paper delivered to the Llafur Day School on History, Historians, and the Public in Wales, April 2007. Indicative examples include, Edmund Stonelake, *Aberdare Trades and Labour Council Jubilee Souvenir, 1900-1950* (Aberdare, 1950); anon, *Action! Struggle! Achievement! A Jubilee History of Pontypridd Trades Council and Labour Party, 1898-1948* (Pontypridd, 1948); Morgan, *VWC*; Hazell, *The Gleaming Vision*.

29 John E. Morgan, 'Letter to Thomas Jones CH, June 1952'. In author's possession.

30 *Reynold's News*, 21 June 1950.

31 The phrase is taken from Smith, *Out of the People*.

32 Francis and Smith, *The Fed* (1980 edn.), 42.

33 Williams, *Democratic Rhondda*, 212.

34 Raymond Williams, *Border Country* (London, 1960). References below are to the Library of Wales Edition. Raymond Williams, *Border Country* (Cardigan, 2006); Dai Smith, 'From "Black Water" to *Border*

Country: Sourcing the Textual Odyssey of Raymond Williams',
Almanac 12 (2007-8), 169-191.

[35] Dai Smith, *Raymond Williams: A Warrior's Tale* (Cardigan, 2008),
450.

[36] Raymond Williams, *Politics and Letters: Interviews with New Left
Review* (London, [1979] 2015 edn), 32.

[37] As above, 368-9.

[38] And Williams continued to struggle with that legacy as evidenced
by his foreword to the 1986 reprint of Gwyn Thomas, *All Things
Betray Thee* (London, [1949] 1986 edn.).

[39] Williams, *Border Country*, 436.

ACKNOWLEDGEMENTS

The origins of this book lie in the stories that I was told by my teachers at Trerobart Primary School in Ynysybwl and Coedylan Comprehensive School in Cilfynydd as a child. At the beginning of the 1990s, with the Lady Windsor Colliery recently gone, they were determined that we, the first generation to have no memory of the pit, would know something about its history and its purpose. My first thanks are to them, especially to Jill and Wynford Price, the late Mike Allen, and to Jonathan Davies. *Labour Country*'s themes will be familiar to everyone who I have talked to since then, so frequently have my thoughts turned to the question of what made South Wales different from (and, yes, similar to) other parts of Britain. In finally building something coherent out of those initial thoughts, spurred on by a mixture of archival curiosity and chance finds in second-hand bookshops, I place on record my gratitude to all those who have played their part in this project. Writing is a lonely activity, and it goes almost without saying that the points of emphasis in this book are my own, but it is also a collective experience for it is a process that relies on discussion, debate, the pooling together of ideas, and a collaborative response to the past. The list of those persons and institutions with some part to play in the making of this book is very long indeed and since I will undoubtedly forget someone, I shall say thank you to everyone here – as they say, you know who you are! But there are a few people and places which I do now get to fully acknowledge in print.

Some of the material in this book began life as dissertations and theses undertaken at Oxford University, Saint Mary's University in Canada, and Swansea University. For their support and guidance, I am grateful to my supervisors and examiners at each. Special thanks are due to Tony Collins, Chris Williams, Doug Vaisey, Sue Bruley, Mike Vance, and Colin Howell and Sandi Galloway. My colleagues at the University of Huddersfield convinced me that this book was a good idea, I hope they think so now it is finished. Especial thanks to Rebecca Gill, Keith Laybourn, Janette Martin, Duncan Stone, Paul Atkinson, Pat Cullum, Katherine Lewis, Jonathan Gledhill, Paul Ward, and Barry Doyle. Thanks also to Ewen A. Cameron of Edinburgh University for support, guidance, and encouragement. Comrades on the Llafur committee kept me going and a particular debt is owed to Martin Wright, Sian Williams, and Alun Burge. Likewise, Ceri Thompson for his enthusiasm, encouragement, and ready offer of a Pot Noodle for making it to Big Pit on the bus. My students and colleagues at the Department for Adult and Continuing Education at Swansea University and at the remarkable WEA/Adult Learning Wales class in Merthyr Tydfil have added to this project in very many ways. The knowledge and memories of Ceinwen Statter, Huw Williams, Maria Williams, Barbara and David Melksham, Mary and Wilf Owen, and Ann Wilson, deserve a big thank you. As does Brian Davies, Paul O'Brian, and David Gwyer at Pontypridd Museum.

The list of libraries and archives, actual and digital, that I've worked in researching this book is substantial and runs to more than a dozen countries. It could not exist, however, without the Glamorgan Archives in Cardiff, the South Wales Miners' Library, the Richard Burton Archives, the Special Collections and Archives at Cardiff University, the National Library of Wales, the People's History Museum in Manchester, the Working Class Movement Library in Salford, the Bodleian Library, the Bristol Archives, Pontypridd Museum, and the local studies departments in the libraries at Pontypridd, Treorchy, Aberdare, Merthyr Tydfil, Dowlais, Cardiff, Newport, Swansea, Leeds,

Huddersfield, Sheffield, Bristol, Bath, Birmingham, and Weston-Super-Mare.

Long ago, I was encouraged to read the great works of Ynysybwl's past – by Glanffrwd, John E. Morgan, and William Hazell, and, sat in the library, under the watchful gaze of Lyn West, my eye turned to a red-covered book with the words *THE FED* on the spine. I took it down to read. Little did I realise, as a teenager, the professional significance of those sessions. It is a delight to get to know the historians who inspired you to start investigating the past in the first place, and I am enormously grateful to Hywel Francis and Dai Smith for their support and encouragement, and in Dai's case, as editor, a necessary critical eye which helped to transform the text. As they shared their ideas and their memories with me, filling in the background of their own research, the men and women in this book first came alive. Through six degrees of separation *Labour Country* is linked to those who knew Arthur Horner, Arthur Cook, Keir Hardie, Mabon, and even Lenin. Historians sometimes dream of such things. Similarly, thanks to Norette Smith, Owen Smith, Richard Davies, Bill Jones, Deian Hopkin, Peter Stead, David Maddox, Alun Williams, Siân James, Christine Chapman, and Ian Rees.

I began writing this book at a time of significant upheaval, in 2014. Unemployment beckoned, and was to last almost the entire period that it took to compose the first draft – two and a half years later. Through the support of friends and family, my father most especially, always there, regardless of the time zone, I was able to continue researching and writing and, eventually, scratch together something approaching ends meet. Thanks Dad! Particular thanks are due (in alphabetical order) to: David Allen, Sam Blaxland, Richard Davies (Neath), Vicky Davis, Victoria Dawson, Emyr Gruffydd, Emma Houlihan, Alex Jackson, Rhian Keyse, Carrie Knox, Jack Maclean, Jenn McClelland, Kieran Murphy, Niall Murphy, John O'Donovan, Rachel Poole,

Martyn Richardson, Michael Ryan, David Selway, Holly Snaith, Norena Shopland, Rachel Sweet, and David Toms.

In many ways, my own experiences in recent years remind me of the first real history I ever heard, the stories and memories of the Depression passed on by my grandparents: my paternal grandfather, Fred, who grew up in Nantyffyllon and Llanharan; my maternal grandfather, Derek, who grew up in Bedwellty in industrial Monmouthshire; my paternal grandmother, Agnes (aka Nan), who grew up in the tenements of Paisley; and my maternal grandmother, Jeanette, who grew up in Bristol. They all ended up living in Somerset, where my parents, sister, and I were born. It was Nan who first taught me about communists, about workers' theatre, and about the to-ing and fro-ing of people across the Atlantic; she taught me about the Depression, as she had experienced it herself as a little girl, about the sorts of collectivism which rarely appears on the pages of history books, about the sights and sounds of the past, and the hopes and aspirations of those who came before. Such are the contours of the history which I have written about in *Labour Country*. I can only wonder what mum would have thought of the book, or of my being a historian, but I hope she would have been proud. I dedicate the book to them both.

INDEX

The index covers the main text only; the endnotes have not been indexed. Entries for towns or villages denote significant events in those locations; scattered references to each location have not been included.

Main headings for index entries are given in full and in the abbreviated form if both are used in the text. In subheadings, abbreviations are used, as follows. AAM: Amalgamated Association of Miners; CPGB: Communist Party of Great Britain; ILP: Independent Labour Party; MFGB: Miners' Federation of Great Britain; MP: member of parliament; NCF: No Conscription Fellowship; NDL: National Democratic League; NUM: National Union of Mineworkers; SDF: Social Democratic Federation; SWMF: South Wales Miners' Federation; SWMIU: South Wales Miners' Industrial Union; TLC: Trades and Labour Council; TURL: Trades Union Reform League.

A Carnival of Voices

EXPLORE MODERN WALES

Series editor: Dai Smith

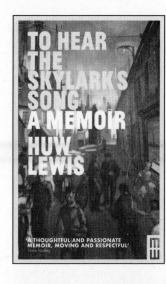

TO HEAR THE SKYLARK'S SONG A MEMOIR HUW LEWIS

'A THOUGHTFUL AND PASSIONATE MEMOIR, MOVING AND RESPECTFUL' Tessa Hadley

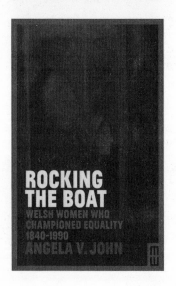

ROCKING THE BOAT WELSH WOMEN WHO CHAMPIONED EQUALITY 1840-1990 ANGELA V. JOHN

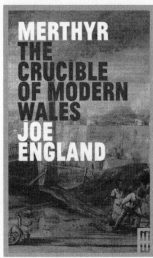

MERTHYR THE CRUCIBLE OF MODERN WALES JOE ENGLAND

www.parthianbooks.com